AFRICAN MIGRATIONS

AFRICAN MIGRATIONS

Patterns and Perspectives

EDITED BY

Abdoulaye Kane AND Todd H. Leedy

Indiana University Press
Bloomington and Indianapolis

This book is a publication of

Indiana University Press
601 North Morton Street
Bloomington, Indiana 47404-3797 USA

iupress.indiana.edu

Telephone orders 800-842-6796
Fax orders 812-855-7931

Library of Congress Cataloging-in-Publication Data

African migrations : patterns and perspectives /
edited by Abdoulaye Kane and Todd H. Leedy.
  p. cm.
Includes index.
ISBN 978-0-253-00308-9 (cloth : alk. paper) — ISBN 978-0-253-00576-2
(pbk. : alk. paper) — ISBN 978-0-253-00583-0 (ebook) 1. Africans—
Migrations. 2. African diaspora. 3. Africa—Emigration and
immigration. I. Kane, Abdoulaye. II. Leedy, Todd H. (Todd Holzgrefe)
    DT16.5.A345   2012
    304.8096—dc23   2012005743

1 2 3 4 5   18 17 16 15 14 13

For those on the move,
and for those left behind

There's a place where I've been told
Every street is paved with gold
And it's just across the borderline
And when it's time to take your turn
Here's one lesson that you must learn
You could lose more than you'll ever hope to find

When you reach the broken promised land
And every dream slips through your hands
Then you'll know that it's too late to change your mind
'Cause you've paid the price to come so far
Just to wind up where you are
And you're still just across the borderline

—Ry Cooder, John Hiatt, and James Dickinson,
"Across the Borderline" (1982)

CONTENTS

Acknowledgments   xi

Introduction:
African Patterns of Migration in a Global Era: New Perspectives
  Abdoulaye Kane and Todd H. Leedy   1

PART 1. PSYCHOLOGICAL, SOCIOCULTURAL, AND POLITICAL DIMENSIONS
     OF AFRICAN MIGRATION

  1. Overcoming the Economistic Fallacy: Social Determinants
     of Voluntary Migration from the Sahel to the Congo Basin
       Bruce Whitehouse   19

  2. Migration as Coping with Risk and State Barriers:
     Malian Migrants' Conception of Being Far from Home
       Isaie Dougnon   35

  3. Navigating Diaspora: The Precarious Depths of the Italian
     Immigration Crisis
       Donald Carter   59

  4. Historic Changes Underway in African Migration Policies:
     From Muddling Through to Organized Brain Circulation
       Rubin Patterson   78

PART 2. TRANSLOCAL AND TRANSNATIONAL CONNECTIONS:
     BETWEEN BELONGING AND EXCLUSION

  5. Belonging amidst Shifting Sands: Insertion, Self-Exclusion, and
     the Remaking of African Urbanism
       Loren B. Landau   93

  6. Securing Wealth, Ordering Social Relations: Kinship, Morality,
     and the Configuration of Subjectivity and Belonging across the
     Rural-Urban Divide
       Hansjörg Dilger   113

  7. Voluntary and Involuntary Homebodies: Adaptations and
     Lived Experiences of Hausa "Left Behind" in Niamey, Niger
       Scott M. Youngstedt   133

8. Strangers Are Like the Mist: Language in the Push and Pull of the
   African Diaspora
        Paul Stoller 158

9. Toward a Christian Disneyland? Negotiating Space and Identity in
   the New African Religious Diaspora
        Afe Adogame 173

10. International Aid to Refugees in Kenya: The Neglected Role of the
    Somali Diaspora
        Cindy Horst 195

PART 3. FEMINIZATION OF MIGRATION AND THE APPEARANCE
        OF DIASPORIC IDENTITIES

11. The Feminization of Asylum Migration from Africa:
    Problems and Perspectives
        Jane Freedman 211

12. Migration as a Factor of Cultural Change Abroad and at Home:
    Senegalese Female Hair Braiders in the United States
        Cheikh Anta Babou 230

13. What the General of Amadou Bamba Saw in New York City:
    Gendered Displays of Devotion among Migrants of the Senegalese
    Murid Tariqa
        Beth A. Buggenhagen 248

14. Toward Understanding a Culture of Migration among "Elite"
    African Youth: Educational Capital and the Future of the
    Igbo Diaspora
        Rachel R. Reynolds 270

Contributors   287

Index   289

ACKNOWLEDGMENTS

This volume emerged from a conversation on a plane to the annual African Studies Association meeting in 2004. Like many projects of this sort, the gestation period has been long but made bearable by the patience of our contributors and support of our colleagues. The editors wish to thank the staff of the Center for African Studies at University of Florida—in particular Leonardo Villalon, Corinna Greene, and Ikeade Akinyemi—for their continued assistance in all phases of this project. We would also like to thank the staff at Indiana University Press and the anonymous reviewers whose suggestions and guidance solidified this collection.

Primary financial support for the project was provided by the U.S. Department of Education Title VI National Resource Center program, with additional resources from the following University of Florida entities: the College of Liberal Arts and Sciences, the Office of the Provost, the International Center, the Office of Research, the Samuel P. Harn Museum of Art, and the Department of Anthropology.

AFRICAN
MIGRATIONS

AFRICAN PATTERNS
OF MIGRATION IN A
GLOBAL ERA

NEW PERSPECTIVES

ABDOULAYE KANE AND TODD H. LEEDY

MOBILITY AS PHENOMENON IN AFRICA

Migration within countries, between countries and between continents, is a central characteristic of the twenty-first century. Castles and Miller (2003) have characterized the end of the twentieth and the beginning of the twenty-first centuries as "the age of migration," referring to population movements across national, regional, and continental borders. Our goal in this volume is to assess the part that Africa and Africans play in this process of human mobility provoked by economic, social, and political forces operating at different yet interconnected levels—local, national, and global.

The various approaches to the study of African migrations necessitate a multidisciplinary approach. The multiple destinations of African migrants and the translocal/transnational connections established between the departed and those left behind compelled us to solicit contributions focused on domestic (rural to urban and, increasingly, urban to rural), regional, and intercontinental migration patterns. The multidisciplinary approach and domestic/regional/intercontinental scope allow these chapters to speak with each other in ways that set this volume apart from previous edited works on the subject (Amin 1974; Manuh 2005; Diop 2008).

There is no better indicator of the level of despair among Africans today than the exponentially growing numbers trying to exit at all costs for a better life elsewhere in urban Africa or Western countries. Since the early 1980s, Africans, particularly the youth, have been voting with their feet. If the wave of democratization that swept Africa in the early 1990s created a sense that political participation would lead to better governance and economic prosperity, then the conflicts in Liberia, Sierra Leone, Somalia, Rwanda, Congo, Sudan, and Côte d'Ivoire have consumed much of this hope. Migration has become—in both in urban and rural areas—an integral part of the community fabric, making it difficult to understand certain phenomena without taking into account the constant flows between rural villages and their "satellites" in African cities or abroad. The example of a marriage taking place at a local mosque in Freetown with the groom in London and the bride in Maryland highlights how African mobility connects the local and the global in unexpected ways (D'Alisera 2004).

The patterns of African migration are evolving in response to changing economic and political realities on both ends of migratory routes. Besides the cosmogonies of displacement and resettlement very common among certain ethnic groups, and the mobility associated with the livelihoods of pastoralist, trading, and fishing communities, colonial rule triggered the movement of most African people (Amin 1974; Curtin 1995; Ferguson 1999; Piot 1999). Colonial capital created sites of raw material production for European industries that attracted rural labor migrants. During the colonial period, both rural-rural and rural-urban migrations in Africa were predominantly male and oftentimes seasonal. If most of the labor migration involved short distances, there were also growing numbers crossing territorial borders and staying longer periods—such as the case of Malian and Burkinabe migrants to the cocoa plantations in Côte d'Ivoire.

Postcolonial migrations have been overwhelmingly oriented toward urban centers. Rural exodus is a common denominator in the way African capital cities grew rapidly during the three decades following African independences. The movements from countryside to city no longer entailed only labor migration by young men; it included women traveling independently or joining their husbands in the city (Lambert 2002; Ferguson 1999). The reconstitution of rural families and the subsequent birth of second and third generations in the city promoted permanent migration. Migrations to neighboring countries in West Africa—where Côte d'Ivoire, Nigeria, Ghana, and Senegal have become popular destinations of intra-regional migration—have substantial economic, and even political, impact. At the same time, long-distance intra-African migration brought West African diamond traders to Central Africa (Bredeloup 2007). Meanwhile, South Africa had long attracted labor migrants, but the end of the apartheid system made the country a desirable destination for long-distance intra-African migrants from outside the region, including West and East Africans.

From the 1950s through the 1980s, migration to Europe followed the historical connections between colonial powers and their former colonies. Francophone Africans largely migrated to France and Belgium while the Anglophones headed to Britain. However, with the tightening of immigration laws in France and Britain at the end of the 1980s, migrants (especially refugees) began to land in countries without any colonial ties to their countries of origin. After European integration, what matters most is simply entering "fortress Europe" (Koser 2003). So Mediterranean countries in particular—Spain, Italy, and Portugal—quickly began to receive large and rapidly growing African migrant groups (Carter 1997).

In the new century, images of traditional boats overloaded with clandestine migrants crossing European borders have been abundant in the media, suggesting an invasion of Europe by desperate and destitute Africans. Musa Dieng Kala's 2008 film *Has God Forsaken Africa* reinforces the impression that all African youth want to exit for Western destinations. If the dreams to exit the continent remain real, fed by an imaginary of the West far removed from the harsh reality of migrant experiences in Europe and North America, media reports fuel a hyper-reality wherein the gates of fortress Europe verge on being overwhelmed by young and unskilled Africans (Stoller 2002; MacGaffey and Bazenguissa-Ganga 2000; Timera 1996; Quiminal 1991; D'Alisera 2004). Yet domestic and regional African migration continues to be far more important and sizable than the flows to Europe, America, and the Gulf region combined (Sander and Maimbo 2003; Bakewell and de Haas 2007).

As to the desperate and destitute character of the candidates to migration, Schmitz (2008) demonstrates that it is most often not the poorest of the poor who are rushing to cross European borders. The cost of travel is frequently in the thousands of dollars, making it impossible for the poor living on less than one dollar a day to participate. The provision of funding by family/village or religious-based social networks is not fully accounted in the analysis of these clandestine migrations, but only a tiny number of African migrants end up crossing European borders. The vast majority of African migrants live close to their communities of origin—in national capital cities or in neighboring countries (Zeleza 2002).

Contributors to this volume explore three main themes in the changing patterns of African migration. First, we look beyond the widely shared visions of straightforward economically determined migration (Adepoju 2008; Amin 1974; Rain 1999). Second, we examine the translocal/transnational connections between African migrant communities and their home areas. Third, we investigate the changes in African immigrant communities as the circular migration of sojourners becomes a more permanent diasporic presence.

THE PSYCHOLOGICAL, SOCIOCULTURAL, AND POLITICAL DIMENSIONS OF AFRICAN MIGRATION

Without downplaying the importance of economic dimensions, there are a variety of other dimensions heuristically critical in any explanations of African migration today. The psychological, sociocultural, and political dimensions offer a more complex reading of decision making, motivations, and the translocal/transnational relations of migrants.

The economic dimension has long been prevalent in migration theories. The widespread use of the "push and pull" factors to explain human mobility indicates some fundamental importance of the economic dimension in understanding migration processes. However, particularly in the African context it is vital to combine "push and pull" with a range of other factors that inform decisions on migration. Bruce Whitehouse (chapter 1) explores the psychological dimensions of how Malian Soninke migrants living in Brazzaville rationalize leaving one poor country for another. In this case, the physical distance separating migrants from their families buffers the constant social pressure on the individual to redistribute, thereby permitting accumulation.

The demands and the social obligation for redistribution are so pressing that only strong personalities can overcome and survive in business near their home villages or towns. So migration becomes a viable option for these Malian migrants to escape the social pressure for redistribution of wealth. Yet physical distance only diminishes but does not negate the social pressure for redistribution. The great majority of these migrants remit money and return resources to their home communities. In the case of Malians in Brazzaville, the psychosocial dimensions move us beyond the focus on labor migrants as a predominant category. Traders, self-employed migrants (e.g., taxi drivers), and informal service providers defy the logic of "push and pull" because their movement is not driven by differential salary and public benefits. Rather, the psychological space allowed by faraway residence, however permanent, actually reinforces opportunities for individual accumulation. Likewise, far away from their communities of origin, migrants are free to take on a variety of income-generating activities that would be socially unacceptable in their home areas.

Another dimension requiring consideration might best be labeled as sociocultural. Across the Sahel region, for example, many groups have a very long history of dwelling and displacement, with some having even adopted mobility as a mode of living. In communities with a long history of migration, we can observe what Durand and Massey (1992) call the "cumulative effect of migration." In such cases, people incorporate migration into their culture and expectations of movement, thereby influencing how people envision their lives, entertain their hopes, and realize their dreams. The growing literature on "cultures of migration" focuses on these aspects of community that are rapidly becoming prevalent all across the continent (Cohen 2004; Hahn and Klute 2007).

Isaie Dougnon (chapter 2) provides a discourse analysis of travel and migration among West African ethnic groups that suggests the great importance of sociocultural dimensions of migration. Dougnon observed that Dogon, Soninke, and Bamana communities often understand migration as a risky and perilous endeavor—in many ways comparable to a rite of passage. The widespread social construct of village as safe place and the beyond as dangerous wilderness places the migrant into space where life is a constant negotiation for survival. Migration becomes a test of masculinity, endurance, and courage. Migrants who succeed in returning home with wealth gain status in their communities in a way parallel to ritual initiates who emerge after successfully accomplishing their rite of passage. They are accorded personal favors, social capital, and notoriety. Dougnon's discussion of migration as rite of passage—testing endurance, virility, and courage—is reminiscent of how young Congolese migrants imagine migration and travel. The term "l'aventure" used to describe the experience of migration underscores the difficulties and risks associated with international migration and the extraordinary capacity of Congolese migrants to overcome obstacles in realizing their dream to become "somebody" (MacGaffey and Bazenguissa-Ganga 2000).

The difficulties and risks have only increased with more restrictive immigration policies in receiving countries. Europe has constructed a veritable fortress along its southern borders with coast guard and military craft constantly patrolling to intercept clandestine migrants crossing to Italy and Spain. French president Nicolas Sarkozy has defended such policies, arguing that Europe should have a "chosen" rather than an "imposed" immigration policy. Of course, his chosen immigration would allow Europe to attract the best and the brightest from poorer countries, while preventing an imposed immigration requires tight border control to keep out unskilled and clandestine candidates.

The politics and policies of border control between Africa and Europe occasioned several international meetings (e.g., in Morocco and Libya) where countries on both ends of migration routes agreed to reinforce control border and coastline controls. Paradoxically, Europe has to a large extent outsourced a significant aspect of its border control activities to the governments of sending countries. Thus it is in Morocco, Tunisia, Libya, Mauritania, and Senegal that the first layers of European border control emerge in an attempt to prevent clandestine migrants from even leaving the country.

Donald Carter (chapter 3) highlights the political dimension of African migration to Italy. Immigration policies in Europe that emphasize border control put the lives of unskilled migrants in peril. Europe has constructed higher fences—both physical and bureaucratic—with serious consequences for the human rights of clandestine migrants. The drama of sinking human cargos in the Atlantic and Mediterranean, of record numbers of human bodies washing ashore or caught up in the nets of fish-

ing boats, cannot be dismissed simply as the cruelty of human traffickers. The "liquid cemeteries" along European coastlines also results from
deliberate policies. Thousands of Africans have perished in attempting to
cross the borders of "Fortress Europe." Thousands more are detained and
interrogated in camps where their human rights are oftentimes violated
repeatedly. Carter raises the crucial issue of ethics and morality in the
formulation of immigration policies. The "chosen migration" of Sarkozy
remains morally questionable as it contributes to the structural reproduction of global inequalities wherein the best human resources of poor
countries are absorbed outward while the unskilled multitudes are prevented from taking up mobility-dependent opportunities.

The "poaching" of African brains, perhaps most notably health professionals, should raise fundamental ethical issues for Western countries.
The exodus of nurses and physicians from Africa to Europe and to North
America undermines the already limited ability of African health systems to operate effectively due to lack of qualified personnel. Despite the
obvious dramatic consequences of the "brain drain" on African countries,
Rubin Patterson (chapter 4) offers compelling possibilities on how African
countries can profit from the skills and professional experience of their
diasporas around the globe. Patterson highlights the efforts made by countries such as Ghana in harnessing the potential of "brain circulation" and
"brain gain" for sending countries. Patterson suggests that African countries adapt models from China and India in their efforts to take advantage
of their best and brightest citizens working abroad.

To a certain extent, brain drain is already mitigated by the flows of
money, material goods, and ideas from African migrants to their countries of origin. The total amount of remittances has been increasing very
significantly since 1990. Studies of remittances have highlighted the fact
that most money sent to Africa by those living abroad goes through informal circuits of transfer, which leads to the underestimation of the total
figures involved. But money is just one element in the various forms of
relations and actions connecting African migrants with their home communities though translocal and transnational networks.

TRANSLOCAL AND TRANSNATIONAL CONNECTIONS: SOCIAL EXCLUSION AND BELONGING

TRANSLOCAL CONNECTIONS

Analyses of postcolonial migrations have focused mainly on the reconstitution of regional, ethnic, and religious identities in urban Africa. The
pioneering urban anthropological studies in Africa largely insisted on the

urban-rural divide and the processes of adaptation and reproduction of local culture in the urban setting (Mayer 1961). The study of hometown associations and sustained migrant connections to rural roots led to the theorization of the "dual system" (Gugler 1971). The dual system reconstructs reciprocal relations between those who have left and those who remained behind. The remittances of migrants in cities as well as the opening of their urban homes to rural guests (students, patients, temporary migrants) were seen both as a moral obligation and an investment useful to the migrant who returns home after retirement (Ferguson 1999). Translocal migrants could mobilize their social capital, wealth, and fame to gain political positions both at local and national levels.

Later studies focused on the same connections but emphasized the translocal relations that seasonal migrants entertained with their rural communities (Lambert 2002; Hahn and Klute 2007). The translocal concept allows exploration of both the connections between migrants and their rural homes as well as the re-creation of locality in the urban centers of Africa. If Geschiere and Gugler's (1998) reexamination of the dual system focuses on continuity and change in the relationship that urbanites have with their villages, the translocal theory seems to highlight the reproduction of localities in African urban contexts by villagers who remain tied to their roots and in constant connection with their rural communities (Lambert 2002).

Geschiere and Gugler (1998) also noticed that the relationship urbanites have with their rural homes expanded rather than declined in recent years despite some fundamental changes in the patterns of flow between rural communities and their urban satellites. One particular aspect they highlight is the important role of the village connection in national politics. Urbanites, especially the political elite, are invested in playing the "politics of autochthony" to access preeminent political positions at the national level.

With the harsh consequences that the structural adjustment plans of the 1980s and 1990s imposed on the African urban populations, some retired urbanites attempt a return to their rural homes as they become unable to afford the high costs of city living on their small pensions. As Ferguson (1999) argues, the translocal migrants who maintained connection to their rural home have better chances of reinsertion than the cosmopolitan urbanites who preferred a more complete urban integration over maintaining relation with their home villages and towns. Geschiere and Gugler (1998) also note the changing meaning of city and village. The customary associations—city with modernity and development, and village with tradition and underdevelopment—are becoming more easily confused. This is due not only to the impact of neoliberal policies on both places, but more importantly by the constant flows of people, images, commodities, and ideas that make drawing the border between urban and rural increasingly challenging.

Hansjörg Dilger (chapter 6) points to the importance of the village connection for urbanites dealing with the HIV/AIDS pandemic in Tanzania. Migrants who established themselves in Dar es Salaam and maintained connections with home by sending remittances or hosting villagers seeking economic opportunities in the city are welcomed home to die after losing their battle with the virus. One may assume similar arrangements are made for AIDS orphans in the city for access to care from their kin in the village. The case study presented by Dilger here confirms that urbanite loyalty to the rural home can also work as insurance to a dignified death and burial. But Dilger points also to the considerable strain placed on the capacity of rural-urban support networks by the impact of HIV/AIDS and the negative effects of neoliberal policies.

Scott Youngstedt (chapter 7) assesses both the translocal and transnational connections in Niamey, which like many African capitals is a city of rural migrants. Hausa urbanites in Niamey create social networks that extend to both rural homes and diasporas outside the country. The "homebodies" in Niamey have constant contact with their family and friends abroad from whom they receive information and financial support for their own attempts to exit for a better life. One of the fascinating aspects of the homebodies in Niamey is the selection processes set up to determine the most promising candidates for migration assistance—those deemed most likely to provide a return on family or community investment. Through this mechanism of support, individuals from poor backgrounds can get the financial help necessary to migrate to Europe and America. This also goes against the widely shared idea in migration studies that the clandestine migrants knocking at the doors of Europe are the poor and miserable—through such assistance networks, they are able to pay large sums of money for the services of traffickers. As Youngstedt points out, migration in Niamey is not just an individual matter but rather a collective enterprise in which the migrant is only one actor. Explorations of transnational connections also point to the particularity of the relations between African migrants and the people they left behind.

TRANSNATIONAL CONNECTIONS

The increasing global flow of goods, people, money, ideas, and images is transforming the twenty-first-century world in unpredictable forms. Globalization has connected remote areas in Africa to global cities in a variety of ways. The cable/satellite news media, in a matter of seconds, bring news from one corner of the world to the most secluded places in the globe (Appadurai 1996).

The attraction of cheap labor from the periphery to the core is especially characteristic of the late twentieth and early twenty-first century capitalism (Basch, Schiller, and Blanc 1994). The result is the movement—both real and perceived—of migrants from poor countries to "global cities" at an extraordinary pace. However, in contrast to nineteenth-century European migrations to the Americas, recent migrants maintain stronger connections with their homes in the global South. The revolution in technologies of communication and mass media have made connections with home more viable, bringing migrants together on a daily basis with their families and friends left behind. Especially in regions with a long history of outmigration, villages do embody Piot's idea of "remotely global" villages (Piot 1999). The villagers are connected to global cities on a daily basis through wireless talk/text, as well as web-based instant messaging conversations.

Loren B. Landau (chapter 5) examines how post-apartheid South Africa has failed to meet the expectations of many young migrants who expected to arrive and share expanded economic opportunities with black South Africans. Despite the Pan-African discourse of Mandela and Mbeki, African migrants in South Africa continue to be depicted as criminals, drivers of high local unemployment, and responsible for much of what is wrong with South Africa. The township violence of 2008 was only the most visible manifestation of the xenophobic attitudes directed toward African foreigners in South Africa. Many South Africans reacted with shock at the open and widespread expression of such sentiments. The reactions of African immigrants are typified by the refusal to seek belonging to the host society and instead a strengthened emphasis on transnational connections already emblematic of Africans living abroad.

Africans in South Africa thereby engage in the same sort of transnational practices as Africans living outside the continent. They send remittances, return home frequently (if they have a legal status), and communicate regularly with the people they left behind. However, in ways very different from increased immigration restrictions in Europe and the United States, the volatile social context of the South African townships following the 2008 episodes has reinforced migrants' sense of not belonging and heightened their need to plan for a future return home. African migrants in South Africa are not interested in taking root and gaining citizenship. Landau also examines identity politics in Johannesburg as South African domestic migrants from different ethnic groups and regions converge to embrace a national South African identity in opposition to the "otherness" of foreigners.

Cindy Horst (chapter 10) analyzes transnational practices of remitting money among Somali refugees living abroad. Patterns of remittances appear very similar across various African migrant communities. They tend to be steady—destined to support the families left behind—and use informal circuits of money transfer wherever they exist alongside formal banking mechanisms. Through a case study, Horst examines the remittances received by Somalis in a refugee camp in Kenya. She illustrates how money from the Somali diaspora has become vital in helping refugee camp families survive the very difficult conditions that persist despite UNHCR assistance. She documents the expected pressing demands for money that family members address to their sons and daughters living abroad. Those left behind commonly express frustration at not receiving sufficient support from their migrant family members. Likewise, migrants complain in unison about the unreasonable demands coming from their family members left behind. For the Somalis living for protracted periods in these camps, remittances are vital in providing support that will allow them to eventually move beyond refugee status. This remains difficult, however, as many studies have already demonstrated, since most remittances from transnational migrants are directed toward immediate consumption needs.

Afe Adogame (chapter 9) examines the negotiations surrounding the construction of places of worship by African Pentecostal churches in Britain and the United States. His contribution reveals the tensions around the placement of worship space as the process can result in the use of identity politics and exclusion in an attempt to preserve a sense of cultural and religious purity. Yet Adogame demonstrates the successes of African Pentecostal churches in successfully negotiating their rights as citizens, by building churches and perhaps their own "Christian Disneyland." The growing number of converts as well as the dynamism of African Pentecostal churches even give an impression of reverse missionary action by Africans in Europe and America. African Pentecostal churches in the United States—like many Muslim mosques—have a particularly transnational character since their highest religious authorities are oftentimes based in Africa or Europe, and in constant communication with their followers dispersed across multiple borders.

Paul Stoller (chapter 8) details the transnational lives of Hausa immigrants in New York City. They engage like many Africans in transnational practices of remittance, regular communication, and return visitation. He argues, however, that they are in many ways caught between home and host countries. As a result, they live in a continually liminal state. While having girlfriends or even wives in America, they never waive their commitment to families left in Africa. But Stoller's informants are Hausa males, which leaves open the question of how women change the dynamic of migration when they join their husbands or arrive by themselves and only marry once in the diaspora.

FEMINIZATION AND THE APPEARANCE OF DIASPORIC IDENTITIES

Underlying these contributions as theoretical unifier is the concept of diaspora. While African migrants often do not seek to assimilate and cut ties with their communities of origin, they simultaneously do not abandon a willingness to claim their rights as citizens in host countries. This phenomenon of maintaining connectedness with origins while negotiating social, economic, and political insertion may be approached in various ways within the framework of diasporic identity. Scott Youngstedt (chapter 7) explicitly addresses the question of how the concept of diaspora can be used to better understand African migration to the West. Rachel Reynolds (chapter 14) examines the way educational capital among Igbo youth contributes to the reinforcement of an ethnic diaspora in America. Diasporas, both old and new, share that political positioning of being "in between" that Paul Stoller (chapter 8) renders in his study of Hausa traders through the concept of liminality.

There are also African ethnic diasporas in African cities, as the contributions by Loren Landau (chapter 5) and Hansjörg Dilger (chapter 6) document. In these instances, migrants express their belonging more directly toward their rural homes where they hope to be buried rather than the city in which they live. The domestic migrants in Johannesburg studied by Landau refuse to belong to the city and do not participate in city politics that would impact their immediate lives. As allochthonous status has become common across the continent, diasporic identity appears often with second-generation migrants born in the city whose perception of belonging is very different from that of their parents.

Women also increasingly migrate alone, especially in areas of significant political instability. Labor migration was for the most part a gendered phenomenon. Men overwhelmingly participated in earlier domestic, regional, and international migration—moving to earn cash that could complement agricultural production. However, as the transition from temporary to long-term migration occurred, women came to join their husbands and thereby provided the basis for establishment of translocal communities in African capitals. A similar process more recently occurred in Europe and the United States as migrants have started to bring over their families.

The recent wave of arrivals from troubled African countries has only accelerated this feminization of African migration. Thousands of women move internally and regionally, crossing international borders in search of stability and opportunity. The arrival of independent African women in Western countries is also becoming a common phenomenon. From domestic workers and hair braiders to nurses and educated professionals, African women undertake transnational migration as individuals, much like their counterparts in Asia and Latin America.

The arrival of women in significant numbers changes the insertion dynamic for immigrant communities. Their presence and the eventual birth of children change how African immigrants envision their future in a host society. The project to return home—completing the migration cycle—in some cases requires revision to integrate support and care for children. Women tend to engage more with the state through social services to ensure the well-being of their children. It is clear, therefore, that women become the foundation of African communities abroad and catalyze the emergence of diasporic identities. The feminization of migration flows may also prompt the renegotiation of gender roles—and the tensions implicit within such processes—as host contexts present different assumptions on equality between men and women. Such tension can be exacerbated by the expansion of economic opportunities for women even as men experience a simultaneous downward mobility.

Cheikh Anta Babou (chapter 12) analyzes how migrants renegotiate gender roles in his study of Senegalese women who own hair-braiding salons. As these women earn far more than their husbands and provide most of the family budget, they challenge—both publicly and privately—the established role of wives who stay home to care for husband and children. In such contexts, it is indeed the husband who will undertake most household tasks, adopting the traditionally defined role of a woman. There are, as Babou indicates, significant conflicts in migrant households whenever men have difficulty accepting new roles they perceive as challenging to their authority or diminishing their masculinity.

However, women face tremendous challenges as both migrants and dependent wives, as underscored by Jane Freedman (chapter 11). That African women would easily move from patriarchal societies to host countries with more rights and protection is challenged by her analysis of women's asylum cases in Europe. In the African conflict zones from which most female asylum seekers originate, targeting women for rape and all manner of physical atrocities is commonplace. In their appeal for asylum, African women must provide an account of what happened to them—a traumatic experience they often are not eager to recount. In contrast to police regulations regarding domestic rape or sexual assault cases, there are no specific guidelines on how to approach the questioning of female asylum seekers when it comes to the psychological scars of war.

Women also reshape migrant cultural and religious identities in host countries. Beth Buggenhagen (chapter 13) provides the example of Senegalese women in New York who belong to the Mouride Sufi order. She depicts women's participation in the *ziarra* of their spiritual guide as an occasion to express sartorial elegance as well as spirituality. In a sense, women's *ziarras* take on the role of Senegalese family ceremonies—becoming a special ritual space wherein women display their elegance and wealth through cloth, jewelry, and money. Women also reproduce important cultural elements in the West through cuisine, hairstyles, and fashion—duplicating and reinterpreting Senegalese canons of elegance in a global city. These cultural expressions, publicly embodied by women, provide visual cues that "Little Senegal" exists in the heart of New York City.

Following family, religion is perhaps the most important element that migrants reproduce in their host country—true for both African Muslims and Christians. Afe Adogame (chapter 9) addresses the rapid deployment of African independent churches in the religious spaces of the United Kingdom and the United States, exploring how creation of sacred space contributes to the geographical representation of religious expression. He examines African independent church negotiations with host-country authorities in determining processes of religious placemaking and ritual space reproduction. Adogame draws upon recent religious ethnography to map the growth dynamics, mobility, and gradual insertion of African churches in Europe and North America. Parallels also emerge with African Muslims negotiating their expression of religious identity through reproduction of sacred spaces, social networking, celebration of religious events, and home connections. Muslim traders in New York also express their religious identity on a daily basis, as witnessed by Paul Stoller (chapter 8) at the Shabazz market and mosque. The West African traders of Harlem—mostly Hausa, Wolof, and Fulani—remain very active in religious practice as well as in welcoming Islamic scholars from their home countries and sponsoring religious conferences. Like their Christian counterparts, and sometimes with greater difficulty, African Muslim migrants constantly negotiate with local authorities and host communities to insert their places of worship into the urban landscape.

The growing flow of African women migrating on their own is slowly but surely changing the landscape of African communities in Europe and North America. With them has come the appearance of a second generation whose sense of self, as Rachel Reynolds (chapter 14) notes, is defined by their "in-betweeness." Despite their youth spent entirely in the United States, second-generation Igbo students study their mother tongue at university—an indication of the appeal of African languages and therefore of the emergence of a diasporic identity.

Both the presence of women and a second generation are already redefining African patterns of migration. Scholars of migration are gradually moving toward the concepts of transnationalism and diaspora as better heuristic lenses to capture the African experience of "dwelling in displacement" (Clifford 1997). Additional longitudinal and interdisciplinary studies need to establish continuity and change in the trends examined within this volume. As African diasporic identities unfold before us, they require close follow-up from social scientists to synthesize cases of daily negotiations of host-country incorporation as well as connections with home into a more dense theoretical approach to African migrations. We hope this volume provides another step in that direction.

REFERENCES

Adepoju, Aderanti. 2008. "Migration in Sub-Saharan Africa." *Current African Issues* no. 37. Uppsala: Nordiska Afrikainstitutet.

Amin, Samir, ed. 1974. *Modern Migration in Western Africa: Studies Presented and Discussed at the Eleventh International African Seminar, Dakar, April 1972.* Oxford: Oxford University Press.

Appadurai, Arjun. 1996. *Modernity at Large: Cultural Dimensions of Globalization.* Minneapolis: University of Minnesota Press.

Bakewell, Oliver, and Hein de Haas. 2007. "African Migrations: Continuities, Discontinuities and Recent Transformations." In *African Perspectives,* ed. P. Chabal, U. Engel, and L. de Haan. Leiden: Brill.

Balandier, Georges. 1955. *Sociologie des brazzavilles noires.* Paris: A. Colin.

Basch, Linda, Nina Glick Schiller, and Cristina Szanton Blanc. 1994. *Nations Unbound: Transnational Projects, Postcolonial Predicaments, and Deterritorialized Nation-States.* New York: Taylor Francis.

Bredeloup, Sylvie. 2007. *La diams pora du fleuve Sénégal. Sociologie des migration africaines.* Toulouse: Presses Universitaires du Mirail-Toulouse.

Carter, Donald. 1997. *States of Grace: Senegalese in Italy and the New European Immigration.* Minneapolis: University of Minnesota Press.

Castles, Stephen, and Mark J. Miller. 2003. *The Age of Migration.* 3rd ed. New York: Palgrave Macmillan.

Clifford, James. 1997. "Diaspora." In *The Ethnicity Reader: Nationalism, Multiculturalism and Migration,* ed. M. Guibernau and J. Rex. Cambridge: Polity Press.

Cohen, Jeffrey 2004. *The Culture of Migration in Southern Mexico.* Austin: University of Texas Press.

Curtin, Philip. 1995. *Why People Move: Migration in African History.* Waco, Tex.: Markham Press Fund.

D'Alisera. JoAnn. 2004. *An Imagined Geography: Sierra Leonean Muslims in America.* Philadelphia: University of Pennsylvania Press.

Diop, Abdoulaye Bara. 1965. *Société toucouleur et migration, l'immigration toucouleur a Dakar.* Dakar: IFAN.

Diop, Momar C. 2008. *Le Sénégal des migrations: mobilités, identités et societies.* Paris: Karthala.

Durand, Jorge, and Douglas Massey. 1992. "Mexican Migration to the United States: A Critical Review." *Latin American Research Review* 27(2): 3–42.

Ferguson, James. 1999. *Expectations of Modernity: Myths and Meanings of Urban Life on the Zambian Copperbelt*. Berkeley: University of California Press.

Geschiere, Peter, and Josef Gugler. 1998. "The Urban-Rural Connection: Changing Issues of Belonging and Identification." *Africa* 68(3): 309–19.

Gugler, Josef. 1971. "Life in a Dual System: Eastern Nigerians in Town." *Cahiers d'etudes africaines* 11(3): 400–421.

———. 1991. "'Life in a Dual System' Revisited: Urban-Rural Ties in Enugu, Nigeria, 1961–87." *World Development* 19(5): 399–409.

Hahn, Peter Hans, and Georg Klute, eds. 2007. *Culture of Migration: African Perspectives*. Berlin: Lit Verlag.

Kane, Abdoulaye. 2001. "Diaspora villageoise et développement locale. Le cas de Thilogne Association Developpement." *Hommes et Migrations* 1229 (janvier-février): 96–107.

———. 2002. "Senegal's Village Diaspora and the People Left Behind." In *The Transnational Family: New European Frontiers and Global Networks*, ed. Deborah Bryceson and Ulla Vuorela. London: Berg Publishers.

Konadu-Agyemang, Kwadwo, Baffour K. Takyi, and John A. Arthur, eds. 2006. *The New African Diaspora in North America: Trends, Community Building, and Adaptation*. Lanham, Md.: Lexington Books.

Koser, Khalid, ed. 2003. *New African Diasporas*. London: Routledge.

Lambert, Michael. 2002. *Longing for Exile: Migration and the Making of a Translocal Community in Senegal, West Africa*. Portsmouth: Heineman.

MacGaffey, Janet, and Remy Bazenguissa-Ganga. 2000. *Congo-Paris: Transnational Traders on the Margins of the Law*. Bloomington: Indiana University Press.

Manchuelle, François. 1997. *Willing Migrants: Soninke Labor Diasporas 1848–1960*. Athens: Ohio University Press.

Manuh, Takyiwaa. 2005. *At Home in the World? International Migration and Development in Contemporary Ghana and West Africa*. Accra: Subsaharan Publishers.

Mayer, Philip. 1961. *Townsmen or Tribesmen: Conservatism and the Process of Urbanization in a South African City*. New York: Oxford University Press.

———. 1962. "Migrancy and the Study of Africans in Town." *American Anthropologist* 64(4): 576–92.

Piot, Charles. 1999. *Remotely Global: Village Modernity in West Africa*. Chicago: University of Chicago Press.

Quiminal, Catherine. 1991. *Gens d'ici, gens d'ailleurs*, Paris: Christian Bourgeois.

Rain, David. 1999. *Eaters of the Dry Season: Circular Labor Migration in the West African Sahel*. Boulder, Colo.: Westview Press.

Sander, Cerstin, and Samuel Maimbo. 2003. "Migrant Labour Remittances in Africa: Reducing Obstacles to Developmental Contributions." Africa Working Paper Series. Washington, D.C.: The World Bank.

Schmitz, Jean. 2008. "Migrants oust-africains: miséreux, aventuriers ou notables?" In *Politique Africaine* 109: 5–15.

Stoller, Paul. 2002. *Money Has No Smell. The Africanization of New York City*. Chicago: University of Chicago Press.

Tienda, Marta, ed. 2006. *Africa on the Move: African Migration and Urbanization in Comparative Perspective*. Johannesburg: Wits University Press.

Timera, Mahomet. 1996. *Les Soninké en France: d'un histoire à l'autre*. Paris: Karthala.

Zeleza, Paul. 2002. "African Migrations in a Global Context." *African Issues* 30(1): 9–14.

PART 1

PSYCHOLOGICAL, SOCIOCULTURAL,
AND POLITICAL DIMENSIONS
OF AFRICAN MIGRATION

1
OVERCOMING THE ECONOMISTIC FALLACY
SOCIAL DETERMINANTS OF VOLUNTARY MIGRATION FROM THE SAHEL TO THE CONGO BASIN

BRUCE WHITEHOUSE

THE "WORLD'S WORST CITY"

Brazzaville, capital of the Republic of Congo, is of modest size by world standards, with a population currently estimated at somewhere between 1.2 and 1.5 million. It is also in many respects typical of cities throughout Africa and the global South, characterized by rapid population growth, high unemployment, and shrinking public resources. While this erstwhile somnolent colonial outpost was once (briefly) renowned as the capital of Free France during the Second World War, during the 1990s Brazzaville became remarkable mainly as the scene of recurring violence by ethno-political factions vying for control of the Congolese state and its substantial oil revenues. These conflicts claimed tens of thousands of lives and forced hundreds of thousands to flee the city. Meanwhile, real income, education, and health indicators dropped sharply (Yengo 2006). The decade of unrest and economic stagnation tarnished Brazzaville's reputation to the point that in 2003 it was actually named the "world's worst city" in a global survey conducted by an international human resources firm.[1]

Herein lies a paradox that has propelled my research since I first visited Brazzaville in 2003. This city, wracked by war, economic decline, and joblessness, is also home to hundreds of thousands of immigrants. The vast majority of them come from across the Congo River in the Democratic Republic of Congo (DRC). But Brazzaville's immigrant population also includes an estimated 30,000 to 40,000 people from the West African Sahel, especially Mali, Guinea, and Senegal. Although Congo has been home in recent years to a few thousand refugees from Rwanda and the

DRC, its West African residents are not forced migrants: they are entrepreneurs, petty traders, and unskilled laborers who have come to Congo to
seek their fortunes at great personal expense and often considerable risk.
Over decades and generations, they have come to constitute a reasonably
successful immigrant community in Brazzaville, an important element of
the city's commercial sector and an enduring part of its social landscape.

What is it that draws these people to Brazzaville? What rewards do
they expect to reap, and what opportunities do they encounter after traveling over 2,000 miles (frequently overland) from their West African countries of origin? As an anthropologist seeking to answer these questions, I
have found that prevailing theories of the determinants of migration are
not always adequate to the task. These theories, which rely overwhelmingly on analysis of economic factors, tend to obscure the social embeddedness of individual migrants, thereby preventing a more complete understanding of human spatial mobility and its underlying motivations. In
this chapter, I demonstrate how established explanations of migration's
causes may be enhanced by considering the social forces that mediate
economic decision-making processes.

MIGRANT MOTIVATIONS: AN OVERVIEW

There is broad agreement among scholars across academic disciplines
that the primary causes of voluntary migration are economic in nature. A
number of theoretical models offer competing but also potentially com-
plementary explanations at both the micro- and macro-levels (Massey et
al. 1994; Brettell and Hollifield 2008). Neoclassical economic analysis emphasizes the role of differing wages and unemployment rates in influencing an individual's decision to move from one place to another, with "high
wage countries" drawing migrants away from "low wage countries." The
value of migration can be understood as the expected standard of living
abroad, minus the expected standard of living at home, minus the costs
of migrating (Carling 2002). The "new economics of migration" focuses
on risk management and economic diversification at the household level, casting migration as the product of conscious strategies by household
heads to protect themselves and their kin from the vagaries of climate and
market conditions. Segmented labor market theory considers the demand
from employers in developed countries for cheap, low-skilled workers
from abroad; this demand creates bifurcated labor markets in host countries, with a high-skill, high-wage upper stratum dominated by natives
and a low-skill, low-wage stratum dominated by immigrants. At the highest level of abstraction, world systems theory stresses economic globalization—the integration of societies into a single capitalist world system—as
the driving force behind international migration, drawing people from

poor countries of the economic "periphery" to the wealthy countries of the "core" (and particularly to a select few "global cities") (Sassen 1991). In all these models, social and cultural factors are secondary. Only after a migration flow has been initiated by wage gaps, economic uncertainty, or labor demand do such factors as social networks come into play, sustaining and expanding the flow by lowering the costs and risks of migration for each successive wave of migrants. Over time a "culture of migration" may be created in migrant-sending societies. Leaving home to seek opportunities abroad becomes the normative course of action in these societies, a virtual rite of passage, particularly as successful returning migrants create a "demonstration effect" (Massey et al. 1994: 737).

The models outlined above have been the subject of numerous critiques, notably by anthropologists who have called attention to the ways migration flows are structured by power differentials and especially gender inequality within sending societies and households (Brettell 2008). But these economic theories remain very much the dominant narratives in explaining human spatial mobility, and there seems to be a general consensus among researchers that material factors—not ideational ones—constitute the real driving forces behind migration. In the words of Alan Gilbert and Josef Gugler, "the evidence is overwhelming: most people move for economic reasons" (Gilbert and Gugler 1992: 66–67).

What, then, can cultural anthropologists, known for paying close attention to the ideational components of people's actions, bring to the discussion about migration and its motivations? We tend to be interested in the webs of meaning that human beings generate and their effects on human behavior; we believe that it is vital to understand how people represent their own actions to themselves and others. With respect to migration, we want to know what people think and what they feel about why they are leaving home. In my own research, most people I have asked about their reasons for migrating have articulated ideational as well as economic motivations. Migrants tend to express a strong desire to see the world and to broaden their horizons, comparing migration to a form of education (Riccio 2004). The "bright lights" and other attractions of far destinations surely have a strong pull, especially for people from poor rural communities.

Anthropologists cannot, however, afford to ignore material factors in their analysis. Indeed, we must study the conjuncture of the material and the ideational. Many of us suspect that ideational motivations alone do not entice people to leave home. It is when they are coupled with economic incentives that they are most likely to become operative, to turn migration from a vague desire to a concrete intention to a reality. My aim here is therefore not to challenge the scholarly consensus behind the economic foundations of migration. Rather, using the case of West African immigrants in Brazzaville, I seek to show how the economic determinants of migration are modulated by social forces, and specifically how unexpected migration outcomes can result from this process of modulation.

The apparent paradox of migration to impoverished or unstable cities has been a longstanding problem for Africanist scholars. Since the colonial era, research has shown that once migration to a destination becomes established, it may continue and even increase in the face of economic disincentives like high unemployment. Disjunctures between urban growth and urban economic opportunity have been observed in African urban areas, including Brazzaville, since the 1940s (Gilbert and Gugler 1992; Balandier 1985; Gondola 1996; Ferguson 1999). I turn now to an examination of some of the social forces that sustain such disjunctures in international migration within Africa, focusing on two interrelated phenomena: on the one hand, social networks; on the other, widely shared imaginaries pertaining to human dignity and modernity.

SAVED BY DISTANCE: SOCIAL NETWORKS AS A PUSH FACTOR

The role of social networks in attracting new migrants has been the subject of considerable research. Each additional migrant in a given migration flow reduces the costs and risks of migration for those left behind, such that someone with a social connection to a migrant is much more likely to become a migrant him- or herself than someone without. The social network in which the individual is embedded therefore acts as a "pull factor," making migration a more enticing option. Studies have shown that social capital—"the aggregate of the actual or potential resources which are linked to possession of a durable network of more or less institutionalized relationships of mutual acquaintance and recognition"—has a strong correlation to the propensity to migrate internationally (Bourdieu 1986; Palloni et al. 2001).

The ability of social networks to dampen economic opportunities in one's home community, thereby acting as a "push factor" encouraging migration, has received rather less scholarly attention. This facet of social relations, the so-called "downside of social capital," became evident through my study of West African immigrant entrepreneurs in Brazzaville (Portes and Landolt 1996; Whitehouse 2007). These entrepreneurs are mostly small- and medium-scale retail traders, and they dominate the sale of imported goods, from food products to clothing to auto parts, in the city's markets. I wondered what induced these individuals (all of them men) to leave their homes in Mali, Guinea, Senegal, or other countries of the Sahel to run their businesses in Brazzaville, where living standards were not necessarily better than in their home communities, where they faced a greater risk than back home of being victims of political violence and looting, and where the official business climate has been rated among the least conducive to private enterprise (World Bank 2007). I also wondered about the other side of the coin: why weren't there more Congolese shopkeepers in Brazzaville's marketplaces? Congolese participation in the private sector seemed clustered in a few areas like local foodstuffs and transportation, while Congolese were all but absent from the retail sale of imported goods.

The explanations received from informants, both West African and Congolese, tended toward culturalistic arguments. Congolese prefer desk jobs, the conventional wisdom went, while West Africans just seem to have commerce "in their blood." But by probing a bit further I was able to elicit another discourse, one pertaining to entrepreneurs' obligations to kin. Many West Africans in Brazzaville told me that they would have been unable to build up and maintain the kind of capital needed to run a business if they had stayed home, because of the volume of claims made on their resources by members of their social networks (mostly kin). In fact, the vast majority of entrepreneurs I interviewed only took up commerce after leaving home, saving start-up capital over many years of doing unskilled labor or ambulant vending in various migrant destinations. For them, migration was an integral part of their strategies for business development and success.

In the West African Sahel, as in much of Africa, it is very difficult to refuse a request from kin. Prevailing norms favor the collective welfare of the kin group over individual private accumulation of wealth, and those who turn down demands from needy relatives risk incurring strong moral and even supernatural sanctions. Parents have an especially powerful moral claim to the wealth generated by their children and can invoke a form of curse known in many Sahelian Muslim societies as *danga* against children who are unwilling to share (Sanneh 1996). In such a social milieu, even acquiring the funds to start up a business, let alone managing one profitably over the long term, is highly problematic. Thus arises what Keith Hart calls the "entrepreneur's social dilemma—how to divide his resources between a public social security fund of reciprocal exchanges between familiars [on the one hand] and private accumulation towards a personalized form of security provided by capital investments [on the other]" (Hart 1975: 28).

Congolese are by no means immune to this dilemma. In fact, in their lineage-dominated society, the constraints on prospective entrepreneurs may be even greater. A number of studies have documented the social challenges faced by Congolese business owners on their home soil (Devauges 1977; Dzaka and Milandou 1994; Tsika 1995). They face the same pressures as West Africans to redistribute their wealth, and the same risk of social stigma if they fail to heed these pressures. With Congolese, however, instead of the threat of *danga*—redolent with Islamic values of filial piety—it is a form of spiritual aggression known as *bunganga* that constitutes the most potent means of compulsion. As in many African societies, in Congo the supernatural acts as an "instrument in the struggle against scarcity" (Dzaka and Milandou 1994: 109). It is also a powerful deterrent to individuals thinking of going into business in their home communities.

Emigration offers perhaps the clearest way out of the entrepreneur's social dilemma.[2] By putting some physical distance between themselves and the bulk of their kin, migrants can insulate themselves from a substantial portion of the claims placed upon their wealth and try to find a more favorable balance between embeddedness in and freedom from their social networks. The most powerful means of making a claim upon their resources—the face-to-face request—is no longer an option, and the alternatives are often difficult or costly. This is why, in the words of a Zambian migrant quoted by Lisa Cliggett, people who have left home are "saved by distance" (Cliggett 2005: 144). They still may send a considerable portion of their profits home to needy relatives, but they can now do so on their own terms, following their own timetables and in accordance with their own circumstances.

If Malian entrepreneurs have been successful in Congo (as well as in many other African countries), some observers have remarked on their under-representation in Mali's own economy, particularly in the most profitable sectors, many of which are controlled by Lebanese (Pringle 2006). Likewise, if Congolese entrepreneurs have been unable to thrive in Brazzaville's markets, they have had more luck in Paris (MacGaffey and Bazenguissa-Ganga 2000). Thus, even given promising formal economic incentives in their home countries (such as high prices, a growing economy, or less government regulation of private business), many would-be entrepreneurs in Africa choose to go abroad in order to escape informal economic disincentives generated by their social milieu. The case of Brazzaville's West African traders suggests that disincentives posed by strong social networks and obligation to kin may actually outweigh the benefits of a stable political environment and a healthy retail economy, at least in the minds of many who migrate.

Much has been written about the power of social networks in developing countries to act as an economic safety net, providing protection to the poor and vulnerable in the absence of state-sponsored welfare and social security programs. In the 1990s the World Bank even held up social capital as the "missing link" in economic development, and development experts identified social networks as a means of harnessing "the genius for survival of the poor," delivering them "from the bonds of bankrupt, downsized nation-states" (World Bank 1997; Elyachar 2002: 508). While social networks do offer significant potential for personal achievement and collective development, we must refrain from reducing them to the opportunities they make accessible. Just as membership in a network can ensure the basic welfare of the needy, it can also stifle individual initiative and penalize success. It is this aspect of social networks and the burdens they create—the downside of social capital—that constitutes a significant push factor driving international migration in Africa.

SOCIAL NETWORKS AND INFORMATION

Social relations have another impact that works in stark contrast to standard assumptions about migrant behavior. Concerns over status and reputation can influence migrants' decisions about whether and when to return home, as well as what kinds of information they should share with people back home concerning conditions in the place of destination. Migrants who have not met with success abroad, rather than lose face by returning home empty-handed, may prefer to remain abroad indefinitely and conceal their misfortune from their kin and peers in the place of origin. Among my informants in Brazzaville, it was the young, unattached male migrants or so-called *aventuriers* who were especially prone to this (Whitehouse 2007).[3] Most of them worked as unskilled laborers and street hawkers. Unlike the better-off traders, they had not yet accumulated much if any wealth and were unable to send remittances home. But it was difficult for them to be open about their situations with people in their communities of origin. They felt considerable pressure to prove themselves as future husbands and fathers and were loath to appear unable to fashion better lives for themselves than the ones they had left behind. So they remained abroad, clinging to scant hopes of one day making it to the fabled diamond fields of Angola or perhaps securing a visa to a Western country. However desperate their situations became in Congo, return was all but out of the question.

When communicating with people back home, such migrants frequently misrepresent their circumstances in the place of destination, exaggerating successes and playing down hardships. In migrant-sending communities, this factor produces an abundance of misinformation about migration and its prospects, leading to a deceptive "demonstration effect" whereby accounts of positive migration outcomes reach home while most negative information is filtered out. This effect creates a systemic bias that favors migration even to destinations where real economic opportunities have become scarce. Brazzaville has been such a destination for several years now, yet young migrants continue to arrive from West Africa with little or no real knowledge of the economic and social difficulties awaiting them there.

Even when accurate information about hardship and lack of opportunity abroad does reach migrant-sending communities, it may have little impact due to widespread suspicions among non-migrants that their migrant kin are deliberately misleading them about life abroad. Non-migrants often believe (not without some justification) that successful migrants conceal their good fortunes from those back home, precisely in order to forestall the types of demands described in the previous section made by needy kin on their resources. Bad news from abroad, or even no news at all, comes to be interpreted as good news. A few years ago outside of Boston I accompanied a woman, recently arrived from Mali for a short visit, to see Lasine, an acquaintance in the area who had come there from Mali a few months earlier. We found Lasine at the landscaping business where he worked long hours. He accosted his compatriot and exhorted her to warn everyone back in Mali that America was not the earthly paradise they imagined it to be. They didn't know about all the hard work, the high cost of living, the loneliness. "Tell them," he urged her, the frustration evident in his voice. But as I have repeatedly found from my own experience in Africa, it is difficult for this kind of evidence to find a receptive audience among prospective migrants. In their eyes, such warnings are in fact proof of the ample opportunities that await them abroad, opportunities their selfish migrant kin would rather keep to themselves. Tense social relations between migrants and non-migrants thus inhibit the transmission of truthful reports about conditions at migration destinations, turning social networks into vehicles for the dissemination of false, or at least deceptive, information.

KANO HIDES A POOR MAN: IMAGINARIES OF DIGNITY AND MODERNITY

I met a young Cameroonian man I'll call Vincent one day in a Brazzaville market. He was self-employed, selling sandwiches as an ambulant vendor. He could earn 3,000 to 3,500 CFA francs in a day in this business, equivalent to US$7–8 at the time. Vincent told me that his living expenses were only about 500 francs per day, so he could accumulate some real savings with which he hoped to pay for future schooling. His business model was admirable, but I felt compelled to ask him why he came to Congo to exercise this trade rather than remaining in Cameroon. Vincent answered that if he were to do this at home, people would feel sorry for him; they'd say, "Oh, look at this son of a respectable father, reduced to selling bread in the streets."

In Cameroon, as in most places, the status of an ambulant vendor is nothing compared to that of a salaried worker or civil servant. Yet Vincent was actually earning more than many Cameroonians—or, for that matter, many Congolese—in those professional categories. In the wake of government austerity measures and the 1994 currency devaluation in the CFA monetary zone, low-ranking policemen and teachers earn no more than $100 per month, while Vincent could save $180 every month if he worked seven days a week (which he did). People looked at him and thought he was suffering, he told me, but he was not bothered by this. He held fast to his goal of going to America someday.

Vincent's example illustrates some of the gaps in neoclassical theories of migration. When people make decisions about whether to stay home or migrate, they are motivated by more than information about wage differentials, labor markets, cost of living, and similar economic factors. Especially in Africa, they are likely to take differentials of status into account as well. At home in Cameroon, working as an ambulant vendor would be degrading for Vincent. Even though selling sandwiches in the street might offer better economic rewards than some of the higher-status forms of employment available, it would be seen as unworthy of a respectable father's son. After emigrating, however, Vincent could take up ambulant vending because it wouldn't make him lose face in the eyes of the people who mattered most to him—his own kin, friends, and home people, whom he would not encounter abroad. I knew many young West African immigrants in much the same situation as Vincent, who came to Brazzaville to work as manual laborers, loading trucks and manhandling pushcarts overloaded with merchandise through the rutted streets. They could easily have found such work in Mali, Guinea, or wherever they had come from, but they chose to go abroad where they could do these low-status jobs without damaging their reputations back home.

In Nigeria, the northern city of Kano has been a destination for migrants from the south of the country for generations. Southern Nigerians sometimes say that "Kano hides a poor man." In Kano, in other words, migrants can conceal not only their poverty, but also their low status as workers from people in their communities of origin. As strangers they can perform labor that would be seen as too degrading for them to accept back home. The Bamanan of Mali, for their part, say that "exile knows no dignity" (Whitehouse 2007). They construct dignity (*danbe*) as a place-bound attribute, intricately intertwined with local social hierarchies and genealogies. When someone enters a foreign land, their inherent worth is not recognized there; their *danbe* is not transferable from their homeland. This imaginary of place-bound dignity can expose migrants to all manner of exploitation and abuse from natives and host-country officials, abuse the migrants tend to tolerate as simply the price of living in exile. It also offers them, however, the opportunity to pursue opportunities—most notably forms of labor—that would have been off-limits to them at home.

GLOBAL HIERARCHIES AND THE "END OF THE WORLD"

Not that anyone can go just anywhere to safeguard their social status. In contemporary Africa, labor has been shown to function as an index of hierarchies pertaining not only to class and gender but also to nationality, modernity, and power. Certain types of work are often reserved for immigrants, and more precisely for immigrants from countries perceived as less developed than the host country. In Abidjan, Côte d'Ivoire, for example, anthropologist Sasha Newell finds that driving a taxi is considered an unworthy occupation for a local, suitable only for immigrants from Burkina Faso and other countries. The preferable type of employment for many native Ivoirians is a desk job in the country's formal sector. In fact, many of Newell's informants in Abidjan said they would rather remain jobless than stoop to a degrading form of work. Engaging in labor seen as beneath one's proper status can lead to social exclusion: an Ivoirian who starts working as a taxi driver may soon find that his friends and neighbors no longer greet him (Newell 2006). Throughout Africa, different kinds of work are ranked along a scale, with some jobs (especially those entailing physical labor) being indelibly associated with backwardness and low status, and other jobs linked to education, high status, and power (Dougnon 2007). As we saw in the case of Vincent, the ambulant sandwich vendor, this scale does not always map onto earnings: even though taxi drivers in Abidjan earn more than the average civil servant, they nonetheless occupy an inferior position in the city's social hierarchy (Newell 2006).

In Congo, the "desk job" has been the ideal to which people, particularly educated young men, aspire. Work in the commercial sector has long been looked down upon. As one of my Congolese colleagues told me, "We Congolese don't have the patience to sit in a shop all day." West Africans, for their part, told me that Congolese just liked to put on fancy clothes and sit in an office awaiting their paychecks. Since the late colonial era commerce has been a "dishonorable occupation" compared to the "valued profession" of civil service work in Congo, and taking a commercial job has been "considered an indication of academic and social failure" (MacGaffey and Bazenguissa-Ganga 2000: 10–11). Although this hierarchy has shifted somewhat over the last two decades of government budget cuts, salary freezes, and a declining urban standard of living, there remains for Congolese a considerable stigma against working in commerce. This stems above all from a persistent binary opposition in the Congolese popular imagination that casts civil servants as educated, modern, and civilized, while traders are unlettered and backward. Never mind that the official wages of a typical Congolese servant today cannot provide for even a small family; in the minds of many *Brazzavillois*, a government job is still preferable to undignified commercial employment, which is to them the proper domain only of immigrants from so-called inferior countries.

To an extent, though, the hierarchies of labor I have described here are place-bound rather than absolute or universal. Like the notions of dignity mentioned earlier, they hold little or no sway over those who go abroad. For this reason many natives of Abidjan and Brazzaville who would balk at keeping a shop, driving a taxi, or sweeping streets at home would be willing to perform these same jobs as immigrant workers in Paris, Marseilles, or New York. Conversely, it would be difficult for them to accept even a well-paying job in Bamako or Bangui, because they rank these cities beneath their own on the scale of development and modernity. Congolese, who tend to represent their country as more "civilized" than its neighbors (with the possible exception of Gabon) because of its close historical ties to France, imagine their place in the global order as intermediary, between more developed, more powerful nations and less developed, less powerful ones.[4]

This point crystallized for me during an interview I conducted in Brazzaville with Draman, the 47-year-old son of a successful immigrant father from Mali and a Congolese mother. His father had passed on, leaving Draman in charge of the family business empire (which included retail shops, trucks, and rental housing) and his many dependents. Draman was struggling with the weight of his obligations to work and family in Brazzaville, and privately he hoped to make a life somewhere else. In a hushed voice, he told me of his dream of living in America, a country he had never visited. When I asked him why he wanted to go there, his reply illuminated an imagined hierarchy of global migrant destinations.

> Americans are the most powerful on earth. Americans are evolved [évolué]. Americans have ease—for them everything's easy, in every domain. If you want to go live there peacefully, you'll be well off. If you want to go work, you'll work. If you want to get medical treatment, you get treatment. It's the end of the world! The end of the world. I think one must start small and grow larger. But one shouldn't. . . . One climbed up, one came to Congo, one goes back to Mali . . . no. If we left Mali to come to Congo, we should leave Congo to go to the U.S. That's the end of the world.

For Draman, leaving Congo for his fatherland, Mali, would be traveling in the wrong direction, downward. One must climb *up* the ladder, ideally continuing until reaching the country at the top—America, "the end of the world." In this respect Draman, Vincent, and many other men I have met throughout Africa share a common imaginary about the "world system" of opportunity and power and about where their countries—not to mention my own—fit into it. While social scientists have occasionally studied the subjective and cognitive aspects of this system of international stratification, these phenomena deserve more thorough analysis, particularly with respect to their impact on migration behavior (Lagos 1963; Ferguson 2006).

CONCLUSION: TOWARD A MORE SOCIAL APPROACH

The evidence reviewed here suggests that we can learn a great deal about why people migrate by analyzing migrants not as isolated *homo economicus* but as fundamentally social beings, for whom the risks and benefits of migration are bound up in socially generated webs of meaning. A more social analysis of migration and its determinants can enable us to overcome what Karl Polanyi called the "economistic fallacy" (Polanyi 1977: 6). This fallacy equates all human economy with markets and their operations and has the effect of defining personhood in terms of productive activity and rational interest, rather than in terms of the "social tissue of relations among persons" (Somers 1990: 152). Neoclassical approaches to economics have been especially condemned as under-socialized (Granovetter 1985). A more complete view of human economy must take into account the embeddedness of individual actors in culturally produced structures of social relations. Migration research in particular must consider the wider cultural and social milieu in which migrants operate and make decisions about where and when to move, what kinds of labor to perform, and which pieces of information to share. Only such an approach can explain the sorts of apparent paradoxes in migration behavior I have described here.

This more comprehensive method enables us to view migration behavior without necessarily judging it as a sign of something out of balance. Governments in the North and South alike still have a strong tendency to pathologize migration and to associate it with social breakdown in the sending societies. Considerable research, however, indicates that even considerable rates of out-migration need not be taken as a sign of social decay. Indeed, as I have argued here, out-migration from a particular place can also be an indication of social institutions at work there which are typically associated with healthy societies, including social networks and generalized norms of reciprocity (de Bruijn, van Dijk, and Foeken 2001; Putnam 2000). What if we came to think of spatial mobility as the norm in human existence, rather than the exception demanding explanation? What if, "other things being equal, people do and will choose to move?" (Lambert 2002: xvii). As sociologist Adrian Favell points out, "Physical movement across space is the natural, normal given of human social life; what is abnormal, changeable, and historically constructed is the idea that human societies need to construct political borders and institutions that define and constrain spatial mobility in particular, regularized ways, such that immobility becomes the norm" (Favell 2008: 271). Current research by scholars of many disciplines suggests that a great deal of contemporary international migration is not a pathological form of displacement, but is instead inherent in the way humans fashion their relationships with their natural environment and with one another. It stems, in other words, from the social and cultural mediation of economic factors.

Finally, as we work to identify the driving forces behind migration, overcoming the "economistic fallacy" means considering gaps not only in living standards and earnings but in status and modernity. As much as anthropologists have stressed the need to abandon meta-narratives of modernity with their hidden teleological and hierarchical connotations of "civilization," we need to recognize that many of the people we study harbor no such desire, and have in fact adopted these same teleologies and hierarchies into their local vernaculars (Englund and Leach 2000; Ferguson 1999; Ferguson 2006). The actions of these people and their migrations in the world reflect their perceptions of global stratifications of wealth, differentials of mobility and immobility, and disparities of power (Bauman 1998; Carling 2002). The migrants I have encountered in Congo, Mali, and elsewhere in Africa would undoubtedly echo the oft-quoted words of science-fiction writer William Gibson: "The future is already here. It's just not evenly distributed yet." As they imagine their world and move within it spatially, they hope to secure a piece of the future for themselves.

NOTES

1. BBC, March 3, 2003. I should stress that the survey in question, carried out by Mercer Human Resources Consulting, was designed to gauge quality of life for expatriate residents; Brazzaville has not scored as low on other urban quality-of-life rankings.

2. The other main strategy involves joining a social group with different internal norms than one's home community. This is most often achieved through conversion to a minority religious denomination espousing a less communitarian ethos than the surrounding society, such as "Wahhabi" reformism in Muslim West Africa (see Kaba 1974) or Pentecostalism in Congo (see Dorier-Apprill 2001).

3. For a typology of Brazzaville's West African immigrants, see White-house 2009.

4. I am indebted to Sasha Newell for pointing out the same worldview among Ivoirians.

REFERENCES

Balandier, G. 1985. *Sociologie des Brazzavilles Noires*. 2nd ed. Paris: Presses de la Fondation Nationale des Sciences Politiques.

Bauman, Z. 1998. *Globalization: The Human Consequences*. Cambridge: Polity Press.

Bourdieu, P. 1986. "The Forms of Capital." In *Handbook of Theory and Research for the Sociology of Education*, ed. J. C. Richards. New York: Greenwood Press.

Brettell, C. 2008. "Theorizing Migration in Anthropology: The Social Construction of Networks, Identities, Communities, and Globalscapes." In *Migration Theory: Talking Across Disciplines*, 2nd ed., ed. C. Brettell and J. Hollifield. New York: Routledge.

Brettell, C., and J. Hollifield. 2008. "Migration Theory: Talking Across Disciplines." In *Migration Theory: Talking Across Disciplines*, 2nd ed., ed. C. Brettell and J. Hollifield. New York: Routledge.

British Broadcasting Corporation. 2003. "Brazzaville—'World's Worst City.'" March 3. http://news.bbc.co.uk/2/hi/africa/2815105.stm.

Carling, J. 2002. "Migration in the Age of Involuntary Immobility: Theoretical Reflections and Cape Verdean Experiences." *Journal of Ethnic and Migration Studies* 28(1).

Cliggett, L. 2005. *Grains from Grass: Aging, Gender and Famine in Rural Africa*. Ithaca, N.Y.: Cornell University Press.

de Bruijn, M., R. van Dijk, and D. Foeken, eds. 2001. *Mobile Africa: Changing Patterns of Movement in Africa and Beyond*. Leiden: Brill.

Devauges, R. 1977. *L'Oncle, le ndoki, et l'entrepreneur: La petite entreprise congolaise à Brazzaville*. Paris: ORSTOM.

Dorier-Apprill, E. 2001. "The New Pentecostal Networks of Brazzaville." In *Between Babel and Pentecost*, ed. A. Corten and R. Marshall-Fratani. Bloomington: Indiana University Press.

Dougnon, I. 2007. *Travail de Blanc, Travail de Noir: La migration des paysans dogon vers l'Office du Niger et au Ghana (1910–1980)*. Paris: Karthala.

Dzaka, T., and M. Milandou. 1994. "L'entrepreneuriat congolais à l'épreuve des pouvoirs magiques: Une face cachée de la gestion culturelle du risque?" *Politique Africaine* 56.

Elyachar, J. 2002. "Empowerment Money: The World Bank, Non-Governmental Organizations and the Value of Culture in Egypt." *Public Culture* 14(3).

Englund, H., and J. Leach. 2000. "Ethnography and the Meta-Narratives of Modernity." *Current Anthropology* 41(3).

Favell, A. 2008. "Rebooting Migration Theory: Interdisciplinarity, Globality and Postdisciplinarity in Migration Studies." In *Migration Theory: Talking Across Disciplines*, 2nd ed., ed. C. Brettell and J. Hollifield. New York: Routledge.

Ferguson, J. 1999. *Expectations of Modernity: Myths and Meanings of Urban Life on the Zambian Copperbelt*. Berkeley: University of California Press.

———. 2006. *Global Shadows: Africa in the Neoliberal World Order*. Durham, N.C.: Duke University Press.

Gilbert, A., and J. Gugler. 1992. *Cities, Poverty and Development: Urbanization in the Third World*. New York: Oxford University Press.

Gondola, C. 1996. *Villes Miroirs: Migrations et identités urbaines à Kinshasa et Brazzaville, 1930–1970.* Paris: L'Harmattan.

Granovetter, M. 1985. "Economic Action and Social Structure: The Problem of Embeddedness." *American Journal of Sociology* 91(3).

Hart, K. 1975. "Swindler or Public Benefactor? The Entrepreneur in his Community." In *Changing Social Structure in Ghana: Essays in the Comparative Sociology of a New State and an Old Tradition,* ed. J. Goody. London: International African Institute.

Kaba, L. 1974. *The Wahhabiyya: Islamic Reform and Politics in French West Africa.* Evanston, Ill.: Northwestern University Press.

Lagos, M. G. 1963. *International Stratification and Underdeveloped Countries.* Chapel Hill: University of North Carolina Press.

Lambert, M. C. 2002. *Longing for Exile: Migration and the Making of a Translocal Community in Senegal, West Africa.* Portsmouth, N.H.: Heinemann.

MacGaffey, J., and R. Bazenguissa-Ganga. 2000. *Congo-Paris: Transnational Traders on the Margins of the Law.* Bloomington: Indiana University Press.

Massey, D. S., J. Arango, G. Hugo, A. Kouaouci, A. Pellegrino, and J. E. Taylor. 1994. "An Evaluation of International Migration Theory: The North American Case." *Population and Development Review* 20(4).

Newell, S. 2006. "Estranged Belongings: A Moral Economy of Theft in Abidjan, Côte d'Ivoire." *Anthropological Theory* 6.

———. n.d. "*Bizness* and Brotherhood: The Moral Economy of Crime." In *The Modernity Bluff: Crimes of Consumption and Urban Youth in Côte d'Ivoire.* Unpublished manuscript.

Palloni, A., D. S. Massey, M. Ceballos, K. Espinosa, and M. Spittel. 2001. "Social Capital and International Migration: A Test Using Information on Family Networks." *American Journal of Sociology* 106(5).

Polanyi, K. 1977. *The Livelihood of Man.* London: Academic Press.

Portes, A., and P. Landolt. 1996. "The Downside of Social Capital." *American Prospect* 26.

Pringle, R. 2006. "Democratization in Mali: Putting History to Work." *Peaceworks* 58. http://www.usip.org/pubs/peaceworks/pwks58.pdf.

Putnam, R. 2000. *Bowling Alone: The Collapse and Revival of American Community.* New York: Simon and Schuster.

Riccio, B. 2004. "Transnational Mouridism and the Afro-Muslim Critique of Italy." *Journal of Ethnic and Migration Studies* 30(5).

Sanneh, L. 1996. *Piety and Power: Muslims and Christians in West Africa.* Maryknoll, N.Y.: Orbis Books.

Sassen, S. 1991. *The Global City: New York, London, Tokyo.* Princeton, N.J.: Princeton University Press.

Somers, M. 1990. "The Intellectual Legacy of Karl Polanyi." In *The Life and Work of Karl Polanyi: A Celebration,* ed. K. Polanyi-Levitt. New York: Black Rose Books.

Tsika, J. 1995. "Entre l'enclume étatique et le marteau familial: L'impossible envol des entrepreneurs au Congo." In *Entreprises et entrepreneurs africains*, ed. Y.-A. Fauré and S. Ellis. Paris: Karthala.

Whitehouse, B. 2007. "Exile Knows No Dignity: African Transnational Migrants and the Anchoring of Identity." Ph.D. diss., Brown University.

———. 2009. "Insights from South-South Migration: Transnational Childrearing and Othered Identities in Brazzaville, Congo." *Global Networks* 9(1): 82–99.

World Bank. 1997. "Social Capital: The Missing Link?" In *Monitoring Economic Progress—Expanding the Measure of Wealth*. Washington, D.C.: World Bank. http://wbln0018.worldbank.org/environment/eei.nsf/3dc00 e2e46240235852567130005a1d4a/aa228cb86afc7ec18525671c00570418/$F ILE/chap6.pdf.

———. 2007. "Doing Business 2007." http://www.doingbusiness.org/ EconomyRankings/.

Yengo, P. 2006. *La guerre civile du Congo-Brazzaville*. Paris: Karthala.

MIGRATION AS COPING WITH RISK AND STATE BARRIERS

MALIAN MIGRANTS' CONCEPTION OF BEING FAR FROM HOME

ISAIE DOUGNON
TRANSLATED FROM FRENCH BY HELENE GAGLIARDI

Death, starvation, overexploitation, poverty, life *sans papier,* states' barriers (arrests and imprisonment), unemployment—just to name a few—are the words most used to redefine migration in order to discourage young Malians from undertaking dangerous trips to Europe or large African cities. What, however, is the real impact of this communication strategy, even coupled with setting up the legal and physical barriers? In fact, we see that in spite of discursive campaigns against migration and small-scale rural development projects to create job opportunities, youth migration from rural and urban Mali is intensifying and the destinations are more diverse. This chapter tries to demonstrate that the policymakers' discourse on the danger of migration is, in fact, at the core of Malian conceptions of traveling outside their community. In most West African societies, "migration" means a pilgrimage into the wilderness. How, given this grassroots' understanding of migration, will state policies be able to stop rural and urban movement toward African and European cities?

Before the colonial period, many African societies were characterized by a sharply bounded community with members living amid the environment that constituted the integral part of humans' lived world. Any movement of individuals outside this community and environment was understood in terms of a threat or danger to their lives. This ancestral conception of traveling has been extended by the challenges of colonial and postcolonial Africa with various frontiers and border checkpoints. The most important aspect of this conception is that the returning migrant is celebrated as hero. A return to the home village means that s/he has coped with the wilderness and been victorious. The newly acquired qualities of this person, based on what s/he has learned or obtained outside, may form a cluster of values that contribute to the migrant's overall identity. Using the definition of "migration" in several Malian national languages, I discuss the meaning of migration and migrants' discourse about crossing borders in the colonial and postcolonial periods, as well as illustrate how current migrants' strategies to overcome all types of barriers—even at the risk of their lives—is rooted in their very definition of migration to seek paid work or to discover the outside world.

MIGRATION IN A LOCAL SENSE

> The one who rises sees something. The one who leaves takes and
> brings back something. The one who stays will get trampled.
> —ARAB PROVERB

It is, in our days, easy to discern—through television, newspaper, or radio—the risks that characterize the lives of young African migrants. It is certainly more difficult to establish analytical categories relevant to the understanding of the essential signification of "to leave" and "to be" far from the natal village in different African societies.[1] Indeed, for at least a decade, we note that the reflection concerning African migrations is limited to flourishing literature on rural and urban poverty, as well as images of drowned migrants in the Atlantic and the Mediterranean. The media shows dead migrants on airport runways or devoured by lions at the Mozambique–South African border. Even more captivating are the images of migrants who desperately attempt to surmount the barbed-wired walls of Ceuta and Mellina. Certain NGOs and frontier security agencies identify, on behalf of their governments, the nationalities of migrants, the route they take, their countries of transit and final destination, as well as their strategy.[2]

We witness in parts of West Africa (Mali, Senegal, and Guinea) a growth of co-development programs and/or of strategies of communication that work to dissuade young Africans from leaving for Europe or big African cities. These programs are often financed by developed countries, supplementing the efforts of the local national governments. Various NGOs and local leaders have organized sensitization campaigns in African villages to awaken in the heart of the youth a certain consciousness that migration is a dangerous and risky enterprise (e.g., they are exposed to horrible images of hundreds of drowned bodies in the Mediterranean and the Atlantic). We therefore witness a multitude of terms that arise in scholarly or press articles, seeking to characterize the tragedy of African migration. The most frequently used terms are "clandestine," "expulsed," "sans papier," "damned of the sea," and "kamikazees." Despite speeches and policies, migratory flows are not declining and instead destinations become more abundant. Facing these failures, questions arise: How do Africans themselves conceptualize the idea of leaving their homes for others? Why do they travel against all odds?

To study migratory dynamism in the *longue durée* within each African society reveals that structural forms of migration cannot by themselves integrally define the historical and sentimental relations between the paternal home and the external world. It has now been some years since politicians and academicians have felt urgency in exploring the current dynamics of migration in Africa. But the question is, with what approach? Should we start with the description of visible consequences of African migration toward Europe and elsewhere? Or should we stick to an analysis of local concepts by which the migrants establish social, material, and cultural relations with the outside world?

I start here with the latter approach. This does not mean that I deny the importance of economic factors for current migration in and out of Africa as described by many scholars and development experts. I have elsewhere described the transition in the Malian Sahel from pre–World War II *migration de prestige*—where cultural values prioritized imported items like umbrella, cloths, perfume—to the "survival migration" of the post-drought period (1973 and 1984).[3] In fact, over the subsequent three decades, many Malian migrants are still in search of cash to invest into housing, shops, small businesses in Malian cities, or modern agricultural technologies and small-scale irrigation in rural areas.

Anthropological approaches to migration first changed from economic push and pull factors to neo-Marxist models in the 1970s (Lewellen 2002). At present, more anthropologists are opting to tackle African migration from historical and sociocultural angles (Moodie and Ndatshe 1994; Manchuelle 1997). I adopt this latter approach, focusing on social values attached to migration and local conceptualizations of risk in migration or traveling. My point here is to show that migration is not a mere relation of individuals to property or earnings but the realization of youthful dreams, of social aspiration.

In many Malian villages (Soninké, Bamana, Peul, Malinké), one has the soul of a migrant from a very young age, as boys take on this role in order to become a man, though often without knowing exactly what it is about. Just like "voyage literature" (which provoked a tourism boom in Europe), seducing stories and songs of emigration have awakened the desire for travel among young people in these villages.

The migrant has foremost a taste for adventure, a taste originating particularly from exposure to the accounts of those who come back from far and unknown countries. In familial conversations, they tell other young ones about their particular sensations experienced while discovering other countries. They influence the young who stayed in the village into believing that the migrant participates in the creation of the country where he visits and works (for instance, the accounts of Malians and Burkinabe migrants on their role in the birth of "Ivory Eldorado" or the former Gold Coast, now Ghana). But it is not enough for the migrant to have souvenirs. He must expose other men to what he has brought back. In order to be complete, the stories demand many objects of prestige (such as clothing and money) and proficiency in foreign languages.

In this chapter, I do not focus on the visible consequences of migrations, but rather on local concepts through which the migrants establish their own relations with the external world. I then analyze how these relations are based on a series of morals that form the identity of the migrants who return to the village. To apprehend the recent intensity of migration in Africa, despite all forms of barriers, we need to understand the significance(s) of the word "travel," the collective imagination of migration, through which the rural youth of Mali experiment, interpret, and frame their voyages and relations with the outside world. We begin with a sociocultural approach—the idea that the meaning given by each Malian society to migration is associated with its migratory traditions and its current perceptions of life abroad.

Our research in Mali shows that the migrants have a clear conception of the problems we invoke today in order to persuade them not to travel. Indeed, the migrants' stories incorporate—just as the colonial reports (British and French) mention on multiple occasions—the nature and consequences of young migrants' exploitation while in search of work. Migrants of yesteryear warn young immigration candidates against the dangers to which they are exposing themselves. Just like their elders in the colonial era, today's young ones are conscious that to migrate is to venture into risks and perils. Several local songs interpret the dangers of leaving their hometown.

In this chapter, I analyze multiple local terms collected within different ethnicities of Mali.[4] These local concepts define the total reality of migration in its dangerous as well as its heroic aspects. For example, the Dogon have two expressions to define migration and the attendant risks. The first one is *bara nu* ("to flee in the wilderness").[5] Bara is, at once, the locality and wilderness that surrounds it, while the term *nu* signifies "to flee." The concept *bara nu*, therefore refers to the person who journeys beyond the land, someone who is not socially or geographically under the control of the village/community.[6]

The second expression is *bara gunu* ("to collect and place"), defining the manner by which migrants, on their way to regions known to have employment opportunities, are approached by recruiters in their trucks. The recruiters propose a job and a compelling salary. With the verbal contract concluded, migrants embark in the truck and arrive to conditions of near-slavery in a cacao or coffee field (from which they are eventually liberated by a third party or run away). As we see, such risk is at the heart of the terminology of young rural individuals regarding migration throughout space and time.

THE VOYAGE AS A RITE OF PASSAGE

One essential point in the popular memory of migration is the importance given to voyage per se—a voyage in which one prepares for death. Many works on migration focus on the descriptions of destinations countries and the installation processes of migrants. Historian David Cressy makes an exception. He gives special attention to the Atlantic crossing in his work on English migration to New England in the seventeenth century. He describes how the crossing of the Atlantic constitutes in itself a vital part in the colonization experience of new lands:

> English emigrants and travellers who journeyed to America in the seventeenth century underwent a crucial seasoning process, a *passage* in several senses of the word. . . . For many of the travellers the crossing was not simply a matter of transportation but rather a primary occasion for seasoning and testing, bonding and socialization, a rehearsal and preparation for community life in the wilderness. (Cressy 1987: 144)

Many Malian societies conceptualize, without doubt, the voyage as a rite of passage.[7]

Within the Dogon the concept *bara nu*, or *jobo* ("to flee toward wilderness"), describe, in an extraordinary manner, a transition from a peaceful state of mind to a state of war. Women cry for the migrants as they would cry for one who is leaving for war. The wilderness and the village are like death and life. The wilderness is understood as not only the actual distance that separates the village from the migrant but also the destination town and every other transit point the migrants will travel through as well.

The inhabitants of these transit localities or destinations can themselves be, on a cultural front, potentially dangerous for the migrant.[8] The Sénoufo use the term *ma-foro* ("to leave your home") to express the movement of an individual that is not under the protection of his own people, one who needs to face the challenges of the new life he encounters. This new life is the antinomy of village life.

Among the Bamana, the ethnic majority of Mali, the word *tunkan* means migrate (*tu*, the forest, and *kan*, to cut; literally "cut the forest") and *tukanrankè* (the man who cuts the forest) signifies that migrants face a perilous exercise. If we take into consideration the immensity of the forest, we can imagine the "supernatural" efforts that a young villager must put forth in order to successfully cut the forest. The metaphor here is even more revealing of the heroic character of the voyage far from the homeland. The Soninké have the word *gounikè*, meaning the man of the vast wilderness (from *gounè*, the vast wilderness) who is a veritable combatant. According to the Soninké, one who leaves through the vast wilderness can be threatened by other men or attacked by animals. Death watches him throughout the entire journey. This is similar to one who ventures into a large city where he knows no one while having no notion of urban life. His situation is comparable to that of the man in the wilderness, without rescue, whose fate lies solely in his own hands.

There are other Soninké terms, synonyms of *gunikè* that are also used today: *yitele tunka* and *wodagana homori*. These depict the migration in the sense of facing a rival or taking on a challenge. To migrate is to build the future before definitely returning to the natal home. To migrate also means destroying the obstacles that can block the enlightenment of the family and the individual. Thus, if a Soninké man has the opportunity to migrate, the risks will not cross his mind and only a bad state of health could prevent him from going. Migration evokes within him a sense of work, the money he will earn, and the help that he will offer to his relatives that stayed in the village. In this society, migration is a synonym for luck. According to them, each should take a chance no matter what the conditions or distance to overcome. So a father may be prouder to have his children scattered around the United States, France, and Canada than to see them as a government minister in Mali, because migration is the source of protection or social security for close ones and distant parents.

In certain Soninké villages, migration as a rite of passage starts at the birth of a young boy. His parents collect and save the money donated during the baby's baptism. When the child turns 12 years old, they give him this money to be used as transportation fees for his very first migration. This first voyage, often within the country (to a regional or national capital), is meant to prepare and teach the child how to become independent. After many years of accumulating experience with internal migrations, the boy develops into an adult who can undertake international migration.

The Soninkés have a strong conception of voyage—it is a combat against death for the beauties of the world. In this cultural milieu, not migrating is not living. One who does not leave the village stays at the bottom of the social ladder. He is seen as a hen that pecks the millet falling from the mortar of a lady while she pounds to prepare *toh*. This essentially means that he eats what others have brought back. Before the voyage, the migrant goes to see a diviner in order to find out the potential dangers or obstacles of which he may be the victim throughout his journey.

Conscious of the migration risks, Soninké migrants grant supreme importance to the sacrifices the village diviner requires from them. These sacrifices are supposed to protect them from all dangers. Certain sacrifices are made in the presence of the entire village community. On the other hand, some sacrifices are made with the greatest discretion because otherwise certain people with the wrong intentions could thwart the adventure. Before departure, the migrant presents his excuses to all his brothers and asks for the benediction and approval of his parents. This is a form of social sacrifice, and it means more than the fetish sacrifices or those of supernatural forces.

According to certain elderly Dogon migrants, in the 1920s and 1930s their voyage was so dangerous that it could take the travelers three days to travel twenty-five kilometers, The density of the vegetation and the presence of animals such as lions, hyenas, and foxes slowed down the pace of the travelers. In these early years of colonization, young recruits that ventured for their military duty or service would often be blocked on the road by lions or other dangers.

In the country of Dogon, the perilous nature of the voyage is associated with the struggle a girl and boy encounter when the community opposes their romantic relationship. In the migrant's story, we witness the narrow correlation between migration for love and the voyage for an unknown world, a land where the two lovers will find the freedom to live for their love.[9] When two individuals love each other and the community opposes their love, the two lovers must flee to live happily under other horizons. On the same level, a man has to migrate to search for objects he desires but cannot find in his homeland, just as this old popular song demonstrates:

Kidjè èju diguè ma so yai ma koye	It is only getting lost in pursuit of good
salamu siri le yana èju le dikè ma so yai	Such a beautiful sword and a beautiful girl
tinè èju digè ma so yai ma koye	It is only getting lost by following a man of good spirit
Ni pa suyi kèjè, yanan èju digè ma	Even if it means crossing seven seas and seven streams.
Olu yai ka su yai, yanna ine teke, nininri ine teke	To migrate is to lose oneself: the women, the singers cry for the migrant.
salamu birè digè ma so yai	It is only getting lost searching for valuable objects.

Kidjè èju diguè ma so yai ma koye	It is only getting lost in pursuit of good
salamu siri le yana èju le dikè ma so yai	Such a beautiful sword and a beautiful girl
tinè éju digè ma so yai ma koye	It is only getting lost by following a man of good spirit
Ni pa suyi kèjè, yanan èju digè ma	Even if it means crossing seven seas and seven streams.
Olu yai ka su yai, yanna ine teke, nininri ine teke	To migrate is to lose oneself: the women, the singers cry for the migrant.
salamu birè digè ma so yai	It is only getting lost searching for valuable objects.
Kidjè èju diguè ma so yai ma koye	It is only getting lost in pursuit of good
salamu siri le yana èju le dikè ma so yai	Such a beautiful sword and a beautiful girl
tinè éju digè ma so yai ma koye	It is only getting lost by following a man of good spirit
Ni pa suyi kèjè, yanan èju digè ma	Even if it means crossing seven seas and seven streams.
Olu yai ka su yai, yanna ine teke, nininri ine teke	To migrate is to lose oneself: the women, the singers cry for the migrant.
salamu birè digè ma so yai	It is only getting lost searching for valuable objects.

In this song, love and migration have the same value. They are as difficult to obtain as a snake's phlegm. The effort of the one who seeks to live his love in freedom is comparable to the effort of one who travels in faraway countries. The risks are numerous in both cases but it is the price that must be paid. The risks emerge from the fact that society does not provide any necessary means at the disposition of the migrant to face the dangers. There are no specific preparations to make: when one decides to leave, he prepares himself for death. The migrant is alone facing the immense wilderness full of misery, diseases, and cruel men.

The voyage into the wilderness represents the first collective or individual experience of a man who desires to be considered fully among the mature. Weeks of walking through the forests, savannas, and fields reinforce their masculinity. No one knows how long the voyage will take. Everything depends on nature and the will of the migrant to face these dangers. In the past, secure roads did not exist and disaster could emerge anytime. The sacrifices and other amulets (magic) were/are a traveler's only guides and protections. Muslims and Christians attribute the success or disaster of their voyage to God, just as the Puritans interpreted the violent winds during their crossing of the Atlantic as an expression of the power and glory of God (Cressy 1987: 137). Whatever the voyage event may be, it can be interpreted as the manifestation of God's will.

In recent stories, just like those of the colonial period, the migrants make reference to disappeared or dead men. The dead—those that their colleagues consider glorious—were never discouraged and would never discourage future candidates. Those who fall are, in reality, torches in the sea or desert that will be raised again to be carried higher and farther.[10] The characteristic young villager, never satisfied with his immobility at the village, would like to always travel—to know and gain more. This is the goal of all migrants.[11]

Another notion, *jobo* (to flee), was always an act of temerity, because it equated to a leap toward the unknown. The village/community could not allow their sons to go on their own into peril. The sons must consequently "flee" or *jobo*. In other words, this is leaving without social authorization and thus living in the wilderness without the consent of the parents. Before it became an acknowledged part of "local culture," migration in a sense of "fleeing" was a violation of village social regulations.

This is why the returned migrant is considered impure and must be purified before reentering village life. He is comparable to a woman who is menstruating. Considered impure, she must spend the entirety of her cycle away from the village. On the seventh day, she reunites with her family after purifying herself with water. The returning migrant must also be purified before entering the village. On the surface, a Dogon migrant is hypothetically impure. He might have eaten meat forbidden for his clan or slept with casted women (a blacksmith or shoemaker, for example). If he came back into the village and drank water from the communal ladle, all the impurities would be transmitted. The reparation for this would be too expensive for the village and his family.

Therefore, when he comes near the village, the returning migrant must signal that there is a "stranger" waiting to be received. To announce this, he either blows a whistle that he bought for the circumstance or he opens a box of perfume and spills a bit in order for the smell to invade the village. Certain inhabitants, familiar with the signal, run in the direction of the whistle's sound or toward the smell of the perfume. Once the migrant is identified, his parents come to get his luggage. Then they have the "purifier" come, who is most often one of the village religious leaders. He ceremonially purifies the returning migrant and serves him water to drink. The objects of purification are made up of a band of local textile, stalks of millet, and sacred water. After the purification ritual, the returning individual first visits the *Hogon* (religious leader) before reuniting with his family. Any contraveners of this required purification were punished by the religious leadership or even by the village gods (Dougnon 2003).

By the 1960s, migration was so anchored into local culture that the wilderness stopped being taboo or impure. On the contrary, it became a new school with which youth should become familiar. Except for Koranic students, seasonal or permanent migration became the goal of boys between the ages of 14 and 30 and girls between 13 and 18 years old.[12] They could now decide to leave themselves. A father or a mother would have a hard time forbidding their children to do what is increasingly perceived as a village tradition. Many household heads even ignored the destination of their children. Or they may (often in vain) try to change their minds by reminding them that they are leaving for regions where their predecessors have been shamefully exploited and came back poorer. They left anyway. The parents no longer had power over them. They could leave suddenly one day without warning anyone. Sometimes, a few from the same village might leave on the same day.

Let us return to the term *baara kuno* (literally "to pick up and place"). This expression today implies child trafficking, exploitation of migrants, or slavery, an ensemble of inhuman and illegal practices in which migrants are victimized in host countries or on the road. In the recountings of elderly Dogon migrants to Ghana, we see the extent of this phenomenon. This is especially prevalent in the north of Ghana where migrants were picked up by drivers and put into slavery. The northern territories were, in fact, a zone of favor for those drivers in search of workers. It was in these localities that the migrants, originally from French Sudan, felt the first physical exhaustion and lack of food provisions. They often searched for work in cities like Bolgatanga, Tamale, Bole, and Wa to earn some money and continue their journey.

Consider this account of a Dogon migrant who provides personal meaning to *baara kuno.*

> In the Dogon country, during winter, we cultivate. During the dry season, certain youth go to Ségou, others to Bamako. We chose Mopti, then Kumasi. From Mopti, we left to Bobo-Dioulasso, where we sold meat. Our clients were usually from Songhaï. The money collected was insufficient to pay the transportation all the way to Kumasi. We decided to walk. We only walked at night; during the day, we rested. This is because, during this time, people were being sold. Despite all of our precautions, a man sold us to an Ashanti. This man was in a truck with an Ashanti driver. He said he would drive us to the Hogon of Kumasi and he would be reimbursed by him. Thus, we climbed in the car. In less than an hour, we arrived in a village, the name of which I did not know. The man told us to get out because

we had arrived. The driver asked the villagers if they wanted to buy some people. There was in the village a Muslim Ashanti who said he needed workers. This man gave money to the driver and drove us to his house. When the night fell, we ran and fled. He caught us and hit us all the way back to the village. A man wrote down our names, and said if we fled again they will find us. For two months, we labored in the cacao fields. The meals were bad. One day, in the middle of the night, I woke my comrades up and said, "Let's flee." We were on the road; we walked only at night, during the day we hid in the forest. We walked a month before arriving at Kumasi.

Bolgatanga, a city in the north of Ghana, was one city where drivers stayed, waiting for ordinary migrants from the French territories. They would propose work to young migrants and transport them to small villages, where they became domestics or forced to work in the fields. Often, the driver proposed to transport the migrants, who already felt the fatigue of the walk to Kumasi, at very low costs. The rest is a common tale: they were made prisoners somewhere in the forest before successfully escaping after a few weeks or months.

Memories of this sort are numerous when the migrants return and tell their adventures to the youngest of the village by the light of the moon. The returnees have plenty of experience with the dangers of migrating. A national campaign to prevent migration by publicizing its dangers would seem like a tautology or a joke to older migrants. They would utterly mock it.

According to the Dogon, Soninké, Bamana, Malinké, Peul, or Songhaï conceptions of migration analyzed above, the youth need to migrate even if it means risking one's life. Like his ancestors who stood up to the dangers of the forest and wilderness, he must surmount the legal and physical barriers to reach European, Asian, or other African countries.[13] The cultural foundations of migration are such that even publicizing the intolerance in receiving countries, the many expulsions, and the barriers to air and sea travel does not change the migratory wave.

If departure is considered a dangerous adventure, the return from the wilderness is perceived as a victory. The one who comes back is considered a hero. During his time in the wilderness, he conquered all difficulties stoically. This is a form of courage that honors not only the migrant but his parents as well. He becomes a role model for his generation. The foreign objects brought back—such as umbrellas, shoes, clothing, fabrics, and bracelets—are proof of success, a success coveted by others who are thus tempted as well by adventure.

In every Malian ethnicity, it is assumed that one will return from migration. To not return is unthinkable. The only reason the migrant would not come back is because of problems that spoiled his relationship with other family members. In such cases, the young man exiles himself from the village. For example, for the Peuls, the terms *ferade* or *perol* are used to designate a migration with no return, caused by familial problem (divorce, incest, theft, murder).[14] In such circumstances, the young man or young woman decides to leave the native region. They leave for far away and never come back to their peers. This is called definitive migration. Once one leaves under the pressure of the community, one never returns. Very often, people who leave their region for social reasons change their identity to avoid being recognized and do everything to evade fellow community members. On the other hand, such cases are fairly rare—the first rule of migration is to return to the village with the fruits of one's journey.

THE RETURNING MIGRANT AS HERO: MIGRATION AND NEW SOCIAL IDENTITY

The migrant is identified as a hunter leaving for the wilderness, eager to come back with game. The hunter is always ashamed to come back empty-handed. He is aware of the recognition and social respect that he will enjoy if he comes back with spoils. To come back empty-handed is a sign of weakness, cowardice, and fear. Rarely is unluckiness implied to explain the hunter's failure. To come back empty-handed signifies that the hunter is not mature enough to slaughter a beast. The migrant is like a hunter who takes on the wilderness with neither blade nor firearm. His only weapon is his courage and his abnegation, two values that merge together to form his new identity, that of an accomplished man.

In the Dogon conception, migration is not the simple fact of linking two geographic regions, but rather an engagement, a determination to overcome or defeat all adversity found in the wilderness. The proof of this accomplishment is without a doubt the return of the migrant to the village. The return is the consecration of the long and difficult voyage. It is like a man nominated to a high position of responsibility after thirty years of experience and hard challenges. This return is celebrated through various ceremonies. During these ceremonies, it is not only the safe physical health of the migrant that we present to the public, but also the material goods that he brought back from unknown countries. If the departure is perceived as heading to your peril, the return, on the other hand, expresses heroism. The exploits of the voyage, as if from a battle-hardened warrior, constitute the primary reason why every young child at the age of migration goes forth without thinking of the risks they may encounter. The social recognition that the migrant obtains upon returning to the village justifies and sharpens his courage to face the wilderness, whatever the adversity may be.[15]

A Bamana proverb says that there are in society three classes of wise men worth discussing: the elderly, the intellectuals, and the ones who have traveled a lot. Migrating is to seek knowledge and well-being, to discover the world, to know life and its difficulties. The Bamanas say that a young migrant who travels in a hundred villages is much more cultivated than an old man of a hundred years. Migration is always positive for the Bamana because the migrant never comes back empty-handed. If he comes back without his goods, he at least comes back with knowledge (or vice versa).

In Mali, we tell a visitor or even a stranger that walks by, "You left your home to come to your home."[16] This conception of the stranger considers the migrant like a message carrier from the culture of another population. This responsibility brings him respect from the society welcoming him.[17] For the Soninké, the migrant is an ambassador of the family, a missionary of his own.

The Bamanas say that a young man who has not migrated has no personal story—his CV is empty—and he will have no experience in his life. A young man who does not migrate is like sauce without salt. The man must travel even at the cost of his life. The following proverb confirms this idea of migration: "The head of a man is like the handle of an axe: we throw it where it breaks." This means that a young boy should not be scared to see his head broken (death) during migration. Migration is the only way to understand life and develop individual defense capacities to face any situation. If he stays at home, without moving, he will be seen as a coward.

The idea of coming back with one's hands full is very prevalent in migration accounts. Those who come back empty-handed are seen as hooligans. Facing this contempt of the community, migrants who fail return to the village during the night, far from the indiscrete looks of the villagers. Their failure is even hidden by parents who give their own money so the migrant can give some to their cousins as gifts, a sign of their migration success.

Except for those who migrate because they are exiled for having committed a social deviance (theft, incest, rape, and lies), migrants are considered like people who are gathering wisdom. The esteem and popular consideration the returning migrant enjoys is so strong that no dangers could make him back down once he has decided to leave.

In the Malinké tradition, migration has similar determining values—bravery, tenacity, and audacity. It gives a positive image of the boy in the eyes of young women. It also expresses kindness and bravery, because when a man returns from migration with a lot of success it elevates the image of his mother as well. We say that success smiles at the child of a mother full of kindness. On the other hand, victory turns its back to a child of a selfish or cruel mother. The success of a young migrant depends on the kindness of his mother's heart. If his mother is generous, she will see her son succeed abroad. This is why we say that each boy is in the "hands of his mother"—the woman is the beginning and the end of the migrant's success.

In the past, after the agricultural season Malinké village chiefs would organize a big party in honor of the young who wanted to migrate. At the occasion, every candidate's mother and father went to visit the marabouts in hopes bringing their child a successful return. When they do return, it is a celebration once again. During their absence, parents stay worried because they are nervous their child may come back empty-handed or be the last one to return. The empty-handed migrant exposes himself, on one hand to his own humiliation and on the other exposes his family to shame because they will not be able to present him to other villagers during the return ceremony.

In Songhaï, *a dira* means to migrate in the sense of leaving and coming back, going to get something away from the village. The migrant must always come back to the village even if he did not get anything. Consequently, if he comes back empty-handed, his cousins mock him that he came back without even a *pirogue* of bamboo or reed. The Songhaïs also use the word *taabuchi*, which comes from the word *taami* (shoes). In multiple Malian ethnicities, the shoes that protect the traveler's feet have a sacred character. For example, if a jealous man wants to harm his neighbor, he can use his shoes to bewitch him. If his spell works, the bewitched man migrates and never comes back to the village. Never coming back is the sign of ultimate malediction. For the Songhaï, if a child begins very early to put his feet in his parent's shoes, they say that this child will become a grand voyager once he grows up.

For the young Songhaï, migrating is showing his parents that he no longer depends on them and that he can contribute to the family's economy. Migrating is initiating oneself to difficulties: hunger, solitude, injustice. The migrant must work hard to come back with something. In that case, he deserves the prettiest girl of the village. It is the dream of all young men to build a beautiful house in the courtyard of his father and become engaged to a girl who will help his mother with domestic tasks. The young men must especially bring back electronic equipment with which to listen to *takamba* (traditional dances and songs). Among the Mininaka, the returning migrant who brings back money is celebrated by the ladies and they run after him. Those who do not bring back anything must lie low or hide once the successful hero-migrant has dropped off his luggage in the village.

The fact of his return and the objects he has brought offer a young migrant the elements for a new identity but one that he must now maintain in a visible manner, especially among the boys of his age group. A series of advantages (or perhaps social values) is automatically associated to his new identity. It offers the returning migrant a reason to pretend he is an individual who possesses certain natural and supernatural knowledge, and in some societies even a spiritual power.[18] The returning migrant can become the village's spokesman for strangers who visit occasionally.[19] He can permit himself to take the pretty fiancée of a man who never left the village. He can become the leader of a group of friends who will become the *grin* of his domicile.[20] The returning migrant's new status will last as long as he continues to show the characteristics and the material goods associated with it.

The discussion that bears on voyage as conflict is fundamental to analyzing the series of values associated with migration. As long as these values stay alive, we need to envisage the possibility of migrants surmounting all the barriers that Europe and the United States currently build to prevent the arrival of young Africans and Latinos. An exhilarating *National Geographic* article (Gorney 2008) insists that no matter the danger, Latino migrants do not back down in their quest to enter the United States. We may tell them in vain that the worst is ahead: that the temperature can rise above 50 degrees centigrade; that there are thefts and rapists on the road; that they can get their feet cut off when they attempt to jump on a moving train. It is pointless; they go anyway. There are hundreds of thousands of Latinos who illegally cross the Mexican frontier each year into the United States. Nobody knows precisely how many migrants attempt the American adventure, but it is estimated that there are at least 150,000 per year. This migration has been dramatically augmented following the civil wars of the 1970s and 1980s in Guatemala, El Salvador, and Nicaragua. The article draws the reader's attention to the fact that no fiction or realistic danger stops the Latinos from reaching the United States: "On a map on del Migrante Casa's entrance wall, someone had attached a note containing distances, in kilometers: Tapachula to New York 4,373. To Houston: 2,930. To Chicago: 3,678. Above the map was a warning poster about the hazards of Texas and Arizona crossings—'Don't risk it, the desert temperature can be fatal.' I had seen no one so much as glance at the poster." In reality, the migrants don't need to be informed of the dangers; they are conscious of them. It is obvious. In their conception, there are no migrations without risks. The question is only how one faces the dangers. What is their strength, their support?

This migrant's attitude to face these dangers is universal. Everywhere in the world, people use their natural rights to travel. When we witness the decision of young Africans to leave, at whatever cost, either for the cultural or social reasons described, or for reasons such as poverty or civil war, we can conclude that they are ready to face the "war" declared by the United States and the European Union. They will walk away winners. If they are not afraid of all these natural dangers, then jail or repatriation will not discourage them. For the moment, the weapons developed by these nations have reached their limits, notably the ones deployed in the sending countries (in order to attack the root of the problem) such as "co-development" (see below) and sensitizing the public to the dangers of illegal migration.

MIGRATION AS COPING WITH STATE BARRIERS

In January 2008, the Burkinabé newspaper *Independence* opined that at the beginning of the twenty-first century, the occidental countries (notably the United States and the European Union) are facing two types of war: terrorism (the hot war) and migration from underdeveloped countries (the cold war). The newspaper projected that the United States and the European Union will not win this latter war because they have created and maintained it. Certain media and scholarly literature maintain that African migration is the devastating consequence of policies that imposed a form of development on African countries—a form that created ethnic conflict and poverty.[21] In this view, the war against migration is simply a further proof of European selfishness.

If we examine the efforts of developed nations to stop, minimize, or simply select desirable migrants, we can understand how migration could be seen as coping with state barriers. It may also be considered a war between wealth and poverty. But an attentive look at migration history shows that it is not poverty that created migration. In Africa, people remember "prestige migration" from an era where nothing was missing for rural youth except objects of European origin (clothing, shoes, perfumes, etc.). Yet during this period, the policy of frontier security existed as well. The colonial empires attempted to control the migration of their subjects, especially to keep the subjects from working in another colonial empire (Dougnon 2007; Harries 1994). Francophone African workers could travel freely in French West Africa and French Equatorial Africa. Their fellow Anglophones were doing the same thing. After World War II, the roads (at least in France, Belgium, and England) were open to numerous Africans during the reconstruction of Europe.[22]

Only in the mid-1990s did France present itself as a victim of African, Arab, and other migrants, subsequently transforming thousands into illegal migrants or hooligans and menacing to deport them at anytime.[23] Why do some observers think that the United States and the European

Union will lose the war against migration, despite their capacities to use every legal, physical, and financial means? If the developed countries are going to lose the war against migration, the question must be asked: What is wrong with their logistics and strategy?

The European Union in particular has had three types of responses to the migratory wave from southern countries. First was the implementation of the Treaty of Schengen, which led to the policy of visa restriction. Seeing the limits of this policy, the European Union moved on to physical measures such as frontier control and forced repatriations. France repatriated several thousand African migrants. The Pasqua law targeted *sans papier* or illegal migrants. At the same time, Spain and Italy have been criticized by other Schengen signatories for not being strong enough against African immigrants. The second response is rooted in the struggle against terrorism since September 11, 2001. The attacks on the World Trade Center have provided the sacred bread that will now feed (as pretext and reason) all manner of migration control and border security.

The third response from the EU was to address the roots of the disease and the means to cure it. This has taken form primarily in the struggle against poverty, coupled with sensitization programs on the dangers of the voyage. Policymakers, European and African alike, have concluded that the struggle against migration will achieve no result as long as African countries stay poor. The creation of jobs has become seen as a surefire alternative. In Mali during the last decade, the French government put forth a development program under the name of "co-development" in the regions where the majority of migration candidates are concentrated. In reality, co-development is nothing more than the economic facade of migration restriction policy. It simply means: stay home, we will provide you, there on the spot, with what you are seeking on our soil.[24] The regions of Kayes and Koulikoro have been the primary beneficiaries of this "aid against migration." I do not discuss co-development further here, but its impact on migration has been almost zero (Katje 2008).

The sensitization campaign aims to give blunt information to those likely to migrate.[25] The communication strategy consists of giving future migrants accurate information on employment opportunities (or lack thereof) and the dangers of illegal work.[26] In an attempt to reinforce this community strategy and to test new measures of restrictions, in October 2008 the EU Commission opened a Mali Center of Information and Migration Management (CIGEM) affiliated with the Ministry of Exterior Malians and African Integration.

Together, all these measures have not satisfied the expectations of the Schengen signatories. We witness the limits of frontier control, or the repatriation of *sans papier*. The security apparatus, with its highly sophisticated devices and their DNA tests in the consulates of sending countries, does not discourage the youth to undertake their perilous voyage. On the other hand, human rights groups criticize detention camps, with their barbed wire walls comparable to the fallen one in Berlin, known as the wall of shame.

The policies of visa restriction and criminalization of the voyage *sans papier* certainly reduced the number of "legal" migrants, but have also augmented the number of "illegal" migrants and consequently the number of victims drowned in the Atlantic or dead in the Sahara. This signifies that the migratory pressure is far from diminishing: on the contrary, it is accelerating. The European Union, by cutting legal forms of access, has therefore multiplied the dangers of the voyage.

Indeed, the dangers of the voyage throughout the illegal routings is at the center of the communication strategy in sending and transit countries such as Mali, Senegal, Mauritania, Guinea, Morocco, and Libya. This strategy of communication also includes publicizing the issues of child trafficking, recruiter traps, and overexploitation of illegal work. But this approach will have to work hard to gain attention.

CONCLUSION

The principal conclusion from this analysis is that the consequences presented to discourage young men from moving are, in reality, at the heart of evolving local concepts of migration. The experience acquired in the crossing of the wilderness is passed on from generation to generation. With so much experience in surviving to reach their destination, the African migrants have made the voyage's experience their story's centerpiece. Almost all old accounts contain remembrances of dangers in the wilderness. The migrants narrate, with powerful details, the events that happened amid the supernaturally powerful, fearful wilderness. In this rite of passage, the hand of God is often called upon, just like courage or the temerity of the traveler. As an English traveler put it to illustrate the tales of Dogon migrants from the 1920s: "To have come so far, and to have endured so much, was surely a sanctifying and a winnowing experience from which great things could be expected" (Cressy 1987: 176).

The generations of the 1970s and 1980s did not face the same experiences in the frightening wilderness. The roads were safer and transportation means more abundant. With the new policy of "migration zero" adopted by certain European and African countries, the generation of the 1990s began to live the experience of the sea and the Sahara. They take on the adventure with no preparations, only God's mercy. We have already counted thousands of deaths and disappearances. The African and European states attempt to forbid the voyage or to warn that the boat may be swept by the tide. The multiplication of boat journeys is proof that this new generation has, in reality, lost nothing of previous generations' capacity to undergo the rite of passage and has no fear to perish in the ocean or the Sahara.

Despite numerous national programs of sensitization in the departure states, the migrants appear undaunted by the peril that awaits them on the roads to Europe, or ignorant of the certain death that awaits them on illegal routes through the Sahara and across the Mediterranean and Atlantic. These programs appear simply as new projects that will require additional funds. It is appropriate to caution against this mercantile treatment of a problem that eventually leads to applying measures of an illusory character and a waste of material and human resources—all in the name of dissuading young men who ultimately leave to wherever, whenever they decide.

The failure of visa restriction measures and the control of the frontiers reveal a poor definition of the migratory problem. In its sociocultural and socioeconomic contexts, the evolving concepts of employment among the African youth have not been sufficiently addressed in preliminary discussions between the European Union and the United States when they were elaborating a plan of attack against illegal migration. When we evaluate young migrants' attitude vis-à-vis rural development projects, we perceive that in addition to ecological causes, another cause for migration appeared recently that we could call developmentalist (Dougnon 2005). The introduction of micro projects, such as the "village perimeters," generates further rural debt. To pay (or not to pay) these debts, the solution remains migration, as it was in the head tax era. No specific study has been undertaken to answer the question of why the development actions undertaken presently have not been able to solve the issue of migration.

Without a deepened study of cultural parameters and economic constraints, the struggle will be vain. We are not currently aware of the future economic development of Africa or the migration trends that will arise as a result. There is, evidently, one solution to the dilemma. African researchers must be able to predict migratory trends both inside and outside Africa. To succeed, they must produce a large knowledge base of certain facts and objectives in the past and the present of African migration (forms, intensity, regions of departure and arrival, etc.).

At the moment, all the policies working to limit migration are facing failure. If migrants are chased from one country, we simply find them (after a few months) in another African or European country—if they do not return directly to the country from which they were expelled! For example, supposedly 90 percent of the beneficiaries of co-development subsequently returned to Paris or headed for other African nations. In the process of struggling against child trafficking, more than 500 children were repatriated to the Dogon country.[27] We know today that more than 90 per-

cent of these "trafficking" victims came back into town after a forced repatriation to their homeland. This means that these young people, despite
their difficult living conditions in the urban center, have never been simply an object of trafficking. In addition, with the interconnection of the
world economy, we would need a global solution to the migratory flows.
Europe may close its doors, but the interests are not exclusively there. The
roads to migration are as numerous as the economic ramifications for the
countries of the North. All these examples show that without a clear and
undistorted understanding of migration, we will not find a durable solution to the problems it causes.

NOTES

1. The best example of such an exercise is that of Clifford (1994), who has
done an analysis of the evolution and cultural, political, social, and economic implications of the diaspora concept in Anglo-Saxon literature. Another
more historical example is Geertz (1979).

2. The approach of the Senegalese NGO *Movement citizen* has led a
study that appears biased, treating illegal migration as a social deviance, a
social flaw developed by the young in poor quarters, struck by unemployment (see Mbow 2008). Such an approach reveals more about ideology than
an objective analysis. Considering illegal migration in the same manner as
delinquency, drugs, and other crimes is inaccurate from a moral and historical standpoint. See also de Haas (2007), whose working paper is important in
current efforts that lead certain researchers to reorient research on African
migration. This means going from a Eurocentric perspective to an intra-African perspective.

3. See my forthcoming paper, "Migratory Trends among Two Malian
Ethnic Groups," to be published by the International Migration Institute.

4. In addition to my own material on the Dogon country, I use materi-
als from my students who majored in sociology during the academic year
2007–2008, collected from among their parents on the different significa-
tions of work migration.

5. Here we use the dialect Tinkiu, the one spoken in the commune of Pel
Koporo Pen and Koproro Na. Notice that the sense of the word "migration"
is identical in every Dogon dialect.

6. In certain Bandiagara regions, migration is identified with the universe, the global world. We use in these regions the term *ganda*. To describe
the migrants we say: *ganda oulembe* (literally, the children of the world, or
those who have seen the world).

7. Very curiously, this is true except among the Kagolo, an ethnic group
close to the Saroké (ethnic champion of migration), where migration was
conceived as the consequence of social deviation. Migrating was only for the
young ones who had sinned, such as theft, adultery, or rape. Since the 1970s,
Kagolos migrate for climate (famine) reasons. To this day, this ethnicity
considers a migrant as someone who leaves to save his family, a true fighter.

8. The Dogon migrants perceived certain ethnicities from the north of Ghana as cannibals and refused to sleep in their village. This accusation was generalized across Africa in an era where interethnic mistrust dominated. Each group accused its neighbor of cannibalism. In Mali, the Dogon were treated by colonists as frightening fetishists who would sacrifice humans during religious holidays.

9. This struggle with the migrants and the lovers reminds us of the fight for freedom of the Black Seminoles in the United States. The Black Seminoles are the descendants of free Africans and runaway slaves who fled South Carolina and Georgia to settle in the Florida forests.

10. In Ghana, Dogon women said they had journeyed too far by installing themselves near the shore of the Atlantic Ocean, but over the past three decades they put into perspective the geographical and cultural aspect of their migration: they see their children going even farther to European and Asiatic countries despite all the barriers that are placed before them (Dougnon 2007).

11. See Gunvor (2007). She analyzes how young Soninké define migration and experience immobility. We see in her analysis that immobility is the harshest punishment for young born and raised in a "culture of migration." This means the risks are not in the voyage but in immobility in the village.

12. According to Balandier (1955), the youth predominated on the labor market in Brazzaville. Other than between the years 1945 and 1951, the migrants represented 86 percent of the adolescents and young from 10 to 30 years of age.

13. Still lodged in the national memory is the pilgrimage of the emperor Kankou Moussa to Mecca in 1324, remembered as the first historical voyage that made the country of Mali a welcoming, diversified land of immigration. With a caravan of sixty men and women and thousands of horses and camels loaded of gold, the emperor of Mali completed a perilous voyage through the most redoubtable deserts in the world. After him, the Orient and Occident began to become of interest in Soudan and Sudanese (Malians) wanted to travel the world. Ever since, the migratory dynamism has stayed the same. We have only changed the eras, the causes, the destinations, the motivations, and the reasons of Malian migrations. The young Malians, to reach their destination countries, are ready to face the same adversity that their Kankou Moussa came across. See Kaké (1975).

14. Among the Sara of Chad, there is a term for migration that could be translated as "fleeing the enemy"—*ndourou kbagnan mbaga*—and another that refers to "movement in search of well-being"—*ndourou lo kingué kindji kokori*. Based in the south of the country, the Sara are known for their wrestling, dancing, and fishing activities (although Chad is landlocked, it is traversed by seven waterways).

15. On this note, see my forthcoming essay "Ghana Boys and Glamour," in which I analyze the new lives of returning migrants whose identity is symbolized by the exploits of the voyage, the control of new knowledge (the English language and Hausa), and the success of work due to the acquisition of clothing and other prestige objects.

16. This formula is utilized by politicians in front of every foreign personality who comes on an official visit to Mali. It is used as an ideological language to brag about Malian hospitality and the pan-Africanism of the founding fathers of Mali.

17. This does not erase the migrant's foreign status that the autochthones would highlight in certain circumstances. Among the Peuls, for example, the tern *n'djolari ou mijahan n'djolari* (literally, going on an adventure) designates the low status of the migrant. The expression has a pejorative connotation. The one who is *n'djolari* (the foreigner) is supposed to be somewhere else. He is, consequently, kept apart from the major decisions concerning life in society. A *ndjola* is not allowed to speak, and we can at anytime let him hear his status of foreigner. The term *ndjola* designates someone who must obey, supplicate himself, and live in strict conformity with the established rules and laws.

18. In 1920s Dogon country, everyone feared the returnees from Ghana because they were seen as people of supernatural powers, capable of casting an evil spell on anyone who did not show them respect. The local wizards feared them because it was believed that if they wanted, they could magically transport all the wizards to one place by the village and demand money in exchange for being freed before sunset. In many Dogon villages, the returning migrants were the first to be converted to Islam and were the first Muslim leaders. See Dougnon (2007) and Bouju (1984).

19. It is a question of the first migration (before the beginning of colonization) when women were basically absent. The danger of the voyage excluded the women from adventure far from the village. Consequently, there exists among the Peul an old form of migration practiced by women called *suuto-gol*, designating the fact that a woman leaves the conjugal domicile to reside in her paternal home or other places. In this case, the woman refuses to tell the true cause of her departure.

20. In Mali, the *grin* signifies an informal group of youth who meet each day around tea to discuss their quotidian lives. They share everything: clothing, shoes, and even intimate secrets. The birth of *grin* in Mali can be situated in the widespread unemployment that ruined two intellectual generations.

21. Meillassoux (1975) argues from a Marxist perspective that the migrations between African villages and Parisians foyers are the result of overexploitation of which the third world has been victimized since the end of World War II.

22. It is important here to cite Stefan Zweig, whose *Die Welt von Gestern* (The World of Yesterday) first appeared in 1942: "Indeed, nothing makes us sensible to the immense relapse into which the world fell after the First World War than the restriction on man's freedom of movement and the diminution of his civil rights" (Zweig 1964: 409–10). Zweig does not hide his bitterness against police and administrative obstruction which block people's voyage.

23. See Mann (2005). He analyzes the political debate (in France and in Mali) centered on how the descendants of those who defended France (Sen

egalese soldiers) and those who worked hard in industries after World War II became *sans-papier* under the "Pasqua laws."

24. It is illusory to believe that after forty years of unfruitful economic cooperation, we should be able to convince rural youth of the efficacy of co-development. The consequences of Structural Adjustment Programs still cause too much devastation (unemployment and the incapacity of the national government to guarantee basic needs) for co-development to be able, magically, to stop migration in Sahel.

25. In Mali, the Ministry of Exterior Malians and African Integration, in collaboration with the International Organization of Migration, just began disseminating a broad campaign of sensitization on clandestine migrations in four regions of Mali: Kayes, Sikasso, Mopti, and Gao.

26. Certain politicians from the North and South started to naively think that the experience of the National Agency for Employment Promotion and Skills (ANAPEC), which already recruited 12,000 women in Morocco to work in Spain with seasonal permits, can be an alternative to illegal migration. Ninety percent of these women came back to their homeland. France followed Spain's lead by recruiting 280 workers in 2007. Other EU countries are interested by this experience, such as Portugal and Ireland.

27. Among these illusory and ineffective measures was the decree N-01-534/ P. RM of November 1, 2001, that required an authorization permit for children up to 18 years old to exit. This permit is only valid for three months and is delivered by the Minister of Security and Civil Protection. The security agents are authorized to return all children younger than 19 years old traveling without this paper.

REFERENCES

Balandier, Georges, 1955. *Sociologie des Brazzavilles noires.* Paris: Cahiers de la Fondation nationale des sciences politiques.

Bouju, Jacky. 1984. *Graine de l'homme, enfant du mil.* Paris: Université Paris X.

Clifford, James. 1994. "Diasporas." *Cultural Anthropology* 9(3): 302–38.

Cressy, David. 1987. *Coming Over: Migration and Communication between England and New England in the Seventeenth Century.* Cambridge: Cambridge University Press.

De Haas, Hein. 2007. *The Myth of Invasion: Irregular Migration from West Africa to the Maghreb and the European Union.* Oxford: International Migration Institute.

Dougnon, Isaie. 2003. "Les Ghana boys et le prestige de l'habit européen au Pays Dogon (1920–1960)." In *Regards sur les Dogon du Mali*, ed. R. M. A. Bedaux and J. D. Van Der Waals. Leiden: Rijksmuseum voor Volkenkunde.

———. 2005. "The Understanding of International Aid among the People of the Timbuktu Region, Mali." London: AEGIS Conference, June 29 –July 2.

————. 2007. *Travail de Blanc, travail de Noir: La migration des paysans dogon vers l'Office du Niger et au Ghana, 1910–1980.* Paris: Karthala.

————. Forthcoming. "Ghana Boys and Glamour: European Clothing among the Dogon, 1920–1960." In *Africans at Home and Abroad: Social Aspiration and Personal Lives,* ed. T. C. McCaskie and Keith Shear. Madison: University of Wisconsin Press.

————. Forthcoming. "Migratory Trends among Two Malian Ethnic Groups—the Songhai and the Dogon—Migrating to Ghana: A Comparative Study." Oxford: International Migration Institute.

Geertz, Clifford. 1979. *Meaning and Order in Moroccan Society: Three Essays in Cultural Analysis.* Cambridge: Cambridge University Press.

Gorney, Cynthia. 2008. "Mexico's Other Border." *National Geographic* 213 (February). http://ngm.nationalgeographic.com/2008/02/mexicos-southern-border/cynthia-gorney-text.html.

Gunvor, Jonsson. 2007. "Migration Aspirations and Immobility in a Malian Soninke Village." M.Phil. thesis, University of Copenhagen.

Harries, Patrick. 1994. *Work, Culture and Identity: Migrant Laborers in Mozambique and South Africa, c. 1860–1910.* Portsmouth, N.H.: Heinemann.

Kaké, Baba Ibrahima. 1975. *Le fabuleux pèlerinage de Kankou Moussa, empereur du Mali.* Paris: L.P.F Danel.

Katje, Danielle. 2008. "Migration and Co-development in France-Mali: New Wine in Ancient Goat Skinned Bottles." Paper presented at the Actuality of Malian Migration Research conference. FLAHS, University of Bamako.

Lewellen, Ted C. 2002. *The Anthropology of Globalization: Cultural Anthropology Enters the Twenty-First Century.* Westport, Conn.: Bergin and Garvey.

Manchuelle, Francois. 1997. *Willing Migrants: Soninke Labor Diasporas, 1848–1960.* Oxford: James Currey.

Mann, Gregory. 2005. "Des Tirailleurs sénégalais aux Sans-papiers: universaux et particularismes." In *L'Esclavage, la colonisation, et après: France, Etats-Unis, Grande Bretagne,* ed. Patrick Weil and Stéphane Dufoix. Paris: Presses Universitaires de la France.

Mbow, Penda. 2008. *L'emigration clandestine, le profil des candidats.* Dakar: Forum CARITAS.

Meillassoux, Claude. 1975. *Femmes Greniers et Capitaux.* Paris: Maspero.

Moodie, Dunbar T., and Vivienne Ndatshe. 1994. *Going for Gold: Men, Mines, and Migration.* Berkeley: University of California Press.

Zweig, Stefan. 1964. *The World of Yesterday.* Lincoln: University of Nebraska Press.

NAVIGATING DIASPORA
THE PRECARIOUS DEPTHS OF THE ITALIAN IMMIGRATION CRISIS

DONALD CARTER

> Ships at a distance have every man's wish on board. For some they
> come in with the tide. For others they still sail forever on the horizon,
> never out of sight, never landing until the Watcher turns his eyes
> away in resignation, his dreams mocked to death by Time.
> —Zora Neale Hurston, *Their Eyes Were Watching God*

The immigration crisis commands center stage in Europe as reconfigured notions of sovereignty, territory, and community challenge traditional concepts of national and cultural belonging. The advent of this post-national world raises illuminating dilemmas concerning European relations with other nations, especially those from postcolonial Africa (Carnegie 2002; Williams 1991; Malkki 1995).[1] In this context of great social and cultural anxiety, different forms of belonging become complicated for members of the African diaspora, as race, gender, and historical legacy render blackness a visible marker of outsider status and as it becomes increasingly difficult to navigate the waters of belonging. This essay explores the new contours of closure in the emergent European Union and the symbolic role of the outsider in the process of reconfiguring ideas of belonging.

On a very hot Turin summer's evening in 2006, just minutes from the site of one of the many Olympic villages—now a kind of tourist beacon on the outskirts of the city—my friend Babacar, who has traveled to his homeland only a handful of times over the last ten years, turned to me and, after a brief outburst in Wolof to his sister and brother-in-law in the next room, shifted into Italian. "Now everyone is dancing," he says. For the better part of an hour we have been watching an endless stream of music videos on Senegalese television. This experience is made possible in part by the new world of African mobility, underscored by Senegalese diasporic spectatorship and enabled by satellite links to Europe connecting the diaspora with the nightly parade of television programming back home. In one of the videos, the momentary flash of a multicolored traditional fishing boat or pirogue brightens the screen and unleashes another kind of response—an unexpected (for me) sadness. Babacar's comment on dancing is a not-so-veiled reference to the lack of opportunity for young people back home, "who look around themselves in their villages" and, finding no way to contribute to the life of their families, look out to sea. Increasingly, young people comb the shores south of Dakar seeking out former fishermen who might captain a tiny wooden canoe with precious little hope of ever making European landfall. This is not just the folklore of the diaspora, as earlier that year in Thiaroye, a poor suburb of Dakar (infamous as the site of a massacre of Senegalese soldiers by French troops in 1944), one of the country's worst naval accidents occurred, taking the lives of eighty-one young people from the village who were attempting to reach Europe in a converted fishing boat.[2] The migration is inspired by a kind of "perfect global storm" in European countries like Italy, where a quiet search has been going on for some time to continually replenish a declining and increasingly aging labor force. In addition, Italy has one of the lowest birthrates in the world. Despite official denials, Europe will be dependent on migrant labor for years to come.[3]

Across the satellite channels, having consolidated the direct window into Senegalese experience, more and more programs referred in one way or another to the exodus of a new generation and reflected back a dimension of its exasperation. It was literally what everyone was talking about from the local news reports to the sports commentators at popular wrestling matches. At some point all seemed preoccupied with the boats. Babacar's sister calls out from the other room, "Many of them leave but where do they go—their families don't hear from them . . . their families don't hear from them." And Babacar picks up the theme: "What has happened to all of these people?" he asks. "We know that they have left but then no one has heard from them again. Many . . . many of them and where have they gone? How can you travel to France in this?" he says, pointing at the passing of a tiny multicolored pirogue. "They must be somewhere but their families never hear from them again—dead," he says in the end, dropping and shaking his head, his voice now all but a whisper.

Long ago Michelet warned us of the sea's passion for erasure. Seeing the tiny pirogue in the video as a symbol of cultural pride, it is clear that they were never meant to attempt such an ambitious voyage. In such places as Sicily, the waters surrounding some of the major points of arrival for foreign migrants by sea have come to be called "liquid tombs" by the local fishing people, who find the evidence of failed voyages so often in their nets that they now avoid vast tracts of the waters frequented by the vessels of this human traffic.

By now the conversation was embracing everyone in the apartment with the weight of the human tragedy that had touched the lives of so many each day. My son Nico, while keeping his sister Eliana entertained, was now straining to follow the conversation across the room from where Babacar and I were sitting side by side. I caught my co-author Heather Merrill's eye, acknowledging the mood change and knowing somehow that the coming moments would require our full attention that we might reconstruct events later. Babacar now turns to Nico and draws him directly into the discussion: "A young man Nico's age, what will he do to look after his family? The old people can do nothing, he needs to help them and has nothing in his pockets, not even enough to replace the jeans that he is wearing, only a few cents a day if that—he cannot live like that and there is no work in Senegal so he takes to the boat. So many of them now . . ."

While my family sat in the small apartment in Turin, Babacar's children lived in a compound in Dakar and rarely saw him. When I first met him almost twenty years ago he had already been traveling between African and Europe for more than a decade. Now he hopes to return, a hope he has been nurturing for years. In the intervening years he has been joined by two sisters, a brother, and countless cousins and friends that he has, in a sense, sponsored. But there are always others who wish to come and they rely on the kindness of people like Babacar. Worsening conditions back home keep him here, but now older he can no longer get the relatively good contract factory jobs he enjoyed previously.[4] Now he must put together odd jobs. In his fifties, like so many migrants and Italians in the volatile labor market today, he waits for benefits and pension payments while caught up in litigation.[5]

Since the 1960s, the population of Senegal has doubled, with a markedly large portion of today's society being young people still dependent on their families. Despite improvements in the economy in recent years, some point to the lack of support for agriculture, slumping returns in the fisheries, rising prices, and taxation as contributing factors forcing so many young people to leave (Riccio 2007: 47). Some of the highest rates of rural-urban migration come from the Mourid regions of the country, with people often turning quickly toward international destinations following the well-worn path of cousins, brothers, sisters, and friends. This new movement has expanded to encompass an entire generation from diverse religious, ethnic, class, and educational backgrounds. The slight turnaround in the Senegalese economy (1995–2006) has done little to stop the call of the sea. The push and pull determinations involve not only conditions in Senegal but the presence of a stable Senegalese diaspora in

Italy and the shifting nature of European immigration practices. Since the first comprehensive immigration legislation in Italy, the legge Martelli (1990), there have been two significant legislative markers for immigration, the legge Turco-Napolitano (1998) and the very conservative legge Bossi-Fini (2002), requiring in effect that the migrants' right to stay in Italy be linked to their employment. The national government in recent years has shifted toward supporting increasingly restrictive measures concerning immigration, with the issue becoming a standard feature of center-right anti-immigrant rhetoric. Public opinion toward migrants has cooled in recent years, resulting in a conflict with the migrant communities that have worked for many years in Italy and that now have begun to demand an easier path to citizenship. In many regions, simply renewing a migrant's permit to stay in the country can take months while waiting for documents to be processed. This means that those who are between jobs while renewing their documents are essentially undocumented and can be forced to return to their countries of origin. Comprehensive immigration reform is currently nowhere in sight, and in its place for the better part of a decade there have been but slight changes in policy rather than a proper debate on immigration. On the Mediterranean, its many islands, and in the lands that jut out into its heart, small cemeteries testify with modest solemnity to the continuing waves of immigration and the dangers its necessity has wrought. This essay is a reflection on this social fact and its implications.

Michelet's warning of the sea's passion for erasure highlights the peculiar nature of this most inhuman domain. Recently, Robert Harrison noted: "Erasure does not mean disappearance only: it means that the site of disappearance remains unmarkable. There are no gravestones on the sea. History and memory ground themselves on inscription, but this element is uninscribable. It closes over rather than keeps the place of its dead, while its unbounded grave remains humanly unmarked" (Harrison 2003). But just as the great photographers like Seydou Keita and others once marked African presence with their portraits, we may for a moment note our objection to the erasure of these young lives without a trace.

DOMINION OF THE DEAD

In one of the worst naval accidents in the recent history of the Mediterranean, a tiny ship went down in December 1996 between Malta and the Strait of Sicily. Some three hundred people lost their lives, of which 283 were young male migrants from India, Pakistan, and Sri Lanka. We know of the incident through the dedicated work of Italian journalist Giovanni Maria Bellu and the valiant fisherman who found evidence of the accident in his fishing nets (Bellu 2004). Many of the young men were en route to new lives in Europe. Whatever we call them they were the beloved of families and they held the hopes and dreams of perhaps a better future for so many. Many came from the same villages and were the best and brightest hope of their small communities. They, like so many from nameless nations who are lost in pursuit of their dreams, mark our times with a series of questions. How do we honor them? What is our responsibility to them and how do we prevent an increase in their number? To call them "clandestine" serves no purpose. They are the terrain on which our times are born—the migrant and the established are inextricably intertwined in their fate. We are in some sense born through the phantom ship that was their transport and must come to terms with our troubled origin.

In his wonderful book *The Dominion of the Dead*, Robert Pogue Harrison explores the insights of Italian Philosopher Giambattista Vico (1668–1744) into the intimate linkage of human community to the dead. In *The New Science* (1725) Vico notes that *"humanitas* in Latin came first and properly from *humando*, burying." Honoring our dead is then an "essential and irreducible" part of the nature of fundamental or inaugural human institutions. In fact, "as Human beings we are born of the dead— of the regional ground they occupy, of the languages they inhabit, of the words they brought into being, of the many institutional, legal, cultural and psychological legacies that, through us, connect them to the unborn." Burial then figures as the "generative institution of human nature," taking here the word "nature" in its full etymological sense from *nasi*, "to be born" (Harrison 2003: xi). Indeed, the notion of unearthing the treasure of other lives, of storing and preserving that which in human traditions is meant to sustain us and those who will follow us on the great journey of human history, is also something that burial must signify.

In this spirit, I would like to consider the lives of those lost in the passage between worlds, the young migrants who set out across the waters of the Mediterranean toward the Promised Land on European shores. These are people who, like the fateful comrades of Ulysses, answered the call of exploration or the daily social and economic conditions that shape obligations to their families and community, prompting them to go beyond their homelands into the unknown. In Canto 26 of Dante's *Inferno* (the Canto of Ulysses), from his great work *The Divine Comedy*, Ulysses calls out to his shipmates: "Consider what you came from—You were not born to live like mindless brutes but to follow paths of excellence and knowledge." They travel beyond the Pillars of Hercules (Strait of Gibraltar), following the counsel of their comrade toward an uninhabited realm that Dante reveals to be none other than the infernal terrain through which he is led by his guide Virgil.[6] Our modern mariners seek out a promised land heralded in their childhood textbooks, in the media, and in the exaltation of a global economy rising up in the "openness" of the emergent

European Union and its expanding economies. Not all travelers reach this promised land. Some fall prey to unpredictable waters like our ancient voyagers, while others succumb to the politics of hospitality in strange new lands. Others still remain in the limbo of an infernal terrain, living a clandestine existence without documents in the world of hidden work, or in detention centers that seem to have all the qualities of infernal prisons and safe houses.

We must remember that those traveling beyond the known world, testing the limits of human potential or transgressing customary cultural boundaries, are subject to real and imagined sanctions as they cross a boundary and through great effort challenge the world of the established. In some societies, the shipwrecked were summarily executed in order to save other members of the society from the potentially contagious nature of their misfortune, the incomplete journey being an ominous portent.

The great Senegalese writer Cheikh Hamidou Kane was one of the first of a generation of African authors to consider in their fiction the fate of European and African journeys or cultural encounters. In *Home and Exile* Chinua Achebe writes of Kane's novel:

> In Cheikh Hamidou Kane's great novel of colonization, *Ambiguous Adventure*, a brilliant, young aristocrat and hope of his people is sent away from his Muslim community in Senegal by the elders to study in Paris. Their decision, which was not reached without deep misgivings, was ultimately made possible by a vision of their son joining the sons of Europe and other continents to construct a new world for all humanity. The young African, Samba Diallo, will, however, discover that, contrary to the optimistic notions of his people, Europe has made no real provision for his participation. The discovery that one is somehow superfluous is there, waiting at journey's end, for the weary traveler from the provinces. (Achebe 2000: 97–98)

In fact, the newcomer is often seen as superfluous to the local context of a world in which he or she must remain on the margin. Yet participation in this distant land has been preceded by missionary encounters, colonization, and an endless parade of school lessons, consumerism, popular culture, and desire without limits that has connected home and future centers of exile for generations. Long before the ticket is purchased to come to the promised land of Europe, this "other world" has insinuated itself into the very fabric of everyday life in the future migrants' homeland. Senegalese often remind me that they also think of themselves as French, but such an identity is more than a simple mist hovering over their lives; it is the language many prefer to speak when discussing politics, it is that place among European nations that they look to as a point of comparison even when they don't live there, and it is the basis and source of the textbooks, journals, and popular culture that they have been breathing in from birth. French news programs still broadcast from Dakar as if it were a suburb of Paris, at times with correspondents of Senegalese origin. Certainly these influences pass in both directions: in some measure every resident of Paris is now aware of the Franco-Algerian and Senegalese presence in their mist and cannot be unaware of the subtle influence of a large resident Muslim population on foreign policy. Even in the most conservative cities like Turin, the presence of migrant populations has impacted culinary arts, theater, and everyday life in untold ways—certainly all that remains is an acknowledgment of this social fact to be made at some point in the future. Today we are far from this juncture and left to consider the fact that in many cases the presence of the newcomer is still thought of as superfluous. For this condition, we might say provisionally that the newcomer is invisible.

Invisibility implies a kind of devaluation of personhood or a denial, as the great cultural critic James Baldwin once wrote, of a basic "human reality . . . human weight and complexity" (Baldwin 1985: 88). It is often when people are, from the perspective of a given cultural logic, designated "superfluous," imponderable as a human presence, that they become invisible. It is through such root metaphors of a culture that we find interconnections of cultural and bodily notions in the production of subjectivity (Jackson 1998: 13). In many societies, ideas surrounding the notion of social and cultural presence or weight are "embodied sensations of amplitude." Michael Jackson, in his *Minima Ethnographica: Intersubjectivity and the Anthropological Project*, emphasizes "substantiality—weight—standing—and voice," as qualities that constitute and reinforce "our sense of existence and autonomy" (Jackson 1998: 13). Other metaphors suggest a relative loss of presence "falling, floating, drifting, being rootless, empty, ungrounded," or "reduced to an inert thing" (Jackson 1998: 13). In short, invisibility is in part a kind of collective master story, a cosmological origin myth of the present. While both the visible and the invisible are in some sense seen, only the established and accepted may gain social relevance.

The hyper-visibility of the socially invisible is then a byproduct of the exclusion process through which they are first classified, labeled, and dismissed. The migrants whose daily attempt to overcome the myriad mechanisms of state immigration control become "superfluous" in part because their very status, real or imagined, makes them illegitimate social persons in the national territory, a kind of "matter out of place," as Mary Douglas (1966) put it. One is too many.

As Madan Sarup reminds us, the stranger marks the ultimate boundary beyond which we find the outer limits of group experience. The nation is imagined in part through the reinforcement of boundary-maintaining mechanisms. The real danger is to fall beyond this community, to exist on its edges in such a way that cultural diversity may be considered a threat to the established.[7] In the common-sense world of the nation, the newcomer is an intruder with different cultural traditions and social practices that lie beyond the dominant norm. Others must either adjust or face exclusion: the foreigner already stands apart from the citizen, but the newcomer, "asylum seeker," or so-called "illegal immigrant" stands outside the very possibility of hospitality, marking a boundary in a sense beyond the social, a liminal world in which the very humanity of the intruder is questioned. As Sarup notes, "The nightmare is to be uprooted, to be without papers, stateless, alone, alienated and adrift in a world of organized others" (Sarup 1996: 11). Such a nightmare is a reality for those who travel the uncharted waters of diaspora, leaving behind all claims to a former life and living in the refuge of their cultural, ethnic, or religious group alone. For the stranger, being "homeless" in the world is not a temporary state but a permanent condition until s/he comes to be embraced by a new social world, a new opportunity of belonging.

Immigration in the new Europe presents a humanitarian challenge not only for those who navigate the coastal waters of Italy, Spain, or Greece, but for those fortunate enough to make landfall—those having reached Europe though "legal" means who must still navigate the often treacherous waters of cultural identity, xenophobia, and the Nation. Certainly we must not forget that even here the market dominates affairs. Would-be employers, human traffic managers, and those states that follow a strategy of increased militarization of borderlands earn vast sums—only in part through the fees exacted from the travelers—while allocating spending within their own borders and/or across them to third-party governments that assist in addressing the "immigration crisis." Indeed, a small fortune is being made in the sale of the tools of this new regime for monitoring, helicopters, speed boats, and surveillance equipment to say nothing of new construction projects, temporary housing and detention centers, and the endless amount of human capital thrown at this problem.

Without a comprehensive multicultural and integration policy for the European Union, however, member nations will experience only partial success in the accommodation of immigrant populations. Conservative anti-immigrant political ideology has carried the day in Italy for many years under the direction of the Berlusconi administration. Scapegoated immigrants have suffered the continual assault of local and national politicians out to make a name for themselves. Blaming immigrants for the volatile economic fortunes brought on by global restructuring has in many cases helped to avoid a straightforward discussion of the national economy, youth unemployment, or the accommodation of migrant communities that are increasingly an integral part of Italian labor and social contexts.

In the basement of a local Catholic church in Turin, just near the Dora River and beyond the great piazza that hosts the Porto Palazo Market, the Mourid enact the prayer circle that young, French-educated Senegalese associate with the rural world of the peanut zone. They attend such ceremonies against their will; these are not our customs, they say, they are singing—meaning that for them the practice of the circle falls outside acceptable Muslim practice. This temporary arrangement for the use of the church grounds, offered by the local priest, was soon to be challenged by parishioners and other priests as improper. While initially the non-Mourid members of the Senegalese community attended such events fearing the sanctions of the Mourid leader, as they moved further out into the city, found their own apartments, and established their own religious centers they rejected the authority of the Mourid leader. Many of the young Mourid preferred to align themselves with more power religious leaders back home in Senegal.

Writing to the Archbishop of Turin, the religious leader of the Mourid invoked a metaphor of common belief in the spirit of the Catholic hierarchies open to other traditions: "A person discovers that he or she does not possess the truth in a perfect and total way but can walk together with others toward that goal" (as a papal encyclical of 1984 puts it). This dialogue of life is encouraged in the spirit of a new "mutual affirmation, reciprocal correction" and exchange between religious traditions. The Mourid leader began, "We think that nothing bad may come of the fact that in a single place of Worship, one prays to the same God, in which we all believe, albeit that we pray with different rituals and believe in the message of different prophets." Such a negotiated presence and affirmation was beyond the scope of the Archbishop, who finally invited Christians to "not lose their religious identity in the face of Islam."

What is happening here is the intricate interpenetration of a system of racial classifications, complicated by the fact that within Italy southern Italians have been thought of as another race in a system of religious and regional intolerance (Carter 1997). The Senegalese ride the crest of this taxonomy. But it has not always been this way: a history of tolerance and coexistence lies buried not so deeply in Europe's past.

THE MEDITERRANEAN

The maritime world and the life of the Mediterranean proletariat, the slave, and smuggler have been linked for centuries across the "ill-defined sea between Africa and Sicily, with its deep waters full of fish, its reefs of coral and sponges, and its islands" (Braudel 1995: 116). In the past, in lands such as Andalusia and Sicily, Islamic and Christian traditions not only converged but also coexisted, balanced by the wisdom of hospitality and the art of commerce. The sea routes in these parts have always carried the licit and illicit, luxury goods, secret communications, and people. Not all cargoes have been welcomed, but all have sooner or later disappeared through the magic of flexible markets. The vital link between Africa and Sicily is now retraced through the tiny ships of human traffickers and the many coast guard and other vessels that attempt to intercept these rickety, barely seaworthy crafts on the open sea. As structural contours of the European Union fall into place, the idea of Europe, at times drawn from notions of common culture, geography, religion, or a diffuse shared political and economic vision clinging loosely to the remnants of a social democratic tradition, appears everywhere to be in crisis. That a kind of revival of interest in the concept of the Mediterranean has come about at this moment is hardly surprising, because an imagined unity of the Mediterranean world has, as often as not, been associated with and mediated by a notion of tolerance and the operation of a more or less humanistic ideology. Fundamental to this tradition for those unfettered by the conceptual apparatus of culture is the granting of a basic humanity and the fact that no culture may rise above or fall below another in our world. Implicit in this is a fundamental human right to exist.

Contemporary practices of incorporation in democratic sovereign states have often been at odds with the claims and expressions of universalistic human rights. But the most recent turn toward militarization in an effort to stem the porous nature of borders runs perilously close to a complete shutting down of legitimate avenues of admittance to the new Europe (Benhabib 2002: 153). The failure to clarify the distinction between admittance and membership and to render transparent the procedures and processes by which permanent residence, asylum, refugee status, and permission to stay are attained and contested in the case of appeal raises serious ethical concerns in the realm of political incorporation, immigration, and human rights. In the absence of a European Union agreement on such issues, ad hoc solutions have begun to crop up among member nations. Collective deportations of newcomers to third-party countries (e.g., Libya) have further raised concerns that migrants have been denied access to lawyers, interpreters, and officials properly trained to handle asylum matters (Carter and Merrill 2005). It is unclear that adequate attention to and respect for the principle of non-*refoulement* (which prohibits the return of anyone to a territory where they would be at risk of serious human rights violations) have been adhered to in many recent deportations of migrants in Italy. The forced repatriation of all potential newcomers and asylum seekers through Italy's agreement with Libya is an example of the ambiguous status of the migrant in Europe.

Detention centers in Libya are virtual holding areas from which migrants are sent back to their alleged country of origin (in the absence of proper identification procedures, the assignment of migrants' country of origin is questionable at best), and through this arrangement hundreds of migrants have been sent home. Amnesty International has criticized the program, suggesting that people are not properly identified or informed of their right to request asylum. United Nations High Commissioner for Refugees (UNHCR) spokesperson Ron Redmond, following Italy's decision to deport some 180 refugees who landed on the tiny island of Lampedusa, renewed his protest, insisting that he regrets "the continued lack of transparency on the part of both Italian and Libyan authorities and regrets that as a result, suspicions that one or both countries may be in breach of international refugee law will be hard to put to rest" (UNHCR 2005). Indeed, Italy and many other countries that practice "forced deportation" may be sending back bona fide refugees. In addition, Libya cannot be considered a safe country of asylum, having at best a troubling human rights record and not having signed on to the Geneva Convention (Messino 2005: 16). Migrants are not only denied the right to appeal their deportation; they are often held incommunicado prior to their departure. No observer group has been allowed access to the entire process, leaving Italian and Libyan authorities as the only arbiters of the deportations (Carter and Merrill 2005).

This shadowy realm indeed creates a new cultural world, linking states in a new configuration posed to fight both terrorism and immigration. Libya, deeply implicated in conflicts in Darfur and elsewhere in the region, has in the recent past contributed to the displacement of populations in an attempt to expand its influence. Now Libya is being tapped to create a bulwark against terrorism and a solution to the immigration crisis in European territory. Recent anti-immigrant riots in Libya raise concerns that conditions may not be favorable to African migrants due to both a pronounced ideology of Arab supremacy and deep anti-immigrant sentiments as the country has increasingly become a transit point in international migration.

Lampedusa, 120 miles southwest of Sicily, with its mysterious clear blue waters, is a small island of some 6,000 souls. It has over the past decade become known as one of the main sea routes into Italy and the primary water channel for migrants coming from Africa. Those reaching its shores have actually come from as far away as Turkey, but whatever the ships' port of departure, people have come to the island from countries including Liberia, Somalia, Iraq, Nigeria, Sudan, Tunisia, Mali, Ghana, Egypt, and Morocco. In an incident reported on October 17, 2003, an Italian rescue ship picked up some eighteen people off Lampedusa. Survivors told officials that seven of their number had fallen victim to the overloaded boat ferrying people to the island's shores, three of them infants ("Seven" 2003). The crew of the rescue ship crew recovered one body, while six others were thrown overboard—a common occurrence on such voyages. As in the case of other deaths at sea, it is clear that "some bodies will never be found, the corpses joining the growing pile of human bones under the Sicilian seas that local fisherman have for months been reporting surfacing in their nets" (Clarke 2002). The small groups of fishermen in the region now call the waters surrounding the island and the straits of Sicily "a liquid tomb."

The Moroccan-born writer Tahar Ben Jelloun wrote of one of the shipwrecks that "the book of the sea is the registry of a marine cemetery that no longer swallows the pirates as it once did, but their victims," as it is certain that such voyages are organized by traffickers (Jelloun 2001). All over the Mediterranean makeshift cemeteries have cropped up for migrants who fall short of their goal to reach a new world. In Lampedusa, the nameless graves now overrun the local cemetery that years ago filled the twenty spaces allotted to the newcomers. At times the island runs out of coffins unable to keep apace of the toll the sea exacts on the travelers, as *New York Times* writer Frank Bruni observes: "In the town cemetery, besides the opulent crypts that many southern Italians favor, is a weed-strewn plot of dirt for the bodies of immigrants, buried under wooden crosses with numbers, not names" (Bruni 2003).

On Lampedusa, the detention center may have been built to house as many as 200 persons but now serves as a temporary home for many hundreds of detainees; in March 2005 it held 732. The newcomers often arrive badly dehydrated and in need of medical attention, which such centers are rarely able to adequately provide. The worst cases are flown to the mainland or to Sicily. This situation is reproduced hundreds of times across Europe, where the conditions of immigration detention centers are primitive and resemble most closely the structure of prisons, surrounded by barbed wire and armed guards. And yet the potential migrants are not terrorist combatants but people who have risked their lives to reach the imagined southern gate of Europe (Carter and Merrill 2005).

Initially, migrants in Italy were transferred to other detention centers or so-called *Centri di Prima Acooglienza* (centers of initial reception), on the mainland or Sicily, but most recently planeloads of migrants have been airlifted directly to "reception centers" in Libya.[8] While identification procedures and the processing necessary for an asylum claim can take months, migrants have been summarily deported from the centers on Lampedusa only days after their arrival on the island, leaving many human rights groups suspicious of official assurances that migrants' rights to asylum have been properly respected. Many of the detainees have been held in less than dignified environmental conditions without the ability to contact the outside world or consult lawyers, interpreters, or relatives (Carter and Merrill 2005). We return to Lampedusa below if only to consider another form of denial, not only of the living but also of the dead.

The new rush toward the militarization of borders may seriously compromise the right to seek asylum under the Geneva Convention and the Universal Declaration of Human Rights (UDHR) and also violate migrants' claim to a constellation of universal human rights that transcends the rights of citizens of the many sovereign states they might wish to enter (Dunkerly 2002; Behhabib 2002: 152). Although there are a number of ways to essentially discipline and punish migrants who wish to gain admittance to European countries, there remains no mechanism for calling sovereign states to order for the treatment of aliens, foreigners, and others. Certainly, defining the identity and subjectivities of the nation-state is a process open to contest and public debate: the lines separating one group from another across ethnicity, social class, race, and sexuality "more often than not rests on unexamined prejudices, ancient battles, historical injustices, and sheer administrative fiat" (Benhabib 2002: 177). As Seyla Benhabib notes in *The Claims of Culture*, "There are still no global courts of justice with the jurisdiction to punish sovereign states for the way they treat refugees, foreigners, and aliens" (Benhabib 2002: 177). The processes of dealing with silences and invisibility within the social order are often contested, historically protracted, and at times run below the threshold of social discourse. The climate of reception is colored also, in the wake of rapid changes in Europe, with a growing anxiety over the rising cost of living, disillusionment and at times despair over the declining efficiency and accessibility of public services, urban decline, traffic, crime, drug use—all seen as symptoms of a growing chaos providing a breeding ground for cultural nationalism, religious intolerance, neo-fascism, and concern with renewed acts of terrorism (Roy 2003: 71).

European philosophical traditions from Rousseau onward have revealed an emphasis on recognition (e.g., Hegel, Adam Smith). "All coexistence is a recognition," as Todorov reminds us, offering a fundamental acknowledgment of the others' existence (Todorov 2001). It is a reciprocal play though which proof of existence is accorded both giver and receiver. Lack of recognition is not just an inconvenient existential modality suffered in silence but rather enters into the lived misfortune of people whose very survival is threatened. I am referring to a fate that results in the denial of recognition that, unlike the effects of derision and hate, may go much further, confronting a person or group of persons with a kind of threat of nothingness. I am talking about a form of indifference or, as I call it, invisibility. Recall that in Dostoyevsky's *Notes from Underground*, while the narrator is willing to accept rejection, he dreads the possibility of being relegated to the denial of recognition altogether. For even in the most humiliating of circumstances one may be acknowledged, but a lack of recognition places one beyond the realm of human coexistence (Todorov 1989; Todorov 2001; Todorov 2002). Recognition marks in a sense the threshold of socially significant human existence. I suggest that the form of denial by sovereign states regarding migrants relegated to deportation without due process at once rejects legitimate legal status and calls into question the migrants' "proof of existence" as subjects with potential claims on a would-be host society. But there is another form of neglect, an invisibility that sets the newcomer at the crossroads of a discourse on immigration and society and, as we see below, that leaves the migrant with no viable place in the social imaginary whatsoever. Such extreme forms of invisibility may even follow one literally to the grave.[9]

In the volatile climate of anti-immigrant sentiment that sets the stage for all manner of violent rejection of the newcomer—promoted by right-wing groups such as Umberto Bossi's Northern League—President Carlo Azeglio Ciampi of Italy has denounced "distrust and hatred" of immigrants who are merely persons "driven by despair." Instead, he states, they must be embraced by Italian civic and Christian traditions, which should inspire feelings of common humanity and compassion. The neoconservative ideology of groups like the League threatens to ruin Italy's claim to being the heart and birthplace of humanism. The anti-immigrant furor has become so strong in recent years that migrants are seen as the containers of a series of contemporary potentialities and are thought to be the source of violence, illness, or contagion, the cause of the degradation of the labor market, urban decline, and a threat to Christian religious integrity (Carter and Merrill 2005). The discourse on immigration tends to criminalize the migrants, who are viewed as a "matter out of place," to be cleared off the shores of Europe like so much driftwood, loaded on Italian air force C-130J airplanes for Libya without regard for individual histories of political persecution, violence, or religious intolerance. Italian politicians even posit the "detention camps" as a humane solution to human trafficking. Interior Minister Giuseppe Pisanu went so far as to compare the traffic with the slave trade "for its dangers and brutality." The traffickers who knowingly subject migrants to less-than-seaworthy vessels for the harsh and often perilous passage to Europe must be stopped. But the deportations figure into the logic of an emergent Italian political identity that has consolidated power since the fall of the first Republic and its party system between 1992 and 1994 (Carter and Merrill 2005). Although it has increasingly consolidated power under the direction of Silvio Berlusconi, the right-wing fringe, attempting to establish partnerships in Europe, has articulated demands for the closure of borders and surveillance and an acute concern with national security. While some scholars predict that Berlusconi may move away from this faction headed by Bossi, and indeed even former coalition partner Gianfranco Fini renounced his more hard-line support of a Fascist legacy in order to become more Europe-friendly, it appears that this anti-immigrant, xenophobic, and anti-centrist position plays well to a disgruntled base (largely in the North) concerned about Italy's standing in Europe, economic growth, and local integrity. In a curious way, the northern politician rejects in an imagined South the very things they hold most dear: a regional connection, local dialects and cultural idioms, and the conviction that some long-standing "heritage" is being preserved (Carter and Merrill 2005). New calls for a "state of emergency" on immigration are more of the same repressive politics. This stance may change once the political page has turned on this administration in Italy. We shall see.

NOTES

1. Many anthropologists have considered the legacy of race, nationalism, and gender in post-slavery and postcolonial societies. I briefly consider these scholars' insights for the contested terrain of this legacy in the European context.

2. Relatives of the young men now comb the coast trying to discourage would-be migrants, joined by political officials, local women's organizations, and others who join in the fight to save a generation.

3. Eastern European migrants tend to return to their countries of origin with improving economic conditions there and thus present only a temporary solution to labor shortages. Their presence in the labor market, however, helps to degrade labor conditions for non-European migrants since informal employment impacts their right to stay but effects no change in European workers' residence status. Other European Union residents can work in the informal sector and legally stay in the country once the job comes to an end, while migrants from outside the EU face deportation in Italy once their job disappears.

4. This is often work subcontracted to firms that hire migrant workers and others on contracts of limited or indeterminate terms; the latter, increasingly rare today, affords workers relative job security and benefits.

5. In medium and large firms, it is common for benefits to be held up in litigation with the trade unions and the employers over the details of agreements made in the past. Workers, both Italian and migrant, are held in limbo while they await the courts' final determinations. Although Babacar won his case for back wages with assistance from the Union, the final allocation of the settlement has yet to take place.

6. I have also in mind the eleventh chapter of Primo Levi's *Survival in Auschwitz* in which the author recalls the canto of Dante devoted to Ulysses in order to teach Italian to a fellow inmate of the camps.

7. Of course, some newcomers, such as health care workers, are welcomed because such skilled labor is desperately needed. But while African health care professionals enter the work force in Europe, Canada, and the

United States, the health emergency in sub-Saharan Africa is reaching a point of crisis as nursing needs in the coming years are likely to double. The lack of skilled professionals, such as doctors, across a wide range of specializations only complicates the emergency in the health system further (Drugger 2004).

8. These centers are also called Centri di Permanenza temporanea e Assistenza (CPTAs) by Italian authorities.

9. I borrow heavily from Todorov's discussion here, especially his notion that humanism was deflected and distorted by scientism, nationalism, and egotism that was inflected into this discourse, particularly during the nineteenth century.

REFERENCES

Abdulafia, David. 2003. "A Globalized Mediterranean: 1900–2000." In *The Mediterranean in History*, ed. David Abdulafia. Los Angeles: Getty Publications.

Achebe, Chinua 2000. *Home and Exile.* New York: Anchor Books.

Arendt, Hannah. 1973. *The Origins of Totalitarianism.* New York: Harcourt, Brace.

Asad, Talal. 2003. *Formations of the Secular: Christianity, Islam, Modernity.* Palo Alto, Calif.: Stanford University Press.

Arie, Sophie. 2003a. "The Fatal Shore: As Thousands of North Africans Risk Their Lives to Reach Italy, Immigration Is Also Proving Dangerous for Silvio Berlusconi's Government." *Guardian*, June 18.

––––––. 2003b. "200 Presumed Dead after Overladen Refugee Boat Sinks: Rescuers Find Little Hope for Survivors on Illegal Migrant Route from Africa to Italy." *Sunday Guardian, The Observer*, June 22.

Baldwin, James. 1985. "Stranger in the Village." In *The Price of the Ticket: Collected Nonfiction 1948–1985.* New York: St. Martin's/Marek.

Barthes, Roland. 1987. *Michelet.* New York. Hill and Wang.

Bathe, B. W. 1973. *Seven Centuries of Sea Travel: From the Crusaders to the Cruises.* New York: Leon Amiel.

Bellu, Giovanni Maria. 2001."Nave Fantasma, ecco le foto cosí morirono 283 clandestini." *La Repubblica*, June 15.

––––––. 2004. *I fantasmi di Portopalo: Natale 1996: la morte di 300 clandestini e il silenzio dell'Italia.* Milano: Arnaldo Mondatori.

Benhabib, Seyla. 2002. *The Claims of Culture: Equality and Diversity in the Global Era.* Princeton, N.J.: Princeton University Press.

Bolzoni, Arrilio. 2001. "Ecco il dossier del naufragio Quattro fogli da archiviare: la Guardia costiera. Nessuno ci parlò dei casaveri ripescati." *La Repubblica*, June 7.

Bossi-Fini. 2002. Legge July 30, 2002, n. 189. Parliamento Italiano, "Modifica alla normative in material di immigrazione e di asilo." *Gazzetta Uficiale* n. 199, August 26.

Braudel, Fernand. 1995. *The Mediterranean: The Mediterranean World in the Age of Philip II, vols. I–II.* Berkeley: University of California Press.

———. 2001. *Memory and the Mediterranean*. New York: Vintage.

Bruni, Frank. 2002. "Off Sicily, Tide of Bodies Roils Immigrant Debate." *New York Times*, September 23.

———. 2003. "Wave of Immigrants Breaks against Italian Island's Shore." *New York Times*, July 11.

Cadalanu, Giampaolo. 2002. "Una Proposta irragionevole che capovolge la realtà." *La Repubblica*, June 14.

Carnegie, Charles V. 2002 *Postnationalism Prefigured*. New Brunswick, N.J.: Rutgers University Press.

Carter, Donald. 1997. *States of Grace: Senegalese in Italy and the New European Immigration*. Minneapolis: University of Minnesota Press.

Carter, Donald, and Heather Merrill. 2005. "Bordering Humanism: Life and Death on the Margins of Europe." Presented at the annual meeting of the Association of American Geographers, Denver.

Cartosio, Maneula. 2002. "Non cureremo la Bossi-Fini: Milan, immigrate in piazza contro la legge: Non saremo servili verso le nuove norme." *Il Manifesto*, June 14.

Clarke, Hilary. 2002. "Desperate Exodus for Survival: Traumatized Local Rescuers Are Still Counting the Bodies after Another Overflowing Boat of Asylum-Seekers Crashed onto Their Italian Shores Last Week." *Sunday Herald*, September 22.

Connolly, William E. 2002. *Neuropolitics: Thinking, Culture, Speed*. Minneapolis: University of Minnesota Press.

Cowell, Alan. 2003. "Boat Carrying African Immigrants Reaches Italy with 13 Dead." *New York Times*, October 2.

Douglas, Mary. 1966: *Purity and Danger*. London: Routledge and Kegan Paul.

Drugger, Celia. 2004. "An Exodus of African Nurses Puts Infants and the Ill in Peril." *New York Times*, July 12.

Dunkerly, David, et al. 2002. *Changing Europe: Identities, Nations and Citizens*. New York: Routledge.

Harrison, Robert Pogue. 2003. *The Dominion of the Dead*. Chicago: University of Chicago Press.

Homan, Thomas. 2003. "Statement of Thomas Homan, Interim Associate Special Agent in Charge, San Antonio, Texas, for Bureau of Immigration and Customs Enforcement, the Department of Homeland Security before the House Subcommittee on Immigration Border Security, and Claims Committee on the Judiciary." June 24.

Horden, Peregrine, and Nicholas Purcell. 2000. *The Corrupting Sea: A Study of Mediterranean History*. London: Blackwell.

Human Rights Watch. 2003. "An 'Unjust Vision' for Europe's Refugees." June 17.

Instituto Nazionale di Statistica. 2002. *Annuario Statistico Italiano*. Rome.

Jackson, Michael. 1998. *Minima Ethnographica: Intersubjectivity and the Anthropological Project*. Chicago: University of Chicago Press.

Jelloun, Tahar Ben. 2001. "La Vergogna Negli Abissi." *La Repubblica*, June 15.

"Key Arrest in Texas Migrant Tragedy." 2003. BBC News. June 16.

La Mattina, Amedeo. 2002a. "Turco: la destra fa solo propaganda: Anche Londra vuole più regola? Ma lì il dibattito non è 'padano.'" *La Stampa*, June 18.

——. 2002b. "Follini: non costruiamo muri, intervista: Marco Follini, leader dell'Udc." *La Stampa*, June 18.

Lacoboni, Jacopo. 2002. "Gli aiuti? Anche ai paesi 'colabrodo." *La Stampa*, June 18.

Malkki, Liisa H. 1995. *Purity and Exile: Violence, Memory, and National Cosmology Among Hutu Refugees in Tanzania*. Chicago: University of Chicago Press.

Margris, Claudio. 1999. "A Philology of the Sea." In *Mediterranean: A Cultural Landscape*, ed. P. Matevejevic. Trans. Michael Henry Heim. Berkeley: University of California Press.

Marozzi, Marco. 2002. "Immigrati, l'Europa si spacca non vince l'asse Italia-Spagna." *La Repubblica*, June 14.

Merrill, Heather, and Donald Carter. 2002. "Inside and Outside Italian Political Culture: Immigrants and Diasporic Politics in Turin." *GeoJournal* 58(2/3).

Messino, Francesco. 2005. *Lampedusa – the Island of Europe's Forgotten Promises*. Amnesty International.

"Mexico Call over Migrant Deaths." 2003. BBC News. May 15.

Michelet, Jules. 2001 [1861]. *The Sea*. Philadelphia: D. N. Goodchild.

"Migrant Headache Dogs Italy." 2003. BBC News. July 2.

Nkrumah, Gamal. 2003. "Controlling the Flow: The Rapid Rise in African Migrants Seeking Refuge in Europe Featured Prominently at the European Union Summit Meeting in Thessaloniki, Greece, Last Week." *Al-Ahram Weekly Online*, June 26–July 2 (issue no. 644). http://weekly .ahram.org.eg/2003/644/in.htm.

Pecoraro, Alfredo. 2003. "Una Strage nel Canale di Sicilia." *Il Manifesto*, June 18.

Riccio, Bruno 2007. "'Toubab' E 'Vu Cumpra': transnazionalitá e representazioni nella migrazioni Senegalese in Italia." Padova: Coop.Libraria Editrce Universitaria di Padova.

Romero, Simon. 2003. "Scene of Horror and Despair in Trailer." *New York Times*, May 16.

Romero, Simon, and Daniel Barboza. 2003. "Trapped in Heat in Texas Truck—18 People Die." *New York Times*, May 15.

Roy, Arundhati. 2003. *War Talk*. Cambridge, Mass.: South End Press.

Sarup, Madan. 1996. *Identity, Culture and the Postmodern World*. Athens: University of Georgia Press.

Sergi, Sergio. 2002. "L'Immigrazione, l'Europa ferma la linea dura." *L'Unita*, June 17.

"Seven Illegal Migrants Die in Italy Sea Crossing." 2003. Reuters. October 17.

Shack, William A. 2001. *Harlem in Montmartre: A Paris Jazz Story between the Great Wars*. Berkeley: University of California Press.

Singer, Enrico. 2002a. "Immigrazione, L'Europe va avanti in ordine sparso: No di Francia e Svezia alle sanzioni contro I paesi che non collaborano." *La Stampa,* June 18.

———. 2002b. "Sanzioni no, ma più aiuti a chi collabora." *La Stampa,* June 19.

Todorov, Tzvetan. 1989. *The Deflection of the Enlightenment.* Palo Alto, Calif.: Stanford University Press.

———. 2001. *Life in Common: An Essay in General Anthropology.* Lincoln: University of Nebraska Press.

———. 2002. *Imperfect Garden: The Legacy of Humanism.* Princeton, N.J.: Princeton University Press.

Valenti, Ricco. 2002a. "La Cassazione "I figli studiano? Niente diritto di soggiorno." *La Stampa,* June 18.

———. 2002b. "Centri d'accoglienza, tuttoo esaurito." *La Stampa,* June 18.

Westbrook, David A. 2004. *City of Gold: An Apology for Global Capitalism in a Time of Discontent.* New York: Routledge.

Wikan, Unni. 2002. *Generous Betrayal: Ethnic Identity Politics in the New Europe.* Chicago: University of Chicago Press.

Wilkinson, Ray. 2003. "Old Problems—New Realities." *Refugees* 3(132).

Williams, Brackette F. 1991. *Stain on My Name, War in My Veins: Guyana and the Politics of Cultural Struggle.* Durham, N.C.: Duke University Press.

Xingjian, Gao. 2000. *Soul Mountain.* New York: HarperCollins.

Ziniti, Alessandra. 2003. "Lampedusa, nuovi sbarchi sfiorata collisione in mare." *La Repubblica,* June 16.

4 HISTORIC CHANGES UNDERWAY IN AFRICAN MIGRATION POLICIES

FROM MUDDLING THROUGH TO ORGANIZED BRAIN CIRCULATION

RUBIN PATTERSON

This chapter takes a step back and examines the new state of play in Africa with respect to brain circulation or the deliberate attempt among southern nations to utilize emigration to advance their socioeconomic development. Numerous modalities exist that illustrate the existence and dimensions of brain circulation on the continent. Researchers could conduct in-depth case studies of nations and comparative analyses to examine closely the strategies of these nations. Another option for researchers is to ascertain primary data or take existing secondary data on dozens of African nations and apply inferential statistics to analyze their brain circulation strategies. Researchers could also apply statistical analysis to cross-tabulated data or even subject extensive panel study data to analysis. All these approaches are valuable and our collective understanding of brain circulation in Africa would be enriched tremendously if we had a combination of studies applying to each of these approaches.

I chose a totally different approach for my study. My work started with a broad reading of brain circulation literature on a widely diverse set of nations, which is a literature primarily reporting that governments today are, in a broad sense, universally embracing the "migration for development" strategy, albeit in different ways and in varying degrees. The proposition that I am exploring is that African states, much like their Asian and Latin American counterparts, are also organizing their versions of brain circulation at the end of the first decade of the twenty-first century. From there, I have engaged several major institutions in Africa that have interacted extensively with many countries on the continent regarding such a development strategy and other development topics. The New Partnership for Africa's Development (NEPAD) and the International Organization for Migration (IOM) for southern Africa reported that they were indeed working on such issues with governments in southern Africa and other parts of the continent. In some instances NEPAD was providing encouragement to nations to pursue such a strategy, and in some other instances IOM for southern Africa was being approached by nations to provide technical support on migration with implications for development. This research strategy is valuable, too, just as are the approaches outlined in the opening paragraph, and it yields unique insights that augment the literature on brain circulation in Africa.

The perspective that I bring to this subject includes the understanding that migration of some talent from nations of the South to nations of the West is inevitable. Failure to develop a migration for development strategy will neither prevent nor discourage such migration of talent from occurring. However, developing such a strategy enables the sending nation to both mitigate the short- to medium-term adverse impacts and maximize the medium- to long-term benefits of migrants returning some of the human, economic, and social capital they acquire in Western countries. It is certainly true that African nations have far fewer highly skilled technical professionals than their Asian counterparts. Alas, acknowledgment of this fact by African highly skilled technical professionals will not deter them from seeking to migrate. Rather than focusing on the fact that African nations can least afford to follow Asian nations in a brain circulation strategy due to an acute shortage of highly skilled technical professionals, I conclude—based on years of interrogating this subject through fieldwork in Africa, Asia, and Latin America—that Africans can least afford not to develop comprehensive brain circulation strategies. Because African nations are destined to lose some of their tiny fractions of professionals, an even greater urgency exists for them to develop and implement plans, mechanisms, and structures to turn the immediate losses into medium- and long-term gains.

I also acknowledge that not all South-to-West migrants are in pursuit of economic gains. The work of many scholars makes that point abundantly clear (Levitt 2001; Manuh 2005; Brinkerhoff 2009; Arthur 2010). That is, every year, the impetus behind the emigration of thousands in the South is associated with a combination of religious toleration, political freedom, intellectual growth, artistic expression, cultural enrichment, or cosmopolitan impulses, among other factors. To my knowledge, no comprehensive, authoritative scholarly study has been conducted in which South-to-West migrants are interviewed and asked to rank the principal reasons for their international migration. Each of the factors cited above is certainly worthy of book-length independent investigations rather than an attempt to examine them holistically in a single publication. Nevertheless, I think we can safely surmise that economic pursuits are among the most prevalent and powerful factors behind South-to-West migration.

It is for these reasons that this chapter concerns itself exclusively with the economic impetus of such migration.

AFRICAN GOVERNMENTS LEARN TO ROLL
WITH THE MIGRATION PUNCHES

International migration is economically, politically, culturally, and socially transforming the modern world in an unprecedented way (Castels and Miller 2003). During the course of the last century, over 100 million migrants took up residence in a country outside their place of birth. Not only is twenty-first-century global migration on track to dwarf its previously staggering twentieth-century forerunner, but humans, like never before, are also visualizing communities and pursuing career trajectories that transcend nation-state boundaries. In the globalization of today and tomorrow, skills are a global commodity to be exported and imported across increasingly porous borders, just as capital and goods have been over the years (Kapur 2005). If there is one universal principle of international migration, it is this: governments of core countries embrace this global migration while their working classes are threatened by it; conversely, governments of peripheral countries have heretofore been threatened by the ease of migrating talent while their professional classes embrace these opportunities. African nations, which are largely in the periphery, operate in accordance with this principle: governments on the continent throughout much of the postcolonial period have been threatened by the migration of skills while citizens look for emigration opportunities to improve their lot in life. As this chapter illustrates, that African migration principle has largely run its course because African governments have suddenly gained a new outlook on the emigration of talent and are in the process of revising their emigration policies.

From all indications, we are on the cusp of significant change in immigration policy across Africa, as governments have taken notice of the potentially huge benefits of the migration-development model. Ambivalence is noticeable among African governments, as they have watched with envy the tremendous boom in Asian and Latin American economies, due in large measure to the migration-development model. However, at the same time, insecure African governments fear the loss of social control due to both migrating talent needed in the society and the movement of that foreign talent back into homeland political affairs.

When it comes to emigration, governments who are threatened by it have three broad options: they can attempt to construct some draconian measures reminiscent of the Cold War in a futile effort to deter emigration; they can take a non-interventionist approach and simply attempt to "muddle through" with whatever the emigration numbers and their effects might be in society at any given time; or they can attempt to shape inevitable migratory events to their respective nation's strategic advantage (i.e., migration-development strategy or brain circulation). African states across the continent, all fifty-three of them, not unlike states around the world, are amending their policies in response to this heightening impulse of global migration. The approaches taken by African states are marked by diversity, as each state has its own idiosyncratic approach to migration based on the nature of both the type of governance in each society and the ruling party as well as their perceived sense of social vulnerability and political insecurity.

Despite the tremendous diversity, all African nations can be judged by the three-category taxonomic continuum above: draconian intervention, non-interventionist, and strategic brain circulation. Fortunately, African states are not pursuing draconian measures to prevent citizens from emigrating, as doing so would constitute a violation of human rights—besides, it is recognized that such efforts are ill-fated. At the other end of the spectrum, African states at present have yet to go through the rigors of systematically setting up the migration-development model with brain circulation.

While some Asian governments and a few Latin American governments were vigorously pursuing the migration-development model between the 1970s and 1990s, many African governments took more of a non-interventionist, "muddling through" posture. Non-interventionist in this context is relative, while both the draconian and the brain circulation approaches to emigration are "all or nothing" propositions. That is, they both see emigration as a factor crucial to the nation's success or, more narrowly, crucial to the stability of the ruling regime. Draconian measures are employed when the state lacks legitimacy, is unable to meet the demands of its citizens, and concludes that it has to take repressive action to keep the doctors, teachers, businesspersons, engineers, and other skilled professionals from emigrating. Hence, draconian measures are taken when regime stability is the utmost concern. Conversely, brain circulation measures are employed when the state makes a virtue of necessity. This is akin to martial arts, as when a fighter takes the energy behind an oncoming blow from an opponent and redirects it against that opponent. In this instance, of course, the opponent is not emigrating citizens but the initial loss of needed talent in the aggregate. Again, based on both reoccurring human history and the unprecedented twenty-first-century global commodification of labor, since we know that talent will most often migrate from South to West, the prudent approach—or, we can say, the martial arts approach—is to help organize and direct the energy in a manner that is beneficial to the sending society. In short, it is a matter of turning an inevitable social action from a negative into a positive. The would-be negative impact on the nation as a result of talented, skilled nationals emigrating can be transformed into a positive impact if the nationals are sufficiently helped to succeed in the core nations where they grow their human, economic, and social capital, and are courted to subsequently reinvest some of that capital back into the homeland. As I have explained previously,

> "Brain circulation" is distinguishable from the "brain gain," as the latter was conceived during the debate from years past. For starters, brain gain was viewed as an automatic overall outcome for poor nations when talented individuals emigrated to rich nations. The brain-circulation thesis, unlike that of brain gain, emphasizes the contingent nature of the process. Emigrant talent from the South to the West can be either an overall brain drain or a brain gain, for it is totally dependent on the extent to which the complex of human, economic, and social capital of the new immigrants from the South is accumulated, the extent to which it is courted by leaders in the homeland in a strategically coordinated manner, and the extent to which there exists an enabling economic and political environment in the homeland for the capital to be put to productive use. (Patterson 2007: 5)

Individual governments in Africa, Latin America, and parts of Asia are busily consulting with experts such as those at IOM, consulting with Asian nations that have successfully employed brain circulation strategies, and engaging their respective diasporas to devise a strategy that makes sense for them. The fact that this development strategy has been around for decades means that there are plenty of data and analyses of best practices to model and worst problems to avoid.

While Asian nations get most of the exemplary attention, other nations that have been involved with their core-based diasporas offer important information, too. Morocco and Mexico make for two interesting examples. Governments of both countries have been interacting with their large diasporas in core societies: Moroccans in France and Mexicans in the United States. Nevertheless, "neither the Moroccan nor the Mexican government had any intention of using migration to advance a strategy of economic change that would include migrants and their communities in such a meaningful way" (Iskander 2010: 305). Neither government started interacting with its diasporas from a brain circulation policy perspective, but over time each has worked pursuant to such a policy with different levels of success. Less successful brain circulation nations such as these can also inform African nations on the way forward.

PURSUING PRUDENT MIGRATION-DEVELOPMENT
POLICY AGENDAS

The first step that governments must take to turn inevitable broad social events into systematically positive outcomes is to conduct policy-informing research. This type of research can only now begin to occur in Africa as governments have finally conceptually embraced the migration-development model for their own countries. Within the past few years leaders in Africa have increasingly and conspicuously embraced this model. An early indication was seen when the African Union (AU) identified the African diaspora as the sixth "region of Africa." Moreover, the AU went on to acknowledge that development in Africa would be neither systematic nor firmly rooted unless the African diaspora has an integral role in the planning and prosecution of that development. African leaders have asked the New Partnership for Africa's Development (NEPAD), as the AU's program for bridging the enormous economic gap between Africa and the advanced industrialized core nations, to advise them on the migration-development model. As was noted, "At a continent-wide level, the African Union has established a 'strategic framework for a policy on migration' and a specific programme on migration within its Social Affairs Directorate" (Black et al. 2006: 10). Similarly, the southern African office of the IOM has been engaged by both NEPAD and individual governments in the region to pursue real-world policy studies on this subject. During interviews at the NEPAD secretariat in a Johannesburg suburb and at the IOM for southern Africa office in Pretoria, the professional staff reported that they had clearly detected a sea change in the views of governments. African governments wish to be further educated on the mechanisms of transitioning from their previous "muddling through" emigration posture to organized brain circulation agendas that generate the broad developmental gains witnessed by the likes of India, Taiwan, the People's Republic of China (PRC), South Korea, Mexico, and others. Not only do they want to be educated about the mechanisms for moving forward but—according to professional staffs of NEPAD and IOM who have been approached by governments within the region—they also want reassurances that there would be no further collapse in social services or that will this be a recipe for future political instability.[1]

Policy-informing research often involves a clearly articulated grand strategy accompanied by abundant rigorous empirical data. The grand migration-development strategy that African governments seek to emulate (in the African context) is the development transformations resulting from brain circulation as experienced by some Asian and Latin American governments. Most early post-independent governments underwent similar maturations regarding the assessment of emigrating talent, particularly to core countries: moving from active discouragement to disillusionment in the face of its inevitability and finally to nascent organized brain circulation. India was a forerunner, as its founding independent president, Nehru, encouraged many of the nation's best and brightest to emigrate to industrialized countries in order to grow their human and economic capital. Some of that capital, he was assured, would eventually be reinvested back into India. Because countries such as India, the PRC, South Korea, and Taiwan were pioneers or early adopters of this development strategy, and their leaders were wholeheartedly committed, they have reaped benefits far beyond other nations' in the South. India began this development strategy in the late 1940s, while the PRC, South Korea, and Taiwan initiated it in the late 1960s. Mexico and other Latin American nations followed in the 1980s. Only a few of the fifty-three African nations pursued this strategy at that time. Under Rawlings, Ghana was an early champion of this approach, and as a result Ghana has been more successful with this development strategy in comparison with other African nations (Arthur 2008).

Pioneers of the migration-development strategy were mobilized around the proposition that, under the right policy and social conditions, emigrating nationals to industrialized societies could be persuaded and would act out of their own volition to reengage and invest into their ancestral homeland. Subsequent adopters of this strategy further clarified the theoretical proposition and thus benefited from the limited empirical evidence of the pioneers and, in turn, generated an abundance of new empirical evidence from their own experiences. Now that African governments are poised to move in this direction, numerous scholars around the world and institutions such as the World Bank and IOM have weighed in, and they have not only attached their imprimaturs to the migration-development strategy, but they have also all contributed to a burgeoning literature.

The brain circulation strategy is framed broadly in the historical-structuralist approach to international migration. As stated above and is indeed already well established, talented and skilled humans have always emigrated from their countries of birth to countries offering greener pastures. However, the world economy of the late twentieth and early twenty-first centuries, where labor has been a global commodity, speaks to a new historical moment with specific structural impediments and opportunities for Africans and others of the global South. Beyond the broad historical-structuralist approach, there is need for both macro-level and micro-level analyses (Massey et al. 1998). Microscopic lenses are needed to understand the agency of individuals, telescopic lenses are needed to understand the structural forces, and theoretical analysis is needed to advise and understand how to make sense of data from switching between the two levels. Fitting for policy applications, policy-informing researchers should neither expect nor need some "grand theory" of African migration (Portes and DeWind 2007); rather, they should seek formulation of a set of "middle-range theories" to advise governments on policy.

Middle-range theories can guide us in ascertaining the following types of requisite data to inform policymakers: migrants by gender, age group, education level, and ethnicity; and levels of remittances, reinvestment, and repatriation by various demographic groups. With more sophisticated macro-level data and finer micro-level data, researchers are more likely to construct the profile of the "typical" migrant and attendant consequences. Extensive compilations of biographical information as well as details regarding the purposes of emigrant travels are needed by governments. Additional studies on African emigration should help governments to move much further beyond simply knowing that the better educated and more skilled individuals are the ones emigrating disproportionately. When sufficient studies have been executed by scholars and commissioned by African governments, IOM, and other nongovernmental organizations, the results should be a clearer recognition of (a) who among the technically talented is most likely to emigrate to the West (since all of them do not emigrate), (b) who is most likely to neither make economic investments back home nor repatriate, (c) who is most likely to reinvest economically back home but not repatriate, and (d) who is most likely to repatriate and under what conditions. Additionally, there is the need to know answers to the following two questions: Among those emigrants who never or only barely reinvested economically back home, what are their principal reasons for being ill-disposed to doing so? For all such categories of technically talented emigrants and would-be emigrants to the West, what are the policy conditions they see as necessary for them to either significantly reinvest economically back home or repatriate? Answers to these questions bear some similarity throughout the periphery countries. Nevertheless, there are important subtleties and *sui generis* cases that need to be thoroughly understood if the likelihood for brain circulation in the African context is to be optimized.

In addition to the southern African region, IOM covers the continent in three other regions. The southern region of IOM, congruent with the fifteen Southern African Development Community (SADC) states, to take just one example, is working toward benchmarking research and governmental data collection methods to ensure, among other necessary attributes, comparability. More broadly, this region is receiving assistance with the identification of important categories of data, the collection and storage of data, the processing and analysis of data, and the accessibility of statistics (Williams and Tsang 2007). Such assistance should provide a much better perspective on intra-region (e.g., within SADC) migration versus migration to the United States, to the European Union, or to one of the other four regions within Africa. Ideally, the AU would have, with the aid of NEPAD and IOM, in tabular form, a compilation of succinctly worded policies for each nation that either promotes or retards migration, a given nation's relationship with its diaspora, and types of regional coordination. Additionally, there is a need to know the degree to which various African nations are establishing policies of dual citizenship and creating ministries to both serve and solicit engagement by their respective diasporas.

African nations are unlikely to emulate those nations who were successful with the migration-development strategies without their respective governments' implementation of conducive migration-development policies, and those governments are unlikely to implement such policies without first ascertaining valid and reliable data of the sort delineated in the above paragraphs. As an example, "The member states of . . . [SADC], while wanting to promote regional co-operation and co-ordination and implement a Protocol on the Facilitation of Movement of Persons, admit that they have insufficient data and information on which to base and develop a workable set of migration policies applicable to most or all countries in the region" (Williams and Tsang 2007: 3). Although having possession of such data by the AU and the governments is not necessarily imminent, there are two major reasons for optimism. First, leaders across the continent have bought into the notion of a migration-development strategy at varying levels of commitment. Second, the AU, NEPAD, IOM, the United Nations Economic Commission for Africa (UNECA), and the regional bodies such as SADC are collectively and individually pushing for such harmonized data and the subsequent accrual of benefits across the continent stemming from the migration-development strategy.

The goals for the AU, NEPAD, IOM, UNECA, and SADC, as well as other regional blocs, are for them to have easily accessible benchmarked data on stocks and flows and policies for each nation, insight into which policies are working and which ones are not, and the ability to determine what any given African nation is doing with reference to migration and development in comparison with nations such as India and Taiwan. The next logical step beyond the collection and assessment of various types of data discussed is to work toward implementation. Here again, documentation is key so as to allow for identification and study of best practices and benchmarking. Among the important best practices will be the means by which to identify large numbers of the diaspora, particularly in global cities in the core, and successful strategies for encouraging them to reengage their respective homelands. Outlines of many of the strategies employed by some Asian and Latin American governments for identifying and engaging their diaspora are in published literature, but much more finely granular data and thoughtful insight are needed to better gauge what is likely applicable in the African context.

CONCLUSION: NOTES OF CAUTION AND OPTIMISM

While it is encouraging that African governments have recognized the potential benefits of implementing a migration-development strategy, one should not underestimate the fact that diaspora engagement alone is enormously inadequate for meeting Africa's twenty-first-century needs. Abounding deep structural barriers can serve to prevent the migration-development strategy from succeeding in certain African countries compared with the way it has worked for others. These structural challenges, along with poor leadership, serve to discourage and foster distrust for diaspora members, which prevent the much-needed input to help remove structural impediments (Waters and Ueda 2007). I do not mean to suggest here, obviously, that the migration-development strategy can work elsewhere in the global South but not in sub-Saharan Africa due to its unique structural conditions. Instead, the point here is to underscore a twofold notion: that this development strategy will be more difficult to successfully implement in some sub-Saharan African nations and that this development strategy is likely to be even more of a prerequisite for these nations to experience transformative progress than it was for the pioneers of this development strategy.

Churchill is noted for having asserted that "you can always count on Americans to do the right thing—after they've tried everything else." However, one could similarly assert that "you can always count on Africans to adopt a necessary strategy for development—long after it has been adopted by others." This tendency of African governments to be late adopters of prudent development strategies was evidenced with information and communications technologies (ICTs). By 1990, the trajectory was theoretically clear although the empirical case was yet to be made: third-world countries needed to quickly roll out broad ICT investment, privatization, and regulatory policies as a means of attracting investment to facilitate economic development. Sub-Saharan African nations on the whole were late adopters of this strategy. Similarly, by the mid-1990s, both theoretically and empirically, the case was established that migration as a means of development through brain circulation had to be included in the policy arsenal of governments in the South. Nearly a decade later, governments in sub-Saharan Africa are finally and conspicuously signaling that they, too, are ready to pursue this development strategy, long after other nations have reaped the benefits. I have elsewhere suggested that sub-Saharan Africans can help pioneer or at least be one of the early adopters of what is likely to be one of the next major development strategies in the future, namely, eco-industrial development (Patterson 2008). Eco-industrial development will necessitate citizens from third-world societies migrating to study and work in key programs and institutions in the West before reinvesting human and economic capital from those experiences to their respective homelands in a manner similar to the way some Asians utilized this strategy over the last generation to help pioneer ICT industries. Too much of the postcolonial experience for too many African countries has been marked by one step forward and two steps backward. But as we observe governments' positions on emigration and the level of economic growth around the continent, perhaps we are observing a much-improved switch: two steps forward and only one step backward.

NOTE

1. During the summer of 2008, I interviewed several NEPAD and southern African IOM experts with various portfolios affected by emigration: homeland development, education, and finance. Moreover, I am contributing to immigration projects at both NEPAD and IOM. Both institutions are located in the Gauteng province of South Africa.

REFERENCES

Arthur, John A. 2008. *The African Diaspora in the United States and Europe: The Ghanaian Experience.* Burlington, Vt.: Ashgate.
———. 2010. *African Diaspora Identities: Negotiating Culture in Transnational Migration.* Lanham, Md.: Lexington Books.
Black, R., et al. 2006. *Migration and Development in Africa: An Overview.* Cape Town: Southern African Migration Project.
Brinkerhoff, Jennifer. 2009. *Digital Diasporas: Identity and Transnational Engagement.* New York: Cambridge University Press.
Castels, S., and M. Miller 2003. *The Age of Migration: International Population Movements in the Modern World.* New York: Guilford Press.
Iskander, Natasha. 2010. *Creative State: Forty Years of Migration and Development Policy in Morocco and Mexico.* Ithaca, N.Y.: Cornell University Press.
Kapur, D. 2005. *Give Us Your Best and Brightest: The Global Hunt for Talent and Its Impact on the Developing World.* Washington, D.C.: Center for Global Development.
Levitt, Peggy. 2001. *The Transnational Villagers.* Berkeley: University of California Press.
Manuh, Takyiwaa, ed. 2005. *At Home in the World? International Migration and Development in Contemporary Ghana and West Africa.* Accra, Ghana: Sub-Saharan Publishers.
Massey, D., et al. 1998. *Worlds in Motion: Understanding International Migration at the End of the Millennium.* New York: Oxford University Press.

Patterson, R. 2007. "Going around the Drain-Gain Debate with Brain Circulation." In *African Brain Circulation: Beyond the Drain-Gain Debate,* ed. R. Patterson. Boston: Brill.

———. 2008. "Preparing Sub-Saharan Africa for a Pioneering Role in Eco-Industrial Development. " *Journal of Industrial Ecology* 12(4).

Portes, A., and J. DeWind, eds. 2007. *Rethinking Migration: New Theoretical and Empirical Perspectives.* New York: Berghahn Books.

Waters, M., and R. Ueda, eds. 2007. *The New Americans: A Guide to Immigration Since 1965.* Cambridge, Mass.: Harvard University Press.

Williams, V., and T. Tsang. 2007. *The Prospects for Migration Data Harmonisation in the SADC.* Cape Town: Southern African Migration Project.

PART 2

TRANSLOCAL AND TRANSNATIONAL
CONNECTIONS: BETWEEN BELONGING
AND EXCLUSION

5

BELONGING
AMIDST SHIFTING SANDS
INSERTION, SELF-EXCLUSION, AND THE
REMAKING OF AFRICAN URBANISM

LOREN B. LANDAU

> I have been here for six years, but I don't think any right
> thinking person would want to be South African. . . .
> They are just so contaminated.
> —SOTHO MIGRANT IN JOHANNESBURG, 2005

AFRICAN URBANIZATION AND THE MEANING OF BELONGING

In the diversity of African cities, dynamic and overlapping systems of exchange, meaning, privilege, and belonging are the norm. These systems stem from longstanding patterns of political and economic domination—apartheid, indirect colonial domination, monopolistic party rule (Zlotnick 2006)—enacted across national territories, mixing together groups that might otherwise have chosen more autonomous trajectories. With differences and diversity heightened by recent mobility, Africa's cities are increasingly characterized by greater disparities of wealth, language, and nationality along with shifting gender roles, life-trajectories, and intergenerational tensions. Through geographic movement—into, out of, and within cities—urban spaces that for many years had only tenuous connections with the people and economies of the rural hinterlands of their own countries are increasingly the loci of economic and normative ties with home villages and diasporic communities spread (and spreading) across the continent and beyond (Geschiere 2005; Malauene 2004; Diouf 2000).

Despite our limited knowledge of African urban realities, planners and scholars continue to adopt analytical and policy tools drawn from European, North American, and (to some extent) Latin American experiences to manage and describe these cities and their populations (Simone 2004). These are valuable reference points, but amidst these cities of constantly "shifting sands" (Bauman 2000), they often lead us to overlook African cities' varied historical trajectories and systems of symbolic and material exchange (Winkler 2006; Diouf 2000; Sommers 2001; Tomlinson et al. 2003; Simone 2001; Landau 2006). Given how quickly new social formations are being fashioned and remade by geographic and social mobility and displacement, it is unclear what forms of inclusion, solidarity, or mutual recognition are desired by those involved (Taylor 1992; Pollock et al. 2000; Habermas 1998). It is similarly difficult to identify who has the authority to set the terms of engagement. In such environments, we see the regular demon of outward conflict, political mobilization, and violence (Horner 2007; Jackson 2006; Wa Kabwe Segatti and Landau 2007; Landau and Haithar 2007). Less visible are the various forms of inclusion, belonging, and identity being forged through the pragmatic strategies of those involved.

Rethinking the nature of belonging means addressing what Kabeer (2005: 1) argues is an "empirical void" where "the views and perspectives of 'ordinary' citizens are largely absent. We do not know what citizenship means to people—particularly people whose status as citizens is either non-existent or extremely precarious—or what these meanings tell us about the goal of building inclusive societies." Given the lack of systematic accounts from across the continent, this chapter uses evidence and anecdotes I have collected in southern Africa to open space for further empirical and conceptual investigations. It works from the starting point that to further our discussions of belonging within African cities, we must look outside policy frameworks and deductive theoretical frameworks to understood where and how inclusion is being negotiated, the actors involved, and the motivations for their participation. If successful, this excursion will encourage greater ecumenicalism in the conceptual categories and normative bases for further investigation and deliberation. However, benefiting from these inquiries necessitates a willingness to explore messy and often contradictory behaviors and beliefs among those being studied. Instead of theory testing, the novelty of these emerging social forms require a willingness to induce: to help build a vocabulary of belonging that maps the practices of those moving in and through Africa's cities.

To these ends, this paper sets out to achieve two modest, interrelated objectives. First, in highlighting the distinctiveness of African cities, it empirically challenges three premises typically informing discussions of urban inclusion: the presence of a dominant host community or political order; states' primacy as both the source of exclusion and the most potent tool for fostering inclusion; and the mutual incompatibility of forms of exclusion and inclusion. To counter, I begin from the ontological premise that despite their sometimes violent exclusion and fragmentation, African cities are also inclusive cities. They are, after all, where almost half the continent's population now lives—and the percentage is growing. More fundamentally, what outwardly appears as exclusion and marginalization may, when viewed through the eyes and words of those involved, reflect pragmatic strategies of incorporation.

The second set of arguments—more speculative than conclusive—relates to the meaning of inclusion (and policies for inclusion) where the premises outlined above do not hold. In doing so, I point to the emergence of distinctive ways of negotiating inclusion and belonging that transcend ethnic, national, or transnational paradigms. Confronted with virulent nativism coupled with restrictive immigration and anti-urbanization regimes, foreigners have reacted with a kind of tactical cosmopolitanism that negotiates partial inclusion in transforming societies without becoming bounded by them. Rather than a coherent philosophy, this is a mish-mash of rhetorical and organizational tools drawing on a diversity of more established discourses and value systems. In doing so, they capitalize on cosmopolitanism's power without being bound by its responsibilities. This paper attempts to contribute to the emerging literature on cosmopolitanism from below, conceptualized not as a philosophy but as a practice and form of experiential culture.

READING AND REVEALING URBAN INCLUSION

This essay draws on an ecumenical set of data in illustrating sub-national and transnational migration dynamics and the socio-institutional responses to them. Most of the information reflected here stems from migration-related research in southern and eastern Africa—beginning with Johannesburg in particular—undertaken between 2002 and 2007. This includes new survey research complemented by formal and informal interviews with migrants, service providers, advocates, and local government representatives.

The 2006 iteration of the migration survey, first undertaken in 2003, is a collaborative project among Wits University (Johannesburg), Tufts University (Boston), the French Institute of South Africa, and partners in Maputo, Lubumbashi, and Nairobi, where it is also being conducted. The 2006 Johannesburg sample—from which I draw perhaps too many of my examples in this piece—included 847 respondents in seven central Johannesburg neighborhoods. Of these, 29.9 percent (253) were from the Democratic Republic of Congo (DRC), 24 percent (203) from Mozambique, 22 percent (186) from Somalia, and 22.4 percent (190) from South Africa. The remainder (1.8 percent) were from other countries mistakenly included in the sample. Overall, 59.7 percent of the respondents were male, generally reflecting official estimates of the inner city's demographic composition. These data are by no means representative of South Africa's migrant stock or of Johannesburg's population, but they nevertheless provide critical illustrations of trends and challenges associated with human mobility. They also highlight the value of comparative work on experiences of migration highlighting similarities and differences among South Africa's international and domestic migrants and its more sedentary population groups. This is critical as transient populations—those who commute regularly into the city or who see their true lives as being elsewhere—are not often considered true city residents even when, as in Johannesburg, they represent a visible minority or majority in particular neighborhoods. In future work, I hope to draw on parallel data from the other studies included in the study.

RECONSIDERING BELONGING IN AFRICA'S CITIES

Before turning to the nature of inclusion in African cities as it is being negotiated within and outside policy frameworks, this essay first challenges three of the primary premises that inform discussions about inclusive cities and, more broadly, inclusive citizenship. Given its necessary brevity, what follows is a schematic review that only indicates where these presumptions fall short in the cases with which I am familiar. Further inquiry in Africa and elsewhere, coupled with more nuanced explanation, will reveal the degree to which my criticisms are justified.

THE PRESENCE OF A SELF-IDENTIFIED
HOST COMMUNITY OR DOMINANT CULTURE

Much of the writing on migration and urbanization explores how a preexisting and self-conscious host community makes space—or does not—for the poor, minority religions, migrants, immigrants, and disempowered genders, ethnicities, and racial groups. The Canadian debate over "reasonable accommodation" and French concerns over the burqa are strong illustrations of this. Underlying discussion about communities accommodating others are assumptions of a set of identifiable dominant values and institutions being challenged, reformed, and occasionally dismissed in the face of heightened diversity. Without denying the existence of self-identified host communities within African cities (or parts thereof), one must be wary of ascribing undue social coherence to Africa's primary urban centers where ethnic heterogeneity, enormous economic disparities, and cultural pastiche are the empirical norms, not exceptions (Larkin 2004; Mbembe 2004; Simone 2004).

Data from the 2006 survey in central Johannesburg is illustrative of the degree to which the urban population is also a "new" population. While it may not be surprising that only 14 percent of the noncitizens we surveyed had been in the inner city for ten or more years, a period almost dating back to the end of the apartheid era, the majority of South Africans (56.2 percent) had also arrived within the past decade. And most of these longer-term citizen residents had come only in the last fifteen years. Equally important, both citizens and non-nationals move frequently after coming to the city, tracing and precipitating changing neighborhood dynamics and their own economic fortunes. Consequently, only 28 percent of South Africans in the Johannesburg survey report having not moved since their arrival in the city, with 50 percent having moved twice or more. Among non–South Africans, the numbers are more striking: only 13 percent of foreigners report having stayed put, with almost three-quarters having moved at least twice. Close to 20 percent report moving thrice and another 31.7 percent four or more times. With such volatility, it is not surprising that only 55 percent of South Africans and 31 percent of noncitizens had occupied their current residence for more than two years, with 19.2 percent of South Africans and 35.1 percent of foreigners having lived there for less than six months.

Although these figures reflect a dynamism that is partially inflated due to apartheid's restrictions and South Africa's economic status, rapid rates of urbanization and international migration are common across the continent. In many places, the almost utter collapse of rural agriculture has resulted in urban growth rates of outstanding proportions. While many of these are domestic migrants, they may have as little in common with the people they find in the city as those coming from across international boundaries. In many places, central urban spaces are becoming filled with growing populations that certainly do not feel they are from the city. Moreover, they may be there only temporarily before dispersing or shifting elsewhere in or out of the city. Indeed, many of those now found in the cities see their residence as temporary or oscillate between rural and urban sites or among cities. Others move frequently to escape the obligations of kin or community, to benefit from them, or simply to lessen costs of urban residence while heightening economic opportunities.

Given the population's volatility, social networks within cities are spread thinly across many people and places. It is little surprise, then, that people sampled in the Wits surveys show remarkably low levels of trust between ethnic and national groups and, more surprisingly, within them. In Johannesburg, there are ethnic and immigrant networks, but these are typically limited to assisting others only to overcome immediate risks, when there are direct, mutual returns, or if a corpse needs to be returned to a country or community of origin (Madsen 2004; Andersson 2006). Even among South Africans, levels of social capital—trust of each other and their public institutions—are remarkably low (cf. Putnam 2007). The population's novelty and distrust may be inflated due to the severity of apartheid spatial planning and the social fragmentation it fostered; but preliminary evidence from other African urban centers rarely reflects a strong normative community. Networks of clan, neighborhood, or co-religionists undoubtedly exist (Nzayabino 2006), but these are often fragmented and functional, organized without an explicit recognition or sense of mutual obligation to those beyond the boundaries of familiarity (Sommers 2001). Among neither migrants nor the ostensible host population can we speak of a community or set of overlapping institutions that can be opened (or is being forced open). This heterogeneity allows for a de facto degree of permeability and co-existence, but without an enacted or articulated collective awareness.

STATE PRIMACY AS THE LOCUS OF EXCLUSION AND BELONGING

Throughout much of the policy-oriented literature on urban inclusion and belonging among immigrants, the state, its agents, and civil society fight, collaborate, and negotiate patterns of inclusion and exclusion. This model assumes a state that is deeply embedded in the social, economic, and institutional lives of those it ostensibly governs. Such approaches may be appropriate in Europe, North America, and some Latin American countries where the state gradually centralized power in the hands of elites before slowly discharging power and authority—albeit unequally—to individuals and corporate bodies (Bendix 1977; Marshall 1950; Dean 1996). In almost no case has this history of incorporation been replicated in Africa or, indeed, elsewhere in the colonial world. Although Africa's colonial and postcolonial cities have been the one geographic site where the state's powers are most evident (Herbst 2000; Hyden 1980; Bratton 2006), an effective, centralized authority has rarely governed residential or commercial activities within the continent's urban centers.

Even in South Africa, arguably the continent's strongest state, such rule required the constant application of force to discipline the populations within urban conglomerations. State weakness is not usually due to centralized opposition to its rule—organized crime, revolutionary social movements, or powerful religious organs—but is instead due to the form of postcolonial political consolidation that has occurred across the continent (Bayart 1993; Chabal and Daloz 1999). Where there are formal laws and institutions, their power rarely extends systematically beyond the central business districts, government bureaucracies, and wealthy residential suburbs. And even here, effective power is often shared in ad hoc ways with private security firms and condominium committees designed to intentionally fragment and delimit rights to urban space (Dirsuweit 2002; Ballard 2005; Caldeira 1996). Elsewhere, urban governance regimes are characterized by patronage politics, irregular policing, and neglect (benign and otherwise). That so many are new to the cities—the one space where African states have historically been visible in citizens' daily lives—means that residents' expectations for the state may also limit their interests in engaging with it or the skills and organizational capacity necessary to do so. Given a history with one or more of the continents' predatory states, one can hardly blame them for wishing to avoid it. Lack of finance and institutional capacity further limits the states' relative autonomy and relevance.

For these and other reasons that cannot be detailed here, the state's position as the center of policy formation, protest, and service delivery is far from assured in Africa's cities. Consequently, many urban residents effectively live in the "brown areas" beyond its direct influence (O'Donnell 2004). These are not necessarily spaces outside the realm of government influence, what Scott (1998) terms "non-state spaces." They are, rather, areas where state action has only indirect or partial influence, influence that is often evident only by efforts to elude or hinder policy. This may come as no surprise to anthropologists, but perceptions of state centrality continue to inform an undue amount of scholarly and policy-relevant work on Africa. It is also deeply frustrating for those wishing to promote integration and tolerance, as there are no obvious policy tools for doing so.

FRAGMENTATION AND MARGINALIZATION AS EXCLUSION

Africa's urban centers undeniably exhibit socioeconomic and political fragmentation, marginalization, and violent exclusion. As a result, millions of people live in slums with tenuous access to the minimum requirements of survival (UNHS 2003). This poverty, violence, exploitation, and political marginalization increasingly shape the activities, expectations, and ambitions of cities' newcomers and long-term residents (Simone 2004; Mbembe 2001). But despite their traumas, trials, and marginalization, Africa's cities are not only sites of exclusion. If they were, growth rates would have stabilized or declined: people would stay "home," return to their countries and communities of origin, or move elsewhere. But for reasons of choice and compulsion, the populations and geographic reach of cities continues to grow. This expanding presence of an ever-diversifying population suggests a kind of de facto inclusivity in which most people are able to meet their survival needs. These are rarely fair or just cities by any normative metric. Nevertheless, the slums, informal settlements, peri-urban zones, and other forms of settlement accommodate and sustain tens of millions, both in the cities and in communities that depend on them.

Much as historians speak about the simultaneous process of economic exclusion and alienation that transformed the rural peasantry and (eventually) the global economy (Polanyi 1957; Mehta 1999), moving to or living within Africa's cities is a process containing both elements of inclusion and exclusion. Unlike the forms of transformation Marx and others describe when force was consciously applied to alienate people from the land and their labor, this process is most often driven by market pressures coupled with individual and family aspirations for prestige, prosperity, or adventure. Through their movements into cities, people are incorporated (and in turn transform) systems of ethics, social engagement, and the exercise of power and authority at local, national, and global levels. Moreover, what at first appears to be exclusion—social, legal, or political marginalization—may be the result of novel strategies of inclusion. I discuss these further below.

RETHINKING BELONGING: GATEKEEPERS AND GLOBALIZATION

Rather than philosophically questioning what inclusion and belonging should mean—though this remains a vital question for philosophers, policy makers, and urban residents— this chapter elaborates what it appears to mean for many of the people living in Africa's urban centers. Through this, I identify the primary architects of urban life and speak further on the limits of planning for diversity in African contexts. In doing so, I recognize that by focusing only on institutions and policy frameworks, scholars too often ignore forms of inclusion negotiated outside the state or means of forging belonging that draw on state initiatives in unpredictable ways. These patterns of "horizontal" inclusion (Kabeer 2005) draw particular attention to the private custodians of membership and to forms of inclusion that may a priori radiate signs of marginalization.

This perspective reveals at least two dimensions of inclusion and belonging that are noticeably absent in my review of the more prescriptive relevant literature on African cities. They do, however, appear under different labels, in sociological and anthropological literature works on migration and cosmopolitanism. The first continues the reasoning outlined above by challenging the mutual exclusivity of inclusion and exclusion. Here we see an emerging form of conscious self-exclusion reflected by the Basotho migrant quoted at the beginning of this chapter. This is at once a form of self-alienation—often in response to ascribed alienation—and inclusion. Whereas non-indigenous plants, for example, cannot survive for long periods without somehow taking root or becoming an integral part of their ecosystem (Comaroff and Comaroff 2001), Johannesburg and a growing number of other African cities host alien populations that are shaping their own idioms of transient superiority, a means through which they actively resist transplantation. Clinging to the status afforded those belonging to the "mobile classes" (Baumann 2000), migrants hover above the soil by retaining loyalties to their countries of origin and orient themselves toward a future outside their country of residence. This emerges from a combination of both original intent (i.e., why people came to a given city), and a counter response to the hostility or exclusion they face when they arrive. Whatever its origins, many migrants deny ever having held aspirations of assimilation or permanent settlement (i.e., total inclusion). Others claim they would refuse such opportunities were they available. For them, status as allochthons is not a badge of shame, but a self-authored form of inclusion into a world that is somehow far greater, more promising, and more elusive than the physical cities in which they live. Instead of transplantation and legibility to the society and political systems in which they live, many foreigners and newcomers alike strive for a kind of usufruct rights: a form of exclusion that is at least partially compatible with social and political marginalization.

The second point emerges from my earlier interrogation into what, exactly, people are seeking to be or becoming included. In African cities—as elsewhere—inclusion is something more than claiming a right to the city or becoming part of a stable, urban community. We must avoid assuming the existence of such communities, but also recognize that for many domestic and (especially) international migrants, moving to a city—or toward larger more networked cities—also represents a step into a global imaginary. Through urbanization, they not only hope to access a place to stay or work, but also to global youth culture, new universal urban lifestyles (however these are understood), or, more concretely, opportunities for onward journeys. Whether they ever realize these ambitions, the city is nevertheless a space where one can access trading and travel opportunities unavailable in rural settings or even in the capital cities of less economically networked countries and communities.

As much as primary African cities are—and have always been—an integral part of global exchange, the global cultures that relatively poor migrants hope to join are not those described by theorists of globalization (Ong 1999; Sassen 2002). These may color their aspirations, but they are not disconnected cosmopolitans or elite professionals. Rather, these global networks are shaped by diasporas of kin, co-ethnics, co-religionists, and co-nationals who provide the infrastructure for a life that is at once in and out of a bounded geography. Within these networks, migrants themselves become conduits of information, money, and values: go-betweens tying home villages and local communities to their city of residence and urban centers around the world. Inclusion in these networks may also facilitate an initial relocation and provide the resources (material and otherwise) needed for business formation, sustenance, and onward travel. Where integration or inclusion into a city of residence is either impossible or undesirable, inclusion into these decent red, largely unregulated, globalized networks may represent a far more significant form of membership. Even when not achieved, it may continue to serve as an aspirational ideal that shapes other more localized strategies and struggles.

TACTICAL COSMOPOLITANISM AS A NEW FORM OF BELONGING

The characteristics I have just described—the desire for usufruct rights, self-alienation, and global membership—are all visible in what I have elsewhere termed "tactical cosmopolitanism" (Landau and Freemantle 2010) based on our extensive work in Johannesburg and preliminary work elsewhere. As noncitizens encounter and attempt to overcome opposition to their presence, they draw on a variegated language of belonging that makes claims to the city while positioning them in an ephemeral, superior, and unrooted condition where they can escape localized social and political obligations. The paragraphs below explore the content of this fragmented and heterogeneous discourse, illustrating foreigners' agency in mitigating xenophobia's effects by at once inserting themselves into city life and distancing themselves from it. While these patterns are particularly pronounced in Johannesburg—a city that has undergone an extraordinary transformation from an isolated, strictly regulated authoritarian site to a truly global city—they are evident elsewhere in forms shaped by context, opportunity, and ambition.

Before describing tactical cosmopolitanism's empirical manifestations, it is worth noting that this is not a coherent or self-conscious collection philosophy or set of tactics. Unlike theoretical or high cosmopolitanism, these are not necessarily grounded in normative ideas of openness or intended to promote universal values of any form. Rather, migrants practically and rhetorically draw on various, often competing systems of cosmopolitan rights and rhetorics to insinuate themselves, however shallowly, in the networks and spaces needed to achieve specific practical goals. Unlike transnationalism, which is often about belonging to multiple communities—or shuttling between them—these are more "decent red" tactics that emphasize individualism, generality and universality, all "central pillars" of cosmopolitanism (Pogge 1992: 48; Roudometof 2005: 121). However, they do so variably, and often contradictorily, in relation to their very personal current needs, interests, and rights. Although it may exist, we do not claim this as evidence of a stable, inclusive "cosmopolitan consciousness." This leaves them, in Jonathan Friedman's words, "betwixt and between without being liminal . . . participating in many worlds without becoming part of them" (Friedman 1995: 78).

There are three particular illustrations of tactical cosmopolitanism I wish to discuss here. The first again draws attention to patterns of self-exclusion and transient superiority that distances this group from a South African national project and cultural assimilation. The second focuses on the particular rhetoric migrants use to claim membership in South Africa—a varied mix of pan-Africanism and other liberation philosophies. The third, and most critical to the tactical component of our argument, is in how they organize to avoid the ethics of obligation to other migrant groups and their home communities. It is this mix of atomization and fluid association that is unique to this form of life: it is not an alternative way of belonging, but a use of cosmopolitan rhetoric and organizational forms to live outside of belonging while claiming the benefits of it.

RHETORIC OF SELF -EXCLUSION

In response to the violence, abuse, and discrimination many foreigners experience in Johannesburg, they have developed a rhetoric of self-exclusion that fetishizes their position as the permanent outsider or wanderer in such a way that "distances him or her from all connections and commitments" (Said 2001: 183; see also Malauene 2003; Simone 2001). So rather than striving to integrate or assimilate, non-nationals' extended interaction with South Africans is leading to a reification of differences and a counter-idiom of transience and superiority. Whatever the source of exclusion, only 45 percent of foreigners we surveyed felt they were part of South African society: 38.6 percent among Congolese and 54.1 percent among the Somali population (compared to 95.7 percent of South Africans who felt they were "in"). Expanding on the epigraph above, one migrant from Lesotho who has lived in Johannesburg for four years reveals many dimensions of a discourse of non-belonging: "I don't think any right thinking person would want to be South African. It's a very unhealthy environment. South Africans are very aggressive, even the way they talk. Both black and white. I don't know what's the word, it's a degenerated façade they are putting up. . . . They are just so contaminated." Ironically, foreigners often brand South Africans with the same flaws levied against them: dishonesty, violence, and vectors of disease. Few trust South Africans, and only a minority speaks of close relationships with them. All this is further complemented (and justified) by a sense that South Africans are uneducated or do not appreciate the opportunities they have for education (or other social services); are promiscuous (female promiscuity is particularly jarring); overly tolerant (especially regarding the acceptance of homosexuality); and unreligious. Imagining themselves as superior and worldly, they look down on the communities around them. While many more foreigners would like their children to learn English or another South African language, they remain wary of ever considering themselves South African.

RHETORIC OF RIGHTS: INCLUSION WITHOUT MEMBERSHIP

Kihato's (2007) work on migrant associations in the inner city described Awelah, a group that rose phoenix-like from the ashes of an Ivorian association that had collapsed after an internal power struggle. Unlike most of the city's previous organizations that are based on ethnic or national foundations, Awelah offers up a new kind of Pan-Africanism. In the words of its founder, quoted at length in Kihato's paper:

> We want to shift our patriotism to the continent, not to a country. We Africans share a history together; we are bound together by a neo-colonialism. When you dig up these feelings all Africans have the same history. This is the link that we have got now, we are African even though we butcher each other but we are African. In our day-to-day living we are all confronted with problems of nationality, ethnicity and so on. But when you have this [broader African] perspective you do not see these problems anymore.

But there is more to this than a desire to build a community of all Africans as an end in itself. Rather, the evocations of Pan-Africanism—drawn from 1960s liberation philosophy, Mbeki's notion of African Renaissance, and the rhetoric of Africa's World Cup played in South Africa in 2010—are particularly designed to erode the barriers that separate foreigners from South Africans. By helping South Africans to realize connections to their continental kin, they undermine the legitimacy of any barriers to inclusion that South Africans may erect in front of them. Ironically, the foundation for such mobilization remains firmly rooted in a transnational articulation of Ivorian identity, as most of the new members come from there. Through this rhetoric and tactics—tactics we are only beginning to explore—migrants adopt a de facto cosmopolitanism that demonstrates a willingness to engage a plurality of cultures as well as an openness to hybridity and multiple identities (Hannerz 1990: 239).

This is not, however, openness without boundaries but rather one that draws on multiple identities simultaneously without ever accepting the overarching authority or power of one. Importantly, their rhetoric is distinctly non-transnational. Nowhere does this new language speak of maintaining ties to a specific location. Rather, it is a tactical effort to gain access to the city, but without a view of becoming exclusively or even partially bound to it or any other concrete locale.

Elsewhere, migrant groups have used South Africa's relatively liberally, if inconsistently, applied asylum laws and its constitution to provide rights of residence and work. However, very few refugees use this language of rights to justify their position in the country. Rather, they call on norms of reciprocity—claiming a right to the city (and the country) based on what their countries did to assist South Africa during the apartheid period. Nigerians, for example, will often claim (with some substantiation) that ANC activists were given full university scholarships in the 1970s and 1980s, opportunities that were not always available to citizens. Mozambicans, Zimbabweans, and even Namibians claim that they personally suffered from wars tied to South Africa's anti-communist campaign and efforts to destroy African National Congress strongholds within their countries. If they did not experience the war firsthand, then they were deprived by an economy that had been destroyed by years of fighting. Others plausibly argue that because South African business derives so much profit from investments in their countries—in both the past and present—that they have a reciprocal right to South Africa's territory and wealth. In this way, South Africa's own transnationalism—past and present—serves as justification for transcending national residential restrictions.

By drawing on religion, African tradition, and almost any other rhetoric that is available, the ever expanding pool of Nigerian-run Pentecostal churches operating within Johannesburg's inner city appear to be fashioning an organizational form that at once bridges barriers with South Africans (and South Africa) while preparing people for a life beyond South Africa. Indeed, in many cases, the churches prepare people for a life beyond any territorially bounded nation. Many of these offer up "health and wealth" promises seen elsewhere in evangelical communities, promises of an alternative to the material deprivation many migrants experience. Although there is not space here to reflect the diversity of testimonies and preaching included in even one five-hour "mass," almost all reflect the lived experiences of people in the city. In some instances, the preaching bares only the faint influence of biblical pronouncements, but is instead fabricated out of contemporary challenges and generalized evangelical Christian philosophy. As one Zimbabwean migrant states: "In the church, they help us in many ways, no matter where you come from, they just help you." The promises and guidance offered within such oration also bring in South Africans to the community, generating one of the rare common spaces between nationals and foreigners in the city.

With their strong links to communities in Nigeria, Ghana, and the United States, the churches also open further connections out of Johannesburg. For many of the churches' founders, South Africa is primarily a place where they can enter global discourse and influence the lives of people across the continent and beyond. In the words of the Nigerian pastor at the Mountain of Fire and Miracles Church, "Africa is shaped like a pistol and South Africa is the mouth from where you can shoot out the word of god." And, consequently, anyone doing the work of God has a divine right to South African territory. Others are exploiting the popularity and themes of Nigerian cinema by also producing DVDs that promote the triumph of good over evil.

Unlike the rhetoric of the street, church ideology is potentially generative of community with social pressures and disciplines that may transform tactics into a counter-hegemonic strategy. However, they presently remain far too fluid, and many of their pronouncements are too pragmatic and flexible to offer a coherent, stable, alternative organizational form. Instead, the churches are often functional units, helping people to find jobs, transcend boundaries, or find ways (physically or spiritually) out of Johannesburg's hardships. If successful, these resources often physically help people out of the city (or at least the inner city) and onto more prosperous grounds.

ORGANIZATION AND ATOMIZATION

Due to its philosophical heterodoxy, "tactical cosmopolitanism" is both enormously flexible and unable to discipline its practitioners. This is clearly illustrated in the dynamic organizational configurations evident among the city's migrants. Mang'ana (2004) and Misago (2005) both report, for example, that even people from the same country are careful to avoid the mutual obligations and politics that come from close association with other so-called exiles. Although there are instances in which migrant groups assert a collective (usually national) identity, these are often based on instrumental and short-lived associations. Amisi and Ballard's (2005) work on refugee associations throughout South Africa, for example, finds an almost universal tendency toward repeated reconfiguration and fragmentation. As Götz and Simone suggest, "These formations embody a broad range of tactical abilities aimed at maximizing economic opportunities through transversal engagements across territories and separate arrangements of powers" (2003: 125). They are not associations founded on preserving identity, but rather use combinations of national, ethnic, and political affiliations for tactical purposes.

In many instances, even people from the same country carefully avoid close association with other "exiles" or cling to multiple points of loyalty that allow them to shift within multiple networks. These act as resources providing the weak links needed to gather information while allowing them to shift affiliations and tactics at a moment's notice (Granovetter

1973). In doing so, they avoid capture by friends, relations, and the state while inadvertently reshaping the city's social and political dynamics. This limits these networks' ability to foster permanent inclusion, but also allows a flexibility of membership and opportunity, with people shifting alliances and allegiances to the degree that it is tenable given their documentation, language skills, and appearance. Somali traders may be a partial exception, but even among this more insular community, fragmentation, mistrust, and other divisions often trump solidary ties.

Rather than integrating or assimilating, the form and rhetoric of organization exploits a migrant's position as permanent outsider in a way that "distances him or her from all connections and commitments" (Said 2001:183). As Simmel notes, these strangers are not fully committed to the peculiar tendencies of the people among whom they live. They can, therefore, approach them with a kind of skepticism, "objectivity," and self-imposed distance. But they are also cosmopolitan for, as Hannerz (1990: 239) suggests they should, many demonstrate a great personal ability to "make their way into other cultures, through listening, looking, intuiting and reflecting," as well as through carefully developed skills for meandering or maneuvering through systems of meaning and obligation.

CONCLUSION: UNDERSTANDING NEW FORMS OF BELONGING IN AFRICAN CITIES

The forms of belonging we see in many African cities are, as Beck (2004: 134) suggests, often "side effects" of efforts to achieve other economic, social, and even political goals. As such, they are not unified, counter-hegemonic or strategic movements seeking to create an alternative, articulated order. Rather, they are a motley collection of actions undertaken by groups that are often fragmented by language, religion, legal status, and mutual enmity. And rarely do they control significant economic resources or organizational capital. They are, however, able to swiftly combine disparate segments of the population according to current necessity and to do so in ways not premised on their moral worth necessarily being realized through national membership (Bowden 2003: 239).

Despite their short-lived, contradictory, and often ineffective practices, these expressions of belonging are nevertheless a powerful force. Even when failing to deliver the intended goals, cosmopolitan tactics occasionally elicit strong reactions from more strategic actors: the police, the business community, or frustrated South African citizens. It is in these counterreactions to migrants' tactical activity that their greatest power lies. So while Lee (2006) argues that "tactical citizenship"—a concept sharing a similar legacy to our notion of "tactical cosmopolitanism"—is simply a reactive and not transformative response, we argue that these reactions,

counter-idioms, and forms of self-exclusion may be fundamentally transformative although not necessarily in intended ways.

Although it is possible that their current fluidity will preserve extraordinary levels of combinatorial freedom, it is likely that the repeated
iterations of hybrid and novel mobilization strategies and rhetoric will
generate new categories of belonging that may eventually crystallize in
ways that exert disciplinary powers of inclusion and exclusion. It is too
early to tell what the nature of these will be, but it is unlikely that they
will conform to existing modes of belonging, even though they are likely
to resonate with aspects of them. Like the marginalized populations that
developed Christianity, Islam, and other transcendent, deterritorialized
memberships, migrants in African cities may pioneer forms of membership that reshape how we understand our relationship to each other, to
space, and to institutions. This may take on the form of "common norms
and mutual translatability" (Robbins 1998: 12) that help overcome the legacy of apartheid and national formation. However, it is unlikely that the
outcome will conform so closely to philosophers' vision or the language of
belonging that scholars of ethnicity and community now employ.

Finally, the discussion of inclusion for those who may be seeking usufruct rights or opportunities for transit raises broader questions about the
issues of rights and duties associated with belonging. Much of the literature on cosmopolitanism—a form of inclusion that recognizes if not
celebrates diversity—demands mutual recognition and a set of at least
minimal reciprocal obligations among all residents. While many authors
focus on state obligations to build inclusive societies and others speak
about countering xenophobia or other forms of discrimination, these im-
peratives typically stem from a model of political community comprising
those who wish to be part of it and where parties at least minimally recognize each other's legitimacy and right to space. In environments where
significant elements of an urban population—citizens and aliens—exist
outside states' cognition or in direct opposition to its stated policies and
to each other, the terms of engagement are significantly altered. Without
the presence of an alternative moral authority, there will be increasingly
heterogeneous normative frameworks operating within Africa's urban
spheres. In such contexts, there is nevertheless a need to think through
alternative ethics of duty and responsibility that correspond to the lives
and aspirations of those most directly affected but do not involve the un-
palatable (and untenable) task of imposing a single set of ideals, values,
and behavioral codes. We must then ask—not only as observers, but also
as members of communities—what our duties are to recognize, support,
or (potentially) regulate and condemn the strangers who are negotiating
inclusion among us. And for those of us who move, these are questions

about our obligations to the multiple communities to which we may claim various forms of membership.

REFERENCES

Amisi, B., and R. Ballard. 2005. "In the Absence of Citizenship: Congolese Refugee Struggle and Organization in South Africa." Forced Migration Working Paper #16 (April). Accessed April 2005 at http://migration.wits. ac.za/AmisiBallardwp.pdf.

Andersson, J. A. 2006. "Informal Moves, Informal Markets: International Migrants and Traders from Mzimba District, Malawi." *African Affairs* 105(420): 375–97.

Ballard, R. 2005. "Bunkers for the Psyche: How Gated Communities Have Allowed the Privatization of Apartheid in Democratic South Africa." Dark Roast Occasional Paper #24. Cape Town: Isandla Institute.

Bauman, Z. 2000. *Globalization: Its Human Consequences.* New York: Columbia University Press.

———. 2002. *Society under Siege.* New York: Polity Press.

Bayart, J. 1993. *The State in Africa: The Politics of the Belly.* London: Longman.

Beck, U. 2004. "Cosmopolitan Realism." *Global Networks* 4(2): 131–56.

Bendix, R. 1977. *Nation Building and Citizenship.* Berkeley: University of California Press.

Bowden, B. 2003. "Nationalism and Cosmopolitanism: Irreconcilable Differences or Possible Bedfellows?" *National Identities* 5(3): 235–49.

Bratton, M. 2006. "Popular Reactions to State Repression: Operation Murambatsvina in Zimbabwe." *African Affairs* 106(422): 21–45.

Caldeira, T. 1996. "Fortified Enclaves: The New Urban Segregation." *Public Culture* 8: 303–28.

Chabal, P., and J. Daloz. 1999. *Africa Works: Disorder as Political Instrument.* Oxford: International African Institute in association with James Currey.

Comaroff, J., and John L. Comaroff. 2001. "Naturing the Nation: Aliens, Apocalypse and the Postcolonial State." *Journal of Southern African Studies* 27: 627–51.

Dean, M. 1996. "Foucault, Government, and the Enfolding of Authority." In *Foucault and Political Reason: Liberalism, Neo-Liberalism, and Rationalities of Government,* ed. A. Barry, T. Osborne, and N. Rose. Chicago: University of Chicago Press.

Diouf. M. 2000. "The Senegalese Murid Trade Diaspora and the Making of a Vernacular Cosmopolitanism." *Public Culture* 12(3): 679–702.

Dirsuweit, T. 2002. "Johannesburg: Fearful City?" *Urban Forum* 13(3): 3–19.

Evans, P. 2002a. "Introduction: Looking for Agents of Urban Change in a Globalised Political Economy." In *Liveable Cities? Urban Struggles for Livelihood and Sustainability,* ed. P. Evans. Berkeley: University of California Press.

———. 2002b. "Political Strategies for More Liveable Cities: Lessons from Six Cases of Development and Political Transition." In *Liveable Cities? Urban Struggles for Livelihood and Sustainability*, ed. P. Evans. Berkeley: University of California Press.

Friedman, J. 1995. "Global System, Globalization, and the Parameters of Modernity." In *Global Modernities*, ed. M. Featherstone, S. Lash, and R. Robertson. London: Sage.

Geschiere, P. 2005. "Funerals and Belonging: Different Patterns in South Cameroon." *African Studies Review* 48(2): 45–64.

Götz, G., and A. Simone. 2003. "On Belonging and Becoming in African Cities." In *Emerging Johannesburg: Perspectives on the Postapartheid City*, ed. R. Tomlinson et al. London: Routledge.

Granovetter, M. 1973. "The Strength of Weak Ties." *American Journal of Sociology* 78(6): 1360–80.

Habermas, J. 1998. *The Inclusion of the Other*. Trans. C. Cronin and P. De Greiff. Cambridge, Mass.: MIT Press.

Hall. S. 1999. "A Conversation with Stuart Hall." *Journal of the International Institute* 7(1).

Hannerz, U. 1990. "Cosmopolitans and Locals in World Culture." In *Global Culture: Nationalism, Globalization and Modernity*, ed. M. Featherstone. London: Sage.

Herbst, J. 2000. *States and Power in Africa*. Princeton, N.J.: Princeton University Press.

Horner, B. 2007. "Somalis in SA: Out of the Frying Pan, Into the Fire." *Sunday Times*, February 25, 1.

Horst, C. 2004. "Money and Mobility: Transnational Livelihood Strategies of the Somali Diaspora." Global Migration Perspectives #9. Geneva: Global Commission for International Migration.

Hyden, G. 1980. *Beyond Ujamaa in Tanzania: Underdevelopment and an Uncaptured Peasantry*. London: Heinemann Educational Books.

Jackson, S. 2006. "Sons of Which Soil? The Language and Politics of Autochtony in Eastern Democratic Republic of Congo." *African Studies Review* 49(2): 95–123.

Kabeer, N. 2005. "The Search for Inclusive Citizenship: Meanings and Expressions in an Interconnected World." In *Inclusive Citizenship: Meanings and Expression*, ed. N. Kabeer. London: Zed Books.

Kihato, C. 2007. "Reconfiguring Citizenship in African Cities." Paper presented to the Inclusive Cities Workshop, Wits University (March 12).

Landau, L. 2006. "Transplants and Transients: Idioms of Belonging and Dislocation in Inner-City Johannesburg." *African Studies Review* 49(2): 125–45.

Landau, L., and I. Freemantle. 2010. "Tactical Cosmopolitanism and Idioms of Belonging: Insertion and Self-Exclusion in Johannesburg." *Journal of Ethnic and Migration Studies* 36(3): 375–90.

Landau, L., and H. Haithar. 2007. "Somalis Are Easy Prey." *Mail and Guardian*, March 2, 15.

Larkin, B. 2004. "Bandiri Music, Globalization, and Urban Experience in Nigeria." *Social Text* 22(4): 91–112.

Lee, C. T. 2006. "Tactical Citizenship: Domestic Workers, the Remainders of Home, and Undocumented Citizen Participation in the Third Space of Mimicry." *Theory and Event* 9(3).

Madsen, M. L. 2004. "Living for Home: Policing Immorality among Undocumented Migrants in Johannesburg." *African Studies* 63(2): 173–92.

Malauene, D. 2004. "The Impact of the Congolese Forced Migrants' 'Permanent Transit' Condition on Their Relations with Mozambique and Its People." M.A. thesis, University of the Witwatersrand.

Mang'ana, J. 2004. "The Effects of Migration on Human Rights Consciousness among Congolese Refugees in Johannesburg." M.A. thesis, University of the Witwatersrand.

Marshall, T. H. 1950. *Citizenship and Social Class and Other Essays.* Cambridge: Cambridge University Press.

Mbembe, A. 2001. *On the Post Colony.* Berkeley: University of California Press.

———. 2004. "Aesthetics of Superfluity." *Public Culture* 16(3): 373–405.

Mbembe, A., and S. Nuttall. 2004. "Writing the World from an African Metropolis." *Public Culture* 16(3): 347–72.

Mehta, U. 1999. *Liberalism and Empire: A Study in Nineteenth-Century British Liberal Thought.* Chicago: University of Chicago Press.

Misago, J. P. 2005. "The Impact of Refugee-Host Community Interactions on Refugees' National and Ethnic Identities: Burundian Hutus in Johannesburg." M.A. thesis, University of Johannesburg.

Nzayabino, V. 2006. "The Dynamics of Humanitarian Assistance: Assessing Faith-Based Organisation's Responses to Forced Migrants in South Africa." M.A. thesis, University of the Witwatersrand.

O'Donnell, G. A. 2004. "Why the Rule of Law Matters." *Journal of Democracy* 15(4): 32–46.

Ong, A. 1999. *Flexible Citizenship: The Cultural Logics of Transnationality.* Durham, N.C.: Duke University Press.

Pogge, T.W. 1992. "Cosmopolitanism and Sovereignty." *Ethics* 103(1): 48–75.

Polanyi, K. 1957. *The Great Transformation.* Boston: Beacon Press.

Pollock, S. 2000. "Cosmopolitan and Vernacular in History." *Public Culture* 12(3): 591–625.

Pollock, S., H. Bhabha, C. Breckenridge, and D. Chakrabarty. 2000. "Cosmopolitanisms." *Public Culture* 12(3): 577–89.

Portes, A. 1997. "Globalization from Below: The Rise of Transnational Communities." UK Economic and Social Research Council Transnational Communities Programme Working Paper Series, WPTC-98-01. http://www.transcomm.ox.ac.uk.

Putnam, R. 2007. "E Pluribus Unum: Diversity and Community in the Twenty-First Century. The 2006 Johan Skytte Prize Lecture." *Scandinavian Political Studies* 30: 137–74.

Robbins, B. 1998. "Introduction Part I: Actually Existing Cosmopolitanism." *In Cosmopolitics: Thinking and Feeling Beyond the Nation*, ed. P. Cheah and B. Robbins. Minneapolis: University of Minnesota Press.

Roudometof, V. 2005. "Transnationalism, Cosmopolitanism and Glocalization." *Current Sociology* 53(1): 113–35.

Said, E. 2001. *Reflections on Exile and Other Essays*. Cambridge, Mass.: Harvard University Press.

Sassen, S. 2002. *Global Networks, Linked Cities*. London: Routledge.

Sandercock, L. 1998. *Towards Cosmopolis: Planning for Multicultural Cities*. Chichester: John Wiley and Sons.

———. 2005. "Designing with Diversity: The Satanic Verses as Design Manifesto in an Age of Migration." Keynote Address, EDRA, Vancouver, April 27.

Scott, J. 1998. *Seeing Like a State*. New Haven, Conn.: Yale University Press.

Simmel, G. 1964. *The Sociology of George Simmel*. Trans. Kurt Wolff. New York: Free Press.

Simone, A. 2001. "On the Worlding of African Cities." *African Studies Review* 44(2): 15–41.

———. 2004. *For the City Yet to Come: Changing African Life in Four Cities*. Durham, N.C.: Duke University Press.

Sommers, M. 2001. *Fear in Bongoland: Burundi Refugees in Urban Tanzania*. New York: Berghahn Books.

Taylor, C. 1992. *Multiculturalism and the Politics of Recognition*. Princeton, N.J.: Princeton University Press.

Tomlinson, R., et al. 2003. "The Postapartheid Struggle for an Integrated Johannesburg." In *Emerging Johannesburg: Perspectives on the Postapartheid City*, ed. R. Tomlinson, R. A. Beauregard, L. Bremner, and X. Mangcu. New York: Routledge.

UNHS. 2003. *The Challenge of Slums: Global Report on Human Settlements*. London: Earthscan.

Wa Kabwe Segatti, A., and L. Landau. 2007. "Displacement and Difference in Lubumbashi." *Forced Migration Review* 27: 71–72.

Winkler, T. 2006. "Kwere Kwere Journeys into Strangeness: Reimagining Inner-City Regeneration in Hillbrow, Johannesburg." Ph.D. diss., University of British Columbia, Vancouver.

Zlotnick, H. 2006. "The Dimensions of Migration in Africa." In *Africa on the Move*, ed. M. Tienda, S. Finley, and S. Tollman. Johannesburg: Wits University Press.

SECURING WEALTH, ORDERING SOCIAL RELATIONS

KINSHIP, MORALITY, AND THE CONFIGURATION OF SUBJECTIVITY AND BELONGING ACROSS THE RURAL-URBAN DIVIDE

HANSJÖRG DILGER

When Francis Lukio died in Dar es Salaam in 1999, he had been the main pillar of support for his rural and urban extended family.[1] When the harvest in his home village failed—or when school fees or hospital bills had to be paid—his relatives relied on Francis's financial support. Other family members—especially the young men from his patrilineage, but also a couple of his wife's relatives—were brought to Dar es Salaam with Francis's help, where he found them a job or paid for their education and training. When Francis passed away at the age of forty, he lived with his wife and their two children in the spacious house he rented in one of Dar es Salaam's more affluent outer-city areas. His house had also become the home of two of his younger (biological) brothers, one of his nephews, his wife's sister, and finally a son of his father's younger brother. All these relatives depended on Francis to varying degrees and were deeply troubled by the long illness he suffered from and which finally led to his premature death.

In this chapter, I explore how relations of kinship solidarity and wealth distribution, established in the context of rural-urban migration in Tanzania, have been affected by the multiple social and economic reconfigurations in the country and the HIV/AIDS epidemic from the mid-1980s onward. I argue that kinship-based arrangements of reciprocity and wealth distribution—which rely to a large extent on the resources of one or more relatives who have established themselves successfully in Tanzania's urban centers—are influenced adversely by neoliberal reform processes as well as the high rates of illness and death among the middle generation caused by HIV/AIDS.[2] Taken together, these phenomena present an enormous challenge for individuals, families, and communities with regard to securing wealth and managing social and moral cohesion across often-large geographical distances.

I argue that the deaths of urban breadwinners have severe implications for the surviving families' ability to sustain themselves socially and economically in the context of rural-urban mobility. At the same time, they draw attention to the way in which subjects and subjectivities are being made and remade in the context of migratory processes and the ongoing dynamics of social differentiation in eastern Africa. Thus, while rural-urban mobility has shaped people's perceptions, hopes, and desires concerning a "good" and "adequate" life in Tanzania for a long time, the growing presence of suffering and death sheds new light on "the concrete constellations in which people forge and foreclose their lives around what is most at stake" (Biehl et al. 2007: 5).

In the following pages, I first provide an overview of the rural Mara region on Lake Victoria, where I have carried out fieldwork since the mid-1990s, and then argue that migration and mobility have become central characteristics of the region from the mid-nineteenth century onwards. While social and family conflicts have probably always been an intrinsic feature of migratory processes in the region, migration-based networks of solidarity have been affected by the introduction of structural reforms and the onset of the HIV/AIDS epidemic in the mid-1980s. Both events have added increased strains on the life situations of rural and urban populations who had to struggle not only with cuts in salaries and employment opportunities in the public sector, but also an increasingly stratified healthcare and education system that relied more and more on the financial contributions of individual citizens. Finally, people were confronted with the unexpected burden resulting from the growing number of deaths of partners, friends, and relatives caused by HIV/AIDS.[3]

Drawing on the case study of Francis Lukio and his family, I argue that the social and moral challenges and conflicts that have evolved around HIV/AIDS-related illnesses and deaths of migrating family members are reflective of wider struggles concerning the distribution of wealth and property as well as questions concerning subject formation, identity, and belonging. The efforts and struggles that people in western Mara undertake in securing and (re)establishing social cohesion over large spatial distances are revealing of the way in which individual and collective desires, hopes, and moral priorities are negotiated in the face of growing social and economic pressures as well as experiences of death and dying.[4] That these processes and struggles are often inherently gendered becomes obvious not only with regard to the multiple endeavors and strategies of families to find a cure for their relative's illness and/or to provide a proper burial for the deceased. Kinship-based systems of solidarity and support are also challenged by the situation of widows who may present a threat to their in-law's strategies of wealth containment and their endeavors to manage the future well-being of their own and the deceased's family.

A HISTORY OF SOLIDARITY AND TENSION: RURAL-URBAN MIGRATION IN NORTHWEST TANZANIA

The western part of the Mara region in northwestern Tanzania is located close to the shores of Lake Victoria, bordering on Kenya in the North. The area is populated mostly by the Luo, a minor ethnic group who migrated from what is today western Kenya to the Mara region in the mid-nineteenth century.[5] Today, people in western Mara live mostly from a combination of income-generating activities, ranging from farming and fishing to small-scale businesses and trading activities and, in many cases, the employment of one or more family members in Tanzania's public or private sector. In recent years the establishment of a fishing business, which is part of a large fishing industry connecting the eastern shores of Lake Victoria to fishing cooperatives in Kenya and the international market, has resulted in a modest economic boom in the area. Before the arrival of the fishing industry, however, the region was characterized by growing poverty, periodic droughts and crop failures, and especially the outward migration of the younger generation to urban centers like Arusha, Mwanza, or Dar es Salaam.

Mobility and migration have been central characteristics of the western Mara region for a long time. Though Tanganyika had become a German colony as early as 1890, the area caught the colonizers' attention only in the late 1890s when—after a short yet brutal military intervention—a military post was established on the shores of Lake Victoria in 1898 (Reh 1993/1994). Beginning in the late nineteenth to early twentieth century, the children of local leaders and more wealthy families were (forcefully) recruited for schooling in Musoma and Mwanza, where the German rulers had established schools in their efforts to establish a three-tier education system in the country. In addition, some men from the Mara region were forced to participate in the construction works along the Tanzanian railway, leading to an early system of out-migration that merged into the dynamics of voluntary labor migration following World War I when colonial power was handed over to the British.

By World War II, the migration of predominantly male family members in search of seasonal work to the settler plantations in neighboring Kenya was interrupted when local men were recruited for military service in the south Asian colonies. Labor migration flourished again from the 1950s onward when people from Mara started to look for work as cooks or construction workers in the colonial centers. During this period, migration processes became more extended and increasingly involved the migration of women who started to accompany their husbands and male counterparts to the centers of migration in Tanganyika and neighboring Kenya.

The establishment of a socialist system at the end of the 1960s placed severe restrictions on the migratory system in Tanzania as people were huddled together in the artificially created *Ujamaa* villages, which were expected to become the basis of an economically self-sustaining nation. However, despite the multiple efforts of the government to curtail the movement of populations from rural to urban areas, the urban centers remained attractive to potential migrants, many of whom were willing to pay bribery fees in return for a job in town. How attractive the life in urban Tanzania became in the decades after dependence is exemplified by the rapid growth of Dar es Salaam, which served as the country's capital city from independence until 1973. Between 1967 and 1978, the population of Dar es Salaam grew from 272,821 to 769,445 and increased to 1,623,238 by 1988 (Obrist 2006: 77). In 1967, only around 32.5 percent of the city's total population originated from Dar es Salaam (Vorlaufer 1973: 81), with the rest of the population originating from regions all over the country. The attractiveness of Dar es Salaam for people in western Mara in the 1960s is reflected in a short story by Agoro Anduru, who grew up in a village in the region and who remembered in 1989 how "life in the town" had become for him—as well as for many other young and educated people from the rural area—the projection of all their desires and hopes toward a "civilized" and "modern" life:

> I remember in those days politicians praised farming saying it was the only hope for the young nation and urged jobless young men and women in the towns to go back to the land. But the picture which we, who had tasted the fruit of education, had of a farmer was not all that glossy. The farmers I was seeing in my village were a poor lot, badly dressed and rather primitive. In our heart of hearts we knew that a better standard of living lay in the salaried jobs and living in the town. The town held irresistible attractions for the youth. It was in the town that you had a taste of what we were told life was like in Europe, which according to what we had been taught all along was the very center of the universe. It was in the town that you could see such things as the cinema and be within reach of those amenities, which were like miracles to the rural breed like us. (Anduru 1989: 58)

While rural-urban migrants started to settle more permanently in Tanzania's urban centers from the late 1960s onward, close relations were maintained with rural families and communities from the beginning. Even today, rural-urban ties are an integral part of rural and urban families' strategies to secure economic survival as well as the social and moral well-being of relatives across large geographical distances. In particular, rural and urban families expect family members who work or trade in the city to support their parents, uncles, and siblings in times of need and crisis and to reinvest some of their acquired wealth in the education and economic advancement of their younger relatives (Flanagan 1982; Tripp 1997: 30–59; Trager 1998). This may involve rural families sending their children to their more wealthy relatives in urban areas who take care of their children for an extended period of time and provide for their schooling. Conversely, urban children may be sent to stay with their rural families if urban living costs become unaffordable.

On another level, rural-urban ties involve decisions and actions that are made by urban dwellers with regard to central areas of life planning, such as marriage and residential location. For example, most male Luo migrants I encountered during fieldwork in Dar es Salaam considered it a natural part of their life cycles to build a house in their home village and to return to the rural areas at a later stage of their lives. Many young Luo men in the cities also preferred to marry a wife from their home region, as Luo women are generally held to be "more reliable" and (even more important in the era of AIDS) to possess "moral integrity." Finally, relationships across the rural-urban divide were characterized by the uncountable travels and visits of rural and urban family members in villages and towns to their rural relatives for Christmas or to attend the burial of a deceased relative or, in the opposite direction, to stay with their urban families for an extended period of time to pursue a trading activity or to look for treatment and healing in the flourishing medical sector of urban settings.

While relationships between rural and urban families in Dar es Salaam and Mara are maintained and reproduced on multiple levels, it should not be concluded that life in the "dual system" (Gugler 1971) is characterized exclusively by its functionality and/or the fulfillment of economic, social, and moral needs. Peter Geschiere and Josef Gugler (1998: 311) have critically remarked that studies on migration and mobility in sub-Saharan Africa have often analyzed rural-urban relationships with regard to their security aspect. From this perspective, rural families were described primarily as a stabilizing force in the uncertain course of migration, whereas urban families were said to provide the necessary means for their rural relatives' economic survival and for establishing access to education and the outside world in general. In this view, the fulfillment of mutual social, economic, and moral obligations was said to culminate in the home burials of migrating family members, which represented the ultimate reaffirmation of the deceased's spiritual and ancestral belonging to his or her respective patri- or matrilineage.

That rural-urban relations have never unproblematically fulfilled the mutual needs and obligations of rural and urban families is exemplified by the moral discourse that has evolved around migratory processes in the western Mara region in which the benefits of migration are matched by the dangers it represents to the cohesion of social and familial units. Rural families are particularly critical of relatives who have acquired some wealth in the towns and forget their rural families, refusing to give the latter their share of what they have earned. The migrants, on the other hand, complain that their rural relatives' expectations are excessively high and that the demands they are confronted with from their parents, brothers, or uncles are often disproportionate. In general, deviant, that is, selfish behavior is met by moral condemnation—sometimes also by accusations of witchcraft directed predominantly at the migrants themselves, but sometimes also at rural family members suspected of being after their more successful migrant relatives' money (Dilger 2008; Geschiere 1997). The case study of Francis Lukio exemplifies that accusations of witchcraft have come to play an important role in the context of HIV/AIDS, too—and have become entangled further with gender- and age-specific conflicts resulting from migratory processes in northwest Tanzania.

ALL THINGS WILL BE PLANNED BY THE FAMILY: BURYING THE DEAD AND CARING FOR THE LIVING

A couple of weeks after Francis Lukio's burial, his nephew Albert recounted the manifold and painful efforts his family undertook in finding a treatment for his uncle. After several unsuccessful attempts to treat Francis's slowly progressing illness at a number of hospitals and private clinics in Dar es Salaam, Francis's wife and one of his brothers started to seek the advice of traditional healers. Costly treatments and rituals were initiated after one of the healers claimed that a mischievous colleague had "thrown a spirit" (amemtupia majini) at the ailing Francis, who had worked in a well-paid position at Tanzania's national income tax department. However, when Francis's state continued to deteriorate, opinion in his family turned increasingly against his wife, Rachel, who was accused of wanting to push her in-laws out of their common home in Dar es Salaam. Rachel was also suspected of having an ongoing love relationship with a man from the neighborhood who, according to Francis's brothers, had even received some of their brother's hard-earned money through their sister-in-law. When Francis's family claimed that Rachel "was killing her husband with her lover's shadow" (amempiga na tipo), she was forbidden to continue nursing her sick husband—and even prevented from approaching her husband's bed during the final weeks before his death.

Accusations against Rachel kept flourishing over the next couple of weeks and were not even laid to rest by the arrival of Rachel's mother, who had traveled to Dar es Salaam in order to support her daughter in the conflict with her in-laws. When Rachel and her mother brought medicine for Francis from a healer in Tanga, rumors spread in Francis's family that they wanted to bewitch their ailing relative. These allegations continued after Francis's death and during the burial preparations in Francis's home village on Lake Victoria. At his burial, Rachel and her mother were accused publicly by their in-laws of having killed him, and Rachel's mother was physically attacked by some of her late son-in-law's relatives. It was only a couple of days after the actual burial that the atmosphere began to calm down and that the initial threats of Rachel's in-laws "to chase away" their late relative's wife gave way to efforts to reestablish a more constructive relationship with her.

In a conversation with Francis's father and two of Francis's brothers, I learned that these efforts were driven not only by concerns they had about their relative's children, but, equally important, about the deceased's inheritance. According to national jurisdiction in Tanzania, it is primarily the widows and their children who are entitled to their husband's and father's property. Thus, if Francis's family wanted to secure their own share of the inheritance (which they were entitled to according to customary law), they had to remain on good terms with their relative's widow. From the family's perspective, there was good reason for making such an effort. While the younger family members depended on their uncle's inheritance in order to be able to continue with their education, Francis's older brothers were hoping to reside in the house which their late relative had started to build a couple of years before his death. Francis's father, in turn, had always depended strongly on his son's financial support, as village life provided few opportunities to procure sufficient money to buy clothes or pay hospital and school fees for the children and other members of the family. All these expectations, hopes, and needs could only be fulfilled if Francis's family was able to secure at least partial access to their deceased relative's property, which consisted not only of the plot and the nearly completed house in Dar es Salaam, but also of several bank accounts and some compensation payments from Francis's employer, which were all to be paid under the name of Rachel Francis. My conversation with Francis's male relatives at the burial made clear that the family made strong claims concerning the future management of the deceased's property as well as about the future life course of Rachel and her children—and that the family would therefore not consent to the potential remarriage of their daughter- and sister-in-law:

Osanya:[6] *Could the widow get remarried?*

Michael Lukio: *I wouldn't feel good, as she would take our brother's property with her. The family will plan all these things; however it is still early to think about this: burial guests are still coming in.[7] We still don't know what is going to happen.*

Osanya: *You, the brothers of the deceased, what are your thoughts about the future life of the deceased's wife and children, as well as about his property?*

Dishon Lukio: *As our brother hasn't built a house in the village yet, we will build a house for our sister-in-law in which she can live with her family.*

Hansjörg: *And the house in Dar es Salaam?*

Michael Lukio: *The house in Dar isn't finished yet. We still have to make plans to complete the building.*

Hansjörg: *Who is going to live there?*

Michael Lukio: *Our elder brother lives there.*

Dishon Lukio: *Once it is finished, even the deceased's wife can live there. Here in the village she might face problems trying to secure her income. In town, she can establish a small trade and take care of herself and her family.*

Osanya: *Where will she get the seed capital she will need to establish a trade?*

Dishon Lukio: *Once her house [in Mara] is finished, we will sit down together and discuss possibilities to find the necessary capital (mtaji) for the trade. The widow shouldn't feel like now that her husband has died that she is all alone. She should be able to lead a good life, and we have to make plans so that she won't lead a life full of grief.*

Mzee Lukio: *My son Francis told me that he had planned to build a house [here in the village]. If he had recovered, he would have built a house and returned to live here. He would build small houses for his mothers,[8] and he would also finish his house in Dar es Salaam.*

In a conversation the same afternoon, Rachel confirmed the allegedly harmonious relationship that had evolved, according to the Lukio family, between her and her in-laws in the wake of her late husband's burial. However, a few hours later when Osanya and I accidentally met her at the market in the village, she complained strongly about the lack of support that she claimed to be receiving from her brothers-in-law and her father-in-law. In particular, she said, she was in need of support for her youngest child, who had fallen seriously ill and for whom she still had to pay the outstanding bills in the nearby health clinic. She contended that she did not receive "a single cent of help" from her late husband's relatives—despite the fact that she had given all the illness and burial payments from her husband's employer to her father-in-law.

In this situation, Rachel displayed a thorough understanding of her own and her children's economic and social situation as well as about her various options and rights to improve this situation and to claim her husband's inheritance with the help of the national law. However, while the conflicts preceding and following her husband's death might have been sufficient reason for her to enter into direct confrontation with her in-laws, Rachel was anxious to maintain an amicable relationship with her late husband's family. Thus Rachel—who only completed a primary school education and had only limited possibilities for earning income by her own means—made no substantial efforts to secure her late husband's inheritance for her and her children. On the contrary, she authorized her brother-in-law, Dishon Lukio, to enter into negotiation with Francis's employer about outstanding payments and benefits from her late husband's salary and his insurance. When Rachel herself started to fall sick a couple of weeks later, she moved back to her parents' compound and was taken care of by her mother. From there, she gave further instructions for the building of the house on her father-in-law's compound, where she planned to live together with her children in the near future.

KINSHIP, BELONGING, AND GENDER IN THE CONTEXT OF RURAL-URBAN MIGRATION AND HIV/AIDS

The case of Francis Lukio and his family is illustrative of the way in which persons and relationships and identities in Tanzania are crafted in the context of rural-urban migration and HIV/AIDS, and how social cohesion and belonging are being established in the face of the ruptures and tensions that are caused by neoliberal reform processes as well as by high rates of illness and death among the socially and economically productive middle generation due to the epidemic. Structural adjustment programs in Tanzania—which were implemented under President Ali Hassan Mwinyi in the mid- to late-1980s and continued under the rule of Benjamin Mkapa between 1995 and 2005—have led to rising living costs and growing social and economic inequalities, especially in rural areas (Lugalla 1995). Furthermore, drastic cuts in the public employment sector have put growing pressure on men and women of all ages to reorganize their lives socially and economically and have pushed women and men increasingly into the expanding informal economy where they have become engaged in establishing small-scale businesses and trading activities (Tripp 1997).

In light of HIV/AIDS, the growing involvement of women and men in business and trading activities has led, according to my informants in rural Mara, to a growing emphasis on economic transactions in sexual relationships and to an increased blurring of gender and generational hierarchies. A morally conservative discourse has evolved that encourages submissiveness and decency, particularly in the sexuality of women, and emphasizes the importance of trust and moral integrity for the selection of sexual partners. From the perspective of many of my informants in the Mara region—old as well as young, strongly religious or not—young women's "greed" has become a metaphor for the moral dangers of a monetized and individualistic modern society in which the dissolution of former so cial hierarchies based on gender and age has allegedly led to decreased control over family members and, at the same time, to increased sexual promiscuity and the spread of HIV/AIDS (Dilger 1999, 2003; Weiss 1993; Haram 1995; Setel 1999).

The moralistic and stigmatizing discourse on HIV/AIDS, gender relations, and the dangers of social and sexual mobility is not restricted to the discursive level but has very concrete effects on the ways in which families deal with HIV-infected and AIDS-sick relatives, as well as with the dependents of those who have died from HIV/AIDS. This becomes particularly obvious with regard to the discourses and practices that have evolved around the illness, care, and burial of family members infected with and dying from HIV/AIDS, and that reflect constructions of gender, relatedness, and the social person in the rural areas. In western Mara, family discussions about the social and moral causes of a relative's affliction comprise a wide range of non-medical discourses that are all assumed to lead to a form of physical ailment whose symptoms are very similar to HIV/AIDS. Central issues in such discourses on witchcraft and the violation of moral and ritual prescriptions are the jealousies evoked by the wealth and social advancement of the affected person as well as the moral failures of women and men who are said to behave immorally in relation to their sexuality and/or with regard to the members of their own or their husband's extended families. In addition to witchcraft, HIV/AIDS is often associated with a polluting disease called chira that is said to result from the violation of social and ritual prescriptions relating to central areas of the social and reproductive order (especially agricultural work, house-building, and the more critical periods of life, such as the death of a relative). Most of these prescriptions concern the regulation of proper sexual behavior and closely follow the principle of seniority, which in a general way rules the relationships within Luo lineages.[9] The observation of such rules of order is of fundamental significance since non-observance may lead to *chira*, which is fatal if not treated with traditional medicine (Dilger 2006, 2008).

On another level, the illness and death of a person in western Mara triggers questions about the way care is provided, where a person will be buried, and how the future life course of the deceased's dependents will be organized. In the era of HIV/AIDS, such questions are complicated by the fact that many men and women die at an age where their social status has not yet been fully confirmed, and where relationships between the sick and dying and their families have often been strained by conflicts caused by migration and processes of socioeconomic mobility. As has become evident in the case of the Lukio family, questions concerning care and belonging are often more easily solved with regard to young and middle-aged men who are mostly taken care of by their patrilineal kinship networks, especially by their mothers and their (biological as well as nominal) brothers. In the case of Francis Lukio, a major challenge for the family was therefore not so much which of his relatives would be doing the actual nursing and caring, but rather how the young man could be integrated properly into his patrilineal kinship network after his death. As the statements of Francis's father and brothers at his burial make clear, a major goal of the migratory process for a man is to build a house on his father's compound and to return ultimately to settle down in his home village—two central aspects of a social process that is considered inevitable and that is nowadays interrupted by the untimely deaths of numerous young men and relatives.

The situation of young to middle-aged women who have not been married or have been married for only a short period of time upon their own or their husband's death is often more difficult. This is due to the fact that women and girls are generally perceived to belong to their father's patrilineage until the time of their marriage, when they and their (future) children are expected to become part of their husband's patrilineal family. If a woman has been married only for a short time—and if the transition to her husband's family has not been completed by the full transmission of her bride price—her social status is particularly vulnerable, especially in the times of disease and crisis. Thus, while even older women tend to return to their families of origin in the case of severe need or illness, the uncertain status of young women in their husband's or partner's family is reflected by the multiple discussions that surround the burials of young women in the time of AIDS and that often raise severe conflicts about the place as well as the costs of their burial (Dilger 2005, 2008; Whyte 2005). The situation of young widows is particularly telling in this regard, as questions concerning their social and moral belonging become enmeshed further with discussions surrounding the performance of mourning rituals and the widow's socioeconomic status.[10]

NEGOTIATING WIDOWHOOD IN KINSHIP-BASED
SYSTEMS OF CARE AND SUPPORT

In a collection of essays on "Widows in African Societies," Betty Potash (1986a) has argued that the socioeconomic support for widows through their late husband's families in sub-Saharan Africa has never been a self-evident issue. In contrast with the alliance and dependency theories of structural-functionalists, which assumed that widows were supported materially and socially by their in-laws or by a selected levir, she claims that such an assumption has always been based on "oral traditions" and "anthropological folklore" rather than on ethnographic evidence (Potash 1986a: 31f.). While widows often received access to the productive resources of their late husbands' extended families and were sometimes supported in their daily work activities (especially agricultural work), their in-laws and levirs seldom played a substantial role in contributing to the larger material and social well-being of the widows and their children. Furthermore, as the institution of the levirate never represented a formal contract associated with specific duties and rights, the levir's contribution to the widow's family's livelihood was always considered a voluntary activity and not as the fulfillment of a duty (Potash 1986b: 61).

That the relationships between widows and their in-laws were complicated even before the outbreak of HIV/AIDS is shown in the short story "The Widow" by Agoro Anduru, written in the late 1970s. This story shows that the care and support for widows and their children in rural Tanzania was compromised by processes of migration and the estrangement of urban dwellers from life in rural areas (Anduru 1981: 24–68). The protagonist of Anduru's story is a widow who moves to her in-laws' home village after the death of her husband and is confronted with the claims of her brothers-in-laws, who want to "inherit" her (i.e., cleanse her sexually). The widow and her children also face considerable difficulties in reintegrating into the economic and social routines of village life, which generates growing discontent and scorn from her relatives and other villagers. The resulting tensions and conflicts culminate in a quarrel between the widow and the other village women, who refer critically to the widow's former life in town in which she was said to have behaved haughtily and selfishly toward her husband's relatives:

> In all these six months her husband's people hurled cutting remarks at her. Her own children could not match the brute strength of the village children and whenever she protested when her child was roughed up, the mother of the boy or the girl who had bullied her child would tell her: "Touch my child and I'll teach you sense today! While you were in the town you turned people out of your house,

thinking they were after your husband's money. Today you bring us
children who cause a lot of quarrels among adults in the village!"
(Anduru 1981: 55)

On another level, the conflicts between widows and their husbands' families in contemporary Mara are reflected by the case of Rachel Francis,
who—after falling sick herself—had to return to her family of origin in
order to be cared for. In this context, Rachel received very little material
support from her in-laws for her own and her children's livelihood, and the
little she received had to be invested largely in the house that she built
on her father-in-law's compound, which served primarily the purpose of
providing a future home for her children. When I visited Rachel four years
after our first encounter, she and her children had moved to the newly
built house, where Rachel secured her family's income through the trade
of vegetables and local crops in the surrounding village markets.

CONFIGURING SUBJECTIVITY AND BELONGING
ACROSS THE RURAL-URBAN DIVIDE

So far, this chapter has focused on the role of rural communities and kinship networks in the configuration of migrants' identities and subjectivities in the context of socioeconomic restructuring and HIV/AIDS. In this
section I show that "life in town" also presents other (institutionalized)
avenues for urban dwellers in dealing with their life circumstances that
reach beyond their own or their respective partners' families and kinship
networks. In the context of HIV/AIDS, the life trajectories that are de-
vised by these institutions' respective ideologies and practices imply an
individualized form of health-related practice that can hardly be transferred to rural areas where life is subjected to the moral priorities and values of extended families as well as the scrutiny of the larger community.

At the turn of the twenty-first century, several NGOs in Dar es Salaam had established services that were targeted specifically at people infected with HIV and that comprised, among others, the counseling of new
clients as well as medical treatment with basic medications and (limited)
material, legal, and psychosocial support for men and women living with
HIV/AIDS. Beyond the pragmatic advice and the material aid provided
by NGOs, some of these transnationally funded organizations also established support groups for people living with HIV/AIDS in which clients
discussed issues such as disclosure and stigma, the challenge of balanced
nutrition, "safe sexuality" in short- and long-term relationships, the writing of a will, and the lack of material support in times of illness. Through
these extended conversations people with HIV/AIDS (ideally) learned to
refashion their lives and identities as "being HIV-positive" and to acquire

a future-oriented and affirmative approach to dealing with HIV. Only a few support group members I interviewed in Dar es Salaam were capable of initiating this process of reconstructing their individual and collective life worlds on their own. It was only through repeated counseling and identification with the suffering of others that people adopted a self-image of being HIV-positive and translated this self-image into the context of marital and nonmarital relationships, kinship networks, and the wider community.

On another level, several of the HIV-positive women and men I worked with during my research in Dar es Salaam were members of the Full Gospel Bible Fellowship Church (FGBFC), a neo-Pentecostal church founded in 1989 that counted more than 120,000 members nationwide in the year 2000 (Dilger 2007). As Birgit Meyer (1998) and other authors have argued, membership in a Pentecostal church implies a conscious break with the past and the reconfiguration of individual and collective identities along the gospel of prosperity and the ideology of salvation. In particular, neo-Pentecostal churches expect their followers to make a break with the multiple "cultural" and "ritual" obligations they have toward their families, as well as with a number of lifestyles that are considered sinful (such as the consumption of alcohol or engagement in extramarital sexual relationships). Only if these conditions are fulfilled can members of a Pentecostal church be healed from all kinds of physical and nonphysical suffering and become part of a "spiritual family" that is defined in opposition to the worldly family and that aims to disperse any doubts church members might have about the righteousness of their path. This process of community-building is an ambiguous process which implies a high potential for intra-familial conflict, stemming both from unsaved (mostly rural) relatives who try to make church members depart from the path of salvation, as well as from the (mostly urban-based) church followers who persistently urge their families to give up their "dark" and "sinful" ways. At the same time, however, church followers described the FGBFC to me as a beneficial network of care and support that has become particularly useful (as is also the case with NGOs) for the mostly female church members who are mainly young to middle-aged, have low educational status, and have migrated to Dar es Salaam in search of employment or business opportunities. To these women as well as to the male members of the church, most of whom have a similar social background, the FGBFC is appealing essentially because it offers social, moral, and often material orientation in the urban context, which is experienced as risky, anonymous, and increasingly ambivalent.

While neither the AIDS NGOs nor the FGBFC played a major role in shaping the ways Francis Lukio and his family dealt with their relative's illness and death, this does not mean that these institutions would not play an important role in shaping the lives and experiences of other people living with or affected by HIV/AIDS in urban areas.[11] In conclusion, I therefore argue that in order to understand how mobility and migration in Tanzania are structured and experienced by migrants and their social networks in the context of shifting economic, social, and political constellations, we have to pay close attention to the ways in which the lives of rural-urban migrants in Tanzania—not only those who become infected with a deadly disease like HIV/AIDS—are being configured, and not just with regard to isolated locations in a rural *or* urban setting, but also across the rural-urban "divide." Following Jens Andersson, I define urban and rural as a single social universe in which analytical dichotomies and structural contrasts recede in favor of emphasizing the bridges between the two:

> Rather than presenting two distinct—but instrumentally and hierarchically linked—social environments, . . . the rural and the urban constitute a single social universe encompassing both rural and urban geographical spaces. Consequently, dichotomies of rural and urban economic sectors, center and periphery, elite and mass are of little importance. In Buhera district [the location of Andersson's research], social life that does not encompass both the rural and the urban seems unthinkable. (Andersson 2001: 84)

CONCLUSION: THE MORAL ECONOMY OF MOBILITY, MIGRATION, AND HIV/AIDS IN CONTEMPORARY TANZANIA

In a paper on occult economies in neoliberal Tanzania, Todd Sanders (2001) has argued that moral discourses on ritual killings and witchcraft practices in contemporary Tanzania have become an essential way for people in rural and urban areas to make sense of the social and economic inequalities produced by neoliberal reform processes and globalization over the last three decades. Moral discourses on occult practices of wealth accumulation provide a socially embedded answer to people's questions about who profits from current transformations at whose expense and for which purpose. Such discourses and practices have also paved the way for people to establish a sense of control over the multiple visible and invisible forces that have come to shape their lives in the context of globalization and structurally adjusted modernity.

In this chapter, I have shown that moral discourses and practices have become an important resource for people in rural Mara as well to think about and act upon the multiple challenges that are posed to them by rural-urban migration, conflicts and tensions resulting from HIV/AIDS-related illnesses and deaths, and structural adjustment programs. As I have argued elsewhere, moralistic discourses on gender, wealth accumulation, and family solidarity have become deeply entrenched in the ways people are attempting to make sense of a family member's illness and to negotiate morally acceptable terms for dealing with a relative's death. It is through these moral discourses and practices that people construct and reconstruct their individual and collective identities and social ties in the context of shifting economic, social, and political constellations and often over large geographical distances (Dilger 2005, 2006, 2008).

Relationships within kinship networks in western Mara are strained in particular by the fact that the HIV/AIDS epidemic in Tanzania is mostly affecting the economically and socially productive middle generation, thus causing the deaths of numerous women and men at an age at which they are actually supposed to be taking care of their aging parents and other family members and where crucial events and life phases have not yet been completed. In this context, for many families in rural Mara questions about the allocation of wealth and inheritance have become intimately intertwined with the spiritual and emotional belonging of dying or deceased family members and their dependents. Such questions often imply multiple discussions concerning the social unit as well as the (physical) locality of which the respective man or woman is perceived to be a part. In this regard, moral discourses on HIV/AIDS and proper social behavior have become an important source for the social and moral management of the sexually transmitted and potentially deadly disease and for defining a framework for morally acceptable (and healthy) behavior in a time perceived as being full of multiple risks and dangers. Moral notions surrounding the epidemic and its articulation with the social, political, and economic context are also playing a central role in the formation of (gendered) subjectivities and in establishing relationships of belonging in the context of wider social, economic, and political transformations.

In a country like Tanzania, in which about 77 percent of the total population lives in rural areas (United Republic of Tanzania 2002) and where urbanization is caused primarily by immigration processes from the rural regions, these processes often involve people, social groups, and institutions from rural as well as from urban areas. The lives of individual actors in Tanzania are shaped by the continuous movement between villages and cities, as well as by the social, economic, and political transfers taking place across often large geographical boundaries. As I have argued here with regard to the HIV/AIDS epidemic, the temporary uncoupling from traditional rural life arrangements, which shapes the lives of work and trade migrants in Tanzania to varying degrees (and is strongly propagated in neo-Pentecostal discourse, for example), is brought into question by cases of the severely ill or deceased such that burials on rural family grounds and "dying at home" represent an essential part of a proper life course for most migrants and their families. In order to understand what position rural-urban migrants assume within this geographic continuum, it is on the one hand important to understand how this continuum is differentiated through the specific distribution of social, economic, and cultural-religious resources, and in particular how, through this distribution, gender specific ruptures in the context of neoliberal reform processes and the HIV/AIDS epidemic are created and compensated for. On the other hand, it is also important to question how individuals move between the different social units of the urban-rural continuum, which boundaries or connections are drawn between the various units (in the Lukio case, NGOs, churches, and extended families) due to the stigmatization of HIV/AIDS, and how such constellations are articulated in interaction with global economic transformations and health politics.

NOTES

1. All informants' names in the text have been changed.

2. While it has been repeatedly emphasized that HIV/AIDS has become "a disease of poverty" affecting the most disadvantaged social groups worldwide, it should not be forgotten that the disease is also affecting those who have managed to advance socially and economically and who—in the case of HIV/AIDS and other "untimely" afflictions—may present a severe burden for their rural and urban families. As has been shown elsewhere (Weiss 1993; Dilger 2006, 2008), men and women who get sick with HIV/AIDS in urban areas, who have often played a central role in sustaining the well-being of their rural and urban families, are returning to their home villages at an advanced stage of their illness. They are being cared for by their rural relatives and are ultimately buried on the grounds of their family compounds.

3. In 2001, 9 percent of the Mara region's blood donors tested HIV-positive. In Dar es Salaam, the overall infection rate among the adult population was 18.8 percent (United Republic of Tanzania 2001).

4. While anti-retroviral therapy was introduced in Tanzania in 2004, there were still 96,000 people dying from HIV/AIDS in the country in 2007 (compared to 110,000 in 2001) (UNAIDS 2008: 217).

5. While Luo speakers in Kenya represent 13.8 percent of the total Kenyan population, there are only about 280,000 Luo speakers in Tanzania, which has a total population of 34.6 million people (http://www.ethnologue .com/show_language.asp?code=luo; accessed October 4, 2007). The Suba and Kine ethnic groups—who had settled in the area before—were assimilated by the Luo immigrants through marriage, but also as a consequence of violent disputes (cf. Reh 1993/1994; Braun 1994). Today, the descendants of the Suba and Kine speak of themselves as Luo (although most of them are able to further specify their ethnic origin; Reh 1993/1994) and maintain that "the traditions of the Luo" (Kiswahili, *mila ya Wajaluo*) are the standards against which decisions at important stages of life (e.g., birth, marriage, house-building, or funerals) are set.

6. My research assistant (name changed).

7. As in other parts of Tanzania, burials in Mara can last for several days, if not several weeks (as was the case with the burial of an old man which I attended in 1995). Over the last ten years, burials have become shorter due to a lack of resources and complaints about the series of funerals people have to attend in the context of AIDS.

8. Francis's biological mother and her co-wives are intended here.

9. In the case of agriculture, for example, these prescriptions imply that a compound owner must have sexual intercourse with his first wife before he can begin a new phase of fieldwork (e.g., sowing seed or harvesting).

10. It is not possible here to go into the practice of sexual cleansing, which is closely connected to the institution of the levirate (see below) and which I have described elsewhere in more detail (cf. Dilger 2005, 2006, 2008).

11. My first encounter with Francis Lukio took place in the FGBFC, where his brothers brought him for healing prayers. However, the prayers did not prove to be effective in Francis's case and he died a few days later. Francis also apparently underwent an HIV test during various examinations in hospitals and clinics in Dar es Salaam. However, as was the case with many other men and women infected with HIV in Tanzania at the turn of the century, the diagnosis was not conferred to Francis himself but to his male relatives, who kept the diagnosis secret from their dying relative (cf. Dilger 2008; 229n12).

REFERENCES

Andersson, Jens A. 2001. "Reinterpreting the Rural-Urban Connection: Migration Practices and Socio-Cultural Dispositions of Buhera Workers in Harare." *Africa* 71(1): 82–112.

Anduru, Agoro. 1981. *Temptation and Other Stories.* Dar es Salaam: Press and Publicity Centre.

———. 1989. *A Bed of Roses and Other Writings.* Dar es Salaam: Press and Publicity Centre.

Biehl, João, Byron Good, and Arthur Kleinman. 2007. "Introduction: Rethinking Subjectivity." In *Subjectivity: Ethnographic Investigations,* ed. João Biehl, Byron Good, and Arthur Kleinman. Berkeley: University of California Press.

Braun, Dorothee. 1994. *Annäherung an Erfahrungen mit kulturellem Wandel bei Luo-sprechenden Bevölkerungsgruppen in Nordtanzania.* Diploma thesis, Free University of Berlin.

De Bruijn, Mirjam, Rijk van Dijk, and Dick Foeken, eds. 2001. *Mobile Africa: Changing Patterns of Movement in Africa and Beyond.* Leiden: Brill.

Dilger, Hansjörg. 1999. *Besser der Vorhang im Haus als die Fahne im Wind. Geld, AIDS und Moral im ländlichen Tanzania.* Münster and London: Lit Verlag.

———. 2003. "Sexuality, AIDS and the Lures of Modernity: Reflexivity and Morality among Young People in Rural Tanzania." *Medical Anthropology* 22(1): 23–52.

————. 2005. *Leben mit AIDS: Krankheit, Tod und soziale Beziehungen in Afrika. Eine Ethnographie.* Frankfurt am Main: Campus.

————. 2006. "The Power of Aids: Kinship, Mobility and the Valuing of Social and Ritual Relationships in Tanzania." *African Journal of Aids Research* 5(2): 109–21.

————. 2007. "Healing the Wounds of Modernity: Community, Salvation and Care in a Neo-Pentecostal Church in Dar es Salaam, Tanzania." *Journal of Religion in Africa* 37(1): 59–83.

————. 2008. "'We Are All Going to Die': Kinship, Belonging and the Morality of HIV/AIDS-Related Illnesses and Deaths in Rural Tanzania." *Anthropological Quarterly* 81(1): 207–32.

Flanagan, William G. 1982. *The Extended Family as an Agent in Urbanization: A Survey of Men and Woman Working in Dar es Salaam, Tanzania.* Ann Arbor, Mich.: University Microfilms International.

Geschiere, Peter. 1997. *The Modernity of Witchcraft: Politics and the Occult in Postcolonial Africa.* Charlottesville: University Press of Virginia.

Geschiere, Peter, and Josef Gugler. 1998. "Introduction: The Rural-Urban Connection—Changing Issues of Belonging and Identification." *Africa* 68(3): 309–19.

Gugler, Josef. 1971. "Life in a Dual System: Eastern Nigerians in Town." *Cahiers d'études africaines* 11(43): 400–421.

Haram, Liv. 1995. "Negotiating Sexuality in Times of Economic Want: The Young and Modern Meru Women." In *Young People at Risk: Fighting AIDS in Northern Tanzania,* ed. Knut-Inge Klepp, Paul M. Biswalo, and Aud Talle. Oslo: Scandinavian University Press.

Lugalla, Joe. 1995. *Adjustment and Poverty in Tanzania.* Münster: Lit Verlag.

HIV/AIDS/STI Surveillance Report (Report No. 16, January–December 2001). Dar es Salaam: Ministry of Health, Tanzania (Mainland), National AIDS Control Programme.

Meyer, Birgit. 1998. "'Make a Complete Break with the Past': Memory and Postcolonial Modernity in Ghanaian Pentecostal Discourse." In *Memory and the Postcolony: African Anthropology and the Critique of Power,* ed. Richard Werbner. London: Zed Books.

Obrist van Eeuwijk, Brigit. 2006. *Struggling for Health in the City: An Anthropological Inquiry in Dar es Salaam, Tanzania.* Frankfurt a.M.: Peter Lang Verlag.

Potash, Betty. 1986a. "Widows in Africa: An Introduction." In *Widows in African Societies: Choices and Constraints,* ed. Betty Potash. Stanford, Calif.: Stanford University Press.

————. 1986b. "Wives of the Grave: Widows in a Rural Luo Community." In *Widows in African Societies: Choices and Constraints,* ed. Betty Potash. Stanford, Calif.: Stanford University Press.

Reh, Mechthild. 1993/1994. *Suba und Luo in Tansania. Geschichte und Gegenwart.* Unpublished ms., University of Bayreuth, Collaborative Research Initiative "Identity in Africa" (SFB 214).

Sanders, Todd. 2001. "Save Our Skins: Structural Adjustment, Morality and the Occult in Tanzania." In *Magical Interpretations, Material Realities: Modernity, Witchcraft and the Occult in Postcolonial Africa*, ed. Henrietta L. Moore and Todd Sanders. London: Routledge.

Setel, Philip W. 1999. *A Plague of Paradoxes: AIDS, Culture, and Demography in Northern Tanzania*. Chicago: University of Chicago Press.

Shipton, Parker. 1989. *Bitter Money. Cultural Economy and Some African Meanings of Forbidden Commodities*. Washington, D.C.: American Anthropological Association Monograph Series.

Trager, Lilian. 1998. "Home-Town Linkages and Local Development in South-Western Nigeria. Whose Agenda? Whose Impact?" *Africa* 68(3): 360–82.

Tripp, Aili Maria. 1997. *Changing the Rules. The Politics of Liberalization and the Urban Informal Economy in Tanzania*. Berkeley: University of California Press.

UNAIDS. 2008. *Report on the Global AIDS Epidemic*. Geneva.

United Republic of Tanzania. 2001. *National AIDS Control Programme*. Dar es Salaam.

———. 2002. *Population and Housing Census*. Dar es Salaam.

Vorlaufer, Karl. 1973. *Dar es Salaam. Bevölkerung und Raum einer afrikanischen Großstadt unter dem Einfluß von Urbanisierungs- und Mobilitätsprozessen*. Hamburg: Deutsches Institut für Afrika-Forschung.

Weiss, Brad. 1993."'Buying Her Grave': Money, Movement and AIDS in North-West Tanzania." *Africa* 63(1): 19–35.

Whyte, Susan Reynolds. 2005. "Going Home? Belonging and Burial in the Era of AIDS." *Africa* 75(2): 154–70.

7

VOLUNTARY AND INVOLUNTARY HOMEBODIES

ADAPTATIONS AND LIVED EXPERIENCES OF HAUSA "LEFT BEHIND" IN NIAMEY, NIGER

SCOTT M. YOUNGSTEDT

This chapter explores the important roles played by Hausa communities in Niamey, Niger, in the ongoing creation of the global Hausa diaspora.[1] For centuries Hausa have been a "traveling culture" (Clifford 1997) famous for their skills in building long-distance trading networks. Most Hausa of Niger eke out a living through circular migration, raising millet, sorghum, and beans under difficult Sahelian conditions during three- to four-month rainy seasons, and also focusing on labor or trade in the informal economies of Niamey and dozens of other West African cities—many of which have longstanding disapora communities of Hausa settlers—during long dry seasons.

During the past fifty years, Hausa have creatively adapted to post-colonial conditions and global neoliberalism through accelerating rural exodus and long-term or permanent out-migration within West and North Africa and to more distant locations in Europe and North America. An impressive body of literature examines the culturally specific ways Nigerien and Nigerian Hausa experience and navigate transnational processes while establishing communities in Ibadan, Nigeria (Cohen 1969), Accra, Ghana (Pellow 2008), Kumasi, Ghana (Schildkrout 1978), Lomé, Togo (Agier 1983), Abidjan, Cote d'Ivoire (Toure 1990), Chad (Works 1976), Morocco (Maghnia 2001), Tunisia (Jankowsky 2001), Libya (Yamba 1995), Sudan (Yamba 1995), Saudi Arabia (Yamba 1995), Paris (Thomas 2006), and New York (Stoller 2002; Youngstedt 2004a), among other places. Indeed, some evidence strongly suggests that are at least as many Nigeriens living outside the country as within it (particularly if this includes first- and second-generation emigrants).

This chapter aims to make an original ethnographic contribution to globalization studies in general and to the understanding of the global Hausa diaspora in particular by focusing on the ways that Niamey—and the people and communities "left behind" there—functions as an integral node in the increasingly dispersed and growing Nigerien Hausa diaspora. I begin with a brief review of the diaspora concept in social theory. I insist on the critical importance of revaluing home in transnational migratory circuits and diasporic processes. Next, I consider overlapping migratory patterns and diasporic formations by examining Niamey as a destination for rural Nigerien immigrants; movement within the city; Niamey as a central staging ground for international migration; patterns of international migration among Nigerien Hausa; and circular migration including intra-national and international routes. Finally, the chapter addresses four key, interrelated dynamics that characterize socioeconomic transnational connections and adaptations in Niamey: (1) decision-making processes about who should migrate and who should remain at home; (2) the feelings of those "left behind" in Niamey; (3) the ways by which the recent introduction of and rapid integration of cell phones in Niger facilitates transnational connections and the sending and receiving of remittances; and (4) contemporary Nigerien Hausa appraisals of remittances and perceptions regarding the commoditization of social relationships.

This chapter draws from ethnographic research—including participation observation, interviews, and life histories—in Hausa communities of Niamey over the past twenty-two years. The statistical data presented in this chapter were collected in December 2007 and January 2008 through interviews consisting of five sets of questions about migration histories with 130 Nigerien Hausa, including 124 men and six women (see Table 1).[2] My longitudinal research enabled me to select a reasonably representative sample of Hausa men in Niamey with respect to age, occupation, and hometown. Thus, this discussion is highly gendered as it focuses on the experiences of men. This is due to rigid gender boundaries in Niamey that restrict my access to women. Nevertheless, I found opportunities to informally discuss migration experiences with many Hausa women over the years.

I recognize that Nigerien Hausa women navigate complex migratory trajectories that illustrate contemporary global trends of the "feminization of migration." That is, "women play a significant role in all regions and in most types of migration" (Castles and Miller 2009: 12). Nigerien Hausa women migrate almost as often as men do within Niger. There are more women (611,173) living in Niamey than men (610,893), and in Niger as a whole there are essentially as many women (1,549,387) living in urban areas as men (1,555,187) (République du Niger 2010: 1). However, Hausa

Table 1. Demographic Profile of Sample of Hausa Migrants in Niamey 2007–2008, N=130

Ages

15–19: 22 (.17)	40–49: 9 (.07)
20–29: 69 (.53)	50–59: 4 (.03)
30–39: 26 (.20)	

Number of Years in Niamey

Less Than 1:	54	(.42)	21–25:	8	(.06)
1–5:	27	(.21)	26–30:	1	(.01)
6–10:	20	(.15)	46–50:	1	(.01)
11–15:	4	(.03)	Born in Niamey:	6	(.05)
16–20:	9	(.07)			

Occupations

Services:	63	(.48)
Traders:	41	(.32)
Unemployed:	15	(.12)
Students:	11	(.08)

Services:	63		
Security Guards:	12	Electricians:	2
Butchers:	9	Taxi Drivers:	2
Domestic workers:	8	Mechanics:	2
Tailors:	6	Carpenters:	2
Laborers:	5	Bicycle Repairmen:	1
Cooks:	5	Painters:	1
Shoe shiners:	3	Tea Sellers:	1
Clothes washers:	3	Grain Grinders:	1

Traders:	41		
Multiple item traders:	21	Single item traders:	20

Unemployed:	15

Students:	11

women are far less likely to independently migrate internationally than men are. Many Hausa women experience being left behind by migratory husbands, whereas very few Hausa men experience being left behind by migratory wives. Women often function as the anchors of the Hausa communities of Niamey and as key actors in the transnational connections that define the global Hausa diaspora. Effectively serving as household heads to ensure social reproduction, many take on difficult burdens of extra work when their husbands fail to send remittances, while others assume responsibility for investing remittances.

REVALUING HOME IN DIASPORIC PROCESSES AND TRANSNATIONAL MIGRANT CIRCUITS

Social theorists have reached a consensus regarding a general definition of diasporas (Clifford 1997: 246–50; Cohen 1997; Manger and Assal 2006: 12–15; Safran 1991: 83–84; Sanjek 1991), which simultaneously recognizes that there are many different specific and often overlapping diasporas differentially constituted and experienced by impetus (e.g., trauma, trade, labor, or education), history, size (absolute and relative to host populations), class, and gender, among other social variables. The core characteristics of diasporas include dispersal and scattering "from an original centre" (Safran 1991: 83), memories and myths that often glorify the homeland, adaptations and "cultural flowering" (Cohen 1997) in tolerant host communities, difficult relationships with hosts, the development of transnational identities, and a commitment to continuing support of the homeland that serves as a basis for the "group's consciousness and solidarity" (Safran 1991: 83) and inspires a return movement. Transnationalism rests at the core of the diasporic experience; "the empowering paradox of diaspora is that dwelling *here* assumes a solidarity and connection *there*" (Clifford 1997: 269; emphasis in original). Thus, the dynamics of diasporas involve both roots and routes (including movements away from and back to home); that is, "unlike don't-look-back emigration, diaspora includes occasional, frequent or long-postponed returns home" (Sanjek 1991: 324).

The lack of scholarly attention paid to Niamey reveals a problem or blind spot with the way that anthropologists and other social scientists have approached African migration and diasporas. Despite the theoretical recognition of the connection between "here" and "there," the vast majority of research—on the Hausa and other African diasporas—considers how migrants establish new communities in diaspora whereas very little focuses on "original centers" and how home sites—in this case, Niamey—contribute to the formation of diasporas and are influenced by them and returning migrants. This chapter aims to fill this gap by centering on social processes and people in Niamey. Ethnographies of "home" are just as important as analyses of scattered diaspora communities in order to appreciate how "separate places become effectively a single community 'through the continuous circulation of people, money, goods and information'" (Rouse 1991: 14; cited in Clifford 1997: 246).

Definitions and typologies of diaspora are useful for broad cross-cultural comparison, but they sometimes risk reifying core concepts such as "original center" or "homeland" and obscure heterogeneous experiences. The locations and meanings of home are often contextual, contested, ambiguous, and nebulous. Among Nigerien Hausa, home means different things to different people in their "traveling culture," in which migration is the norm due to the fluidity of ethnic boundaries in Niger, diverse family histories of migration, the variability of individual career trajectories, and generation gaps. In Niamey, middle-aged and elderly Hausa who were born in rural Niger before settling in Niamey often perceive of home (usually their villages and towns) very differently from the first large cohort youth born and reared in Niamey—many of whom regard Niamey as home.

Clifford's comparative study emphasizes that travel away from home may be "negatively viewed as transience, superficiality, tourism, and rootlessness . . . [or] positively conceived as exploration, research, escape, transforming encounter" (Clifford 1997: 31). This dichotomous view is reflected in two contrasting yet roughly equally popular Hausa proverbs. Hausa youth and young adults typically prefer "*tahiya ta hi zaman gida*" (traveling is better than staying at home). Hausa in their forties and older usually conclude "*zaman gida ta hi tahiya*" (staying at home is better than traveling)—at least for themselves.

A male youth's completion of his first dry-season migration away from his rural home to a city such as Niamey, capped by a successful return home with gifts and stories before the rainy season, functions as an auxiliary, preliminary rite of passage to adulthood among rural Nigerien Hausa males. It demonstrates resolve, ambition, and the ability to secure cash in a capitalist economy, all of which are necessary to marry—or achieve manhood. Most Nigerien men and women are on the move or in transit (seasonally, circularly, intra-nationally, or internationally) most of time from the age of about fifteen years old until about forty-five. "The market is dead here so we must leave home to support our families, and ourselves," explained one young man whose view reflects the thoughts of millions of Nigeriens.

Once they reach their mid-forties, most men and women hope to return home—however defined—and begin a gradual process of retirement. They are often exhausted from years of travel and come to revalue the peace and comforts of home. Those who have lived abroad for significant lengths of time in large urban areas typically spend a few years in Niamey before returning to their hometowns. However, increasing numbers of Hausa who were born in rural Niger are choosing to retire in Niamey.

Perspectives on migration and home are contextual in other ways. Staying at home may be negatively viewed as demonstrating lack of ambition, resignation, or cowardice. In other cases, staying at home may be viewed positively as evidence of commitment to family and community, reliability, or courage. For example, a man who is a successful trader in Niamey may be considered prudent for staying put, rather than lacking in ambition. In contrast, impoverished men may find international migration the most viable means to support their families.

The phrase "left behind in Niamey," used earlier, seems to imply that those left behind are insignificant "homebodies" out of touch with their family and friends in the global Hausa diaspora. On the contrary, people "left behind" in Niamey play a crucial role in generating the Hausa diaspora through preparing and sponsoring the migrations of family and friends. They are linked in financial and personal networks—now more tightly integrated than ever through the use of cell phones—that make them part of one transnational diasporic community. Furthermore, "left behind" is relative in other ways. First, most Hausa in Niamey are migrants themselves who hail from villages, towns, and cities across south-central Niger. Second, the vast majority of Hausa in Niamey has previously migrated abroad, or intend to do so in the future, or both. Finally, Hausa of Niamey include involuntary and voluntary "homebodies"—and these conditions shift over time. Thus, there are few true "homebodies" in Niamey as most peoples' lives are defined by transience and liminality rather than permanence and completion. As Clifford (1997: 37) explains, "with everyone more or less permanently in transit" (or at least thinking about migration), the question becomes "not so much 'Where are you from?' as 'Where are you between?'"

Even though Hausa men and women spend most of their lives in transnational and national migration circuits, very few forget about their *gida* ("home"), variously defined. About 80 percent of Nigerien Hausa are born in small, rural villages of south-central Niger, and among these most regard their place of birth as home. Idrissa (2009: 161) similarly emphasizes, "While living in urban settlements like Niamey or Maradi, most Nigeriens who are not indigenous to the place will reflexively refer to their *terroir* ('traditional countryside') as their first identity of origin—almost never to their ethnicity." Most men seek to retire and eventually be buried in their home villages. For example, Nigerien and other West African immigrants in New York City have established formal associations—such as L'Association des Nigeriens de New York—from which family and friends can draw to transport bodies home for burial (Stoller 2002: 167). Even those who were born in diaspora, say Accra, and have never even been to Niger often identify their father's natal village in Niger as home. However, as increasing numbers of Nigerien Hausa spend most of their years in Niamey—often with more family and friends there than at "home"—Niamey has become a second home. Indeed many Hausa now find it acceptable or desirable to be buried in Niamey.

OVERLAPPING MIGRATORY PATTERNS AND DIASPORIC FORMATIONS

NIAMEY AS A DESTINATION FOR RURAL NIGERIEN MIGRANTS

Hausa migration has played a key role in the historical growth of Niamey as Hausa became a slight majority around 1980 and have retained that position ever since. Niamey has become a second home to many Hausa migrants and a primary home to a new generation of youth coming of age today. However, it is important to remember that Hausa communities in Niamey are diaspora communities by definition, even though Niamey is within Niger. The following dialogue illustrates this point. I have had many similar discussions over the years, particularly with middle-aged men. Typically the encounter begins with a stranger in a market or in a taxi whom I greet, and we engage in brief conversation to negotiate prices or destinations. Then, as the encounter is coming to a close, my newfound acquaintance praises my ability to speak Hausa (this is evidence of Hausa graciousness and not necessarily of my linguistic skills).

TAXIMAN: *Where did you learn Hausa so well?*

SMY: *Here in Niamey.*

TAXIMAN: *No, really? You must have learned it Maradi or Dogondoutchi.*

SMY: *I've been there, but I really learned to speak Hausa in Niamey.*

TAXIMAN: *But this is a Zarma city.*

SMY: *Almost everyone here speaks Hausa here, right? Even more than Zarma?*

TAXIMAN: *Yes, I think that is true. See you later.*

SMY: *Arrive safely.*

The taximan's assumption that I must have learned Hausa in Hausa-land because Niamey is a "Zarma city" reflects the perception—particu-larly among the middle-aged—that Hausa are away from home in Nia-mey. Simultaneously his acknowledgment of the prevalence of Hausa speakers in Niamey points to the reality that in fact Hausa constitute the majority of Niamey's population, and almost everyone in Niamey speaks Hausa. Indeed, Hausa have built dense social networks and communities in Niamey. These are organized around family, hometown, occupational, congregational, and conversation group affiliations. Their connections, friendships, and marriages are not defined solely by Hausa ethnicity. In Niamey their communities are interwoven with those of many other ethnic groups due to Nigerien *brassage* ("cultural and ethnic blending"). Youth fifteen to twenty-five years old who were born and reared in Niamey (or moved there as children) typically feel that Niamey is really home even if they have some symbolic attachment to their father's rural hometown. They do not ask me where I learned to speak Hausa.

MOVEMENT WITHIN THE CITY

Hausa are constantly on the move within Niamey (as well as to and from it). Men typically cover ten-kilometer circuits on foot everyday in the city for work (or looking for work), prayer, and social networking. This is partly because they have time on their hands, as most are either unemployed or underemployed. But this is not the only reason. The daily rounds of Hausa men in Niamey are motivated by the quest for a vibrant social life of intelligent conversation and clever humor filled with a wide range of friends and acquaintances. Niamey is an "outdoor culture" particularly for men. Most men spend little time at home regardless of their marital status or employment status. Most jobs in the informal economy are outdoors. Most prayers are conducted in open-air mosques and in sidewalk gatherings that sometimes expand to block off roads. The "average" man also participates daily in several street corner conversation groups that are scattered throughout the city.

Most Hausa women of Niamey also circulate daily throughout the city, though a minority is partially or fully secluded. Their places of work are often distant from home. Women make trips to markets nearly every day to purchase cooking supplies. Many Hausa women spend a great deal of time visiting family and friends, participating in naming and wedding ceremonies, and women-centered social networks and formal associations.

Monthly and annual movements and migrations from one domicile to another are due to two primary factors: the high cost of rent and the circular migratory patterns of many Hausa who spend dry seasons in Niamey and wet seasons farming in their villages. Most Niaméens are renters. A few have been renting the same apartment or compound for decades, but most move every few years both near and far within the city. Moves are almost always based solely on financial considerations. Many are constantly ready to move if they hear of better deals or their fortunes change

for better or worse. Seasonal migrants that are not well connected in Niamey have to find new lodging every year. Other circular migrants find
more stability in Niamey by forming groups (based on kinship, hometown
connections, friendships) to share rent and make arrangements such that
at least one man in the group will reside in the lodging at all times during
the wet season, so that those who go home to farm can easily relocate to
Niamey after the harvest. Some of these rental relationships last a decade
or more.

NIAMEY AS A CENTRAL STAGING GROUND FOR
INTERNATIONAL MIGRATION

Decisions about who will leave the country take place across Niger. Most
of the practical planning for international migration occurs in Niamey
rather than in rural villages, for it is in Niamey that Hausa find higher
concentrations of people with international migration experiences and
connections, ready access to official travel documents, and—for the well-
to-do—Niger's only international airport. Nigerien Hausa have made Niamey a place where they can get urban diaspora experience with many of
the comforts of home. Indeed, it is far more common for Hausa to spend a
few years learning urban social skills in Niamey before migrating abroad
than it is for Hausa to depart rural homes directly for foreign destinations.
This is a specific example of the global pattern whereby migrants first
move from rural areas to cities in their home countries before embark-
ing on secondary international migratory journeys (Castles and Miller
2009: 4).

Niamey is a place that many people want to leave. Movement and
transience define the ethos of Niamey where migration is a constant topic
of conversation. It is a city of dreamers and dreams—both realized and
frustrated. Simultaneously Niaméens recognize that leaving (and returning or staying) requires broad social networks and support. Since people
are constantly going and coming, Nigeriens must constantly nurture old
relationships at a distance and cultivate new connections. That is to say,
Hausa maintain a sense of solidarity and community in Niamey despite
and because so many are eager to emigrate.

Migratory dreams and aspirations are expressed in many ways. *Fada*
("formal conversation") groups are often named after desirable global destinations, and names such as Brooklyn, L.A., and Paris are spray-painted
on walls throughout Niamey. Men I met twenty years ago as newcomers
in Niamey who are now in their forties and fifties regularly ask me to
take them home with me to the United States. Many are joking but not
all of them, including Salissou, who explained, "I am serious. I will do
any kind of work, even sweeping streets and emptying trashcans. And I

won't cause any trouble for you or your family." Issaka, a twenty-five-year old man who has grown up in Niamey, talks incessantly about his desire to move to the United States, even though his father is destitute, he has no formal education, and he speaks neither French nor English. He wears T-shirts with U.S. Embassy logos from around the world that he has purchased in Niamey's used clothing markets. His friends usually call him "Americain" rather than Issaka, and he has taught them to greet him with what he regards as cool African American handshakes. "I love you guys," he told his *hira* mates, "but if get the chance to go to the U.S. I will never come back." However unrealistic, his identity is defined by this American dream.

PATTERNS OF INTERNATIONAL MIGRATION

For many years, Nigerien scholars and many well-informed citizens have been telling me that there are at least as many Nigeriens living outside the country as within it, particularly if both first- and second-generation emigrants are counted. My recent research provides strong evidence that this may be the case. Among my sample of Hausa migrants in Niamey, 82 percent have at least one family member or friend who is living abroad. Moreover, among those 82 percent, each person has on average two family members and friends living abroad. This snapshot of the global Nigerien Hausa diaspora includes 71 percent of migrants in twelve West African countries, 12 percent in North Africa, 9 percent in Europe, 6 percent in North America, and 2 percent in Saudi Arabia (see Table 2). This roughly matches World Bank (2006) data that lists Cote d'Ivoire, Burkina Faso, Nigeria, Chad, Benin, Togo, France, Italy, Germany, and the United States as the top ten destination countries for Nigerien emigrants in 2005.

Furthermore, the ongoing economic crisis in Niger and the reported intentions of Hausa in my sample suggest that international migration will remain important. Two-thirds are planning to migrate abroad and they identify ninety destinations (see Table 3). Among these ninety destinations, 61 percent are in West African nations; 17 percent are in European nations; 10 percent are in North African nations; and less than one percent each are in the United States and Saudi Arabia and Asia. In addition, only one-third of respondents who have no current plans to migrate abroad have never left Niger. Seventy-two percent of the Hausa in the sample have previously migrated abroad.

CIRCULAR MIGRATION INCLUDING INTRA-NATIONAL AND
INTERNATIONAL ROUTES

Much of the migration to and from Niamey is circular, including both seasonal rural-urban migration within Niger and international migration

Table 2. Frequencies and Locations of Family and Friends Abroad

Family or Friends Abroad, N =130

Yes:	106	(.82)
No:	24	(.18)

Locations of Family and Friends Abroad, N=225

West Africa:	160	(.71)
North Africa:	27	(.12)
Europe:	20	(.09)
North America:	14	(.06)
Saudi Arabia:	4	(.02)

West Africa:	159		
Nigeria:	38	Mali:	7
Cote d'Ivoire:	26	Cameroon:	6
Togo:	23	Senegal:	6
Benin:	22	Gabon:	2
Ghana:	19	Guinea:	1
Burkina Faso:	8	Congo:	1

North Africa:	27		
Libya:	17	Morocco:	1
Algeria:	6	Egypt:	1
Tunisia:	2		

Europe:	20		
France:	9	Italy:	1
Belgium:	4	Netherlands:	1
England:	1	Norway:	1
Germany:	1	"Europe":	1
Switzerland:	1		

North America:	14		
U.S.:	13	Canada:	1

Middle East:	4		
Saudi Arabia	4		

Table 3. Migratory Intentions, Experience, and Preferred Destinations

Intentions to Migrate Internationally, N=130

Yes:	86	(.66)
No:	44	(.34)

Previous International Migration Experience among Those with Intentions to Migrate, N=86

Yes:	62	(.72)
No:	24	(.28)

Previous International Migration Experience among Those without Intentions to Migrate, N=44

Yes:	29	(.66)
No:	15	(.34)

Intended Migratory Destinations, N=90

West Africa:	55	(.61)
Europe:	15	(.17)
North Africa:	9	(.10)
North America:	6	(.07)
Middle East/Asia:	5	(.06)

West Africa:	55		
Ghana:	13	Burkina Faso:	4
Cote d'Ivoire:	9	Cameroon:	4
Togo:	8	Mali:	2
Benin:	7	Senegal:	1
Nigeria:	6	Central African Rep:	1

Europe:	15		
"Europe":	5	England:	1
France:	4	Germany:	1
Belgium:	3	Switzerland:	1

North Africa:	9
Libya:	7
Algeria:	2

North America:	6
U.S.	6

Middle East/Asia	5		
Mecca:	2	Pakistan:	1
India:	1	"Asia":	1

that keeps Nigeriens out of the country for months, years, or even decades at a time. This means that people are constantly leaving and returning to Niamey with infusions of diverse experiences, stories, skills, fashions, languages, and money. Migrants from Niamey influence the lives of family and friends in Niamey whether they return or not. Many are gone for indefinite lengths of time, during which people must reorder social structures in order to adapt while anticipating long-awaited returns.

DYNAMICS OF TRANSNATIONAL CONNECTIONS AND ADAPTATIONS IN NIAMEY

SELECTING MIGRANTS

In Niger, group considerations and assistance are almost always crucial to migration decisions. The further the destination, the less likely that prospective migrants can handle costs and preparation independently. While a few have the means to migrate on their own, most Nigerien Hausa rely on extended family, *hira* ("informal conversation") groups, or *fada* ("formal conversation") groups to support their migration even if they are only moving a few hundred kilometers within the country or to a neighboring country. Others look to individual relationships with wealthy patrons for help with travel costs and expenses associated with resettlement.

Individual families and *hira* and *fada* conversation groups typically perceive that they can only afford to invest in one or two member's international migration and thus engage in careful and difficult decisions regarding who is considered worthy of sponsoring. Prospective Hausa migrants compete indirectly for this scarce resource. They do not appear simultaneously before a "jury" of their kin and peers listening to each other's appeals or trying to directly outdo their rivals. The process plays out during informal palavers that take place over months and years in which individuals seek to demonstrate valued qualities, establish positive reputations, and orally make their cases. In family palavers, many voices are heard but a man's father has the final say. In conversation groups, decisions are reached by democratic consensus except that those prepared to contribute more have more power. Men spend hours considering the qualities of those who have successfully secured migration sponsorship. Men who are friendly, hard working (particularly if they are perceived to have occupational skills that are portable to other urban areas), linguistically adept (in African languages, French, and, increasingly, English), cell phone–owning, humble, devout Muslims with proven track records of supporting family and friends through migration to Niamey are generally regarded as the best candidates.

Migration sponsorship is perceived as a group investment, counterbalanced by the inherent duty of the emigrant to send remittances home.

Individuals make contributions according to their means and the degree of trust that they have in would-be migrants. The amount given in support influences the amount expected in return. Not only are migrants obliged to repay the loans that allowed their travel, they are expected to regularly send remittances for as long as they are away from home.

Occasionally families and conversation groups choose individuals who have never stated desires to migrate abroad but who demonstrate the desired qualities of trustworthy migrants, highlighting the value of migration as a communal, adaptive strategy. These chosen ones sometimes resist, chafing at the burdens that international migration entails, including homesickness, separation from wives, and high expectations of generosity. However, they typically relent due to informal pressure, occasionally including hiring *marok'a* ("praise-singers") to publicly extol their virtues.

FEELINGS OF THOSE "LEFT BEHIND" IN NIAMEY

At independence in 1960 only 12 percent of Niamey's 30,000 residents were Hausa. Today slightly more than 50 percent of Niamey's 1.2 million residents are Hausa. This constitutes a highly unusual transformation given that Niamey rests some 150 kilometers east of the westernmost boundaries of "traditional Hausaland." Hausa have made Niamey "a home away from home." They take pride in their role in the growth of Niamey and value particular aspects of the quality of life there. In referring to Niamey, many Hausa simply say that they are "thanking Allah that they have food, water, and decent clothing," and indicate that these basic necessities are not always available in their home villages. Many other Hausa express appreciation for the "cosmopolitan civilization" of Niamey. Finally, most Hausa deeply value the peace (*kwancen hankali*) and the paucity of violence in Niamey, especially as they have become more aware of war (*tashin hankali*) and violence in West African cities through mass media or their own travels. Aliou, a beef jerky salesman who has lived in Niamey for twenty years, succinctly summarized feelings shared by many: "We have everything here—conversation, religion, friendship, and peace (a man can sleep on the road without being disturbed)—but money."

"Voluntary homebodies" eloquently express their worldviews. Soulley, a fifty-year old man, explained, "If I can get what I want in Niger I have no business going to a foreign country because as a famous Hausa singer put, 'there is no place like home.'" Hassane, a thirty-five-year-old man with the perspective of experience, similarly declared, "I do not intend to return to a foreign country, because if a man cannot get what he wants in Niger, he will not be able to get what he wants in a foreign country."

Table 4. Achieved Goals in Niamey, N=130

Yes:	14	(.11)
No:	100	(.77)
Partially:	16	(.12)

Hausa migrants, however, have experienced increasing difficulty in earning a decent living in Niamey over the past twenty years. Today only about 10 percent of men have achieved their principal goals in Niamey (see Table 4). These goals typically include establishing oneself in an occupation that will become increasingly lucrative over time, allowing one to live in some modest material comfort, marry before the age of thirty, and regularly send money home. Many cite steady inflation and expensive rent, food, and taxes as the biggest drawbacks of Niamey, making it nearly impossible to get ahead. Furthermore, a significant minority suffers in dire poverty in Niamey, lacking the resources to simply return home.

While enduring economic decline, the cost of bridewealth has risen at a rate faster than the overall inflation rate, leaving many frustrated thirty- and forty-year old bachelors. The declining pool of eligible and financially stable young bachelors similarly discontents women. Many reluctantly accept marriages with much older men in polygynous marriages. Although many Hausa women in Niamey do not mind polygyny and some prefer it to monogamy, most first-time brides prefer to be the first brides of their husbands, and a substantial and growing minority strongly prefer monogamy.

In this context of economic decline, most Hausa men desire onward migration from Niamey to a foreign destination to try their luck for at least a few years. "Involuntary homebodies" who desire to leave the country but who are unable to secure the resources to do so may be deeply frustrated, particularly if their appeals for sponsorship have been rejected. While they retain hopes for future migration, they patiently wait for news and remittances from family and friends, especially if they themselves have invested in the sponsorship of migrants.

Despite the "feminization of migration" among the Hausa, married women are more likely to be left behind by migrant husbands in Niamey than to be international migrants. Hausa custom—as is the case in most Nigerien cultures—"dictates" that wives should reside in the homes of the parents of their husbands while their husbands are in diaspora, even if they were not doing so before their husbands departed—and most do. Women's experiences in this arrangement vary and are influenced by the interaction of personalities, the generosity of their husbands, the size of their in-laws' homes, the degree of privacy they are afforded, and the length of the time their husbands are away from home. Although Hausa women understand the necessity of their husbands' migrations given the lack of economic opportunities in Niger, they typically find this living situation to be very stressful, as they are often expected to carry out expanded domestic labor in large extended families, may face rude in-laws, and must cope with separations from their husbands for years at a time. Some find this so intolerable that they move out despite their husbands' wishes (Stoller 1999). Stress associated with long-term absences of husbands is a common factor in divorce, as I learned through a number of cases.

Many women make other arrangements during the absences of their husbands. Some women simply refuse to live with parents of their husbands and insist on living alone or with their own families. Moreover, not all husbands have living parents. Women head about one in five households in Niamey (Youngstedt 2004c). In contrast to the possibility of enduring hardship, some women find advantages in being "left behind" as they come to appreciate their independence—in some cases in which they live with supportive and kind in-laws and particularly if they are living alone with their children (Stoller 1999). They feel liberated from the domestic demands of their husbands and relish more opportunities to pursue their occupations and to socialize with family and friends. Furthermore, if their husbands are successful in diaspora and regularly send money home, they enjoy a higher standard of living. Women often have divided feelings about their husband's returns in these situations. Some come to wish that their husbands would return home only periodically, just long enough so that they can have children.

TRANSNATIONALISM, CELL PHONES, AND REMITTANCES

Hausa in Niamey use cell phones to serve core values, for navigating local economic matters, as important status symbols or the latest markers of modernity, and to promote literacy. I focus here on the ways that Nigerien Hausa employ cell phones to strengthen and expand transnational connections and a sense of community in diaspora, and for securing remittances. The regular communication afforded by cell phones has changed the meaning and feeling of being "left behind" or away from home. Keeping in touch is important. It is expensive. It is commoditized. But it is worth it.

Hausa are making revolutionary changes to their far-flung diaspora by utilizing mobile phones to create new and unprecedented opportunities for communication across distances. Prior to the late 1990s, Hausa separated by migration communicated with each other primarily by proxy; that is, news and cash and gifts were given to individuals traveling back and forth through networks of communities dispersed across Africa and delivered in person. For a few years in the late 1990s and early 2000s, email accessed at new, public cybercafés in Niamey became a popular means of communication and remittance negotiation with émigrés, particularly for the literate and relatively well-off and their friends. Since 2001 and accelerating ever since, cell phones have been adopted as the primary technology facilitating symbolic and financial communication linking the Nigerien Hausa diaspora. Using cell phones as their main tool of time-space compression, the vast majority of Hausa migrants in Niamey today—including 85 percent of people in my sample—communicate regularly with their family members and friends abroad (see Table 5).

Hausa in Niamey use cell phones to communicate more frequently with international migrants than was feasible in the past. Cell phone owners can be contacted at any time at virtually any place. This constitutes both their primary advantage and their primary disadvantage, as anyone who owns one knows. Hausa consider the synchronic communication offered by cell phones as far more personalized and immediate than that afforded by other asynchronic channels, such as handwritten letters, e-mail messages, or couriers. Literacy is not required to place and receive cell phone calls, however, those who are literate can save money by sending text messages rather than placing calls.

Most international calls received and placed by Hausa in Niamey are brief—two to five minutes—and consist primarily of greetings and family news updates. "Just a one to two minute call home every one to two months to let everyone know that things are fine is acceptable," according to Ousseini, whose son is working in Paris. In addition, the question of money is always lurking in international conversations. Usually it is put off until just before the conclusion of the conversation (in other cases, migrants are simply informing those in Niamey that they have sent or will send money). Hausa in Niamey now use cell phones to communicate their specific needs with international migrants: medicine for an ill child, a sheep for Tabaski (*Eid al-Adha* in Arabic; the "feast of sacrifice" commemorating Abraham's willingness to sacrifice his son), food to survive, and expenses for baptisms, marriages, and funerals. Migrants in diaspora find it more difficult to deny requests made during phone conversations than they do when requests are sent through letters, email, or couriers. Abdoulrazack, a Hausa man who has been living in Ypsilanti, Michigan, for more than decade, commented on this: "Years ago my family sent me letters. They are not literate, so they dictated letters to my cousin. Somehow I could ignore their pleas for money in these letters. I just sent money whenever I had a little extra. Now, when I hear my mother crying on the phone, I melt and run straight down to the Western Union outlet."

Cell phone communication exacerbates the pressure that many migrants feel to support family and friends left behind in Niamey. Many migrants rise to this challenge by purchasing cell phones as gifts for those in Niamey and expressing their strong desire to keep current with news at home. Many live frugally in diaspora in order to send as much money home as possible. In contrast, many Hausa in diaspora communities grow so weary of steady streams of phone calls from family and friends in Niger asking for money that they use two phone numbers—one that they share with people that are likely to ask for money and another that they share with people who are unlikely to ask for money. Another strategy entails purchasing calling cards and using public phones to call home so that one can remain in touch with home on one's own terms. Ousmane, working as a butcher in Senegal, explained, "I paid for my bus ticket to Dakar. I do not owe anyone anything. Besides, I earn a very modest living here. I would rather save money to visit home once a year or so and to give gifts in person so I know that the money is not squandered."

Cell phones have emerged as the primary media for securing the remittances upon which increasing numbers of people are virtually entirely dependent for everyday necessities, and for emergencies. Remittances are notoriously very difficult to measure. Many Nigerien Hausa prefer to send cash through proxies who return to Niamey, and this is not accounted for in official statistics. Many remittances are wired, primarily through Western Union, though Moneygram has emerged as a competitor in recent years. In the last couple of years, it has also become possible to wire money through cell phones to bank accounts. Some evidence indicates that remittances are increasing. According to World Bank (2009) data, Nigerien workers sent home remittances totaling $14 million in 2000, $66 million in 2005, and $78 million in 2007 and 2008 (it might not be coincidental that these increases parallel the acceleration adoption of cell phones). Olivier de Sardan's (2007) analysis indicates that remittances from the Nigerien diaspora were likely more significant in mitigating Niger's famine in 2005 than state and international humanitarian assistance.

In my sample, 36 percent of respondents report having received remittances from family and friends abroad, and among them 61 percent indicated that they themselves received remittances whereas 39 percent indicated that it was sent to their parents to manage for their families (see Table 5). More than four in five received only money, while a few received gifts such as cell phones and clothes. The average remittance, on roughly an annual basis, was 121,785 FCFA ($270). To put this into perspective, the annual per capita income in Niger is about $250. This average remittance obscures inequality; that is, remittances ranged from 10,000 FCFA ($22) to 750,000 FCFA ($1,666). Sixty-one percent of men who indicated specific monetary figures, received between $22 and $166. Eighty-seven percent of those who received money reported that it made a significant difference in their lives, whereas only 13 percent complained that they did not receive enough to really help them.

Table 5. Communication with and Remittances from the Nigerien Hausa Diaspora

Regular Communication via Cell Phones with Family and Friends Abroad, N=106		
Yes:	90	(.85)
No:	16	(.15)

Received Remittances from Family or Friends Abroad, N=106		
Yes:	38	(.36)
No:	68	(.64)

Recipient of Remittances, N=38		
Self:	23	(.61)
Parents:	15	(.39)

Types of Remittances, N=38		
Money only:	31	(.82)
Cell phone and clothes:	4	(.11)
Money and gifts:	3	(.08)

Size of Reported Annual Monetary Remittances, N=28 ($1 = FCFA 450)					
10,000–30,000 FCFA	6	(.21)	300,000 FCFA	1	(.04)
31,000–60,000 FCFA	8	(.29)	400,000 FCFA	1	(.04)
61,000–90,000 FCFA	3	(.11)	500,000 FCFA	1	(.04)
91,000–120,000 FCFA	6	(.21)	750,000 FCFA	1	(.04)
121,000–150,000 FCFA	1	(.04)			

Average Size of Reported Annual Monetary Remittances, N=28
121,785 FCFA

Impact of Remittances for Recipients, N=38		
Important	33	(.87)
Not Important	5	(.13)

Hausa of Niamey are eager to own cell phones despite the relatively exorbitant costs to purchase and use them, because they recognize their immense social and economic value. In December 2008 the prices for new, basic model phones made by major brands such as Nokia, Motorola, and Samsung began at about $55, while models produced in China could be found for about half this price. A year later, in December 2009, the price had been reduced by almost half, to about $35. Despite this deflation, $35 is still the average monthly income among Hausa of Niamey. A thriving market in used phones permits consumers to purchase functional phones for less than $10. Using a phone requires procuring recharge cards through which call time is paid for by loading a unique PIN number each time one wants to add credit to an individual account. The system facilitates the sharing of cell phones because users can determine the precise cost of each call.[3] While cell phones are beyond the means of more than half of Hausa in Niamey, many people who can barely afford some of the basic necessities of everyday life make extraordinary efforts to acquire one. Many men paying $30 a month to rent apartments own $50 cell phones and spend 50 cents a day making phone calls.

MIGRATION AND REMITTANCES: THE GOOD, THE BAD, AND THE UGLY

Migration is a core adaptive strategy and a means of survival for Hausa, involving establishing and maintaining transnational diasporic connections that are designed to lead to improved opportunities for individual migrants and infusions of remittances to family and friends in Niamey and across Niger. The social performance of migration is differentiating. Its success rests on synergy between individuals and groups. Some migrants succeed whereas others fail, including some who are never heard from again. This can be due to particular circumstances, and the personal qualities and skills of individual migrants as well as good and bad choices made by groups about whom to sponsor. Much is at stake. Not only are the reputations of individual migrants on the line, but, more important, the reputations, investments, and finances of families and communities in Niamey are at risk. In a context of economic scarcity, contestations over remittances are becoming more frequent and have influenced the perception that social relationships are increasingly commoditized in Niamey. The older generation laments this shift; as one man cited earlier summed it up, "Today, chasing money drives people crazy." The younger generation, particularly those who were born or reared in Niamey, is more likely to see an individualistic, cash-oriented economy as a simple fact of life.

Lively discussions and heated debates regarding remittances have become a staple theme in Hausa street corner conversation groups and family meetings in Niamey, due to the increasing importance of remittances in social reproduction and survival. Almost all people who received cash remittances praise and humbly thank the donors. Indeed, those who fulfilled the cultural expectation to support family and friends will receive hero's welcomes upon returning to Niger. But the situation is complicated as jealousy can creep into relationships for a number of reasons. For example, some men who are generous with remittances are otherwise regarded as immoral or unlikable for any number of reasons. As one man poignantly observed, "Now respect can be purchased with remittances. My brother in Greensboro, North Carolina just sent home $500. Many people in the family cannot stop praising him even though they know he drinks whiskey every day and has not prayed for years."

While they suffer in dire poverty, many Hausa in Niamey are upset with their relatives and friends abroad. Many Hausa of Niamey claim that their comrades in diaspora are growing ever more selfish. I do not have evidence to support the claim the migrants are sending less money home, but I think that this perception reflects a declining economic climate in Niamey and the global economic recession. That is, Niaméens need remittances now more than ever. Almost two-thirds of respondents with family or friends abroad report that they have not received any remittances, including 14 percent who have received no news at all from their migrant compatriots (see Table 5). Commenting on this, many Hausa simply say, "Today it's every man for himself." In Niamey's street corner conversation groups and family discussions, Hausa spend more time and energy complaining about irresponsible international migrants—expressing especially deep exasperation regarding those who never even bother to call or send an occasional email message—than they do praising generous family or friends in diaspora. For example, neither his family nor his friends have heard from Mamane Ousmane, who left Niamey for New York City more than a decade ago shortly after his father died. His mother, Hadija, expresses her exasperation about this almost daily in comments such as "We do not need money from him; we just want to know that he is alright." His brother, Tidjani, says that the family would be satisfied to receive even a one-minute phone call during holidays. His friend Djibrilla concluded that, "His mother or other family could have died and he would not even know it. It is very strange, he must really hate Niger to behave like this."

Many Hausa in Niamey fail—due to lack of knowledge or frustration—to recognize the difficulties faced by their migrant brethren and sisters in diaspora communities that typically rest precariously on the margins of the global economy, despite their own, often difficult, experiences abroad. Economic conditions in the nations where Nigerien Hausa have been and currently are most likely to migrate—Nigeria, Cote d'Ivoire, Togo, Benin, Ghana, and Libya—are only marginally better than in Niger. Most Hausa in the diaspora desperately yearn to send money but cannot as they are barely making ends meet. Hausa of Niamey often have grossly inflated expectations of those who manage to make it to Europe or North America. In a comment that echoed dozens of others, a man severely criticized his own brother who has been living in New York City for six years without sending any remittances: "Any Hausa in New York who is not fully supporting at least fifteen people in Niger is either lying and living the high life or incredibly foolish and lazy."

Contestations regarding exactly whom should receive remittances and on what they should be spent have also intensified. Sons sometimes resent and resist their fathers' demands to turn over remittances to them to manage for their families. Wives left behind by their migrant husbands typically reside with their husbands' parents, as mentioned earlier. In many cases this relationship is severely strained by jealousy and competition for gifts, in a context in which loyalty to affinal and consanguineal relationships is measured monetarily. Wives and parents-in-law trade accusations and counter-accusations of hording or squandering the remittances sent home by husbands or sons (Stoller 1999). Migrant men face difficult and uncomfortable questions from each.

Hausa in Niamey prefer to control how they will spend remittances, and resent international migrants who try to assert control. This is especially true among those who helped to sponsor international migrants. Most migrants who send money home expect or ask for it to be spent on everyday necessities such as food, rent, and medicine, while a few send home cell phones (or "top-up" cell phone accounts) or clothes rather than money. Today, they increasingly resist homebodies' requests for money to support "luxuries"—such as purchasing sheep for Tabaski, or hosting expensive naming and wedding ceremonies. Their stance on "rational" investment parallels one of the core messages articulated by the Izala reformist movement. Though only a minority of 'yan Izala (members of Izala) are international migrants, the similar financial strategy favored by migrants and 'yan Izala represents a common solution to a common problem—severe poverty.

CONCLUSION

In summary, Niamey serves as an integral node and symbolic home of the increasingly dispersed Nigerien Hausa diaspora. I have argued that understandings of traveling cultures are necessarily incomplete if they fail to pay attention to home sites and concepts of home. For it is at home that global processes generate the conditions that motivate migration, it is at home that people launch their migratory careers, and home is inexorably changed by those who are away whether or not they remain in contact and whether or not they return. Hausa in Niamey make calculated investments in the sponsorship of migrants expecting to receive remittances in return. While many are disappointed by the inability or unwillingness of their migrant family and friends to come through for them, others have become almost entirely dependent on remittances for their survival. A few others have seen their standards of living rise significantly due to the generosity of their migrant comrades. Hausa have rapidly deployed cell phones since their introduction in 2001 for maintaining and building personal and economic relationships and facilitating multi-local community connections, including the sending and receiving of remittances. Migrants now feel much more pressure to send money home when they can easily be contacted in a very personal way than before the spread of cell phones. Conflicts over remittances are becoming more common with so much at stake. Many middle-aged and elderly Hausa bemoan that struggles over remittances symbolize the divisive nature of money and broader disturbing trends in the commoditization of social relationships.

NOTES

1. I deeply appreciate the invitation offered by Abdoulaye Kane and Todd Leedy to participate in "Migrations In and Out of Africa: Old Patterns and New Perspectives," the 2008 Gwendolen M. Carter Conference of The Center for African Studies at the University of Florida. I gratefully acknowledge the helpful insights of conference participants Beth A. Buggenhagen, Cathleen Coe, Rachel R. Reynolds, and Paul Stoller. I sincerely thank my Nigerien colleagues Djibrilla Garba and Cheiffou Idrissa for offering their critical perspectives. Sara Beth Keough—my colleague at Saginaw Valley State University—offered constructive suggestions for which I am thankful. Most importantly, I thank the Nigeriens who graciously and patiently shared their experiences with me.

2. Interview questions include the following: (1) Where are you from? Why did you come to Niamey? How were you able to come to Niamey? How is your life here in Niamey? (2) How long have you been in Niamey? What are your successes and your problems in Niamey? Have you found what you are seeking? (3) Have you ever migrated to foreign countries? Which countries? Why? When? How many years did you spend abroad? Why did you return to Niamey? (4) Do you intend to migrate to a foreign country? Why? Where? How? When? (5) Do you have family or friends who are living in foreign countries? Where? Do you receive news from them? Did they send you money? How much? Did it solve your problems?

3. Zain dominates the market in Niger. The current rates for calls in Zain's most basic plan in Niamey include 25 cents per minute between Zain subscribers, 39 cents per minute to other mobile subscribers and fixed lines, 16 cents per minute for a family and friends plan, 30 cents per minute for international calls within the ECOWAS zone, and 60 cents per minute for international calls to the rest of the world. Zain's SMS rates are 5 cents per text message between Zain subscribers, 15 cents per text message to other mobile subscribers, and 24 cents per text message to the rest of the world (Zain 2010).

REFERENCES

Agier, M. 1983. *Commerce et Sociabilité: Les Négociants Soudanais du Quartier Zongo de Lomé (Togo)*. Paris: OSTROM.

Castles, S., and M. Miller. 2009. *The Age of Migration: International Population Movements in the Modern World*. 4th ed. New York: Guilford Press.

Clifford, J. 1997. *Routes: Travel and Translation in the Late Twentieth Century*. Cambridge, Mass.: Harvard University Press.

Cohen, A. 1969. *Custom and Politics in Urban Africa: A Study of Hausa Migrants in Yoruba Towns*. Berkeley: University of California Press.

Cohen, R. 1997. *Global Diasporas: An Introduction*. London: University College London Press.

Idrissa, A. 2009. *The Invention of Order: Republican Codes and Islamic Law in Niger*. Ph.D. diss., University of Florida.

Jankowsky, R. 2001. "The Globalization of Music in Tunisia." Paper presented at Fulbright-Hays Seminars Abroad Program: The Challenges of Globalization in Morocco and Tunisia. Tunis.

Maghnia, A. 2001. "The Musical Tradition of the Gnaoua in the Age of World Music." Paper presented at Fulbright-Hays Seminars Abroad Program: The Challenges of Globalization in Morocco and Tunisia. Rabat.

Manger, L., and M. Assal. 2006. "Diasporas within and without Africa—Dynamism, Heterogeneity, Variation." In *Diasporas within and without Africa—Dynamism, Heterogeneity, Variation*, ed. L. Manger and M. Assal. Uppsala: Nordiska Afrikainstitutet.

Olivier de Sardan, J., et al. 2007. "Analyse rétrospective de la crise alimentaire au Niger en 2005." *Document de Travail* 45. Niamey: LASDEL and Paris: Agence Francaise de Développement.

Pellow, D. 2008. *Landlords and Lodgers: Socio-Spatial Organization in an Accra Community*. Chicago: University of Chicago Press.

République du Niger. 2010. *La Population du Niger en 2010*. Niamey: L'Institut National de la Statisque.

Rouse, R. 1991. "Mexican Migration and the Social Space of Postmodernism." *Diaspora* 1(1): 8–23.

Safran, W. 1991. "Diasporas in Modern Societies: Myths of Homeland and Return." *Diaspora* 1(1): 83–99.

Sanjek, R. 1991. "Rethinking Migration, Ancient to Future." *Global Networks* 3(3): 315–36.

Schildkrout, E. 1978. *People of the Zongo: The Transformation of Ethnic Identities in Ghana*. New York: Cambridge University Press.

Stoller, P. 1999. *Jaguar: A Story of Africans in America*. Chicago: University of Chicago Press.

———. 2002. *Money Has No Smell: The Africanization of New York City*. Chicago: University of Chicago Press.

Thomas, D. 2006. *Black France: Colonialism, Immigration, and Transnationalism*. Bloomington: Indiana University Press.

Toure, A. 1990. *Sacrifices dans la ville: le citadin chez le Devin en Cote d'Ivoire*. Abidjan and St. Maur: Editions Douga.

Works, J. A. Jr. 1976. *Pilgrims in a Strange Land: Hausa Communities in Chad.* New York: Columbia University Press.

World Bank. 2006. Migration and Remittances Factbook. Accessed February 9. www.worldbank.org/prospects/migrationandremittances.

Yamba, C. B. 1995. *Permanent Pilgrims: The Role of the Pilgrimage in the Lives of West African Muslims in Sudan.* Washington, D.C.: Smithsonian Institution Press.

Youngstedt, S. M. 2004a. "The New Nigerien Hausa Diaspora in the U.S.: Surviving and Building Community on the Margins of the Global Economy." *City and Society* 16(1): 39–67.

———. 2004b. "Creating Modernities through Conversation Groups: The Everyday Worlds of Hausa Migrants in Niamey, Niger." *African Studies Review* 47(3): 91–118.

———. 2004c. "Household Forms and Composition: Sub-Saharan Africa." In *Encyclopedia of Women and Islamic Cultures, Volume 2,* ed. S. Joseph. Leiden: Brill.

Zain. 2010. "Un Monde Merveileux." Accessed March 16, 2010. www.ne.zain.com.

8 STRANGERS ARE LIKE THE MIST

LANGUAGE IN THE PUSH AND PULL OF THE AFRICAN DIASPORA

PAUL STOLLER

> Yeow harandang no, nd'a a mana bia, a ga woyma.
> (Strangers are like the mist; if they haven't disappeared by
> the morning, they will surely be gone by afternoon.)
> —SONGHAY PROVERB

Issifi Mayaki is a stranger in New York City. Born in a small village near Tahoua in north central Niger, Issifi has lived in New York City for almost twenty years. He comes from a Hausa family of religious clerics who, besides having taught the Koran to the children of the village, have long been engaged in long distance commerce. As a young man Issifi left Niger and took up residence in Abidjan, Cote d'Ivoire, where his father taught him the trading business. He sold watches and traded kola nut. In time, he began to buy and sell African textiles—especially to American diplomats and Peace Corps volunteers. He set up a small African art shop at the Abidjan market. Having heard so much about America, he decided to seek his fortunes in New York City. And so he traveled to New York with a large and valuable inventory of antique cloth, which, due to a misunderstanding and a degree of naiveté, was stolen from him. Stuck in New York City without the resources to return to West Africa, he resiliently found an apartment, got an informal loan, and in no time at all found himself on 125th Street in Harlem, selling audiotapes and compact discs of popular music under the marquis of the Apollo Theatre. In time, he began to invest again in cloth, which he bought from West African suppliers (Stoller 2002). Issifi continues to sell cloth in Harlem. Because trading affords him a decent living, he wears fashionable clothing, uses a Blackberry, and drives a relatively new car—a good life in New York City.

When he came to the United States, Issifi left behind a wife and three children, who continue to live in his natal village near Tahoua. Now that cell phones are commonplace in rural Niger, Issifi speaks to his family once a week. He has not seen his father, mother, wife, or children in almost twenty years. Issifi also has had an American common-law wife, who has a child from a previous marriage. They lived as a family in a Harlem apartment until two years ago, when Issifi returned to the single life, complaining that an American woman could never understand an African man.

Issifi is tired of the complicated life of a stranger in New York City. In a recent conversation, he said he longed to give up "Western life" and return to Niger, where he would live simply and study the Koran. He said that in the United States he felt very much like a stranger and that sometime soon, like the mist, he would simply like to disappear and find himself at home.

Many people in Niger and Mali, in fact, like to say, "Strangers are like the mist; if they haven't disappeared by morning, they will surely be gone by afternoon." For any immigrant, the notion of "home" continuously pulls on his or her sensibilities. Like the patient suffering from a disease that has no cure, immigrants are often in a state of continuous liminality. In the liminality described by the late Victor Turner (1969), a person undergoing an initiation ritual is "betwixt and between, neither this nor that." Once a person is initiated, however, the liminal status ends and he or she rejoins society with a changed but clear-cut identity. No matter their legal status, professional standing, or educational level, most immigrants never fully escape their liminality. Like patients whose chronic illnesses are in remission, which places them forever between the end points of health and disease, most immigrants are continuously betwixt and between the poles of home and host country—caught in a vortex of conflicting desire and obligation. Indeed, even if they have been long settled in New York City, most of the West African immigrants I know continue to miss the smells, tastes, and sounds of home. Many of them pine for at-home, face-to-face conversations with friends and family. Are immigrants ever "home" in the host country? In the end, immigrants may well be like the mist. In time, they might dissipate into the air.

For almost twenty years I have followed a group of West African immigrants, mostly Songhay-Zarma and Hausa men from Niger as they migrated, settled, and worked in New York City as taxi drivers, security guards, grocery delivery men, and, like Issifi Mayaki, street vendors. Like most immigrants, these men are liminal figures. Although many of them call themselves "Les New Yorkais," they remain for the most part alienated. They say that they miss the quality of life in Niger, the smells, tastes, and sounds of their homeland. They say that "next year" they will return home. And yet they remain in New York City. Some have returned definitively to Niger only to return one year after their "permanent" departure. Many are now raising families in America. Their children, who know little about the cultural life of West Africa, speak English rather than Songhay or Hausa. Some want their children to visit Niger so they might be introduced to their ancestral language and culture and be exposed to social codes of "respect" for their elders. Given the pervasive power of American culture, they realize that these visits are no solution to the problem of language loss and cultural erosion. In the end, they all say that they want to return home. Considering their economic and social entanglements in America, can they simply return to Africa? Can they, like the mist, melt into the air?

It is clear that African immigrants are becoming more and more woven into the social and economic fabric of life in the United States. There are vibrant communities of Nigeriens in New York City and elsewhere. These rooted communities are now firmly established. They will not disappear tomorrow morning or afternoon. It is equally clear that the push and pull of immigrant life constructs a degree of sociocultural and linguistic alienation—especially so when diasporic communities deepen their roots in North American localities. Even though most of the West African immigrants I know have cell phones and are in regular contact with their loved ones at home, this contact has neither reduced significantly the sting of their liminality nor the stress of their alienation. In this essay, I discuss the linguistic, social, and cultural ramifications of this alienation and then suggest how academic institutions might reach out to African immigrants to ease the burden of continuous liminality and enrich the cultural life in their increasingly multi-generational communities.

THE PULL OF NORTH AMERICA

What factors have compelled thousands of francophone West Africans to travel to North America? In the past, many scholars have argued that repressive immigration policies gradually made France a less attractive destination. That is no doubt part of the story. Most scholars, however, seek a broader explanation. They believe that the increased migration of "third world" peoples, including West Africans, devolves from global restructuring. This restructuring has prompted the growth of multinational corporations, and, following David Harvey's analysis in *The Condition of Postmodernity* (1989), has imploded space and time. These alternations have encouraged the outplacement of manufacturing from the first to the third world, the outsourcing of industrial parts and business services, and the downsizing of corporate payrolls. The emergence of these global markets has brought on the feminization of the workforce in export processing zones, eroded large sectors of the American middle class, and propelled the rapid growth of informal economies (Kantner and Pittinsky 1996).

The neoliberal extension of economic forces has led less to the global integration of human and economic resources and more to the polarization of rich and poor. This polarization is strikingly evident in sub-Saharan Africa, in which the number of poor rose to an estimated 313 million people in 2001 (World Bank 2005). This disturbing statistic, which today, given the economic realities of "the Great Recession," no doubt underestimates the ever-growing polarization of rich and poor, nevertheless underscores the exponential growth of hunger and malnutrition in Africa.

New York City has been no stranger to the forces of economic polarization. As New York has become what Saskia Sassen (1991) has termed a "global city," the gulf between New York's rich and poor has widened considerably. New York has long been, in the words of John Mollenkopf (1991), a "dual city" of economic and spatial dislocations. This series of dislocations has created a space for the growth of such informal entrepreneurial activities as street vending.

The complex of social and economic forces compelled thousands of West Africans to come to North America. Those who arrived in New York City thought they might well be able to earn decent wages in the formal sector. After arriving they found out, not unlike Issifi Mayaki, that their lack of fluency in English, their limited technical skills, and unresolved immigration status made working in the formal sector a virtual impossibility. Facing this hard reality, many West Africans entered the unregulated informal economy.

The term informal sector has come to replace more pejorative terms like the black market and the underground economy, for what makes an activity informal is not its substance, the validity of the goods produced, the character of the labor force, or the site of production, but the fact that "it is unregulated by the institutions of society, in a legal and social environment in which similar activities are regulated" (Castells and Portes 1989: 12). The parent who purchases day care service without filling out social security forms, the unlicensed gypsy cab drivers who serve poor neighborhoods, the craftsperson building furniture in an area not zoned for manufacturing activity, the immigrant woman reading pap smears or sewing teddy bears in a poorly lit suburban garage, and the unlicensed African street vendor are all participating in the burgeoning informal economy that characterizes a global city like New York (Coombe and Stoller 1994: 252).

Despite the economic difficulties he confronted, Issifi Mayaki had little trouble adapting to the economic realties of a transnational space like New York City. Based upon his family's long involvement in the culture of trade, Issifi knew that the key to commercial success entailed a sense of economic anticipation—of trends and/or tastes—and a degree of flexibility. Using these longstanding skills, Issifi quickly understood what he could successfully sell in Harlem. And so he mounted his enterprise in Harlem, first on a sidewalk card table and later in a small shop in a market. As the years as passed by, he has become more and more comfortable with English and more and more adapted to the cultural peculiarities of living in the United States.

Although there is an emerging folklore about the outstanding commercial abilities of West African immigrants, the picture of their economic adaptation is a complex one (Millman 1997; Perry 1997). There are, indeed, many "success" stories like that of Issifi. Hundreds, if not thousands, of West Africans have come to places like New York City and made themselves a good life. In my view, however, there are just as many West African immigrants who have struggled economically in North America. My research in New York City suggests that language competence is the major factor in the capacity of West African immigrants to adapt to economic circumstances. A second factor, which goes hand in hand with linguistic capacity, is cultural competence—knowing the standards of behavior in a myriad of contexts. West African immigrants who speak relatively fluent English and who have established business relationships with non-African immigrants and with Americans have mounted successful enterprises. Those West African immigrants whose English is halting and who have limited social networks outside the African community have faced considerable economic difficulties (Stoller 2002; Stoller 2008). Some of these men, especially those immigrants over fifty years of age, have returned to West Africa and their families.

During the almost twenty-year period that I have been doing research among West African immigrants in New York City, a number of important changes have occurred. In the early 1990s most West African immigrants were single males, most of whom had left their families (parents, siblings, wives, and/or children) at home in Niger or Mali. To save money, these men often shared sub-standard apartments in the poorer neighborhoods of the Bronx, Harlem, or Brooklyn. Sometimes, they might even share a Single Room Occupancy (SRO) hotel room, as did Issifi Mayaki at the Hotel Belleclaire on the Upper West Side of Manhattan. Other men lived in what I have called "vertical villages," apartment buildings in which the vast majority of tenants hailed from West Africa. The communal ethos of the West African village helped to shape the life in these vertical communities, in which the men spent much of their time with one another at street markets or with their compatriots at home.

As time passed and they became accustomed to life in the United States, they gradually began to move into larger apartments with perhaps one roommate. The number of vertical villages declined and fewer West African immigrants lived communally in New York City. In time, West African immigrants extended their social and economic networks to non-African people in New York (Asians, West Indians, Latinos, and Americans). The process of integration had several important results. First, it provided an impetus for West African immigrants to improve their proficiency in English. Second, it enhanced West African competence in American culture. Third, it opened space for family life. In some cases, West African immigrants arranged for members of their family to come to New York City. Issifi Mayaki, for example, arranged for his brother to come and live with him in his Harlem apartment. In other cases, men would bring their wives and children to New York and set up households in Harlem or the Bronx. Some of these arriving women remained at home with their children. Some of them, however, took classes in professional schools, technical institutes, or local colleges. Some women established their own enterprises, including cloth shops, restaurants, and hair-braiding salons. In still other cases, West African immigrants married American women. In some of these transnational families, the West African men moved into households and, like Issifi Mayaki, became informal stepfathers. In other circumstances West African men have fathered, given their tradition of patrilineal descent, African children who happen to live in North America. In conversations with my friends in New York, I learned that family life brings them much pleasure, but also triggers a great deal of stress that adds to already embedded feelings of alienation.

ALIENATION AND THE PULL OF AFRICA

Almost all the West Africans I have known during my research in New York City have expressed feelings of alienation. As previously mentioned, even those immigrants who have established families in New York City or have regular cell phone conversations with their loved ones back home say that they often feel lonely, isolated, and misunderstood. Although degrees of alienation vary with an immigrant's capacity of social and cultural resilience, alienation, which has its roots in language use, cultural practices, and religious beliefs, has impacted the lives of most of my West African immigrant friends.

Consider language use. At the Malcolm Shabazz Market on 116th Street in Harlem, most of the shoppers speak English or Spanish. None of them have learned a West African language. This creates a considerable linguistic gulf between West African merchants and their North American buyers. Most of the West African merchants who sell at the Malcolm Shabazz Market speak English with varying degrees of competence. All of them know enough "market English" to sell their products. Some of them, as I have indicated, have a relatively sophisticated command of English, which enables them to build transnational trading networks in New York, which, in turn, empowers them to expand their enterprises. Traders like Issifi Mayaki attend night school, in his words, to learn to "speak English properly."

When the traders talk among themselves at the market they often speak Dyula, a major trade language in West Africa, which is derived from Bamana. If traders do not share a mutual African language, they converse in French. With members of their own ethnic group, of course, they speak Songhay, Hausa, Bamana, Fulani, or Wolof. Most of the market traders are multilingual. Boubé Mounkaila, a leather bag trader who is a principal character in my book *Money Has No Smell*, speaks Songhay, Hausa, Bamana-Dyula, French, some Wolof, and, of course, English. And so when North America buyers walk through the aisles of the Malcolm Shabazz Market, they enter a culturally alien space, a place where incomprehensible and strange sounding African languages are spoken. It is not unusual for English-speaking buyers to say, "What are those Africans saying about us?" as they briskly walk through the market.

Some visible cultural practices at the market also open up gulfs of misunderstanding. West African traders in Harlem think it is rude to eat alone. At lunch time, market goers are likely to see small groups of traders seated around a table. On the table is a container of rice onto which they pour a variety of sauces—*mafe*, sauce *feuille*—or they consume a pilaf like the Senegalese favorite *tchebudan*, which is resplendent with fish, vegetables, and scotch bonnet peppers. If a stranger wanders by, the traders will sometimes invite him or her to sit down, take a spoon, and eat—even if he or she is not hungry. If you refuse such an invitation, it can be an insult. When you eat a few mouthfuls of food, even if you are not hungry, you demonstrate respect. As a Songhay person would say upon receiving such an invitation to food: *ay a ka ga taba* (let me come and taste). With that the people in the group will smile and make room for their guest, who will then praise the wonders of tasty African food. For West Africans, eating is a fundamentally social act. It is a group activity. You never buy food for yourself; you buy for the group, however that group might be defined.

Market behaviors are also culturally contoured. Most of the West African merchants in New York City come from families and/or ethnic groups that have extensive histories of long distance trade. That is certainly the case for traders who are Hausa, Malinke, Soninke, and Wolof. These West African traders in New York City are beneficiaries of a longstanding culture of trade in which commercial activity is seen as a means of extending social ties. This is how trade languages developed in West Africa and why Bamana/Dyula and Hausa are such widely spoken languages. Following the logic of the culture of trade, one works hard to build social ties with trading partners and clients, and thus a climate of trust is created. In such a climate, you trust your "brother" trader with your goods. In such a climate, you extend credit without worry. In such a climate, you can leave your shop and know someone will look after it. In such a climate, you want to make money, but do not engage in cutthroat competition with traders who sell the same kinds of goods. If business is good, according to this logic, sufficient amounts of money will circulate through the network. If business is bad, traders can pool their resources and extend each other loans. In West Africa, there are two kinds of wealth. To be sure, there is wealth in goods and income, but there is also wealth in people. If you are part of a large network, you are protected. Your "brothers," both real and fictive, will look out for you. As the Songhay like to say: *kumba hinka ga charotarey numey* (it takes two hands to establish a friendship).

When strangers come to the Malcolm Shabazz Market they sometimes have trouble finding the owner of a particular business.

"Where's Mamadou?"
"He went downtown," Mamadou's friend might say.
"Are you the owner?"
"No. But I can sell you whatever you want."

Sometimes, this exchange might result in a sale. Often, it does not. North Americans, who often find it difficult to wean themselves from a competitive orientation to business, find it strange that in African markets, including, of course, the Malcolm Shabazz in Harlem, there are so many shops, so close together, in which virtually indistinguishable traders sell virtually indistinguishable goods at virtually the same price. "How can any of them make any money?" they often ask as they inspect the goods on display.

West African commercial values, which are often beautifully expressed in the idiomatic expressions and proverbs of African languages, also lead to misunderstanding, betrayal, and alienation, given that West Africans generally extend trust to their business partners and clients. Boubé Mounkaila used to park his van, which he filled with thousands of dollars of inventory, in a secure lot. One day the lot attendant, whom Boubé trusted, let thieves into the lot and Boubé lost his inventory. In another instance, Issifi Mayaki sent thousands of dollars of antique cloth to a Canadian merchant who then never paid him.

The West African culture of trade, then, seeks, sometimes at great cost, to enhance social relations. Talk, of course, is the glue of those social relations. At the market, traders make time to talk with one another. You often find them seated in small groups, a space of storytelling. When a visitor-client comes to the market, the traders would like him or her to engage in some conversation, tell some stories, and buy some merchandise. These desires are paths to the construction of social relationships. "There's always time for a good story," Boubé Mounkaila is fond of saying. When a person is leaving on a long trip, Songhay people will say to him or her: *Ni go g'iri fajaandi* (literally, "you will make us bored," which in its own way means "we'll miss your talk"). Then the same interlocutor will say: *kala ni kayan* (until your return), which keeps open the expectation that a social connection established through talk will remain strong and be once again reestablished upon the traveler's return. For many North Americans, these examples of "fellowship" seem antiquated—out of step with the turbo-charged pace of life in a place like New York City.

These different appreciations of time and talk can lead to further misunderstandings. Many West Africans see American society as socially impoverished. They say that Americans eat alone, run from place to place to keep "on schedule," and don't take time to talk with one another—especially if one doesn't have an appointment. Many North Americans see the West African penchant for taking time to visit one another and tell stories as a waste of time—a quaint practice of the "pre-modern" era.

Profound religious differences between West African immigrants and their North American neighbors also lead to cultural misunderstanding and social alienation. The vast majority of West African merchants in New York City are Muslims, a religion about which most North Americans are ill informed. For the West African merchants, Islam is central to their lives. They rise before sunrise to recite early morning prayers. They stop what they are doing four other times during the day to pray. During the month of Ramadan, they fast from dawn to sunset. They observe Muslim dietary and alcohol restrictions. They attempt to give to the poor. Many of them have made the pilgrimage to Mecca. "Islam," Issifi Mayaki likes to say, "is a difficult religion to follow." Given the centrality of prayer, Songhay people use these periods of spiritual reflection as markers of time:

"When can I see you, Halidou?"
"*Alula banda*" (after the first afternoon prayer).

Following 9/11, religion has played an even greater role in the West African immigrant identity and alienation. Traders often tell me how Americans simply do not understand the central themes of Islam. "They think," said Boubé Mounkaila, "that we are all terrorists."

Many of my friends think that Islam provides them an inner resilience that enables them to resist the considerable temptations of American social life. El Hadj Harouna Soulay, who once sold scarves and ski caps on Canal Street near Broadway, says that Islam makes him and his family strong. "My Muslim discipline gives me great strength to withstand America. I have been to Mecca. I give to the poor. I rise before dawn so that I can pray five times a day, everyday. I fast during the Ramadan. I avoid pork and alcohol. I honor the memory of my father and mother. I respect my wife. And even if I lose all of my money, if I am able, Inshallah, to live with my family, I will be truly blessed" (Stoller 2002: 166).

These socio-religious distinctions, of course, can lead to social problems, especially if we consider gender expectations. Many of the traders complain about their social relations with American women. Before he settled down for a time with a common-law American wife, Issifi had several relationships in which differing gender expectations sparked conflict. "You know how it is," Issifi said. "There are many differences between African and American women. Two different cultures." In this conversation Issifi said that in Africa, men could do pretty much what they wanted. African women, he asserted, make few demands on their husbands. Wives don't usually question the husband's behavior or decisions. "I respect my wife and she respects me," he said, "but she doesn't consume me. . . . Here," Issifi said, shaking his head, "they want to own you, to control your life. And they're jealous" (Stoller 2002: 3–4). These attitudes eventually doomed Issifi's relationship with his African American female companion. In the end, many of the male traders believe that American women cannot accept that in Islam, a man can have four wives, that the life of a woman in West Africa is more constrained than the life of a woman in the United States.

As should be evident, profound social and cultural differences, in addition to often tenuous legal and financial situations, have led to the social and cultural alienation of many if not most West African immigrants living in New York City. Feelings of loneliness and alienation compel them to yearn for life "at home" with their "families" in West Africa. By the same token, many West African immigrants have established families to confront these problems of isolation and alienation. This tack, as we shall see, is only a partial solution to the problem of transnational alienation in the United States. As their roots grow deeper and deeper in American soil the pull of Africa doesn't disappear, but economic, social, and cultural conditions may diminish some of its force.

WEST AFRICAN SOCIAL LIFE IN NEW YORK CITY

In May 2000 I attended a meeting of concerned African parents in an auditorium in one of the suburbs of Paris. The parents and elders, most of whom were Soninke and Bamana from Mali, expressed genuine concern about their teen-aged children.

"They have no jobs and no hope," one man said.

"They wander the streets in gangs and get into trouble," a woman said.

"They speak French slang and we can't understand them. They don't speak our languages," another woman complained.

An older man rose, and from the hush in the room it was clear that he was an elder who commanded community respect. "They are lost to us," he said. "They don't speak our words. They don't think our thoughts. They don't share our values. They are lost souls. May God help them."

Five years later these "lost souls," which included North African and West African youth, all French citizens, burst upon the international stage when they rioted in suburban Paris streets:

> The rioters feel alienated from French police, judges, prosecutors, defense attorneys and social workers in part because minorities are still underrepresented in all these fields. Many of them have friends and family who experienced police abuse: use of excessive force, racist insults, recurrent identity checks, unwarranted arrests. . . . The fires set in France are a reminder that blacks and Arabs, in contrast to white adolescents, are youth whose masculinity and attitude is a threat. They are expressing their powerlessness, venting their anger and serving a long overdue notice on French society, a cry that well may have global resonance. (Terrio 2006: 4–5)

Clearly, the North African and West African teenagers are alienated politically from a French society, which, in theory, embraces an all-encompassing fraternity but in practice exercises a pernicious discrimination. Many commentators, however, have not thoroughly discussed the cultural alienation of these youth. They are neither French or North African nor West African. Having "lost" their home language and culture, they are, in the words of the Soninke elder, "lost souls."

The social conditions of the West African diaspora in New York City are far different from those in France. In many respects, West Africans and North Africans in France are far more entangled in French society. Many of these French residents have lived in France for more than a generation. The children of these families, many of whom are adolescents, are French citizens who speak French, but not the African languages of their parents. Many of these children have never been to West Africa or North Africa and have little desire to visit. This set of circumstances has prompted a kind of linguistic and cultural vacuum that led to the deep alienation that triggered the 2005 youth riots in suburbs of the major cities of France.

In New York City, by contrast, West African families so far seem less entrenched in American society, which, unlike France, seems to more readily acknowledge, if not understand, linguistic and cultural difference. In America, adult traders, who are and will forever remain immigrants in the United States, have expressed feelings of deep-seated alienation. The children of the traders, most of whom are quite young, have not, by contrast, articulated any sense of social or cultural frustration. What's more, the texture of this alienation has not resulted in the explosion of West African anti-social violence in New York City.

If anything, West Africans are increasingly the targets of anti-social and xenophobic violence that is sometimes generated by linguistic and cultural ignorance. Who can forget the tragic murders of Amadou Diallo and Ousmane Zongo? The latter man, known as the "mask doctor," worked at "The Warehouse" in the Chelsea section of Manhattan, a field site for my research on the trade in African art that I conducted between 1999 and 2003. Other West African immigrants have been periodically robbed or, worse yet, killed on the streets of New York. While some of these tragic acts can be attributed to the arbitrary nature of sporadic street crime, there have been incidents that express a kind of cultural hatred of West Africans. Take the tragic case of Ali Kamara, who in August 2005 was beaten to death—perhaps with a baseball bat—on a Harlem sidewalk. "Two African-American men are believed to have taunted Kamara, asking him to kill a cockroach on the street because he 'lived with animals over there in Africa,' said Diakite Aboubacar, a friend of the victim. When Kamara refused he was attacked" (Tornkvist 2005: 2).

There are, then, profound social costs that linguistic and cultural ignorance can exact. At the very least, it triggers a sense of alienation that compels West Africans to feel isolated, misunderstood, and lonely. Linguistic and cultural ignorance, however, can sometimes trigger tragic events as in the cases of Amadou Diallo, who was senselessly shot as he tried to show the police his papers, or of Ousmane Zongo, who, when confronted by undercover detectives, fled his oppressors and was shot to death, or Ali Kamara, who was killed for maintaining his cultural dignity.

Despite these social and culture tensions, the economic necessities of a global economy, the forces of which continue to expand the gulf between rich and poor, compel a steady flow of West Africans who immigrate to New York City. The benefits of an even depressed New York City economy seem to outweigh the social and cultural and psychological costs of the street.

As mentioned at the outset of this essay, increasing numbers of the traders have recently established families in New York City. Some of these families are uniquely West African; other families reflect the transnational nature of contemporary urban spaces. And so there are families with West African fathers or African American or Anglo mothers who have "cosmopolitan" children. In one family, a man from Niger lives with a woman from Japan. They have two children, a seven-year-old girl and a five-year-old boy. His children speak English and know little, if anything, of their West African heritage. The father wants to send them "home" to Niger, but he doesn't know when he'll be able to do so. "They should speak my language," he says. "I want them to know our way of life. I want them to learn respect for their elders. They won't get that here." Will these young children grow up to be "lost souls"?

ACADEMIC OBLIGATION

During my time in Niger I had the great privilege to sit with and listen to the late Adamu Jenitongo, a famous sorcerer who lived in Tillaberi, a town on the banks of the Niger River 120 kilometers north of Niger's capital, Niamey. Over a period of almost twenty years, I learned a great deal form this man. He never lectured me; rather, he taught by example. Over the years I observed how he conducted himself and, in time, the seeds of truth he planted in my being germinated and grew to maturity. He taught me that the education of a *sohanci* (sorcerer) consisted of three stages. At the beginning novices memorized incantations, learned how to mix herbal medicines, and witnessed scores of healing rituals. After many years of quiet observation and intense memorization, novices became apprentices to senior figures. In time, the elders gave their apprentices more and more responsibility. If an apprentice demonstrated a deep resilience, then he or she would be introduced to the great secrets and would eventually become master sorcerers. The masters, of course, became the spiritual guardians of their communities and would use their knowledge to preserve the harmony of their villages. But the ultimate responsibility of the master was not to demonstrate her or his power, but to pass precious knowledge on to the next generation (Stoller 2004, 2007, 2008).

The same set of principles, I think, should be applied to the academy. What is the purpose of our work? Why study Songhay sorcery, Bamana social change, or Wolof exchange networks? Why write about the semantic categories of African languages? If he were here, Adamu Jenitongo would probably say: "Once you have mastered your work, you pass your knowledge on to the next generation." Extending this insight to the academy, we could say that our purpose is to produce knowledge that will improve the quality of life—the classic definition of wisdom.

Put in more practical terms, academics, including scholars of African language and culture, have, in my view, the obligation (1) to extend their knowledge to their communities and (2) to advocate for the peoples they have written about in their scholarly works. For example, there is a wealth of knowledge, practices, and, indeed, wisdom embedded in African language and culture. This rich and nuanced body of knowledge needs to be communicated to the wider public to help to reduce cultural misunderstanding that feeds the cross-cultural ignorance that sometimes results in violent acts. This same knowledge can reach an increasing number of African children and teenagers in the United States. Will they become "lost" like their brothers and sisters in France? Or will they find another path?

Like the master sorcerer, scholars of African language and culture can follow the wise path of Adamu Jenitongo and extend their wisdom to the next generation. In so doing, we will help to refine knowledge of the African language and culture. In so doing, we will help to improve the quality of social life in diasporic communities. African immigrants in America are no longer strangers who will soon dissipate like the mist, which means that the challenge is to embed the precious knowledge of African language and culture in new soil, a precious knowledge that will root as deeply and strongly as the sturdiest desert palm tree.

More concretely, scholars of the African diaspora, who are well versed in the legal trials and social tribulations of immigration policy, should become players in the public discourse of the immigration debate, a discourse filled with myths and inaccuracies that vilify immigrants, including people who left West Africa to follow the twists and turns of the immigrant life in New York City. Given the climate of contemporary debate about immigration, Africanists might want to follow the lead of an increasing number of public anthropologists who advocate directly for the populations among whom they have lived (Low and Merry 2010).

REFERENCES

Castells, M., and A. Portes. 1989. "World Underneath: The Origins, Dynamics and Effects of the Informal Economy." In *The Informal Economy: Studies in Advanced and Less Developed Countries*, ed. A. Portes, M. Castells, and L. Benton. Baltimore: Johns Hopkins University Press.
Coombe, R. J., and P. Stoller. 1994. "X Marks the Spot: The Ambiguities of African Trading in the Commerce of the Black Public Sphere." *Public Culture* 15: 249–79.
Harvey, D. 1989. *The Condition of Postmodernity*. London: Blackwell.
Kantner, R. M., and T. L. Pittinsky. 1996. "Globalization: New Worlds for Social Inquiry." *Berkeley Journal of Sociology* 40: 1–21.
Low, S., and S. E. Merry. 2010. "Engaged Anthropology: Diversity and Dilemmas: An Introduction to Supplement 2." *Current Anthropology* 51(S2): 203–26.
Millman, J. 1997. *The Other Americans: How Immigrants Renew Our Country, Our Economy, and Our Values*. New York: Viking.

Mollenkopf, J., and M. Castells, eds. 1991. *The Dual City: Restructuring New York*. New York: Russell Sage.

Perry, D. 1997. "Rural Ideologies and Urban Imaginings: Wolof Immigrants in New York City." *Africa Today* 44(2): 229–60.

Sassen, S. 1991. *The Global City: New York, London, Tokyo*. Princeton, N.J.: Princeton University Press.

Stoller, P. 2002. *Money Has No Smell: The Africanization of New York City*. Chicago: University of Chicago Press.

———. 2004. *Stranger in the Village of the Sick: A Memoir of Cancer, Sorcery and Healing*. Boston: Beacon Press.

———. 2007. "Embodying Knowledge: Finding a Path in the Village of the Sick." In *Ways of Knowing*, ed. M. Harris. London: Bergdahl.

———. 2008. *The Power of the Between: And Anthropological Odyssey*. Chicago: University of Chicago Press.

Terrio, S. 2006. "Who Are the Rioters in France?" *Anthropology News* 47(1): 4–5.

Tornkvist, A. 2005. "Kamara Murder." Columbia School of Journalism, September 22.

World Bank. 2005. *World Development Indicators 2005*. Washington, D.C.: The World Bank.

9

TOWARD A CHRISTIAN DISNEYLAND?

NEGOTIATING SPACE AND IDENTITY IN THE NEW AFRICAN RELIGIOUS DIASPORA

AFE ADOGAME

On July 17, 2005, under the headline "African Church Plans Christian Disneyland," Scott Farwell of the *Dallas Morning News* reported that "the Redeemed Christian Church of God—Africa's largest and most ambitious evangelical church—plans to build a 10,000-seat sanctuary, two elementary school-size lecture centers, a dormitory, several cottages, a lake and a Christian-themed water park in Floyd, Texas."[1] The description of the gigantic development project as a "Christian Disneyland"[2] came from one of the church's senior pastors, though its meaning is ambiguous.

In addition, the concept of a Christian Disneyland of course evokes the famous American theme park in Anaheim, California, built and marketed as "the happiest place on Earth."[3] Walt Disney's words at its dedication ceremony on July 17, 1955, are quite instructive: "To all who come to this happy place—welcome. Disneyland is your land. Here age relives fond memories of the past and here youth may savor the challenge and promise of the future. Disneyland is dedicated to the ideals, the dreams, and the hard facts that have created America . . . with the hope that it will be a source of joy and inspiration to all the world." Occupying over 160 acres, Disneyland has now been replicated as Disney World (in Florida), Tokyo Disneyland, and Euro Disneyland (now called Disneyland Paris).[4] That Farwell's article appeared on the fiftieth anniversary of Disneyland's official opening is striking given that the original Disneyland in Anaheim and the under-construction North American Redemption Camp of the Redeemed Christian Church of God (RCCG) in Texas will boast extensive acres of domesticated landscapes and a myriad of facilities. Such wide-ranging attractions are important for leisure and tourism, but they also partly carry religious, spiritual, ecological, and social import. Beneath the façade of aesthetics within these facilities lie crucial negotiations that have been enacted via layers of economics, culture, religion, and identity. I contend that place-making processes and space reproduction or appropriation rarely operate in a social vacuum; they are often entangled in the intricate politics of negotiation by different actors, including policymakers, social/cultural/political pressure groups, and local interests; and they are conditioned by a multiplicity of local, contextual, and global factors. In the case of minority groupings—diaspora and new immigrant religious communities in particular—the dynamics of such concerns as power and identity, which often shape emplacements and the invention of new ritual places in host geo-cultural contexts, are essential to understanding the politics of belonging, place-making, and translocality.

This chapter teases out some inherent complexities that may anchor processes of religious place-making in translocal contexts. Drawing upon recent religious ethnography, the chapter maps the growth dynamics and religious mobility of African churches in Europe and North America, as well as their gradual insertion within religious maps of the universe, discernible in their construction of religious geographies. I explore how and to what extent they are creating new identities through sacred space reproduction and religious place-making processes. I argue that place-making is, in actual fact, a strategy toward public self-positioning, a mark of location in local-global maps of the universe; but also that mediated space and new media appropriation is indeed a process of emplacement, albeit a local-global, virtual one. Although this chapter draws its examples specifically from African immigrant religious communities, it does not in any way suggest that such politics of negotiation are peculiar to them. In fact, such negotiated politics are characteristic of minority, immigrant (religious) groupings quest toward (religious) place-making in new host geo-cultural contexts, as the example below demonstrates.

With the caption "No minarets, but a place to pray—Athens factory gets spiritual makeover" (*International Herald Tribune*, July 5, 2007), Niki Kitsantonis drew public attention to the fact that the burgeoning Muslim community in Athens had lobbied the Greek authorities for several years, without success, to build them a house of worship. But quite unprecedentedly, Muslim worshippers in the meantime found a temporary solution, "a converted factory in the city's southern outskirts." As he reports, "Initiatives by successive governments to build a new mosque in the capital ran into objections from the Orthodox Church and protests from citizens who associate mosques with four centuries of subjugation under the Ottoman Empire and political rivalry with Turkey, Greece's Muslim neighbor." As a 2007 survey of 1,500 Athenians disclosed, "More than half of Athen's five million residents oppose to the creation of a mosque to serve the Muslim immigrant community, which numbers about 500,000." Although our scope here is neither Muslim communities nor any specific focus on

Greece, this interesting report best eulogizes the politics of religious emplacement that often confronts immigrant religious communities, particularly in Europe and the United States, as I attempt to illustrate below.

Space (religious) contestations are far from limited to any host immigrant contexts. They occur in original homeland contexts as well, although such emplacement politics manifest differently and are shaped by specific local and/or global conditions and realities. The history of religious politics in Nigeria is one that is undoubtedly characterized by complex, controversial issues of a wide-ranging nature. Religion often assumes a matter of political significance and unprecedented tension in Nigeria owing to its pluriformity and inherent ambivalences (Adogame 2004b). There is remarkable evidence of religious expansion and resurgence within Christianity and Islam, but also in forms of indigenous and exogenous religions.

Increasing religious mobility, diversity, and incessant religious violence and conflict raise crucial issues regarding the shaping, (re-)construction, and (re-)negotiation of boundaries between and within religious groups in Nigeria (Adogame 2010c: 489). Contestation intensifies religious self-definitions that in turn thicken and escalate conflict. Religious tension and violence in Nigeria have a clear connection with the proliferation of uncompromising Muslim and Christian activism, a relationship that has led to a growing culture of religious violence, particularly in northern Nigeria (Adogame 2004b, 2010c).

Petitions, complaints, and allegations, by Christians and church organizations, about instances of discrimination and marginalization have escalated with the declaration of Sharia criminal law in virtually all northern Nigerian states. Such petitions vary: systematic denial and/or difficulties in obtaining land and accommodation for religious purposes; delays in securing permission to build churches; the non-appointment of Christians to political offices; and alleged demolition of church buildings on the pretext that they were illegally constructed. Christians also petition the government over the use of state media and denial of airtime in state radios, discrimination in public schools, and the use of public facilities for religious purposes (Kukah 1993, 2003; Falola 1998). The allegations also suggest a systematic clampdown on freedom of religious expression or a conscripted space for Christian evangelism. In states like Kano, Zamfara, and Sokoto there are reported cases of cancellation of initial land allocations and demolition of religious buildings on the grounds that they were illegally built in originally residential plots.

Thus, in northern Nigeria, the contestation of power and religious space, particularly between Christians and Muslims, has generated an atmosphere of mutual distrust and suspicion, thus challenging religious freedom and tolerance and hampering any meaningful interfaith dialogue and coexistence. It is important to mention that this unhealthy tension between Christianity and Islam is less volatile in southern, western, and eastern Nigeria, where the relationship appears to be more cordial. In these parts of the country, religious space emplacements play out fairly differently with more proven indices of religious freedom and tolerance. In such a scenario, the mobility and spread of the two churches, RCCG and the Kingsway International Christian Center (KICC), is more remarkable and far-reaching. Besides, the leaders of both churches hail from southwest Nigeria, thus also accounting for their huge concentration of branches and demographic spread in contrast to northern Nigeria. The above suggests the complexity of religious place-making processes even within a specific national polity.

RECONCEPTUALIZING SPACE, RETHINKING PLACE?

The theory and interpretation of space, place, and spatial identity have remained contentious in socio-scientific discourses. Nevertheless, Doreen Massey's reconceptualization of place aptly critiques essentialized notions that places are stable, static, and unchanging and inherently enable the enactment of history within them.[5] Her analysis of contemporary society illuminates the significance of space and spatial relationships where places are processes and not enclosures with a clear inside and outside, but characterized by multiple identities. A "locale" in Massey's (1993: 148ff.) understanding of localities is not a bounded entity but one that evolves as a network of social relations and practices. She rightly perceives "localities" as "articulated moments," as constructions out of the intersections and interactions of concrete social relations and social processes in a situation of co-presence (Massey 1991: 277). Thus, localities are dynamic, always in the making, and often contested. Localities are significant in maintaining cultural resilience and difference, but can also be sites of cultural mixing, synthesis, and transformation. In the face of movements and intermixing that now characterize space-time compression and discourses around the global village, can we still decipher any sense of a local place and its peculiarity? Social scientists should pay closer attention to the ways in which the uniqueness of a particular locality modifies and transforms wider economic, social, political, cultural, and religious trends in space-time.

The dynamics of emplacement and the politics of religious place-making needs to be understood against the backdrop of the sense of place and its variables of legibility, the perception of and preference for the visual environment and the compatibility of the setting with human purposes. Thus, a conceptualization of sense of place for which places are not merely objects but objects for subjects is expedient.[6] Such a progressive or global sense of place includes a consciousness of its links with the wider world, which integrates in a positive way the global and the local (Massey 1994). There are real relations with real content—economic, political, cultural, and religious—between any local space and the wider world in which it is set. It is a sense of place, an understanding of "its character," as Massey argues, which can only be constructed by linking that place to places beyond. She concludes, in fact, that "what we need is a global sense of the local, a global sense of place."

In another vein, the sense of place is often a reflection of places that lack a sense of place, sometimes referred to as placeless or inauthentic. Placeless landscapes could be perceived to have no special relationship to the places in which they are located—they could be anywhere (Augé 1995). Augé coined the term "non-place" to refer to places of transience such as motorways, hotel rooms, airports, supermarkets, or the spaces before computers, TVs, and cash machines that do not hold enough significance to be regarded as places. With this in view, he maps the distinction between place—encrusted with historical monuments and creative social life—and non-place—to which individuals are connected in a uniform manner and where no organic social life is possible. For Augé, a non-place comes into existence when human beings do not recognize themselves in it. Non-places begin with uprootedness; they provide the "passive joys of identity loss." While anthropological places create the organically social, so non-places create solitary contractuality. Thus a space that cannot be defined as relational, historical, or concerned with identity will be a non-place, and these non-places are the real measure of our time (Augé 1995: 77–79).

In actual fact, migration, travel, and mobility have the potential to create what Massey calls a "global place," a sense of globalization whereby place is put into the context of other places and experiences, in contrast to the context of its own history. Thus, Massey's repositioning of space, spatial identities, and the sense of place and identity are integral in this chapter to our understanding of the politics of religious emplacement and place-making processes that inform how African-led Pentecostal churches such as the RCCG and the KICC are negotiating ritual, geographic, mediated, and virtual spaces in translocal contexts. In an interesting essay, Krause draws useful insights from Massey's understanding of localities in exploring transnational African churches in the Lea Valley industrial park of North East London (Krause 2008). In this essay she interrogates ways in which place-making involves finding one's place within a specific spatial-political situation; the (non)engagement with the place as a social place; how space is appropriated through aesthetic and ritual practices; but also how spatial meaning is created within the Destiny Changing Church in North East London.

MAPPING NEW RELIGIOUS GEOGRAPHIES OF PLACE

Elsewhere (Adogame 2004a, 2005, 2007, 2010b, 2010d), I have demonstrated instances of how African-led churches are gradually inserting themselves into new geo-cultural spaces through the construction and reproduction of religious geographies. Integral to religious place-making processes, some African-led churches in Europe and the United States have grown to acquire immense properties and real estate. In many large cities such as London, Hamburg, Paris, Cologne, Amsterdam, Berlin, New York, Chicago, and Dallas, erstwhile warehouses, abandoned church buildings, cinemas, disco halls, and pubs have been acquired at huge financial costs. What is being witnessed is the acquisition and renegotiation of space, whereby "desecrated space" due to "worldly" activities is taken over and resacralized for ritual ends. There are further examples of new African-led churches in the diaspora that have erected buildings of their own or those that currently lease and use hotel premises as temporary ritual space pending the acquisition of more permanent places. Business centers, lodging and accommodation facilities, religious book centers, guidance and counseling units, recreation and rehabilitation centers, cyber cafés and computer training centers, musical halls, music and video shops, and shopping malls are also owned by these churches. Thus, some African-led churches in Europe and the United States appropriate and use non-places (hotels, pubs, cinema, community centers) as places of transcience since they cannot acquire spaces or religious places or historical monuments, even though many have become desolate.

The relevance of African-led churches is not only located in the unique expression of African Christianity they exhibit; they also constitute international ministries and groups that have implications on a global scale. The impact and import of the exportation of African-led churches, driven by a vision of winning converts, is that it offers a unique opportunity to analyze its impact at local levels such as in diaspora. Many African-led churches are increasingly taking up extra-religious functions such as social welfare programs. Thus, their focus is not only the spiritual wealth of members but their social, material, and psychological well-being as well. Beyond their church vicinity, they have taken up functions such as assisting drug-ridden youths, the socially displaced, the underprivileged, refugees, and asylum seekers (Adogame 2005).

The social anatomy of African-led churches is complex and variegated. A majority of the membership are not illiterate, but rather elites of their countries or those who have ventured out in search for the "golden fleece." In most recent times, the membership has been characterized by skilled and unskilled factory workers, the unemployed, asylum seekers, and refugees. Thus, these religious communities largely remain the locus of identity, community, and security for African immigrants. They have come to fill a spiritual vacuum and offer "a home away from home" for many disenchanted Africans; they have also become avenues where people can go to feel important and valued. Irrespective of member's cultural backgrounds, a sense of belonging and community is rekindled in the church and a kind of religious and ethnic identity is also engendered through the process.

In this chapter I further demonstrate ways in which African-led churches are creating new spatial identities through religious place-making processes and what local responses and land politics such processes elicit. In this way, we can better understand the interconnectedness between social contexts in which space is (re)produced and the contextual factors that shape it. Two of several examples will suffice here.

The Nigerian-born Muslim-turned-pastor Matthew Ashimolowo established the KICC in 1992 with an initial membership of 200 adults and 100 children. KICC's international headquarters in East London is now believed to be the largest single Pentecostal congregation in London, with attendance of about 3,000 in each of the three scheduled Sunday worship services (cynically described as having "the largest church building in the UK in terms of bums on pews").[7] It is arguably one of the fastest growing African-led churches in Europe. KICC has gradually spread within the South East Region of England with branches in Wimbledon, Wembley, Hackney (Darnley Road), Luton, and Birmingham. KICC Sunday chapels are also located in southeastern England locales such as in Ashford, Bedford, Croydon, Dagenham, Edmonton, Finchley, Grays, Downage, Surbiton, Milton Keynes, Thamesmead, Tooting, Wood Green, and Richmond.[8] Beyond the United Kingdom, the church has also spread by establishing branches in the founder's home country of Nigeria and in Ghana.

In August 1998, KICC moved to 57 Waterden Road in Hackney Wick, a 9.5 acre-facility named the Miracle Centre that has a 4,000-seat auditorium and parking for more than 1,000 cars. The church had further proposed to build "a 10,000-seater arena that is to be the first of its kind in Europe . . . a 5,000 seater church building and a four floor office—a state-of-the art facility providing: 5,000 seats for worship, 1,000 place children's church, 600 place teenage church, a counselling and prayer centre, class rooms for bible school, 100-place nursery, 400-seat restaurant, a fully equipped gym. A place for the total healing of the total man and the total nation."[9] KICC's plans to redevelop its existing site, a converted warehouse, were allegedly rebuffed by the Borough of Hackney Council partly on grounds that it was inconsistent with the vision for the Lower Lea Valley regeneration area.[10] The site redevelopment proposal in East London was, however, truncated by the unprecedented earmark of its London Hackney site in the Olympic zone, to make way for the 2012 Olympic Games.[11] KICC's expansionist relocation plans and the planned construction of a multidimensional, mega-church project have been largely marred by local politics of emplacement. While the intricacies of these negotiation politics go beyond the purview of this chapter, it nevertheless provides some glimpses of how local, contextual factors often shape place-making processes—especially those connected with immigrant, minority groups. Quite ironically, the success of the 2012 Olympic bid provided an added impetus for spatial relocation and gentrification in the London metropolis. The industrial brownfield site Beam Reach became the most prominent site and target for relocation.[12] Consequently, the Olympic Delivery Authority (ODA) and the London Development Agency (LDA) supported KICC in its plan to redevelop and turn the site of Beam Reach, Havering, into its "permanent new home."[13]

Thus in July 2007, KICC and LDA submitted a full planning application toward the acquisition of "Plots 10–12, Off Consul Avenue and Manor Way Beam Reach 5 Rainham, Essex" for "a phased mixed-use development for temporary and permanent accommodation, uses and works comprising, an 8000 seat multi-use auditorium (13,750sqm gross floor space on two levels), four storey office, four storey multi-use building, chapel, multi-storey car park, new access and landscaping."[14] As Stuart Watson reports,

> For years, the London Development Agency's flagship industrial scheme in Rainham has languished, tenantless and unloved. But now it has chosen as the location for two highly controversial buildings: London's biggest church and a huge new prison. The Agency would like to be on the side of the angels and has supported the relocation of Kingsway International Christian Centre from its site in the Olympic zone, despite local misgivings. It is far less keen on the Home Office's proposal for a 1,500-offender category B prison that would house the second most dangerous type of inmates, including murderers and rapists.[15]

Nevertheless, this joint planning application from KICC and LDA for a £70 million, 8,000 seat mega-church project was refused by the London Thames Gateway Development Corporation's Planning Committee (LTGDC) on February 22, 2008.[16] As the LTGDC explained its verdict on its website:

> The proposed development on a 13.5 acre site including a 500-seat chapel, 8,000-seat auditorium, office building, 1,000-seat multi-use building, and multi-storey car park for 1200 cars plus cycles and motorcycles is part of land already allocated for high quality manufac-

turing known as the Beam Reach 5 Business Park. . . . Following extensive stakeholder and public consultation and a very detailed analysis of the various key issues, including the justification put forward by the applicants for their scheme, the planning committee took the decision to refuse the application. It was concluded that a combination of the designated use of the site for employment uses, serious concerns over the plans to get people to and from the site by both cars and public and private bus services and the extent to which a community facility for the local community would be provided justified refusal. There were significant concerns about the ability of the applicants to get the large numbers of people involved to and from the site, both for KICC events and other events, whilst not being too dependent on private vehicles. This was seen as affecting the ability of the local transport infrastructure to cope with a sudden increase in traffic movements. With limited public transport, overspill parking and an increase in carbon emissions from large numbers of visitors traveling into the area, the development would negatively impact on local residents. The committee also concluded that the lack of public transport means that the site is not appropriate for a community facility.[17]

Ostensibly in a bid to further justify its decision, Councilor Conor McAuley, chair of the LTGDC planning committee, reiterated the corporation's modus operandi in which he contended that the Development Corporation has an important role to play in developing sustainable regeneration programs across the London Thames Gateway. He argued that while the applicants submitted a comprehensive proposal for developing this employment site, it is important that this be evaluated as part of established proposals for the area and the sustainability of the proposals in transport terms. Thus, he concluded, "after serious consideration, the planning committee felt that concerns over the effectiveness of the proposals to get people to and from the site, the conflict with the planning policy land use allocated for the site, and the impact on the local community outweighed the exceptional use that the applicant sought to argue in favor of the proposal."[18]

Although Beam Reach, as an industrial development area located on the borders of Dagenham and Rainham, has poor public transport access, public concerns were raised over increased traffic in the area in a controversial manner.[19] Local authorities and the community remain ambivalent about relocation to Beam Reach in spite of KICC's promises to continue to contribute to local charities and carry out local community work, and its planned adoption of a comprehensive "green travel plan" that would include a fleet of minibuses for commuting members and visitors to the church.[20] Reacting to the development, the church, through its chief executive officer, Dapo Oluyomi, expressed "extreme disappointment" at the corporation's action:

> The meeting of the Thames Gateway Development Corporation planning committee on 14th February was at the same time an uplifting and extremely disappointing event for everyone at KICC. Hundreds of our members who live in the Rainham area turned out to show their support in a positive and dignified manner. . . . This decision flies in the face of the wide-ranging support for our plans. The community has backed us with over 16,000 signatures to petitions or letters of support sent to the London Borough of Havering and the Thames Gateway Development Corporation. KICC's proposals for addressing the transport of our members to and from the site were developed in consultation with Transport for London and the Highways Agency who have not objected, particularly in the light of our proven track record in this area. Support also came from bodies such as the Greater London Authority which recognizes KICC's plans both in benefiting the local community and meeting a strategic and unique need.[21]

The LTGDC's refusal generated further controversy as portrayed by the media, but also attracted sympathies and protests from local publics. The Christian Choice councilor Alan Craig, leader of the Christian Peoples Alliance (CPA) and CPA councilors on Newham Borough Council in London, and the London mayoral candidate for the Christian Choice ticket described LTGDC's decision to reject plans to build an 8,000-seat Pentecostal church in Havering:

> As a direct result of Machiavellian maneuvering by Ken Livingstone's London Development Agency . . . the LDA is knowingly culpable, they have deliberately left this thriving large church swinging in the wind with no permanent home and no prospect but to appeal to the government to overturn this unjust decision. It's appalling, especially given there were no legitimate planning reasons to refuse the application. It is also a perfect illustration of the authorities' *prejudice against Christianity* [emphasis added]. If KICC was an entertainment complex, you can be sure they would have been treated more sympathetically—especially if its management was *white*. The LDA has failed to deliver on its promises and has simply out-maneuvered the church in order to get the Hackney land. Church-goers in London have to wake up and smell the coffee. They can give their verdict at the May 1st London elections, when just 5% will win a seat

on the London Assembly. Our aim as the Christian Choice is to be a strong team at the political negotiating table, fighting in the GLA to voice Christian concerns on a range of issues of importance to all Londoners.[22]

The above statement is undoubtedly controversial in several respects and evokes nuances of a religious, political, and ideological nature that can be further unpacked and analyzed. An aspect of the above statement strikes a local politics chord and a race discourse. It also resonates with a cross-section of the British public's impression of discrimination against Christianity, which is a feature of ongoing secularization process in Britain.[23] Nevertheless, it portrays how this singular decision has been contested by KICC, religious organizations, and a cross-section of the public that was sympathetic to its cause.

On September 18, 2008, KICC and the LDA lodged a planning application appeal to the London Borough of Havering.[24] Pending the determination of the appeal, the KICC is currently worshipping in temporary premises in Walthamstow (Waltham Forest), holding six services every Sunday, having been obliged to move from their Hackney Wick site to make way for the 2012 Olympics. Although KICC has so far been served enforcement notices against the use of a major gateway site in the Lower Lea Valley in East London, the church through its town planning consulting agency—Rapleys LLP—successfully appealed against the issue of an Enforcement Notice by securing a significant extension in the compliance period, sufficient to allow KICC to find alternate premises and negotiate with relevant public bodies to acquire the site to commence construction of the Olympic Park.[25]

Another instance of an African-led church that is increasingly reshaping its religious geography is the RCCG, a typical example of an African pentecostal church, which has spread globally from Nigeria to about seventy countries with over two million members, scattered within Africa, America, Europe, Asia, Australia, the Middle East, and other parts of the world (Adogame 2004a, 2005, 2007). Elsewhere, we have demonstrated how the reproduction of the Redemption Camp becomes one of the significant ways in which the RCCG is gradually inserting itself on the American geo-cultural landscape. The Redemption Camp (aka Redemption City), located along the Lagos-Ibadan Expressway in Nigeria, doubles as RCCG International headquarters and the most important sacred space of the church. It is the venue that hosts their most popular religious programs and festivals, such as the Holy Ghost Service (an all-night prayer, healing, and miracle service). It has metamorphosed into the International Holy Ghost Festival, drawing at least a million participants at any one event. It was recently renamed the Holy Ghost Congress and takes place annually at the specially prepared Holy Ghost arena at the Redemption City.[26] The camp now sits on over ten hectares of land, and its geography is diversified with structures hosting a large auditorium, conference center, guesthouse and chalets, and a presidential villa set aside for government functionaries and politicians who visit the camp. Also situated at the site are a maternity center, an orphanage, a post office, a gas station, bookstores, supermarkets, a bakery, and a canteen. Other significant facilities include two banks, Redeemer's University, a secondary school, and a bible school. An estate consisting of residential buildings has come to characterize its topography. Thus, the significance of the Redemption Camp lies not only in the religious and spiritual functions it serves for members and non-members alike. It also has come to represent an avenue where social, economic, cultural, ecological, and political functions meet at a crossroads.

By 2003, the Redeemed Christian Church of God North America (RCCGNA) had fully acquired a multimillion-dollar property of over 400 hectares in Floyd (Hunt County), Texas, for a replication of a Redemption Camp, similar to the International headquarters in Nigeria.[27] The new Redemption Camp serves as RCCGNA headquarters and is currently being developed to include physical structures such as the Holy Ghost Ground, chapels, a bible college, baptismal pool, recreational center, administrative building, library, banquet and seminar halls, shopping mall, restaurants, community center, guesthouses, residential accommodations, and an impressive driveway.[28] It is perhaps this planned concentration of facilities within a religiously encased local space that led to its description as a Christian Disneyland.

There are currently a total of twenty-two zones in RCCG North America: nineteen in the United States and the Caribbean and three in Canada. Each country is divided into zones; states and provinces are grouped together to form a zone.[29] At the 2003 RCCGNA annual convention held in Dallas, over 120 parishes were listed.[30] By September 2008, 334 parishes were listed on the RCCGNA official website.[31] RCCG's religious cartographical maps of North America quite consciously illuminate the physical, demographic spread of parishes but also how the North American terrain has been mapped and partitioned for missionary, evangelistic ends. The desire and enthusiasm toward establishing parishes in North America is not unconnected with global vision and goals, as expressed in the RCCG mission statement:

> It is our goal to make heaven. It is our goal to take as many people as possible with us. In order to accomplish our goals, holiness will be our lifestyle. In order to take as many people with us as possible, we will plant churches within five minutes walking distance in every

city and town of developing countries; and within five minutes driving distance in every city and town of developed countries. We will
pursue these objectives until every nation in the world is reached for
Jesus Christ our Lord.[32]

In the case of RCCGNA, this statement took on a qualifying addendum in
view of demographic peculiarity in the North American region. It also exemplifies how and to what extent contextual factors can shape the growth
of a religious movement and serve as a dynamic of change in a new context. For planting new parishes in North America and Caribbean countries, the location to any existing parish must be at least thirty minutes
driving distance. "We believe in positioning our worship centers close to
the people hence in North America we are challenged to establish parishes in every State, County, City and in fact within 30 minutes driving
distance."[33] Samuel Shorimade expressed the significance of evangelism
in the RCCGNA: "The United States was often described in some circles
as God's own country, but this country has become very slack morally
and spiritually. So God is making us [RCCG] bring worship and praise to
them [US] as well as in rediscovering God."[34]

The first RCCG parish in the United States was founded in 1992 in
Detroit, Michigan. From 1994 onward, new parishes sprang up in Florida,
Texas, Massachusetts, and other states. In Dallas, the initiative to establish a parish was mooted by Nigerian employees and trainees on intern-
ship programs, special projects with Mobil Oil, and some other oil industries whose headquarters were located in Dallas. From this pioneer parish
the Dallas–Fort Worth metroplex became host to fourteen full-fledged
RCCG parishes in 2003. There were twelve existing parishes in the city
of Houston and others located in different parts of Texas (Adogame 2004a:
31–32) Just as new parishes continue to spring up across U.S. cities, so are
local parishes acquiring real estates that are developed into "local religious empires" characterized by magnificent state-of-the-art edifices.

Beyond the consideration of the aesthetics of place and ecological import of the resacralized that undercut space lie politics that undercut processes of place-making. Just as we discussed in the KICC example above,
the reproduction of the RCCG Redemption City, a burgeoning Christian
Disneyland in Floyd, Texas, has evoked local responses. In fact, one may
argue that the ways in which the local media shot this development project into public attention may have impacted and considerably shaped the
texture of local discourses and responses.[35] I would argue that such contextual factors and local responses have a corresponding impact on the
development of the religious community itself. Such ambivalent responses enable the RCCG to reposition, repackage, and explore new strategies,
albeit of a political nature, resulting in the production of a distinctly new,

spatial identity. Two seemingly provocative news headlines, "A Texas Town Nervously Awaits a New Neighbor" and "Racist Gods Fret as Redeemed Church Takes US by Storm," vividly capture the local attitude among the public.[36] As Romero expressed:

> Blackest Land, Whitest People: Until the mid-1960s, those words were painted on the water tower and on a sign near the square in this North Texas town, a once-segregated cotton-ginning center. . . . The people of Hunt County . . . are about to get a rare opportunity to break with the past. The Redeemed Christian Church of God is a fast-growing evangelical church with mostly black adherents but that espouses a multicultural mission.

Nigeria Daily reporter Sam Omatseye much more pointedly remarks: "In a script that is unveiling like a flip-flop of history, a rural town of white people is growing nervous about the 'invasion' of blacks, especially blacks from another country, which happens to be Nigeria." As one local inhabitant reportedly expressed, "I don't have problems with black people, I just feel uncomfortable in large numbers of them. They live different, they think different, they have different cultures."[37] As Omatseye further reported:

> The choice of Floyd has baffled not only the inhabitants of Texas but Americans who think it too audacious. Part of Texas belongs to what is known as redneck America, a term that describes an entrenched culture of racial bias. . . . But the RCCG chose neither Dallas nor Houston, nor even Austin, which enjoy a variegated racial mix, but Floyd, a rural backstreet. The RCCG says the choice of Floyd was not the province of man. God pointed the way.

Although some of Omatseye's observation may be contested, he has unearthed a fragment of racial discourse that often characterizes a racially segregated context such as the United States. Nevertheless, it is amid this uncertain climate of reception that the RCCGNA may have worked out strategies that seek approval and recognition of local and national policy makers, thus guaranteeing for them some legitimacy to express and profess their religion in a new cultural context. The formal invitation of state and city government authorities to annual religious functions and programs is suggestive of the political dimension of the church. One example will suffice here. The governor of Texas and the mayors of Dallas and Arlington were among special dignitaries invited to participate in the Seventh Annual Convention of the RCCGNA, which took place in Dallas in 2003. Although these public figures may not have attended the event, they each sent letters to the convention that were expressly marked

by narratives of credence, warm reception, and recognition. Mayor Elzie
Odom of Arlington, in a letter dated March 17, 2003, extended a "warm
welcome" to attendees of the convention on behalf of the citizens of Arlington: "Dear Friends, . . . The Dallas–Fort Worth Metroplex is a growing
and dynamic area. . . . The people of north Texas are pleased to share their
well-known hospitality, outstanding attractions, and unique lifestyle to
make your visit most enjoyable."[38] Letters from Governor Rick Perry and
Dallas mayor Laura Miller were also characterized by their welcoming
tones:

> Welcome to Texas, as you convene the 7th annual Convention of the
> Redeemed Christian Church of God. With diverse landscapes, vary-
> ing climatic conditions, and elevations ranging from sea level to the
> majestic Guadalupe Peak, the Lone Star is a land of striking contrasts
> and great natural beauty. Moreover, we welcome you to our rich tap-
> estry of people and cultures, evidence of the many who have come
> from far and near to call this great state home. Our proud heritage is
> reflected in our architecture, and I encourage you all to explore and
> enjoy the best of Texas. Anita [Perry] and I wish you all the very best
> for the future.[39]

> Greetings! On behalf of the city of Dallas and my colleagues on the
> Dallas City Council, it gives me great pleasure to welcome you. . . .
> As you prepare to participate in this event, I encourage each one of
> you to use this occasion as an opportunity for fellowship and to gain
> a better understanding of the role you play in our society, present
> and future. Best wishes for a successful and exciting anniversary, and
> please visit again soon.[40]

In actual fact, the tone of these letters appears on the surface to run contrary to the hostile local responses expressed above. It is, however, unclear
whether these artificial political relationships with constituted political
authority ever go beyond the ceremonial exchange of letters or how far the
RCCG taps into this political goodwill and approval offered by state and
local leadership. In any case, it may play a decisive role in the long run as
the RCCG continues to chart its path into the new host context. It is not
uncommon for the RCCG General Overseer, Enoch Adeboye, to pay cour-
tesy visits on state functionaries and public office holders while attending
RCCGNA programs in U.S. cities. This is suggestive of the interconnectedness of religion and politics—the political dimension of religion as well
as the religious dimension of politics.

Anthias's (2001) analytical framework, premised on the idea of "translocational positionality," is instructive here in that it facilitates the interrogation of other constructions of difference, beyond culture, based upon

various identifiers and signifiers. As Tettey notes, "Such a tool makes it possible to look beyond immigrant communities as homogenous groups that are bound by a collective identity in relation to others and opens up analytical insights into different narratives of belonging and otherness in the context not only of the host societies but of the societies of origin, as well" (Tettey 2007: 230). Tettey successfully employs the framework of "translocational positionality" to analyze the multiple ways in which Ghanaians in Canada connect with their communities and country of origin via religion, in spite of the distance that their location in Canada imposes. As Tettey remarks, "This dialectical approach facilitates the appreciation of the multiple, simultaneous, fluid, and sometimes conflictual positions occupied by individuals and groups as they negotiate their sense of self and consequent attachments to culture, religion, ethnicities, places, and nations" (Tettey 2007: 230)

The growth and development of African-led churches such as KICC and RCCG in Africa, Europe, and North America is indicative of how they translate into local-global environments. The reconstructed religious space may also symbolize the reproduction of religio-cultural and spatial identities as well as the construction of a new immigrant religious identity, thus creating and reinforcing a kind of locality (as opposed to globality) at the religious level. Nevertheless, the varied social, cultural, and religious entanglements that weave local-global spaces together are in themselves pertinent, especially the ways in which religious worldviews and praxis are resilient but also transformed through translocal processes mutually. Furthermore, different localities will not only shape the development of religious traditions or movements differently, but also the politics of religious place-making.

New African-led churches and religious organizations have appropriated new media technologies such as websites, TV, and interactive technologies in the transmission of their religious ideologies, as a recruitment strategy for new clientele, but also as a way of maintaining links and contact to members and branches transnationally (Adogame 2005: 510). RCCG and KICC's geographical expansion also results from conscious mission strategies and individual networks, but also indirectly from the frequent mobility of its members. The mobility and increasing itinerancy of religious leaders and members play a crucial role in religious expansion, and thus has implications for place-making, sometimes giving it a transnational twist. The complex mobility of the RCCG and KICC leaders, Enoch Adeboye and Matthew Ashimolowo, respectively, is an indication of the transnational tendencies of this new brand of African Christianity. Their travel schedules portray them as "world class travelers," with frequent trips to virtually all continents of the world. They engage in cross-continental travels virtually every month, sometimes in multiple directions between Nigeria, London, and Texas. This mobility is, however, not limited to these contexts, as frequent visits are undertaken by leaders and members to branches in Europe, the United States, and other parts of Africa, as well as to attend religious programs of churches and religious organizations with which RCCG and KICC have ecumenical links. The significance of these frequent travels does not simply lie in the number of cities or countries visited but more on the motive of the travels and the activities that took place during these travels. The nature of the events further eulogizes both their transnational dimension and the socio-religious, cultural, political, and economic implications in local-global contexts.

CONCLUSION

This chapter has demonstrated how African-led churches such as KICC and RCCG are gradually inserting themselves into new geo-cultural spaces through the construction and reproduction of religious geographies. Beyond the consideration of the aesthetics of space lie other issues woven around power dynamics; identity questions, public attitudes, and receptivity; government and legal regulations on properties and real estate and their uses; the economic base of immigrant churches; and the local networks and global links they engender to assert and insert themselves in the newly constructed spaces of worship. A host of contextual factors are essential to understanding how these churches negotiate ritual spaces, but also the ways in which they construct and reconstruct religious, cultural, and spatial identities.

NOTES

1. Scott Farwell, "African Church Plans Christian Disneyland," *Dallas Morning News*, July 17, 2005.
2. See Christian Disneyland at http://www.christianebooks.com/christiandisneyland.htm (accessed December 6, 2007).
3. See full details on the Disneyland Resort homepage, available at http://www.disneyland.com/. In 1998, the theme park was re-branded as Disneyland Park to distinguish it from the larger Disneyland Resort complex. Disneyland holds the distinction of being the only theme park to be designed, built, opened, and operated by Walt Disney. Currently the park has been visited by more than 515 million guests since it opened, including presidents, royalty, and other heads of state.
4. In 1983 Tokyo Disneyland was opened and its success spurred interest in building a European park. Euro Disneyland (140 acres) was renamed Disneyland Paris in 1995 and is located twenty miles outside of Paris.
5. Doreen Massey, a contemporary British social scientist and geographer, is one of the most profound thinkers in contemporary human geography. Her extensive writings on the importance of space/place, cities, globalization,

and so on have undoubtedly marked critical turning points in the socio-scientific discourses of place and spatial identities. See for instance Massey 1991, 1993, 1994, 2005.

6. Yan Xu, "Sense of Place and Identity," background research report, East St. Louis Action Research Project, University of Illinois, fall 1995. Available at http://www.eslarp.uiuc.edu/la/LA437-F95/reports/yards/main.html (accessed October 20, 2007).

7. See Stuart Watson, "Reach for the Heavens," available at http://www.propertyweek.com/story.asp?sectioncode=39&storycode=3087216 (accessed August 17, 2008).

8. See KICC official church website, available at http://www.kicc.org.uk/ (accessed November 12, 2006) and "Introduction—KICC Beam Reach," at http://kiccbeamreach.org/index.html (accessed September 3, 2008).

9. See KICC website, http://www.kicc.org.uk/ (accessed November 12, 2006).

10. Watson, "Reach for the Heavens."

11. KICC's announcement of its planned relocation is available at http://www.kicc.org.uk/Church/Relocation/tabid/50/Default.aspx and http://kiccbeamreach.org/index.html.

12. The site comprises some 5.5 hectares of broadly level and open land, and forms part of a larger parcel of industrial land (35.6 hectares) that the London Development Agency purchased from Ford Motor Company in 1999 and is now marketed as Beam Reach.

13. See Greater London Authority, Planning Report PDU/1630/01, November 2, 2007. Beam Reach 5, Rainham. London Thames Gateway Development Corporation (London Borough of Havering) Planning Application No. PA/06/01525 and Greater London Authority. Planning Report PDU/1630/02. February 4, 2008. Beam Reach 5, Rainham. London Thames Gateway Development Corporation (London Borough of Havering) Planning Application No. PA/06/01525.

14. See KICC's Full Planning Application Number LTGDC-07-149-LBHG-U0006.07 to the London Borough of Havering (20/07/2007). Also available at the Borough of Havering Council website, at http://planning.havering.gov.uk.

15. Watson, "Reach for the Heavens." The LDA, the Borough of Havering Council, and the local community were vehement in their opposition to relocate a prison in Beam Reach on grounds that it does not meet the regeneration agenda.

16. In October 2005 the London Thames Gateway Development Corporation became the strategic development control authority for its areas of responsibility in the Thames Gateway. The corporation has the power to determine certain strategic types of planning application, for instance those with over fifty residential units and those with over 2,500 square miles of commercial floor space. It has no powers to prepare statutory planning polices and no direct powers regarding planning enforcement.

17. See Press Release Regeneration for East London—"London Thames Gateway Refuses Planning Application" on February 15, 2008. Available at

the London Thames Gateway Development Corporation official website, available at http://www.ltgdc.org.uk/news/pressreleases/detail.asp?newsID =125. See also "Applications Received by LTGDC" at the LTGDC Corporation Planning List, available at: http://www.ltgdc.org.uk/planning/receive/ and http://www.ltgdc.org.uk/media/applications/index.html.

18. See Press Release Regeneration for East London—"London Thames Gateway Refuses Planning Application" on February15, 2008.

19. See, for instance, "Anger over Plans for Super-church in Rainham," in which residents were alleged to have spoken out against plans to move the country's largest evangelical church to Rainham (November 19, 2006), available at: http://www.bbc.co.uk/london/content/articles/2006/11/19/lebo_ church_feature.shtml (accessed March 15, 2007).

20. See KICC proposed social programs for the Beam reach local community, available at http://kiccbeamreach.org/social_programme.html.

21. Blog from Pastor Dipo Oluyomi, Monday, February 18, 2008. Available at: http://www.kiccbeamreach.org/blog/?m=200802.

22. See the documentary titled "KICC: Church 'Hung out to Dry': Alan Craig and Paula Warren take on the LDA," available at http://uk.youtube. com/watch?v=Myq75L5eC58, http://www.meetpaulawarren.com/?cat=4, and http://www.thechristianchoice.org.uk/. See also Black UK Online Magazine, available at http://www.blackukonline.com/index.php?option=com_content &task=view&id=438&Itemid=1.

23. A BBC *Heaven and Earth Program* survey says that Christians in the United Kingdom feel they are discriminated against. See for instance http://news.bbc.co.uk/1/hi/uk/6463527.stm. It reported that more than one in five Christians in the United Kingdom faces discrimination in their local communities because of their faith.

24. See KICC planning application details: Town and Country Planning Act 1990: Appeal by KICC and LDA in "Appeal Reference: APP/A9580/A/08/2082331. Site at Beam Reach 5, Off Consol Avenue and Manor Way, Rainham, Essex." Also available at London Borough of Havering website, http://www.havering.gov.uk/index.aspx?articleid=14001#detailid2377 (accessed September 23, 2008). See also James McGlashan (KICC Chief Operating Officer), "Submission of Appeal on Planning Decision," available at: http://kiccbeamreach.org/blog/ (accessed September 23, 2008).

25. See Rapleys, Town Planning Consultancy Press Releases: "Planning Application for KICC, London" and "Enforcement Notices," available at http://www.rapleys.co.uk (accessed September 12, 2008). Rapleys LLP agency submitted the major planning application on behalf of KICC and LDA.

26. The Holy Ghost Congress presently attracts a huge attendance estimated at over two million, thus leading some observers to describe the religious festival as the largest Christian gathering on earth. See Lee Grady, "Nigeria's Miracle: How a Sweeping Christian Revival is Transforming Africa's Most Populous Nation," *Charisma and Christian Life* 27(10) (May 2002): 38–41.

27. Author interview with Pastor (Dr.) Ajibike Akinyoye at the RCCGNA headquarters, Dallas, Texas, March 9, 2004. Cf. Laolu Akande, "Multi-million Dollar Redemption Camp Underway in U.S.," *Guardian*, April 8, 2003,

available at http://odili.net/news/source/2003/apr/3/100.html or http://www
.rccgna.org/news.htm.

28. Ibid.

29. The RCCG North America area comprises the United States, Canada,
and the Caribbean. For more details on the RCCGNA administrative structure, see Adogame (2004a: 31–32). See also the RCCGNA network, available
at http://www.rccgna.org/zones.asp.

30. "The Latter Rain," 7th Annual RCCG North American Convention
Program, Dallas, June 2003.

31. See Parish Directory for a current list of parishes (branches) in North
America listed according to parish/city, state/zone, available at http://www
.rccgna.org/login/pdirectory.asp?offset=0 and http://www.rccgna.org/bocus
.asp (accessed September 5, 2008).

32. See the official website of the RCCG, http://www.rccg.org, created and
maintained by the RCCG Internet Project, Houston, Texas.

33. See "Addendum—Our Poise," The Redeemed Christian Church of
God, North America and Caribbean Statement of Fundamental Truths, a
publication of RCCGNA, n.d., 39–40.

34. Author interview with Pastor Dr. Samuel Shorimade at the RCCG Cor-
nerstone Worship Centre for All Nations Parish, Cambridge, Massachusetts,
November 23, 2003. Pastor Shorimade is the founder and current pastor of
the parish.

35. See Scott Farwell, "African Church Plans 'Christian Disneyland,'"
Dallas Morning News, July 17, 2005, and "Redeemed Christian Church of
God Buys Multimillion Dollar Property in Dallas, USA," May 10, 2004,
available at http://www.rccgna.org/renews/templates/news.asp?articleid
=9&zoneid=2 (accessed August 10, 2004). Cf. Laolu Akande, "Multi-million
Dollar Redemption Camp Underway in U.S.," Guardian, April 8, 2003,
available at http://odili.net/news/source/2003/apr/3/100.html or http://www
.rccgna.org/news.htm. See also "Redemption Camp, Texas USA," Christian
Character, a publication of RCCGNA, June 2002, 2–5.

36. Simon Romero, "A Texas Town Nervously Awaits a New Neighbor,"
New York Times, August 21, 2005, and Sam Omatseye, "Racist Gods Fret
as Redeemed Church Takes US by Storm," Online Nigeria Daily News,
August 21, 2005, available at http://nm.onlinenigeria.com/templates/default.
aspx?a=4781&template=print-article.htm (accessed June 12, 2007).

37. Quoted in Sam Omatseye, "Racist Gods Fret as Redeemed Church
Takes US by Storm."

38. Letter of Welcome from Mayor Elzie Odom, Mayor of Arlington, to the
Redeemed Christian Church of God Seventh Annual North America Convention, March 17, 2003.

39. Letter of "Greetings" from Rick Perry, Governor, State of Texas, Office
of the Governor to the Seventh Annual Convention of the Redeemed Christian Church of God, April 25, 2003.

40. Letter of "Greetings" from Laura Miller, Mayor, City of Dallas, to the
Seventh Annual Convention of the Redeemed Christian Church of God,
May 29, 2003.

REFERENCES

Adogame, A. 2004a. "Contesting the Ambivalences of Modernity in a Global Context: The Redeemed Christian Church of God, North America." *Studies in World Christianity* 10(1): 25–48.
———. 2004b. "The Politicization of Religion and the Religionization of Politics in Nigeria." In *Religion, History and Politics in Nigeria*, ed. K. Chima and N. Ugo. Lanham, Md.: University Press of America.
———. 2005. "African Christian Communities in Diaspora." In *African Christianity: An African Story*, ed. Ogbu U. Kalu. Pretoria: University of Pretoria.
———. 2007. "Raising Champions, Taking Territories: African Churches and the Mapping of New Religious Landscapes in Diaspora." In *The African Diaspora and the Study of Religion*, ed. T. L. Trost. New York: Palgrave Macmillan.
———. 2010a. "Transnational Migration and Pentecostalism in Europe." *PentecoStudies: An Interdisciplinary Journal for Research on the Pentecostal and Charismatic Movements* 9(1): 56–73.
———. 2010b. "From House Cells to Warehouse Churches? Christian Church Outreach Mission International in Translocal Contexts." In *Traveling Spirits: Migrants, Markets and Mobilities*, ed. G. Hüwelmeier and Kristine Krause. New York: Routledge.
———. 2010c. "How God Became a Nigerian: Religious Impulse and the Unfolding of a Nation." *Journal of Contemporary African Studies* 28(4): 479–98.
———. 2010d. "Pentecostal and Charismatic Movements in a Global Perspective." In *The New Blackwell Companion to the Sociology of Religion*, ed. Byran S. Turner. Chichester: Wiley-Blackwell.
Anthias, F. 2001. "New Hybridities, Old Concepts: The Limits of Culture." *Ethnic and Racial Studies* 24(4): 619–41.
Augé, M. 1995. *Non-places: Introduction to an Anthropology of Supermodernity.* Trans. John Howe. London: Verso.
Castles, S., and M. Miller. 2003. *The Age of Migration.* 3rd ed. New York: Guilford Press.
Falola, T. 1998. *Violence in Nigeria: The Crisis of Religious Politics and Secular Ideologies.* Rochester, N.Y.: University of Rochester Press.
Krause, K. 2008. "Spiritual Spaces in Post-Industrial Places: Transnational Churches in North East London." In *Transnational Ties: Cities, Migrations and Identities*, ed. Michael P. Smith and John Eade. New Brunswick, N.J.: Transaction Publishers.
Kukah, M. H. 1993. *Religion, Politics and Power in Northern Nigeria.* Ibadan: Spectrum.
———. 2003. *Human Rights in Nigeria: Hopes and Hindrances.* Pontifical Mission Society Human Rights Office. http://www.missio-aachen.de/humanrights. Accessed June 2007.
Massey, D. 1991. "The Political Place of Locality Studies." *Environment and Planning* 23(2): 267–81.

———. 1993. "Questions of Locality." *Geography* 78(2): 142–49.

———. 1994. *Space, Place and Gender.* Minneapolis: University of Minnesota Press.

———. 2005. *For Space.* London: Sage.

Park, C. 1994. *Sacred Worlds: An Introduction to Geography and Religion.* London: Routledge.

Tettey, W. 2007. "Transnationalism, Religion, and the African Diaspora in Canada: An Examination of Ghanaians and Ghanaian Churches." In *African Immigrant Religions in America*, ed. Jacob K. Olupona and Regina Gemignani. New York: New York University Press.

10

INTERNATIONAL AID TO REFUGEES IN KENYA

THE NEGLECTED ROLE OF THE SOMALI DIASPORA

CINDY HORST

This chapter focuses on the neglected role of transnational assistance provided within refugee communities in understandings of international aid to refugees in Kenya.[1] It builds on earlier work that argues that international aid systems that provide relief aid or technical assistance to refugees fail to respect the complex gift-giving norms in refugee communities (Harrell-Bond et al. 1992, Harrell-Bond and Voutira 1994, Harrell-Bond 2002). I maintain that it is important to look not only at social norms of gift-giving, but also at actual and current social practices within refugee communities. In the Dadaab camps of northeastern Kenya, assistance is provided not just by the United Nations High Commissioner for Refugees (UNHCR) and various NGOs but also by Somalis within and outside the camps. Furthermore, an unknown but considerable number of refugees do not reside in the camps but live in Nairobi, by and large unassisted by the international community (Campbell 2006; Lindley 2007b). A large proportion of these urban refugees survive through remittances sent to them by relatives in the United States, Europe, and elsewhere.

Thus, Somalis across the world play a crucial role in enabling the survival of refugees in Kenya, with that assistance often being further distributed among relatives, friends, and neighbors. And yet, the international aid community fails to acknowledge the full scale of this assistance provision, with two serious implications. First, this lack of acknowledgment leads to perceptions of refugees in terms of their needs rather than their agency (Horst 2006b; Malkki 1995; Malkki 1996; Zetter 1991). Second, the disregard for assistance provided within refugee communities, whether locally or transnationally, has implications for the effectiveness of international assistance practices.

The data presented in this chapter stem from fieldwork carried out in Dadaab and Nairobi over various periods in 2007 and 2008.[2] My main argument is that refugees need to be acknowledged not just in their role as assistance receivers but also as providers of aid, balancing the power dimensions implicit in the act of giving. The chapter first discusses the context in which Somali refugees survive in Kenya, in a protracted refugee situation, and the monopoly on assistance that is commonly assumed by international aid providers. A second section discusses assistance provided by relatives abroad to Somali refugees in Kenya through the lens of international aid provision by distinguishing emergency aid, care and maintenance, and sustainable development aid. This discussion aims to illustrate the fact that international aid providers do not hold a monopoly on any of these kinds of aid provision. It also shows that knowledge of the social interactions between assistance providers and receivers is crucial for understanding the gift-giving norms ultimately impacting the appropriateness of international aid practices.

SOMALI REFUGEES IN KENYA: A PROTRACTED REFUGEE SITUATION

Many refugees across the world have lived in refugee camps for a decade or more, being classified as living in protracted refugee situations (Crisp 2003). Recently, this phenomenon has received increased attention again, partly because of an awareness of the human rights implications of living in limbo for such extensive periods of time and, particularly at present, because of the security implications (Loescher et al. 2007; Loescher et al. 2008). A textbook example of a "protracted refugee situation" is Dadaab. The town of Dadaab lies in the Garissa district in Kenya's Northeastern Province. It is situated some 500 km from Nairobi and 80 km from the Kenyan-Somali border. Since 1991–92, there have been three refugee camps near Dadaab: Ifo, Hagadera, and Dagahaley. The camps currently host 288,348 refugees, with Somalis making up the large majority of the population (CEDAT 2010). Over the last three years, with worsening conditions in south/central Somalia, the population has doubled, putting severe pressure on the already overstretched camp structures.

The camps are located in a semi-arid region that is otherwise largely inhabited by nomadic pastoralists. This environment greatly limits livelihood opportunities, and it is highly unlikely that the refugees would survive there without assistance from the international community. At the same time, it is highly unlikely they would survive only on assistance from the international community (Horst 2006b). Food distributions are insufficient and the distribution of non-food items rare. The aid agencies offer incentive worker opportunities for refugees, which pay very small amounts. These are the only jobs refugees can engage in legally, as they are not allowed to move beyond the camps or work formally in Kenya. Although the 1951 Geneva Convention Relating to the Status of Refugees, to which Kenya is a signatory, allows refugees free movement as well as the ability to set up an independent livelihood, in many signatory countries such rights are not observed. Regardless of their location and length of stay in countries of asylum, refugees in Africa are treated as temporary guests (Kibreab 1999: 399). Thus, the government of Kenya also prefers to see the refugees confined in camps and penalizes any initiative by refugees to invest or settle outside the camps (Kagwanja and Juma 2008; Perouse de Montclos and Kagwanja 2000). Whereas the U.S. Committee for Refugees and Immigrants and others have advocated the importance of a rights-based approach in the provision of aid to refugees in camps, these refugees are rarely portrayed as persons with rights (USCRI 2004).

The international aid regime claims a monopoly on assistance based on the perception that the UN and NGOs are the sole providers of aid and that refugees are solely receivers. Agencies operate according to the norms of charity rather than using a rights-based approach or operating in accordance with the gift-giving norms common in the communities they work in. Furthermore, the actual assistance provided by Somalis is not acknowledged, except on the abstract level of yearly remittance flows. The impression that a number of international staff members working in the camps have is that international aid enables survival in these camps and that refugees themselves only receive aid and do not contribute to their own livelihoods, let alone assist others. It is, for example, a common perception among agency staff that refugees are extremely demanding: they demand to be given aid while being dependent on it unnecessarily (Papadopoulos 2002).

In a conversation on solutions for these long-term refugee camps, a staff member suggested that with the introduction of sophisticated biometric information on the refugees, UNHCR would be able to reduce the number of registrations in the camps. This, according to him, would mean that refugees would not have additional rations to sell and would have to develop their own livelihoods. His observation overlooks the fact that almost all refugees in Dadaab have sources of income additional to the food rations provided, either through (self) employment or remittances (Horst 2006b; Horst 2007a). And yet, assumptions that refugees are demanding and fully dependent on international food aid remain widespread (Malkki 1996: 385; Turner 2010: 62). This is partly related to the fact that the camps are seen as isolated areas that are cut off from the rest of Kenya and the world, from where people should not and do not move. And yet, migration has played a crucial part in people's livelihoods in the camps, as those who have moved away from them have enabled those who have remained in Dadaab to survive.

Indeed, one of the ways in which refugees defy the assumption of being helpless victims waiting to be assisted by the international community is by avoiding or moving out of camp-like situations (Jacobsen 2006). Many Somali refugees in Kenya live in Nairobi, although their exact numbers are impossible to establish. General estimates have it that about 18 percent of refugees worldwide live in urban centers, with these numbers still growing, as opposed to 26 percent in camps and centers and the remainder "dispersed" elsewhere (Jacobsen 2006: 273).

The vast majority of Nairobi's urban refugees live in Eastleigh, a densely populated low-income area of Nairobi, where the informal economy is flourishing (Campbell 2006: 402). These refugees cannot expect to receive handouts or other livelihood support from UNHCR or other agencies. Looking for education, resettlement opportunities, or a job, Somalis who move from the camps often require the assistance of others to establish themselves in Nairobi (Horst 2006b: 140). Among those interviewed in Nairobi, a very large proportion receives remittances in order to be able to live in town. At the same time, many of those living in Nairobi support family members remaining in the camps on a monthly or occasional basis.

"INTERNATIONAL AID" EXAMINED: TRANSNATIONAL ASSISTANCE PRACTICES

International humanitarian aid practices have been examined through theories on gift-giving, building on the principle that the exchange of goods is not a mechanical but a moral and social transaction. Mauss's (1954) work has been used by Harrell-Bond et al. (1992, 1994, 2002), and subsequently by others, to explain the power dimensions of giving and receiving entailed in humanitarian assistance to refugees. Harrell-Bond et al. (1992) argue that in the humanitarian context, providing assistance implies giving to a deserving or worthy (absolutely destitute) recipient, being fully aware that no reciprocity can be expected. International aid systems to refugees fail to pay respect to the complex and often quite different social norms of the receiving group and their understanding of gift-giving and charity. I want to take these observations one step further by arguing that it is not only vital to understand the gift-giving *norms* of the refugee communities to which assistance is provided; a great deal can be gained by understanding actual gift-giving *practices* as well. The assistance provided by Somalis, both within Kenya and transnationally, is crucial for survival in the camps and in urban settings (Horst 2006b; Horst 2007a).

In recent years, interest in transnational assistance by refugees, particularly in the form of remittances, has increased (Diaz-Briquets and Perez-Lopez 1997; Horst 2007a; Lindley 2010; Riak Akuei 2005). The crucial importance of remittances for Somalis in Somalia and Somali refugees in the region has now been widely acknowledged (Gundel 2002; Lindley 2007a; Lindley 2010; Perouse de Montclos 2007). At the macroeconomic level, the country depends heavily on remittances in order to function. Remittances significantly outweigh export income and Official Development Aid (ODA) in Somalia. The United Nations Development Programme (UNDP) estimated that remittances to Somalia in 2004 totaled between US$700 million and 1 billion (Omer and El Koury 2005), whereas more recent estimates range up to 2 billion (Lindley 2010). This is at least double current international relief and development assistance to Somalia.

At the household level, remittances are essential for daily consumption but are also used for investments, such as constructing houses and establishing businesses. Somaliland has a well-developed private sector and more successful business enterprises compared to other conflict-affected countries due to these remittance inflows (Ahmed 2000). Financial remittances as well as other transnational flows have furthermore enabled the provision of vital services commonly provided by the state including education, health care, and infrastructure. Somali organizations established abroad invest in health and educational facilities including hospitals, schools, and universities (Hansen 2004; Hoehne 2010; Horst 2008a; Kent and Von Hippel 2005; Lindley 2005). It is not only those remaining in or returning to Somalia who benefit; remittances also have a substantial impact on the livelihood options of Somalis in the region, including, for example, those living in refugee camps or urban areas in Kenya and Cairo (Al-Sharmani 2006). While the literature mainly stresses the vital role remittances play in enabling the survival of many Somalis in the region, insights have so far not been used to address perceptions of refugees solely as receivers of assistance or to understand assistance norms and practices among Somalis.

REMITTANCES: EMERGENCY AID, CARE AND MAINTENANCE, AND SUSTAINABLE DEVELOPMENT AID

In order to examine assistance practices among refugees in greater detail, I wish to introduce a number of quotes from Rashid Ibrahim. Rashid is a young Somali father who has lived in Dadaab since 1992 and during the time of the research was residing in Eastleigh estate in Nairobi in an attempt to complete a bachelor's degree in information technology. His wife and baby girl live in Hagadera, one of the Dadaab camps, with his parents. Rashid is very well positioned in that he has many relatives and friends in Western countries, who enabled him not only to survive in Dadaab and Nairobi but also to continue his education. He is following in the footsteps of his father, who is an elder and a religious leader in Hagadera. Furthermore, Rashid has been a research assistant for me and other researchers for many years. I have selected excerpts from the various interviews I conducted with him because he has an excellent understanding of the complexities of assistance relations within the Somali community. This understanding is based not only on his own experiences but also on the experiences of a wide range of people whom he has assisted with advice and mediation and whom he has interviewed. The selection presented here is based on insights gained during the field research and from analyzing the interview data.

Different types of remittance-sending practices among Somalis are discussed in very similar ways as international assistance practices. In this chapter, I distinguish three categories: emergency aid, care and maintenance, and sustainable development aid. Remittances of the first type are sent reactively and infrequently; those of the second type are sent proactively and regularly, whereas the last type of remittance-sending practice occurs proactively and infrequently.

The first type of remittance-sending practice, the type provided in times of emergency, is a response to sudden, unexpected expenses. Such expenses occur in times of communal or personal disaster, such as droughts, floods, diseases, or death; this type of aid is mostly requested by those in the region of origin. Emergency aid is, for example, provided during ongoing conflict to deal with emergency health care needs, price inflation, and the need to migrate from an insecure area (Carling, Erdal, and Horst forthcoming). While remittances aimed at providing emergency aid also occur in non-conflict settings, in these contexts such practices are of a much smaller scale and occur less frequently.

For those in a position to provide remittances, emergency needs have to be prioritized, as they can be a matter of life and death. Rashid indicates a difference between these types of contributions and remittances that deal with regular living expenses or *biil* (Lindley 2010). While the first type gives a person the right to call any of his or her relatives and friends elsewhere for assistance, the second type does not automatically do so. Rather, as we will see, "care and maintenance" type of remittances are only an absolute obligation to close relatives. Rashid engages in discussions with his cousin in Norway on how best to distinguish levels of need and urgency relation to emergency requests:

We are trying to figure out who he can assist in Somalia and how he can assist, what his priorities should be. If someone is getting married you need to assist him, and if someone is sick and needs to go to hospital you need to assist him, but you do not expect to assist a cousin from this or that family to come and say "just send me money," if there are no clear problems. So we were saying maybe we can contact the family elders in Somalia to know which problems are very urgent and need assistance and which do not.

Rashid's transnational discussions indicate, first, that it is not always possible to obtain the full information necessary to prioritize emergency needs for people who are not present locally. The solution the two cousins choose, of relying on respected family members to prioritize local needs for them, is one that is not uncommon. The quote furthermore shows that among Somali remittance senders, attempts are made to judge the many requests they receive as accurately as possible. These are interesting observations in light of the very similar concerns international aid agencies face.

The second remittance category, for care and maintenance, is only a priority for close relatives. The main reasons for this fact are that, first, such needs are not as urgent as those associated with emergency aid and, second, they require a substantially greater, long-term dedication from the remitter. This type of monthly assistance is an obligation, especially for parents, children, spouses, and siblings. It is important to realize that if these family members were to live in the same locality, they would also be expected to assist one another (Carling 2008). Moreover, the reason for the migration of one of the family members is often exactly because it will enable someone within the family to provide for the others: migration and transnational exchanges occur in the context of existing social relations (Monsutti 2004). Rashid indicates the many subtleties in expectations between close family members when he describes the responsibilities his younger sister in the United States has toward him and his parents:

I feel that my sister has the responsibility to assist me when she can, and I feel that I have the same. But I am her brother, and I am older than her. What I know is, to my parents, she has to do it. And if she is working, if she is getting an income, and she is not sending, in that case, some kind of problems might arise. If she doesn't have, if she is not working, if she's a student, maybe it is ok. There were months when my sister did not send, but by that time she said she bought a car because she could not work without a car and the family accepted it. But if she is in America and she is not sending anything to her parents, that one brings conflict. Of course, her parents will not be happy: why is our daughter not assisting us? That's the question where it starts.

What is illustrated here is that, despite the many subtle differences in the expectations faced by potential remitters, related to gender, age, ranking in the family, and economic position, nuclear family members abroad are ultimately expected to take care of their relatives who live as refugees in the region. Aunts, uncles, and cousins may also be included if there is a very strong bond or if they have special needs. Rashid's sister assists her *abti* (maternal uncle) in Somalia because he is an amputee with additional health problems. She agreed with her mother that she would assist her *abti* "as an obligation." In fact, it is often the case that, when extended family members are supported in their care and maintenance costs, it is because of coaxing from close family members. This commonly happens, for example, when parents no longer need this type of assistance because they are resettled in the United States or Europe, and argue that the "spare" money can now be used to support one of their siblings. The level of obligation related to such regular remittance-sending patterns is a very distinct feature. At the same time, however, the question of the sustainability of such practices is one that is asked by Somali remittance senders and receivers in ways quite similar to debates on international aid provision to refugees.

A last type of remittance sending practices, which is infrequent because it can only occur if remittance senders have extra resources or if specific livelihood strategies are agreed upon between senders and receivers, is sent as a form of sustainable development aid. This type of assistance has the longer-term purpose of allowing the receiver to develop an independent, sustainable livelihood. When monthly remittances are sent that enable the daily survival of people who would in normal circumstances be able to sustain themselves, the issue of dependency is a concern both for senders and receivers. Senders do not want to continue sending remittances indefinitely and at times prefer to send larger amounts that allow the receiver to move to places where he or she has better livelihood opportunities, to obtain educational certificates and diplomas, or to start up a business. Such arrangements are by and large also preferred by those receivers of remittances who have the capacity to take care of themselves economically, given a chance.

There are considerable risks involved in sending larger sums of money, both for the sender and receiver. Remittances that aim for more sustainable results are supposed to be used for very specific purposes. Yet these larger sums are mostly sent to individuals who also struggle to pay their monthly bills and are rarely able to deal with sudden unexpected needs. As such, there is a risk that the money sent with a long-term perspective in mind will be used for more immediate needs and thus not reach its goal. In addition, regional refugees face many obstacles, including legal restrictions and the general political and economic climate in which they live, which may prevent them from building a sustainable livelihood with the sum received.

Though senders and receivers live far apart, mechanisms to reduce the risks for the senders of remittances operate transnationally as well as locally. Rashid was at one point offered 3,000 dollars by his mother-in-law so that he could start up a business. He was not willing to take up this offer, as he explains:

> I said, "Let me first explore the market," although I already knew that I was not going to accept her offer. There is no way I can work with 3,000 dollars. There was a time she sent 2,000 dollars to her brother and after two months he asked for his monthly bill. When she asked where the 2,000 was, he said, "It has gone." Then there were a lot of shaming words that were said in the market; people in the diaspora and here were exchanging shameful words. So. . . . I know what people can say if I take responsibility. So when I am taking responsibility I have to see that what I am doing is viable. It will not be said that "Rashid started a business and it did not yield profit"; they will say, "Rashid misused the money," yes. That money was given to me, obviously. Whichever way it gets lost, whether it is official or non-official, it will be on me. People will say, "Rashid has taken the money from his mother-in-law, and he used it." Some enemies will say he has chewed it [referring to the practice of chewing qat among Somalis]; some enemies will say he gave it to others.

As such, although this last type of remittance sending-practices is most preferred by all involved, because it addresses issues of dependency that might arise in care and maintenance support, it is also the least common. First, sustainable development aid requires much higher amounts of support at once, which is often difficult for the senders, many of whom live abroad as asylum seekers or refugees. Second, the risks and stakes are higher—not only in terms of losing the money but also losing the respect of family members and friends.

CONCLUDING REMARKS

The analysis of transnational assistance practices through the lens of international aid brings interesting parallels and differences to light. Many of the challenges and dilemmas faced in providing emergency aid, care and maintenance, or sustainable development aid are faced by Somali remittance senders and international aid organizations alike. In emergency situations, needs are always far greater than resources, while at the same time it is not always possible to obtain the full information necessary to prioritize them. Providing regular and continued "care and maintenance" support to refugees becomes an obligation when they have no alternative ways of providing for themselves, but this always leads to questions of sustainability and dependency. These are addressed by sustainable development aid, which is much preferred by refugees but rarely provided to them. In the case of international aid agencies, this is largely because of the different mandates, bureaucracies, and funding mechanisms of the humanitarian and development sector (Frerks 2005). In the case of Somali remittance senders, it is related to their limited capacity and the greater risks involved.

Mauss (1954) has taught us that "gift giving" is not a mechanical but a moral and social transaction. As such, the social interactions between assistance providers and receivers, as well as their perspectives on gift giving and charity, need to be understood when providing aid to refugee groups. Somalis see assistance to those in need as an absolute responsibility of the individual as a member of a larger whole, whether this is the family, clan, community, or *umma*. It is a religious and cultural obligation to assist those who are struck by a crisis situation and to contribute to the livelihoods of one's close relatives in need. Conversely, it then also becomes a right to receive such assistance. These are long-existing assistance practices in which migration has always played an important role (Horst 2006a; Kleist 2004). After 1991, the fact that economic and political conditions in Somalia are bad and regional refugees live in situations of great duress has added extra weight to existing obligations. Somalis feel a great sense of responsibility to transfer money, especially because of the level of deprivation they know their relatives face (Carling, Erdal, and Horst forthcoming).

Drawing parallels between assistance provided within a refugee community and by international agencies is useful because there is a gap in our current understanding of assistance practices to refugees. Among many humanitarian assistance providers, refugees are still understood as receivers of assistance only, and this assistance is seen to be provided by international aid organizations. Such an understanding has tremendous implications for the power ascribed to the different actors involved and, ultimately, for actual practices as well (Zetter 1991; Horst 2006b). Acknowledging the importance of assistance provided by Somali refugees locally and transnationally is vital. Among Somalis, providing assistance to those who need it is the responsibility of those who can do so, and receiving aid thus becomes a right of those in need. Both senders and receivers share a great concern about the independence and dignity of the receiver, and more sustainable types of aid are preferred over "monthly bills" when senders would in normal circumstances be able to provide for themselves. These are issues that providers of international aid need to take into account when developing programs in refugee camps.

I have argued that understanding the dilemmas faced by Somali assistance providers, the choices they make, and the solutions they find will prove useful in developing new ways of thinking about international aid in protracted refugee situations. At the same time, it is important not to underestimate the difficulties related to assistance norms and practices among Somalis as well. The strong sense of responsibility regarding remittance relations may be more demanding than expected senders can handle (Horst 2007b; Lindley 2010; Riak Akuei 2005), while receivers may also fail to achieve what is expected of them. This could lead to the poverty cycle that Lindley (2007a) has warned against, in which senders face such great pressures that they incur overwhelming debts in order to be able to fulfill all the demands on them, and receivers are unable to substantially improve their conditions. Despite the preferences of senders and receivers, remittances rarely consist of substantial amounts for sustainable purposes, but they can be mainly classified as aid for emergency or "care and maintenance" money. Besides, remittances hardly ever address structural conditions that obstruct socioeconomic opportunities. In order to enable both assistance practices among Somalis and international aid practices to have greater impact, however, it is crucial to start exploring these issues as well as the opportunities that may arise from building bridges across currently parallel systems.

NOTES

1. An earlier version of this chapter was published as Horst 2008b. See http://hup.sub.uni-hamburg.de/giga/afsp/index.
2. The ethnographic data presented was collected for two ongoing research projects: Globalization of Protracted Refugee Situations (GPRS) and Remittances of Immigrants in Norway (RIN). The GPRS project was hosted by York University and funded by the Social Science and Humanities Research Council (SSHRC) in Canada; the RIN project was hosted by the Peace Research Institute Oslo (PRIO) and funded by the Research Council of Norway (RCN). In addition to conducting participant observation and collecting semi-structured interview data myself from agency staff and refugees in both places, I provided training to three refugees to conduct interviews for both projects. A total of sixty semi-structured interviews were conducted with refugees in Kenya for both projects, of which thirty-four were interviews with refugees in camps and twenty-six with urban refugees. The data analysis furthermore benefited from earlier fieldwork among Somalis in Kenya, starting in 1995.

REFERENCES

Ahmed, I. 2000. "Remittances and Their Impact in Postwar Somaliland."
   Disasters 24(4): 380–89.
Al-Sharmani, M. 2006. "Living Transnationally: Somali Diasporic Women
   in Cairo." *International Migration* 44(1): 55–77.
Campbell, E. 2006. "Urban Refugees in Nairobi: Problems of Protection,
   Mechanisms for Survival and Possibilities for Integration." *Journal of
   Refugee Studies* 19(3): 396–413.
Carling, J. 2008. "The Human Dynamics of Migrant Transnationalism."
   Journal of Ethnic and Racial Studies 31(8): 1452–77.
Carling, J., M. B. Erdal, and C. Horst. Forthcoming. "How Does Conflict in
   the Country of Origin Affect Remittance-Sending? A Mixed-Method
   Study of Financial Priorities and Transnational Obligations among So-
   malis and Pakistanis in Norway." *International Migration Review.*
CEDAT. 2010. Complex Emergency Database Newsletter. Brussels: Centre
   for Research on the Epidemiology of Disasters. *CEDAT Newsletter* 15:
   November.
Crisp, J. 2003. *No Solutions in Sight: The Problem of Protracted Refugee
   Situations in Africa.* New Issues in Refugee Research. Geneva, UNHCR.
Diaz-Briquets, S., and J. Perez-Lopez. 1997. "Refugee Remittances: Concep-
   tual Issues and the Cuban and Nicaraguan Experiences." *International
   Migration Review* 31(2): 411–37.
Frerks, G. 2005. "Refugees between Relief and Development." In *Refugees
   and the Transformation of Societies: Agency, Policies, Ethics, and Poli-
   tics,* ed. P. Essed, G. Frerks, and J. Schrijvers. Oxford: Berghahn.
Gundel, J. 2002. "The Migration-Development Nexus: Somalia Case Study."
   International Migration 40(5): 255–81.
Hansen, P. 2004. *Migrant Transfers as a Development Tool: The Case of
   Somaliland.* DIIS Working Paper Series No 15. Copenhagen: DIIS.
Harrell-Bond, B. 2002. "Can Humanitarian Work with Refugees be Hu-
   mane?" *Human Rights Quarterly* 24(1): 51–85.
Harrell-Bond, B., and E. Voutira. 1994. "In Search of the Locus of Trust: The
   Social World of the Refugee Camp." In *Mistrusting Refugees,* ed. E.
   Daniel and J. Knudsen. Berkeley: University of California Press.
Harrell-Bond, B., E. Voutira, and M. Leopold. 1992. "Counting the Refugees:
   Gifts, Givers, Patrons and Clients." *Journal of Refugee Studies* 5 (3/4):
   206–25.
Hoehne, M. 2010. *Diasporic Engagement in the Educational Sector in Post-
   Conflict Somaliland: A Contribution to Peacebuilding?* DIASPEACE
   Working Paper Series no. 5.
Horst, C. 2006a. "Buufis amongst Somalis in Dadaab: The Transnational
   and Historical Logics behind Resettlement Dreams." *Journal of Refugee
   Studies* 19(2): 143–57.
———. 2006b. *Transnational Nomads. How Somalis Cope with Refugee Life
   in the Dadaab Camps of Kenya.* Oxford: Berghahn.

———. 2007a. "The Role of Remittances in the Transnational Livelihood Strategies of Somalis." In *Global Migration and Development*, ed. T. Van Naerssen, E. Spaan, and A. Zoomers. London: Routledge.

———. 2007b. "The Somali Community in Minneapolis: Expectations and Realities." In *From Mogadishu to Dixon: The Somali Diaspora in a Global Context*, ed. A. Kusow and S. Bjork. Trenton, N.J.: Red Sea Press.

———. 2008. "The Transnational Political Engagements of Refugees: Remittance Sending Practices amongst Somalis in Norway." *Conflict, Security and Development* 8(3): 317–39.

———. 2008b. "A Monopoly on Assistance? International Aid to Refugee Camps and the Role of the Diaspora." *Afrika Spectrum* 43(1): 121–31.

Jacobsen, K. 2006. "Refugees and Asylum Seekers in Urban Areas: A Livelihoods Perspective." *Journal of Refugee Studies* 19(3): 273–86.

Kagwanja, P., and M. Juma. 2008. "Somali Refugees: Protracted Exile and Shifting Security Frontiers." In *Protracted Refugee Situations: Political, Human Rights and Security Implications*, ed. G. Loescher et al. Tokyo: United Nations University Press.

Kent, R., and K. Von Hippel. 2005. "Social Facilitation, Development and the Diaspora: Support for Sustainable Health Services in Somalia." Paper presented at Understanding the Challenges & Development Potential of Somali Remittances Conference, Washington, D.C., December 1–2.

Kibreab, G. 1999. "Revisiting the Debate on People, Place, Identity and Displacement." *Journal of Refugee Studies* 12(4): 384–428.

Kleist, N. 2004. "Nomads, Sailors and Refugees: A Century of Somali Migration." Sussex Migration Working Paper. University of Sussex, Centre for Migration Research.

Lindley, A. 2005. "The Influence of Remittances and Diaspora Donations on Education." Paper presented at Understanding the Challenges & Development Potential of Somali Remittances Conference, Washington, D.C., December 1–2.

———. 2006. *Migrant Remittances in the Context of Crisis in Somali Society: A Case Study of Hargeisa*. Humanitarian Policy Group Working Paper. London: ODI.

———. 2007a. *The Early Morning Phonecall: Remittances from a Refugee Diaspora Perspective*. Oxford: Centre on Migration, Policy and Society (COMPAS).

———. 2007b. *Protracted Displacement and Remittances: The View from Eastleigh, Nairobi*. UNHCR Working Paper Series.

———. 2010. *The Early Morning Phone Call: Somali Refugees' Remittances*. Oxford: Berghahn.

Loescher, G., J. Milner, E. Newman, and G. Troeller. 2007. "Protracted Refugee Situations and the Regional Dynamics of Peacebuilding." *Conflict, Security and Development* 7(3): 491–501.

———, eds. 2008. *Protracted Refugee Situations: Political, Human Rights and Security Implications*. Tokyo: United Nations University Press.

Malkki, L. 1995. *Purity and Exile: Violence, Memory, and National Cosmology among Hutu Refugees in Tanzania*. Chicago: University of Chicago Press.

————. 1996. "Speechless Emissaries: Refugees, Humanitarianism and De-historicization." *Cultural Anthropology* 11(3): 377–404.

Mauss, M. 1954. *The Gift: Forms and Functions of Exchange in Archaic Societies.* London: Cohen and West.

Monsutti, A. 2004. "Cooperation, Remittances, and Kinship among the Hazaras." *Iranian Studies* 37(2): 219–40.

Omer, A., and G. El Koury. 2005. "Regulation and Supervision in a Vacuum: The Story of the Somali Remittance Sector." In *Remittances: Development Impact and Future Prospects,* ed. S. Maimbo and D. Ratha. Washington, D.C.: World Bank.

Papadopoulos, R. 2002. *Therapeutic Care for Refugees: No Place like Home.* London: H. Karnac Books.

Perouse de Montclos, M. A. 2007. "A Refugee Diaspora: When the Somali Go West." In *New African Diasporas,* ed. K. Koser. London: Routledge.

Perouse de Montclos, M. A., and P. Kagwanja. 2000. "Refugee Camps or Cities? The Socio-economic Dynamics of the Dadaab and Kakuma Camps in Northern Kenya." *Journal of Refugee Studies* 13(2): 205–22.

Riak Akuei, S. 2005. *Remittances as Unforeseen Burdens: The Livelihoods and Social Obligations of Sudanese Refugees.* Global Migration Perspectives. Geneva: GCIM.

Turner, S. 2010. *Politics of Innocence: Hutu Identity, Conflict and Camp Life.* Oxford: Berghahn.

UNHCR. 2007. *Dadaab Operations in Brief.* Nairobi: UNHCR Sub-Office Dadaab.

USCRI. 2004. *World Refugee Survey 2004 (Warehousing Issue).* Washington, D.C.: U.S. Committee for Refugees and Immigrants.

Van Hear, N. 2001. "Sustaining Societies under Strain: Remittances as a Form of Transnational Exchange in Sri Lanka and Ghana." In *New Approaches to Migration? Transnational Communities and the Transformation of Home,* ed. K. Koser and N. Al-Ali. London: Routledge.

Zetter, R. 1991. "Labelling Refugees: Forming and Transforming a Bureaucratic Identity." *Journal of Refugee Studies* 4(1): 39–62.

PART 3

FEMINIZATION OF MIGRATION
AND THE APPEARANCE OF
DIASPORIC IDENTITIES

11

THE FEMINIZATION OF ASYLUM MIGRATION FROM AFRICA

PROBLEMS AND PERSPECTIVES

JANE FREEDMAN

One of the accepted characteristics of contemporary migratory flows from Africa to countries of the global North is "feminization." The newness and extent of this feminization are matters of some debate, but one area where there is a clear increase in women migrants is in asylum migration. This growth comes at a time when governments in many states are introducing increasingly restrictive and repressive policies with regard to asylum seekers. Regarded as "false" refugees by much of the media and public opinion, asylum seekers are more and more often seeing their claims rejected by the authorities who determine national refugee status. In addition, restrictions on the welfare and social rights of asylum seekers and increasing use of detention, dispersal, and deportation have made the living conditions for many asylum seekers particularly difficult (Bloch and Schuster 2005; Valluy 2005). While supposedly gender neutral, these policies may have specific gendered impacts that are ignored by policy makers but that may lead to particular insecurities for women seeking asylum. Further, women may adopt specific strategies for seeking asylum in order to try to conform to the particular constructions of who is a "real" refugee. A gendered analysis of the way that asylum seekers are constructed through asylum determination procedures shows that although in some circumstances it may now be easier for a woman to be granted refugee status on the basis of gender-related persecution, this is dependent on her ability to conform both to an appropriate image of the "convention refugee" and to representations of proper modes of "female" behavior.

This chapter seeks to explore the experiences of African women seeking asylum in industrialized countries, specifically within the European Union. I argue that restrictive legislation and policies within the EU have not stemmed the increasing flow of women wishing to seek asylum, and that on the contrary the causes of asylum migration from Africa are ever more present. The current policies and legislation have, however, pushed some women into situations of great insecurity and have made them reliant in many cases on the services of smugglers or traffickers to reach Europe. Paradoxically, European Union policies designed to crack down on trafficking and illegal migration have often just increased the demand for such services, and gendered structures of inequality may mean that women are more vulnerable to exploitation in this case. The chapter is based on research carried out in various European countries from 2005 to 2008, including interviews with asylum seekers, policy makers, and representatives of various NGOs and associations involved in the support of asylum seekers and refugees.

WOMEN ASYLUM SEEKERS: THE "INVISIBLE MINORITY"?

One of the difficulties in researching the "feminization" of asylum migration from Africa is a lack of accurate gender-disaggregated statistics. While UNHCR has called on states to provide gender-disaggregated data on asylum seeking and refugee populations in order to ensure a more accurate and comprehensive knowledge of such populations, there are still large gaps in the available data.[1] These gaps have led some to overestimate the proportion of women in refugee and asylum-seeking populations, arguing for example that "the faces of refugees are overwhelmingly female: women and children represent eighty percent of the world's twenty seven million refugees and displaced people" (Oosterveld 1996: 570). This type of claim is used to try to reverse a previous "invisibility" of women in research and policy making on asylum seekers and refugees, and to press for further national and international actions. However, a basic problem with these statistics is that they conflate women and children into a single category, thus obscuring even further the real nature of the statistical differences between men and women.[2] The amalgamation of women and children into one category of "vulnerable" refugees is an important feature of the representations of women refugees in humanitarian actions, representations that can have major impacts on the way in which gender is treated in issues of refugee protection (Rajaram 2002). According to the UNHCR, women make up about one half of the total populations of concern to them. Breaking down the available data for 2006 by gender reveals that less than half of the overall population of concern is accounted for—only 13.9 million out of 32.9 million persons. Of these roughly half are women, although the proportions vary greatly depending on the refugee situation and the region of asylum (UNHCR 2006). Women are the majority in some refugee camps, resulting from "mass influx" situations following civil wars, for example, but they have historically been less represented among those seeking asylum in industrialized countries. Available statistics show that in Europe, for example, women make up only about one third of the total asylum claimants (Bloch et al. 2000; Freedman 2007).

The reasons there have historically been fewer women than men claiming asylum in industrialized countries are linked not to a lack of persecution and violence against women, but to structural gender inequalities that may make it more difficult for women to migrate. Gendered relations and structures of power play an essential role in the decision of whether or not to migrate (Binder and Tosic 2005), and although it would clearly be wrong to continue to regard the figure of the migrant as male, there are specifically gendered barriers that make it harder in some circumstances for women to leave their countries of origin. In some countries it may be problematic for a woman live alone or with children without the protection of her husband or another male relative. Prevalent norms may prevent a woman from working outside the home or traveling outside alone. In these circumstances, the idea of leaving her home or community and traveling long distances in order to reach another country to claim asylum may seem almost unimaginable. Further problems arise in relation to financial resources necessary for travel. Women may find themselves in a situation of economic dependence that makes it very hard for them to find the necessary resources to pay for their journey. The increased use of smugglers to help asylum seekers reach an industrialized country makes this problem even more acute, with the necessity of paying for one's passage adding yet another obstacle in the way of women with few financial resources. Many women asylum seekers interviewed for this research explained the problems that they had encountered in trying to raise money for their journey, or the way in which they had swapped services (including sexual relations) in order to bargain with those who would help them reach Europe.

Women who travel alone may also expose themselves to dangers of violence or sexual abuse on the journey, the fear of which may mean that they choose to stay and endure persecutions at home. The danger of becoming a victim of sexual abuse is very high, both within the country of origin, during the journey, and also in the host country (Binder and Tosic 2005). These dangers may be exacerbated by policies designed to prevent asylum seekers from reaching countries in the global North, policies that force many to use the service of smugglers and thus make themselves more vulnerable to exploitation and extortion. For women, this may take the form of sexual exploitation or forced prostitution. One Guinean woman recounted her experience of traveling to France, a journey of over four years: "Coming here was like a journey through hell. It took me four years to arrive. I went by foot, and then by bus and boat, and bus again. I worked along my way to get money. Once I met a man who said he would help me. But then he wanted me to work for him and that was too much shame for me. When I got here I was so tired, and tired of living."[3] This woman's experiences of the difficulties of the journey from Africa to Europe, and of vulnerability to sexual exploitation or abuse, are representative of the experiences of many women.

Another key difficulty faced by many women in making their decision to migrate or not relates to the care of their children. A woman may be reluctant to travel with her children under forced migratory circumstances because they also become exposed to the dangers of the journey. Other women may decide to leave their children in their country of origin with relatives or friends, but the decision to separate from one's children may be very painful, as the testimonies of women asylum seekers makes clear. One of the respondents interviewed for this research explained how she had left her three children with her neighbor in Rwanda when she had to flee suddenly following the murder of her husband. "The hardest thing for me is that I am not with my children, and I don't know what is happening to them. The neighbor who is looking after them is a good friend, but I haven't managed to phone her for a long time."[4] Ironically, the fact that a mother has left her children behind in her country of origin may make it harder for her to be granted asylum: she is stigmatized by authorities in the receiving country as a bad mother.

All these issues explain why there are fewer women than men seeking asylum in industrialized countries. However, as stated above, the proportion of women among asylum seekers reaching Europe has been growing consistently in recent years, and this is especially true for asylum seekers from Africa. Statistics from France, for example, indicate that the percentage of women among the total asylum claimants grew from 29.6 percent in 2001 to 36.5 percent in 2007.[5] However, this overall growth in the proportion of female asylum claimants masks important differences depending on the country of origin. In France in 2007, for example, 51 percent of all asylum claimants from the Democratic Republic of Congo were women, while only 22 percent of Turkish asylum claimants were women.[6] This difference illustrates a more general trend that is mirrored in other European countries. In the UK in 2006, 56 percent of Zimbabwean and 45 percent of Somalian asylum claimants were women, as compared to only 13 percent of Iranian and 6 percent of Afghan claimants.[7] Research carried out by the Refugee Women's Resource Project (RWRP) in the UK attempts to analyze these differentials with respect to gendered dynamics of forced migration. The report notes that "the proportion of women asylum-seekers is higher for countries where civil unrest and/or war are widespread. It is lower in countries where the primary focus on human rights violations is political and civil rights abuses and where women's rights are repressed" (RWRP 2003: 35). These figures reinforce the arguments outlined above that describe the difficulties women have in undertaking any kind of forced migration, suggesting that it is more likely that they will leave a country only when it is absolutely the last choice, such as in times of civil war or conflict where their lives are in immediate danger. They are less likely to flee when persecution is in the form of general violations of their human rights, such as discriminatory laws or practices in some countries.

In addition, however, to these more negative explanations of why women do not flee from some countries, we could add some positive explanations examining the reasons why more women are undertaking forced migrations from some African countries. Clearly a proportion of this asylum migration is linked to the high level of conflict, and the outbreak of "new" forms of war in which civilians have become the primary targets. Although it would be wrong to simply equate civilians with women and children (Carpenter 2006), it is evident that these are conflicts in which women civilians have suffered high levels of violence and where sexual violence against women has become prevalent (Alison 2007). Many of the women interviewed for this research had been victims of rape and sexual violence during conflict situations. And as one NGO employee explained: "It's horrible to say, but with women from some countries like DRC, for example, you don't even have to ask the question—you just know what they have suffered. And when we have to ask them to explain their stories for the asylum claims, it feels like we are part of the violence—making them re-live it again."[8] Unfortunately, the prevalence of rape and sexual violence may lead in some cases to a normalization of such violence that can lead decision makers and judges to taken it less seriously as grounds for granting asylum, as discussed below.

A further explanation for the feminization of asylum migration from Africa emanates from the authorities who determine refugee status: in some cases they are seeing more asylum claims linked to "social" issues such as female genital mutilation (FGM) or forced marriage since the introduction of the status of subsidiary protection as a substitute for that of convention refugee status. Thus the French refugee status determination body, Ofpra, in its 2006 annual report, points to a particular growth in the number of women asylum seekers from Guinea and Nigeria who are fleeing from FGM or forced marriage, and women from Algeria claiming asylum on the basis of persecutions suffered because of their westernized life style. For those who would like to see these types of persecution recognized as legitimate grounds for claiming refugee status under the Geneva Convention, it is perhaps worrying that the Ofpra report refers to these types of claims as emerging in "parallel with classic political problematics arising from the Geneva Convention," and it makes a very strong link between the emergence of these types of claims and the introduction of a new form of subsidiary protection (Ofpra 2006).[9] Some interviewees working within NGOs expressed a fear that this perception of gender-related persecutions such as FGM and forced marriage as "non-political" would mean that women claiming refugee status on these grounds would never receive convention refugee status but only subsidiary protection, with much less guarantee of protection.

A final explanation for the increasing number of asylum claims from African women can be seen in the increase in trafficking in women to the EU. As noted above, the ever more restrictive controls at the borders of Europe have somewhat paradoxically created a huge demand for the services of people smugglers and traffickers. There are still many ongoing debates over the definition of trafficking and its scale. As with other forms of clandestine migration, it is impossible to give any accurate figures regarding trafficking, but both police sources and NGOs in Europe have remarked on a rise in the number of foreign women working as prostitutes, and according to these sources many of these women are working for organized networks. One NGO working with prostitutes in the French city of Toulouse, for example, has noted a huge increase in the presence of Nigerian and Ghanaian women working as prostitutes in the city, many of whom are working to repay "debts" incurred while paying for their entry into France. The link between trafficking and asylum is not often made in policy-making bodies, but, according to UNHCR guidelines, victims of trafficking should be entitled to refugee status if they have a well-founded fear of persecution on return to their country of origin. Further, social workers at various associations and NGOs working with victims of trafficking recount that many of the women trafficked have been victims of violence and persecution in their country of origin.[10] They may have been victims of forced marriage or threatened with FGM, for example, and thus been forced to flee. Other women who are later trafficked may have been persecuted for their ethnic or religious identity and have suffered violence that has forced them to move to another part of the country, where they are then prey to traffickers. One Nigerian woman interviewed had fled from her village after both her parents were killed in political violence, and then met a man who offered to bring her to France. When she arrived she was forced to work in prostitution to repay her "debt" to this man. Another woman from Ghana fled a forced marriage and also ended up working as a prostitute to pay her debts to the man who helped to bring her to France. The prevalence of gender-based forms of persecution and the lack of legal channels for arriving in Europe to make an asylum claim make these women vulnerable to traffickers. These women may well have grounds for claiming asylum, but because they are under the control of the trafficker, it is the trafficker who will write their asylum claim and it will not contain their real story. Traffickers encourage women to make asylum claims as a way of keeping them in France "legally," but all aspects of this claim are tightly controlled. It is difficult for these women to then tell their real story to the authorities to gain effective protection.

TAKING GENDER-RELATED PERSECUTION SERIOUSLY?

One of the consequences of the feminization of asylum migration has been the emergence and problematization of the question of gender-related forms of persecution and of the ways that these could be dealt with under existing international and national conventions and legislation. The term gender-related persecution encompasses persecution inflicted on women because they are women, but also persecution for other reasons that takes a particular form because the victim is a woman. In some instances the two elements may be combined, but this is not necessarily the case. As Macklin explains:

> Gender may explain why a woman was persecuted. Gender may also determine the form that persecution takes. Sometimes, it may even be a risk factor that makes a woman's fear of persecution more well-founded than that of a man in similar circumstances. Though one or more of these links between gender and persecution may be present simultaneously in a given case, they are not synonymous. The idea of women being persecuted *as* women is not the same as women being persecuted *because* they are women. (Macklin 1995: 259)

Although some progress can be noted in the degree to which authorities determining national refugee status have begun to accept some forms of gender-related persecution as grounds for granting refugee status, there are still large gaps in the protection afforded to the women who arrive in Europe. It should be noted that discretionary power plays a large role in refugee status determination, and that a large range of actors are involved, including both public authorities and NGOs or associations who help asylum seekers to frame their claims.

The international laws and conventions on refugees (principally the 1951 Convention on the Status of Refugees, or Geneva Convention), which supposedly offer protection to all on a gender-neutral basis, are in fact often undermined by deeply gendered practices that fail to offer protection to women because their persecution is not recognized as such. It can thus be argued that while the Geneva Convention and other international agreements on refugees and asylum supposedly offer protection to all on a gender-neutral basis, the procedures for granting protection have often been undermined by deeply gendered practices that fail to offer protection to women because their persecution is not recognized as such. Women may also fail to receive protection because of the failure to take into account barriers such as the difficulty in recounting their experiences before immigration officials and judges. As argued above, the definitions of persecution that has been adopted by national authorities when interpreting the Geneva Convention have been diverse, but many have been based on definitions of human rights that have been constructed from a male perspective. As Crawley argues, the interpretation of refugee law has evolved through an examination of male asylum applicants and their activities that has both reflected and reinforced existing gender biases within states: "It is men who have been considered the principal agents of political resistance and therefore the legitimate beneficiaries of protection from resulting persecution" (Crawley 1999: 309). Thus when considering the practical implementation of the Geneva Convention in national legislation and procedures, it is clear that gender bias still remains. Although there has been some limited progress in different countries toward the recognition of gender-related persecution and measures have been put in place in some contexts to provide specific assistance and support to women seeking asylum, this progress remains piecemeal and rather arbitrary, with decisions still depending to a great extent on the discretionary power of immigration officials and judges, and on the views and actions of a number of other actors, including NGOs and associations supporting asylum seekers. The progress represented by such individual decisions does not correspond to a real shift away from much of the gender bias present in the application of asylum laws and processes.

One of the major effects of this transposition of liberal definitions of human rights into the interpretation of the Geneva Convention has been to reinforce the division between public and private found in much of liberal rights discourse. Historically, as many feminist theorists have already pointed out, liberal rights discourse reinforced the division between the public and the private spheres—where the public sphere referred to non-domestic life and the private to domestic and family matters—ignoring discriminations and harm to women that took place within the private setting of home and family. Thus huge areas of women's lives are left outside the scope of legal protection and redress. While demands from women's movements that the scope of rights be extended has led to a reframing and redevelopment of the criteria for advancing women's rights across a number of spheres (Charlesworth and Chinkin 2000), this issue of the demarcation of public from private still remains. The underlying assumption of the public-private division thus undermines asylum law and practice by creating situations wherein much of what women do and what is done to them may be seen as irrelevant to the law. The threat of forced marriage or female genital mutilation, for example, may be considered threats of a private nature, as they take place within the sphere of the family or home, and therefore they may not be considered to come under the scope of the Geneva Convention and thus not be grounds for granting asylum to women. Similarly, forms of persecution related to women's private behavior (for example, their refusal to adhere to certain dress codes) or to violence that takes place within the private sphere of the family (violence committed by a husband, father, or another family member) may not be recognized as grounds for granting refugee status.

This public-private division might be argued to be particularly acute in cases of domestic violence, which is a type of violence often dismissed as irrelevant to asylum claims, even when the women who experience it can expect no help or protection from the police or state authorities in their country of origin. Because this type of violence takes place within the family, and is indeed perpetrated by family members, it is somehow perceived as less severe than other types of violence experienced in the public sphere (Copelon 1994). A woman who is severely beaten by her husband or father can thus expect less recognition from immigration officials and judges than one who is beaten by the police in her country of origin. Crawley, for example, recounts the experience of two women from Ghana who had both suffered severe domestic violence at the hands of their husbands. One of the women recounts the violence thus:

> My husband started chasing girls after my son was born. He wouldn't come home. If I said something about it he would beat me, with his hands, his belt. I had a very swollen face. He beat me for three years. He said if I tried to stop him he would cut me with knives and kill me. He didn't want me to divorce and his family has to divorce me. (Crawley 1999: 318)

Although the abuse this woman and her compatriot suffered was so severe that they both fled the country without their children, their asylum claims were described as "frivolous." The adjudicator at the appeal hearing of one of the women claimed that as far as he understood the law, "being beaten up by your husband is not a ground for asylum however deplorable it might be" (Crawley 1999: 319). This type of official reaction shows the way in which violence that takes place within the home is considered less serious and worthy of immigration officials' consideration than other forms of violence, even though a woman who is beaten in her home every day by her husband may under other criteria be considered just as much a victim of persecution as a political prisoner who is beaten by a guard in his prison cell.

Similarly, sexual violence and rape may not be considered on the same level as other types of violence; they are deemed personal or private, a result of private feelings of lust or desire and not a form of persecution or torture. Rape and sexual violence are often effectively normalized and considered as part of the universal relations between men and women. This normalization or relegation of rape to a private affair between individuals means that it might not be taken seriously when women make claims for asylum. Although many studies have pointed to the extensive use of sexual violence against women, particularly in conflict situations (Pearce 2003), this type of violence is still not always recognized as a form of persecution that can justify the granting of refugee status. The true scale of this sexual violence is probably unknown, since, as the UNHCR concludes, numerous incidents are never reported, often because of the shame of the women involved (UNHCR 1995). However, is it estimated that over 50 percent of refugee women have been raped (Pearce 2003). Sexual violence may be an explicit tool of political oppression, or it may be part of generalized violence in situations of civil war. Its effects on women are both physical and psychological harm. Women who have experienced such violence may also be perceived as having dishonored their family or community by engaging in sexual intercourse, even if forced, and so may find themselves rejected. Nevertheless, as noted, such women may not receive refugee status since it is often not recognized as a form of "serious harm" under the Geneva Convention. As Macklin argues: "Some decision makers have proven unable to grasp the nature of rape by state actors as an integral and tactical part of the arsenal of weapons deployed to brutalize, dehumanize and humiliate women and demoralize their kin and community" (Macklin 1995: 226).

In Germany, for example, women have been refused asylum on the grounds of rape during times of ethnic conflict, because "widespread rape by hostile militia has been dismissed as the common fate of women caught in a war zone and not recognised as persecution" (Ankenbrand 2002: 48). A report by the Black Women's Rape Action Project and Women Against Rape in the UK describes a similar phenomenon of the rejection of asylum claims by women who have been raped, as the political nature of this type of violence is not acknowledged and rape is not recognized as persecution. The report provides an example of a Ugandan woman who was raped by soldiers during an interrogation about her alleged support for rebels in the country. The Asylum Appeal Adjudicator rejected her claim, dismissing the rape as an act of "sexual gratification" and not persecution under the terms of the Geneva Convention. This judgment was upheld in the High Court, where the judges argued that the woman was not a victim of persecution but merely of "dreadful lust" (BWRAP and WAR 2006). Further, the conditions under which female asylum seekers are interviewed about their experiences often make it almost impossible to talk about the sexual violence perpetrated against them.

A further barrier to the recognition of gender-related persecution within current definitions and interpretations of the Geneva Convention is the way in which persecutory practices that may be common in third-world countries are assigned to cultural difference and are thus viewed as part of the order of things. This normalization of persecutions through their ascription to cultural differences that should not be challenged by Western states feeds into the debates over the possibility of defining universal women's rights, or whether these rights should be culturally sensitive. Liberal rights discourse has been criticized for its false universalism and its inability to accommodate cultural diversity. In international arenas, some of the resistance to universal standards for women's rights has in fact been led by conservative states and religious NGOs (Sen and Correa 1999; Molyneux and Razavi 2002), but this universal rights discourse has also been criticized by some feminists, who have argued that it does not take account of differences among women and reproduces an ethnocentric and Western model of rights that supports the idea of Western cultural superiority (Mohanty 1991). The difficulty is thus to determine how far any defense of "cultural difference" is actually a defense of practices that amount to an attack on women's rights and to persecution of women. As Rao points out, the arguments against universal rights based on the need to maintain cultural difference actually serve a variety of interests and may in fact be employed by regimes that do not favor women's emancipation (Rao 1995). Claims to defend traditional cultures often involve control of areas such as family life, which lead to the subjugation of women within the domestic sphere. As Molyneux and Razavi argue: "The fact that the roles and symbolism associated with femininity together with patriarchal authority and masculine privilege are often made into cultural signifiers places women's individual rights in conflict with those seeking to impose 'traditional,' 'authentic,' or 'national' customs on their people" (Molyneux and Razavi 2002: 15).

These conflicts between women's individual rights and those who seek to impose "traditional" or "cultural" practices upon them can easily lead to persecutions of women, but claims for asylum based on these persecutions may not be recognized as legitimate if the imperative of recognizing cultural difference prevails. For example, in a recent decision, the British Court of Appeal rejected an asylum claim from a Sierra Leonean woman who feared forced genital mutilation if she were returned to her country. One of the judges argued that the practice of female genital mutilation was clearly accepted by the majority of the population of Sierra Leone and was not in those circumstances discriminatory (RWRP 2005). After considerable lobbying by feminist groups, this decision was later overturned by the House of Lords, which ruled that the claimant could be considered as part of a "particular social group" of women from

Sierra Leone who were at risk of FGM. However, in other cases it is still assumed that if FGM is the prevailing norm in a country of origin, then a woman cannot claim to be persecuted because she resists the practice, and that, further, it would be wrong to label such a practice as persecution because it is a common practice of this "other" culture. The problems of constructing refugees as victims of these "other" cultures are discussed further below.

Additional barriers to the recognition of women's asylum claims include the conditions under which claims are made and heard. UNHCR guidelines recommend that an asylum seeker should be able to request an interviewer and interpreter of the same sex when making her claim; however, in many European countries this is still not the general practice. The trauma of having to recount one's experiences of persecution, in some cases several times, is for some women akin to being forced to relive that violence. As one woman from Cote d'Ivoire explained:

> It was horrible because I didn't want to keep telling my story to everyone. It really wasn't easy to talk about my life, because I'm a person who has my dignity. I felt really bad because I saw all my past again. . . . That's it. . . . In order to get out of my situation . . . first at the Ofpra and then at the Commission . . . The images of what I had lived through flashed through my head again, and I became really cold. . . . The friend who was supporting me took my hand and said I was completely cold, I wasn't in my body anymore. . . . It was no longer me. . . . I was cold. . . . The French state forces you to go through that and to tell your story again and again in order to have your papers.[11]

However traumatic may be the experience of recounting one's story repeatedly and in as much detail as possible in order to claim asylum, there is no other way for a woman to convince authorities that she is a genuine asylum seeker. Little psychological support is available to traumatized asylum seekers who are faced with this grueling legal process. The system for judging asylum claims makes few allowances for the reactions of those traumatized by persecution or violence. Many claims are rejected because the asylum seeker is unable to explain clearly in front of immigration officials or judges what has happened to her. In such a case her claims will be judged as not credible.

There are also important material difficulties facing asylum seekers who arrive in Europe. An idea that has become commonplace in debates over the number of asylum seekers reaching different countries is that the welfare benefits available to these asylum seekers in each country can act like a magnet to attract greater and greater numbers. This idea, together with the perception that asylum seekers place a huge financial burden on national governments, has led to the restriction of many of the welfare rights to which asylum seekers were previously entitled.

In Europe, this process can be seen as a reduction of welfare benefits and support offered to asylum seekers to the level of the lowest common denominator, even though disparities remain in the level of benefits available. In 2003 the EU introduced a Reception Directive that should have been transposed in all member states (with the exception of Ireland and Denmark, which opted out) by February 2005.[12] The Reception Directive is supposed to ensure minimum standards for the reception of asylum seekers in all states that are meant to guarantee a "dignified standard of living." This standard of living seems in many cases not to be a reality, however, and often the rights of asylum seekers to housing and other benefits are well below the level of those granted to other citizens. As Düvell and Jordan explain, a process of "benchmarking" has taken place within the EU over the types of accommodation provided for asylum seekers, the level of social benefits, and the duration for which an asylum seeker is allowed to claim them. In each case, member states have chosen to adopt models from other countries that are seen as best limiting the number of asylum applicants. Thus Germany and Sweden have been the models for the dispersal of asylum seekers to accommodation across the country, and programs for restriction of benefits have been copied from the Netherlands and Denmark. "The overall effect has been a leveling-down of welfare provision and an attempt to speed up decisions in most countries" (Düvell and Jordan 2002: 505).

Although this leveling down of welfare provisions affects all asylum seekers, it is again true that gendered inequalities may mean that women are left even more vulnerable and insecure. The lack of suitable accommodation, for example, is a serious problem. The UN Commission on Human Rights report on Italy, for example, highlights the terrible conditions facing some African asylum seekers in Rome who are living in abandoned buildings in the city's Tiburtina Station (commonly known as the "African Hotel"). The special rapporteur met one young woman who was living in a room with twenty other people, and pointed out that women and teenage girls living in these circumstances ran a high risk of sexual abuse (UN Economic and Social Council 2005).

Some of the women interviewed for this research had also experienced homelessness, like one Guinean woman who spent three weeks sleeping in Paris's Gare du Nord. An Eritrean woman in London explained: "I was thrown out of my hostel and forced to sleep rough. Sometimes I slept at Victoria Station, sometimes on night buses. I was terrified of being attacked." Another woman expresses the difficulties of her life as an asylum seeker: "Our daily life is a race for survival. We spend our whole day running around trying to find enough food, somewhere to sleep, clothes for our children, never mind trying to find a lawyer to help with our asylum claim."[13] The procedural and material difficulties outlined add to the insecurities and vulnerability of these women who arrive in Europe to claim asylum, and these make it more difficult for them to go through all the legal procedures to have their claim recognized.

STRATEGIES FOR SURVIVAL

I have outlined some of the sources of insecurity and vulnerability facing African women who arrive in Europe to make an asylum claim. It would be wrong, however, to see these women as merely victims. Faced with persecutions in their countries of origin and restrictions on their rights in Europe, they have developed many different strategies for survival, and in some cases they have organized and mobilized collectively to defend their rights, despite the obstacles to such collective action. One of the major barriers to asylum seekers' self-organization and mobilization is their very precarious legal status, which makes it difficult to plan or carry out any long-term projects. Lesselier points to the way in which various attempts to create autonomous associations for asylum seeking and refugee women in France have led to short-lived mobilizations, which have foundered both because of the precarious legal status of the women involved and because of a lack of recognition for this type of organization both from within official government structures and from other NGOs and associations (Lesselier 2007). In addition, women may find it more difficult to organize because of the subordinate role that they have been assigned in many societies. This means that male asylum seekers may not allow women to take an equal role in associations or political mobilizations.

When successful, these types of independent mobilizations can be a way of developing a more formal status for those granted some form of protection and a means of integration into the host society. For example, Sales and Gregory refer to the case of Somali women from a local refugee organization who now works with social services in London (Sales and Gregory 1998). Perhaps even more important, these types of associations can provide an arena where women asylum seekers or refugees can express their own political agency and escape from the dominant representations of themselves as merely victims. As one of the founders of the All African Women's Group in the UK explained: "Being together with other women has really helped us to fight. We know that we can help each other, it's very important for women to come together and share our experiences and help each other. We've managed to change our lives."[14] She described how the group was formed in the wake of protests against the effects of Section 55 of the 2002 Immigration and Asylum Act, which removed the right to welfare support for asylum seekers who failed to make an application "as soon as is reasonably practicable" when arriving in the country. A group of Eritrean women claiming asylum were refused housing by the Refugee Council under the terms of this act and organized a public protest outside the Refugee Council offices in London. This group was joined by women from other African countries who shared similar experiences. Semret Fesshaye, an Eritrean woman who was one of the group's initial members, describes the importance of this self-mobilization: "Traditionally, asylum seekers in this country have remained silent for fear of deportation. We have allowed others to speak on our behalf, but because the situation we find ourselves in here is disastrous we are starting to speak up for ourselves" (Fesshaye 2003).

This point about allowing women asylum seekers and refugees to speak for themselves seems to be key if there is to be any real progress in protecting their rights. Too often, the campaigns to help refugee and asylum-seeking women employ dominant representations that both portray women refugees as helpless victims and reinforce the difference between "us" and "them"—Western women and the racialized "other." This division can be traced back to a primary dichotomy that has been established in international politics between those states that produce refugees and those that accept refugees (Macklin 1995). Following the logic of the Cold War period, when the countries of the Western bloc believed that refugees all emanated from the other side of the Iron Curtain and that political persecution could not happen in their own countries, democratic Western states in the post–Cold War era have assumed that they cannot produce refugees because they have laws and policies designed to protect the human rights of their citizens. The refugee-producing countries are "others," countries that do not respect human rights in the same way. The problems inherent in this type of distinction are evident from the discussion of gender-related persecution and particularly of domestic violence. While domestic violence occurs in all countries, the connection is rarely established between violence against women "here" in the West and violence against women "there" in other countries. As a result, the persecutions that take place in those "other" countries are attributed to immutable social and cultural characteristics, and the real dynamics of gender inequality underlying all types of gender-related violence, whether "here" or "there," are not analyzed. This critique might serve as the basis of a wider criticism of the ways in which the voice of women asylum seekers and refugees is ignored in the framing of issues relating to gender specific persecution. The discursive opportunities that exist are not open to these women for reasons of political, social, and economic marginalization and exclusion. The NGOs and associations that make claims for gender-specific policies and legislation do so on behalf of refugee and asylum-seeking women, as these women themselves have little or no voice in the process. Speaking for women asylum seekers and refugees leads to representations and framings that rely heavily on preexisting cultural norms, as argued above, and that contain these women in their role of victims. Real understanding of the gendered causes of forced migration would take into account the voices and perspectives of those women who flee, and would adapt solutions for protection to specific experiences and to particular national and local contexts. A goal of feminist constructivist analysis must be to give a voice to those considered marginal in international politics (Locher and Prugl 2001). As Steans and Ahmadi conclude: "Agreements on principles or statements of good intent are of little use if they are not followed up with implementation and enforcement measures or if they are undermined, subsumed or spoken for only by elites. Impediments to women's participation in decision making processes remain, while practices of inclusion and exclusion in relation to NGOs . . . also silence women's voices" (Steans and Ahmadi 2005: 244). If the interests of women fleeing persecution and seeking protection as refugees are truly to be guaranteed, then the voices of these women need to be heard. It is important to listen to the voices of women seeking asylum and refugees if the trap of essentializing their experience and treating them as passive victims is to be avoided. Women do need protection and are vulnerable in some circumstances, but this should not be generalized to assume that they are all just vulnerable victims. Cockburn argues that women should only be treated as mothers, dependents, or vulnerable individuals when they themselves ask for this special treatment. "When, on the contrary, should they be disinterred from 'the family,' from 'women and children,' and seen as themselves, women—people, even? Ask the women in question. They will know" (Cockburn 2004: 29). The major problem inherent in European asylum systems is that women and men claiming asylum often do not get the opportunity to speak for themselves or to properly explain the persecutions they have suffered. The gendered constructions of a "real" refugee mean that women must conform to the ideal of a "victim" as defined within the asylum systems, but the circumstances of many women asylum seekers make this hard to do. Sadly, gender-based violence and persecutions are unlikely to disappear in the near future, and women from Africa will continue to arrive in Europe to claim asylum, but the current context means that these claims are likely to fall on deaf ears.

NOTES

1. Most recently in the *Agenda for Protection* (UNHCR 2003).
2. Cynthia Enloe has explained eloquently the ways in which the utilization of the category "womenandchildren [*sic*]" acts to identify man as the norm against which all others can be grouped together into a single leftover category, reiterating the notion that women are family members above all

and allowing the state and international institutions to play a paternalistic role in "protecting" these vulnerable women and children (Enloe 1993).

3. Interview with author, October 2006.

4. Interview with author, May 2008.

5. Office Français de Protection des Refugiés et Apatrides. Rapports d'activité 2001–2007.

6. Office Français de Protection des Refugiés et Apatrides. Rapport d'activité 2007.

7. UK Home Office, Control of Immigration: Yearly Statistics 2006.

8. Interview with author, January 2006.

9. Subsidiary protection is a lesser form of protection that may be granted to those whom the authorities judge not to qualify for full refugee status under the terms of the Geneva Convention, but who are nevertheless judged to be at risk of inhumane treatment if returned to their country of origin. This form of protection has been generalized across the EU under the terms of the EU Qualifications Directive. Some NGOs interviewed expressed the fear that this subsidiary protection might be widely used to treat claims involving more "social" forms of persecution, such as FGM or forced marriage, which would undermine efforts to ensure that the Refugee Convention was interpreted so as to include such gender-related forms of persecution. Subsidiary protection is less secure than Refugee Convention refugee status as it entitles the beneficiary to only a temporary residence permit and thus lesser access to social and welfare benefits.

10. Interview with author, October 2007.

11. Interview with author, October 2005.

12. Council Directive 2003/9/EC, laying down the minimum standards for the reception of asylum seekers.

13. Interviews with author, October 2006.

14. Interview with author January 2007.

REFERENCES

Alison, M. 2007. "Wartime Sexual Violence: Questions of Masculinity." *Review of International Studies* 33(1): 75–90.

Ankenbrand, B. 2002. "Refugee Women under German Asylum Law." *International Journal of Refugee Law* 14(1): 45–56.

Binder, S., and J. Tosic. 2005. "Refugees as a Particular Form of Transnational Migrations and Social Transformations: Socioanthropological and Gender Aspects." *Current Sociology* 53(4): 607–24.

Bloch, A., T. Galvin, and B. Harrell-Bond. 2000. "Refugee Women in Europe: Some Aspects of the Legal and Policy Dimensions." *International Migration* 38(2): 169–90.

Bloch, A., and L. Schuster. 2005. "At the Extremes of Exclusion: Deportation, Detention and Dispersal." *Ethnic and Racial Studies* 28(3): 491–512.

Bunch, C. 1995. "Transforming Human Rights from a Feminist Perspective." In *Women's Rights, Human Rights: International Feminist Perspectives*, ed. J. Peter and A. Wolper. New York: Routledge.

BWRAP and WAR. 2006. *Misjudging Rape: Breaching Gender Guidelines and International Law in Asylum Appeals.* London: Crossroads Books.

Carpenter, R. C. 2006. *"Innocent Women and Children": Gender, Norms and the Protection of Civilians.* Aldershot: Ashgate.

Charlesworth, H., and C. Chinkin. 2000. *The Boundaries of International Law: A Feminist Analysis.* Manchester: Manchester University Press.

Charlesworth, H., et al. 1991. "Feminist Approaches to International Law." *American Journal of International Law* 85(4): 613–64.

Chimni, B. S. 1998. "The Geopolitics of Refugee Studies: A View from the South." *Journal of Refugee Studies* 11(4): 350–74.

Cockburn, C. 2004. "The Continuum of Violence: A Gender Perspective on War and Peace." In *Sites of Violence: Gender and Conflict Zones*, ed. W. Giles and J. Hyndman. Berkeley: University of California Press.

Copelon, R. 1994. "Intimate Terror: Understanding Domestic Violence as Torture." In *Human Rights of Women: National and International Perspectives*, ed. R. Cook. Philadelphia: University of Pennsylvania Press.

Crawley, H. 1999. "Women and Refugee Status: Beyond the Public/Private Dichotomy." In *Engendering Forced Migration: Theory and Practice*, ed. D. Indra. Oxford: Berghahn.

Crawley, H. 2001. *Refugees and Gender: Law and Process.* Bristol: Jordan.

Düvell, F., and B. Jordan. 2002. "Immigration, Asylum and Welfare: The European Context." *Critical Social Policy* 22(3): 498–517.

Enloe, C. 1993. *The Morning After: Sexual Politics at the End of the Cold War.* Berkeley: University of California Press.

Fesshaye, S. 2003. "Rape, Hunger and Homelessness." *Guardian*, November 1.

Finnemore, M., and K. Sikkink. 1998. "International Norm Dynamics and Political Change." *International Organization* 52(4): 887–917.

Freedman, J. 2007. *Gendering the International Asylum and Refugee Debate.* Basingstoke: Palgrave Macmillan.

Lesselier, C. 2007. "Politiques d'immigration en France: appréhender la dimension de genre." In *Femmes, genre, migrations et mondialisation: un état des problématiques*, ed. J. Falquet, J. Freedman, and F. Scrinzi. Paris : CEDREF.

Locher, B., and E. Prugl. 2001. "Feminism and Constructivism: Worlds Apart or Sharing the Middle Ground?" *International Studies Quarterly* 45(1): 111–29.

Macklin, A. 1995. "Refugee Women and the Imperative of Categories." *Human Rights Quarterly* 17(2): 213–77.

Mohanty, C. T. 1991. *Third World Women and the Politics of Feminism.* Bloomington: Indiana University Press.

Moller-Okin, S., ed. 1999. *Is Multiculturalism Bad for Women?* Princeton, N.J.: Princeton University Press.

Molyneux, M. and S. Razavi. (eds.). 2002. *Gender Justice, Development and Rights.* Oxford: Oxford University Press.

Oosterveld, V. L. 1996. "The Canadian Guidelines on Gender-Related Persecution: An Evaluation." *International Journal of Refugee Law* 8(4): 569–96.

Pearce, H. 2003. "An Examination of the International Understanding of Political Rape and the Significance of Labeling It Torture." *International Journal of Refugee Law* 14(4): 534–60.

Rajaram, P. K. 2002. "Humanitarianism and Representations of the Refugee." *Journal of Refugee Studies* 15(3): 247–64.

Rao, A. 1995. "The Politics of Gender and Culture in International Human Rights Discourse." In *Women's Rights, Human Rights: International Feminist Perspectives*, ed. S. Peters and A. Wolper. New York: Routledge.

Refugee Women's Resource Project [RWRP] (Asylum Aid). 2003. *Women Asylum Seekers in the UK: A Gender Perspective*. London: Refugee Women's Resource Project.

Refugee Women's Resource Project [RWRP] (Asylum Aid). 2005. *Gender Issues in Asylum Claims: Spreading Good Practice across the European Union*. London: Refugee Women's Resource Project.

Sales, R. 2002. "The Deserving and the Undeserving? Refugees, Asylum Seekers and Welfare in Britain." *Critical Social Policy* 22(3): 456–78.

Sales, R. and J. Gregory. 1998. "Refugee Resettlement in Europe." In *Refugees, Citizenship and Social Policy in Europe*, ed. A. Bloch and C. Levy. Basingstoke: Macmillan.

Steans, J., and V. Ahmadi, V. 2005. "Negotiating the Politics of Gender and Rights: Some Reflections on the Status of Women's Human Rights at 'Beijing Plus Ten.'" *Global Society* 19(3): 227–45.

Stivens, M. 2002 "Gender Politics and the Reimagining of Human Rights in the Asia-Pacific." In *Human Rights and Gender Politics: Asia-Pacific Perspectives*, ed. A. Hildson et al. London: Routledge.

United Nations Economic and Social Council. Commission on Human Rights. 2005. *Specific Groups and Individuals: Migrant Workers: Visit to Italy*. E/CN.4/2005/85/Add.3.

United Nations High Commissioner for Refugees.1995. *Sexual Violence against Refugees: Guidelines on Protection and Response*. Geneva: UNHCR.

———. 2003. *Agenda for Protection*. Geneva: UNHCR.

———. 2006. *State of the World's Refugees: Human Displacement in the New Millennium*. Geneva: UNHCR.

Valluy, J. 2005. "La nouvelle Europe politique des camps d'exilés: genèse d'une source élitaire de phobie et de repression des étrangers." *Cultures et Conflits* 57: 13–69.

MIGRATION AS A FACTOR OF CULTURAL CHANGE ABROAD AND AT HOME

SENEGALESE FEMALE HAIR BRAIDERS IN THE UNITED STATES

CHEIKH ANTA BABOU

Hair braiding has become the leading profession of Senegalese female immigrants in North America.[1] It is also embraced by male immigrants working as managers of hair salons. This scorned profession that was traditionally reserved for women belonging to endogamic craft corporations (castes in Senegal) has become in the diaspora a highly sought after and valued career, attracting Senegalese of all genders, ethnic groups, and social statuses. Through an examination of the experience of Senegalese female hair braiders in Anderson (S.C.), Atlanta, New York, and Philadelphia, and their roles in their communities of origin in Senegal, this paper explores the issues of caste, gender, class, and money, and investigates how life in the United States has affected "traditional" views of these concepts.[2] I argue that economic power and changing societal values among immigrants are gradually undermining traditional bases of gender roles and social hierarchies abroad and at home. In Senegal, notions of gender and social status are shaped historically by local Islamic culture, professional occupation, and genealogy, which assign women and men from different families and ethnicities specific positions in society. But these categories of caste, gender, and class are increasingly contested at home and more so abroad, especially among the young and highly educated. In addition, several factors linked to legal status, the family, and the sociopolitical and cultural context in the host country affect the life of immigrants. Changes in these variables are echoed by the immigrant's behavior. In the diaspora, economic success is becoming the defining element of social status, and the gendered conception of work is giving way to pragmatism, where the prospect of earning a comfortable living tends to trump all other considerations.

HAIR BRAIDING AND SOCIAL STATUS IN WOLOF SOCIETY

Hair braiding is perhaps the most widespread form of body art in Africa. Scarifications, skin paintings, and other forms of body decoration are widely practiced by Africans, but they are not universal. The practice of hair braiding, in contrast, is found in all African cultures, ancient and contemporary, rural and urban. In Africa, unkempt hair is often associated with mental illness, grief, or lack of social integration (Sieber and Herreman 2000). In addition to being an art and an aesthetic, hair design was also a signifier of people's ethnicity, gender, and socioeconomic and political status.[3]

Hair dressing was primarily a domestic activity of women. It was an important dimension of female sociability. Family members and close friends did each other's hair and the long hours that women spent together dressing their hair provided a space for gossips and social interactions. The knowledge of the art of grooming hair was passed down from grandmothers to mothers and daughters. Knowing how to take care of one's daughters' hair was an integral part of motherhood.

While in most African societies the art of hair braiding was practiced in the realm of the household between relatives and friends, among the Wolof of Senegal complex hair designs were performed by specialists. These specialists were members of so-called lower castes. The Wolof social hierarchy is comprised of *géer*, non-artisans who occupy the top rank of the social ladder, and *ñeeño*, artisans who are confined to lower ranks.[4] The practice of endogamy and hereditary status among members of these different social strata led to the formation and reproduction of socially segregated craft corporations, such as wood workers, leather workers, blacksmiths, and *griots* (bards). And the social isolation of these craft corporations is so extreme that some scholars describe the Wolof as a caste society (Irvine 1973; Diop 1985; Tamari 1997). Although caste affiliation no longer plays a significant role in the distribution of wealth and power in contemporary Senegal, the stigma attached to caste continues to have a strong sociological significance that informs social interactions, marriage patterns, and people's perception of their self worth (Mbow 2000).

Until the explosion of the hair salon business in Senegal in the late 1970s and early 1980s, the profession of hair braiding was monopolized by casted women. For special occasions, *géer* women had their hair done at their *griots'* house (*ngewel ga*). Each *géer* or non-casted family entertained patron-client type relationships with a corresponding family of *ñeeño* who tended their women's hair. For unmarried young girls, payment was often delayed until they got married. *Géer* families collectively offered gifts of clothes, food, and sometimes money, to their clients. The *ñeeño* also had rights over certain parts of animals slaughtered at their *géer's* house. They were owed gifts at the occasion of family ceremonies such as marriage, naming ceremonies, funeral, and circumcision. In times of need, it was a moral obligation of their patrons to provide them help. For these casted women, hairdressing was not the exclusive source of income: they made and sold goods, mostly cosmetic and erotic products destined for female beautification and bedroom paraphernalia.

The monetization of African economies, stimulated by the introduction of cash crops and taxation by European colonizers, led to an increasing professionalization of hair braiding, especially in urban areas (Biaya 1999: 33). In the late 1980s, the enforcement of draconian policies of structural adjustments established by the World Bank and the International Monetary Fund stimulated male out-migration and encouraged women to leave the household and seek income-generating occupations.[5] Many women in urban and semi-urban areas in Senegal found employment in the restaurant and hair fashion businesses. Ñeeño continued to dominate the hair braiding profession, but the patron-client relationships gradually gave way to business type relationships, where paying customers increasingly requested professional treatment and braiders became increasingly ingenious in their ability to invent new designs and to adapt popular ancient styles. In the 1980s, the introduction of artificial hair extensions by entrepreneurial Senegalese male transnational traders accelerated the process of professionalization. Artificial hair was first imported into Senegal from the United States by Sheikh Gey, an international trader, who later partnered with a Korean businessman to open the first plant for the production of synthetic hair in Senegal.[6] Today, two of those plants operate in Senegal and they supply the local market and neighboring countries. Gey, who was among the first generation of Senegalese migrants to New York, was inspired by African American and Caribbean hairstyles, and he rightly anticipated Senegalese women's attraction to artificial hair extension. Historically, Senegalese women have used natural products such as tree bark and wool to increase hair length.[7] When they began to migrate to the United States, they had already developed hair fashions and styles that would exert great appeal for African American women and men.

SENEGALESE FEMALE HAIR BRAIDERS IN THE UNITED STATES

The first significant numbers of female Senegalese immigrants arrived in the United States in the early 1980s.[8] Like their male compatriots who started the journey a decade earlier, these women had much experience in international trade through their involvement in business ventures across Europe and Africa (Babou 2002: 161–62). In the United States they sold masks and other African artifacts, targeting African American fairs and music festivals organized in many states during the summer, and they returned to Africa for the remainder of the year. By the late 1980s and early 1990s, more women arrived to join their husbands. The Amnesty Law of 1986 allowed many undocumented Senegalese immigrants to regularize their situation, and many united with their wives. In the following decade, the immigration of Senegalese women to the United States accelerated, surpassing perhaps the rate of male immigration, this time involving unmarried adults and younger girls holding student visas or step-migrating from Canada or Europe. Women already established in the United States bought tickets for their sisters and provided them with the documentation to obtain a visa. The leniency of the American consul in Dakar toward women seeking entrance in the United States also helped spur migration.

The first Senegalese hair-braiding salons opened in New York City and Washington, D.C., in the second half of the 1980s.[9] The explosion in hairstyles prompted by the Afro revolution created a great demand for braiders that salon owners tried to meet by luring new Senegalese immigrants into the business. American and Caribbean hairstylists toured African immigrant residences to recruit braiders, some even making the trip to Senegal to look for workers.[10] And they were quite successful in their recruiting drive. For the new Senegalese immigrants, braiding presented many advantages. First, many among them were undocumented and did not speak English. Work in a hair salon was particularly desirable because it did not require a social security number or work permit, and the lack of English proficiency was not an obstacle. Second, although many of these women did not have formal training in braiding, they had learned the craft informally as young girls in Senegal.[11] They could quickly learn the styles practiced in the United States and get up to speed. In fact, many women braiders started first as apprentices in hair salons. They would be hired to do simple braids like cornrows or plaiting while learning the more sophisticated styles such as weaving and "micros." Third, the work environment was also appealing. New immigrants mingled with more experienced women and they could speak in their mother tongues sitting side by side, gossiping and sharing information about life in New York, replicating the atmosphere at home.

Salon owners were equally happy about working with Senegalese. They appreciated that Senegalese braiders were hard working and reliable. Furthermore, as noted by one of them—the owner of *Billy Jean*, one the oldest and most prestigious hair salons in Harlem—salon owners particularly valued the creativity of African braiders.[12] Senegalese women rapidly adapted to rigorous time management and a strict respect of customers' demands that braiding in the United States required. They also brought with them the tradition of innovation that characterizes hair fashions in Senegal. The great impact of Senegalese women on black hair fashions in the United States is exemplified by the adoption of styles typically associated with Senegal, such as Senegalese twists and Casamance, which are now offered by most hair salons (Jackson 2000: 185). In fact, one can argue that Senegalese braiders have succeeded in turning their craft into a highly desirable fashion brand. And just as French women are often seen as the epitome of fashion by white America, black America seems to embrace Senegalese hairstyles as the archetype of beauty.[13]

The popularity of Senegalese-style braiding opened a large window of opportunity for female immigrants in the United States. Braiding was a lucrative business that afforded self-employment and upward mobility to women immigrants. It was not merely a job of last resort that women were compelled to choose because of their immigration situation or because they lacked the professional skills to find employment elsewhere. On a good day during the tax refund period (January-April), which is the high season for braiding, a fast braider can easily make $200 to $300.[14] Large salons such as those of Ndey Astu Aac in Washington or Assan Gey in Atlanta, which employ dozens of braiders, annually produce six-figure incomes for their owners. It is safe to assert that about 70 percent of Senegalese women living in the United States work in the business of braiding. In some areas, particularly in the South, that percentage can reach over 90 percent.[15] A growing number of women are salon owners, but many braiders rent a chair in a salon or sell their services to fellow Africans. While in the beginning many women working with African American hairstylists accepted fixed weekly salaries, now payment is determined as a percentage of the money that the braider generates in a day.[16] The most common practice is to split in half the sum paid by the customer after subtracting the price for the artificial hair.

Although lucrative, braiding is a physically taxing job, putting much stress on the braider's wrists, fingers, legs, and back while requiring her to work standing up for hours. Braiders are also subject to emotional distress. They almost unanimously resent the cultural misunderstandings and tensions that mar their relationships with their African American customers.[17] Clients complain about African braiders' unwillingness to learn English and their tendency to blend workplace and home, how they turn their salons into dining rooms and lounges and spend long hours conversing among themselves in strange languages.[18] There are also complaints about hygiene and the health hazards that the lack of proper sanitation represents for clients. The braiders for their part criticize their African American customers for their cultural arrogance and their propensity to find excuses not to pay the price they bargained for.[19] However, despite the physical and emotional tolls associated with braiding and the negative effect of intense competition, Senegalese braiders are doing extremely well in the diaspora, much better than their male compatriots involved in taxi driving, street vending, or wage labor (Williams 2001).

BRAIDING, WEALTH, GENDER, AND SOCIAL STATUS

Perhaps the area where the expansion of braiding as a profession has its most important impact is gender roles. This impact is felt both in terms of distribution of wealth and power within the household and the larger extended family in the United States and in Senegal, and in terms of division of labor between the sexes. In Wolof Muslim society of Senegal, the roles of wife and husband are clearly defined, at least at the ideological level. Men maintain the authority in the house and they are responsible for providing for their families. This view is clearly expressed by a popular saying inspired by Islamic and Wolof values, *"Jabar: dëkel, dundal, dëkoo"* (it is the husband's responsibility to "to shelter, feed, and satisfy sexually his wife"). A man's worth is measured by the value of the house he is able to build, the quality of life he is able to provide to his wife or wives and children, and his ability to materially support his parents and in-laws. One should be aware, however, that the ways that the ideology of gender inequality is expressed in popular discourse (proverbs, popular wisdom, and even religion) rarely account for the real material conditions of power between the sexes. There are many cultural practices that reinforce the idea of male dominance and female subordination by highlighting women's domestic subjugation, but these cultural practices function as masks of the public power of women expressed in their roles as dynamic economic agents and political actors (Barnes 1990).

As shown in the pioneering work of Esther Boserup (1970) and later scholars, West Africans and Senegalese women in urban and rural areas as well have historically been economically active. But their economic activities, whether tending an orchard to supplement food supplies provided by their husbands or selling goods at local markets, were gender-specific both in their forms and the destination of the money they generated. Women may go out and work, and they often do, but their contribution to the family is not an obligation. And no matter how wealthy they are, it is their husbands' duty to take care of them (Guérin 2006; Perry 2005). A woman's worth is measured by her performance in the domestic sphere: how well she takes care of the household (manages daily expenses, cooks, cleans, educates the children) and how proficiently she manages interpersonal relationships and displays a sense of hospitality. Unlike men who are supposed to invest in inheritable and convertible goods such as real estate, houses, and cars, women carry their wealth on their bodies in the form of consumable goods such as expensive clothes, cosmetics, jewelry, wigs, and other accessories. Women's wealth is also used to build social capital through lavish spending during family gatherings such as naming ceremonies, marriages, or even funerals, and through generous gifts to in-laws, friends, and *griots* (Buggenhagen 2003).

This image of the Muslim Wolof household is, however, rapidly chang-ing, and one of the most important factors precipitating this change is the money that women are making from braiding and other economic ac-tivities. As mentioned earlier, Senegalese women have always been active economically. But more recently, braiders and a growing number of female entrepreneurs are increasingly and openly assuming the roles that men once held, especially in the ways they spend their money.[20] Many suc-cessful women braiders have become de facto providers for their families. Women are also more frequently investing in convertible assets (Guérin 2006: 556). In many cases I have encountered during my field research in Philadelphia, Atlanta, and New York, one can speak of a reversal of gender roles. Many husbands are employed by their wives. They help manage the hair salon, run errands, babysit the children, and serve as chauffeurs. In many instances, women contribute to the payment of rent, utilities, and groceries, and in some instances they shoulder all household expenses. The increase in women's wealth and monetary contribution is gradually affecting the distribution of power and authority within the household. Many women have taken the lead in making decisions about reproductive issues, investment priorities, and work schedules. Women are increasingly mobile and willing to move away from their husbands to seek better work opportunities. Although the women I have interviewed deny that they are subverting the traditional household hierarchy and insist that they remain faithful to Wolof and Muslim values of respect and submission to the husband, they display a mentality and set of practices that scarcely reflect their statements.[21] Many reminded me of two Wolof sayings that better expressed their growing power in the household: *"Goor baaxna, jigeen baaxna"* (It is good to be a man and it is good to be a woman) and *"ñaari loxooy takk tubëy, ñaari loxooy takk sër"* (It takes two hands to tie pants and it also takes two hands to tie a wrap). These transformations noted in the gender relations between immigrant Senegalese women and men are also documented in other migratory experiences. As noted by Saskia Sassen and others, international migration and the formation of transnational households can result in the shifting of gender patterns and the empowerment of women (Sassen 2007a: 9).

The changing power structure within the household is having a criti-cal effect on the stability of marriages in the Senegalese diaspora.[22] Many men are uncomfortable with the increasingly dominant position that women are enjoying in the household and in the extended family. Hus-bands are critical of their wives, who are accused of neglecting their du-ties as caretakers of their houses while devoting too much time to making money. The most frequent complaint is the long hours that wives spend in the hair salons, sometimes over fourteen hours a day in the first four months of the year, forcing the family to eat fast-food and leaving the apartment unclean for days. Some men also reproach their wives for not contributing enough to household expenses.[23] Women immigrants for their part assert their refusal to be confined to the kitchen and emphasize their rights to work, to earn money, to support their parents back in Senegal, and to make provisions for the future. They attribute men's discomfort to the fact that in the diaspora men no longer hold the position of authority they enjoyed in Senegal, a position that allowed them to control the lives and economic resources of their wives (Babou 2002: 163). The tensions caused by the changing power structure in the immigrants' households have led to a high divorce rate among the Senegalese diaspora in North America. According to some estimates, one of every two marriages among immigrants in the United States dissolves within five years, which is a very high divorce rate by the standards of the generally stable Senegalese household (Babou 2002).

Another important transformation prompted by braiding and which is greatly affecting the immigrant household is that wealth accumulated by women braiders is undermining the very basis of traditional Wolof masculinity.[24] Among the Wolof, male adulthood and maturity is fundamentally defined by the ability to build a house. One can earn a decent living, get married, and have children but not be considered responsible in the full sense of the word until owning his own house. In fact, the Wolof word for head of the household, *borom kër*, literally means the owner (*boroom*) of a house (*kër*). An increasing number of women braiders are becoming *borom kër* while men struggle to meet family expenses (in both the United States and in Senegal) and consequently delay the building of a house. All the women I interviewed during my field research declared that their top priority was to build a house in Senegal. Some among them have already built one and are saving to build a second house. There are also women who already own or are contemplating buying a house in the United States. Women still continue to carry their wealth on their bodies, spending large amounts of money on cloth, gold jewelry, makeup, and skin-bleaching products, but they are also increasingly investing in real estate, a domain usually reserved for men. Owning a house has become for a growing number of women immigrants a source of prestige and a measure of success more desirable than building social capital though gift giving to in-laws and praise singers.[25] Conversely, husbands who are unable to build a house feel frustrated and emasculated by their wives' success. Many are trying to reassert their masculinity by resorting to extended polygamy and marrying younger women living in Senegal who are therefore more dependent on them and less likely to present a challenge. The inability of men to fulfill the idealized role of breadwinner and house builder undermines their status and identity.[26]

The incursion of female immigrants in the male-dominated business of house building is not the only socially transforming change that the involvement of women in braiding business has prompted: women's new economic standing is also affecting ideas about the sexual division of labor and castes. I have noted earlier that braiding was traditionally a job exclusively reserved for lower-class women. In the diaspora, this is no longer the case. Men have also invested, though with some discomfort, in the business of hair braiding. They do not touch hair, but they are owners and managers of hair salons. In fact, the first hair salons run by Africans in the United States were opened by Senegalese male immigrants. There are still some prominent male owners of salons in Detroit, Cleveland, and Philadelphia. The president of the Association of African-Style Hair Salon Owners of Philadelphia, which supervises dozens of salons, is a man. Men enjoyed a head start in the business because they were first to migrate to the United States, to regularize their immigration status, and to save enough start-up money. Some among them also spoke English and had some experience managing a business, in contrast to the great majority of early women immigrants who were illiterate housewives in Senegal. However, women braiders were quick to catch up and they have since become more successful than many men. Although the business of hair braiding is as lucrative for men as it is for women, many men still feel uncomfortable doing a job so closely associated with femininity. In the Senegalese Muslim society, men shave but do not braid their hair and they do not work in salons providing service to women.[27] In addition, men lack the skills and cultural wherewithal to deal with a clientele almost exclusively female. Many male owners of hair salons use their wives, sisters, and female cousins as front, thus avoiding as much as possible spending long hours in the salon. Few among them would willingly disclose to friends and members of their family back in Senegal the kind of job they practice in the United States. In fact, most of the time, they take a second job or open a shop in the same building where the salon is located to mask the fact they are involved in hair braiding.

If gender still remains a sensitive issue among Senegalese hair braiders in the United States, there seems to be less preoccupation with caste. Unlike the men who feel much discomfort working in the hairstyle business, most *géer* women seem comfortable practicing a job that clearly violates their social rank. In the hair salons, one finds braiders of all backgrounds and social statuses, from lawyers to members of the prestigious Mbacké Muslim family to college graduates to illiterate homemakers. There are still some women, mostly of so-called noble origin or from affluent families, who continue to shun braiding, or who take the job only as a last resort and manage to quit as soon as they find an alternative means to support themselves. However, the large majority of Senegalese non-casted women in the United States defend their rights to braid and assert that they feel no shame dealing in a business traditionally associated with lower status people. For some of them, the fact that they do their work far away from Senegal for American customers in a very different cultural environment makes the notions of caste and customs irrelevant.[28] These women present braiding as a profession, which, like any other profession, should be opened to anybody having the skills to perform. They reject the customs that forbid them from working with hair and suggest that Senegalese society must abandon caste-based division of labor.[29] Yet most of these women would not agree that their sons and daughters should work as blacksmiths, jewelers, or shoemakers. They also adamantly oppose marriage between casted and non-casted. It is also probable that many among them would abandon braiding upon returning to Senegal. It seems that, as one woman told me in Atlanta, "In the United States, the dollar is the great equalizer: whatever you can do to honestly earn it is all right."[30] What she did not say but which she clearly implied was that in Senegal traditional norms and values still weigh heavily on people's behavior, and the prospect for returning home puts some limit on the depth of changes that the immigrants can carry back home.

NDEYE ASTU AAC: A BRAIDING SUCCESS STORY

The life story of Ndeye Astu Aac of Washington, D.C., provides a good example of the transforming power of money generated by hair braiding in Senegalese communities in the diaspora and at home.[31] Aac was born to a family of blacksmiths in the impoverished Dakar neighborhood of Medina, a quarter created by the French colonial administration for Africans during the epidemic of bubonic plague of 1914. She grew up learning to braid from her friends despite the opposition of her father, who wanted her to focus instead on her education and to get a degree. She did not embrace braiding as a profession but rather as a means for earning pocket money to pay for miscellaneous expenses. Unlike many young girls of her generation, Ndeye Astu was able to successfully combine her duties in the household and her studies. She earned a high school diploma in business and was accepted at the Department of Economics of the University of Dakar. In 1987, she left the university to join her sister, Aram, who had recently moved to New York City.

In New York, Aac hoped to resume undergraduate studies and to earn a degree in banking. In 1988, she met Mbay Caam, also a member of the blacksmith caste, and married him the same year. Caam was among the pioneers of Senegalese immigration in the United States.[32] He came to New York in the late 1960s and was aware of the hair revolution that was taking place in the United States and the money to be made in the business of hair braiding. He contributed start-up money and convinced his wife to abandon school and open a hair salon instead. In 1989, Astu Aac and Mbay Caam opened one of the first African-owned hair salons in the

United States, which they named African Hair Gallery in the Washington neighborhood of Mount Pleasant. They started with three braiders but soon confronted the regulatory tension and controversies that surrounded the business of braiding in the United States in the late 1980s. Astu Aac was not trained in cosmetology and as such she faced the prospect of losing her business if she did not get the appropriate license. She hired a manager to run the salon and joined a cosmetology institute where she graduated, after one a year of training, in hair hygiene.

Aac's hair business started to blossom in the early 1990s. A folklife festival organized in Washington and which featured Senegalese culture offered her an excellent platform to advertise her business. This festival may have been connected to the hair workshop organized by the Library of Congress the same year. She distributed flyers and business cards and talked to the large audience that attended the event. The positive effect of the festival and advertising campaign on the hair salon was immediate. Ndeye Astu evokes with nostalgia the era when in a single day she would receive dozens of clients ("Success Story" 2003). Most of these customers were middle- and upper-class African American women.

To continue to satisfy and maintain the trust of her demanding clientele, Astu Aac took advantage of her connections at the United States' embassy in Dakar to keep a steady flow of skilled braiders she recruited from Senegal. She provided lodging and probably airline tickets to her new employees. Aac also established stringent rules in her salon. Braiders had one day off a week, they were forbidden to converse in Wolof at work, those who came late would not be allowed to work, and if the customer was not happy the braider would not be paid. For Aac, the adoption of these draconian measures was indispensable to success in the tough U.S. work environment. Her method seemed to have succeeded since the business grew so fast that she needed the service of two secretaries and an accountant to manage it.

In 1995, Aac bought her first house in the high-class Washington neighborhood of Klinsman Farm, for which she paid $400,000. She holds investment portfolios at Morgan Stanley and Fidelity Investment. She has opened hair salons in City Place Mall in suburban Washington (Silver Spring, Maryland) and is planning to open more in Los Angeles, London, and Johannesburg. Aac estimates her financial worth at several million dollars.

Braiding has made the young blacksmith girl from impoverished Medina a role model and a star in Senegal. Her accomplishments have inspired many Senegalese pop stars, first among them Yousou Ndour, the Senegalese Grammy winner and world-class musician, who dedicated a song to her as well as the 2003 edition of his celebrated annual concert in Bercy Stadium in Paris. A devout Murid, Ndeye Astu was also the host of the late Sheikh Murtalla, the youngest son of Ahmadu Bamba, founder of the powerful Muridiyya Muslim order in Senegal, during his annual visit to Washington. Aac is intensely courted by the ruling party Parti Democratic Sénégalais in Senegal and she regularly meets with President Abdoulaye Wade when he visits the United States. The attention this woman from a traditionally scorned status group gets from prestigious Senegalese spiritual and political leaders reflects the transforming power of money earned from hair braiding.

CONCLUSION

From a much-disdained profession, practiced exclusively by lower-caste women in Senegal, braiding has become a highly desirable career among Senegalese in the diaspora. It is embraced by women of all social extractions. Men are also involved in hair braiding, even if behind the scenes. Senegalese women in the United States were first attracted to braiding because it did not require the immigration documentation and language skills that the often illiterate and undocumented African immigrants did not possess. However, more women are now choosing braiding as a profession, less because of their immigration predicament and more because it is a lucrative business that has afforded many of them social mobility.

Money made through braiding has become one of the most powerful agents of social change among the Senegalese immigrant community in the United States, and its impact is clearly felt by the people left behind. Braiding is undermining the very basis of household and social hierarchies. Female braiders are increasingly competing with their husbands and brothers as providers for their families in the diaspora and at home in Senegal. Like their male counterparts, women immigrants are also buying and building houses and in the process earning the title of *borom kër* (head of the household) previously reserved for men. Greater economic power has also given women a stronger and more authoritative voice as decision makers in family and financial affairs, more so in the diaspora where deeper changes are occurring at a faster pace. The changing balance of power within the household and families stoked by greater economic success for women in the diaspora is blurring markers of gender and social status.

Women's increasingly dominant position in the household and in the larger extended family is subverting notions of gender roles and is giving new meanings to Wolof conceptions of masculinity and femininity. These changes have not happened without a cost. Men who feel their authority threatened by women's ability to compete in terrains they traditionally dominated (house building, family provider, and decision maker) are trying to reassert their power by resorting to extended polygamy and other means. While they continue to affirm their faithfulness to Wolof and Muslim family values, women are more and more willing to defy societal pressure by contesting their husband's decisions regarding household management or by seeking divorce when they feel that their interests are ignored. The tensions and instability brought about by these changes deeply trouble Senegalese men and women used to stable household life.

This research has also revealed that wealth drawn from hair braiding is gradually changing attitudes toward caste and the gendered division of labor. Although views about the relevance of caste continue to be fraught with contradictions and ambiguities, there seems to be an emerging consensus among immigrants that these customs are things of the past that should be rejected, at least in the context of the diaspora. Money is gradually displacing non-material sources of prestige and authority, such as blood and gender. While established social hierarchies continue to retain much symbolic significance, honor and self-worth are increasingly defined by people's ability to accumulate money and to satisfy economic needs.

NOTES

1. A version of this chapter was previously published in 2008 as "Migration and Cultural Change: Money, 'Caste,' Gender, and Social Status among Senegalese Female Hair Braiders in the United States," *Africa Today* 55(2).

2. I put "traditional" in quotation marks to indicate that I am not using the concept to refer to a timeless and static past opposed to a dynamic, flexible, and changing present "modernity." The idea of a demiurgic Western modernity bound to destroy everywhere obsolescent and unchanging non-Western traditions has largely been abandoned by scholars. Emerging scholarship on culture and globalization insists on the existence of alternative or multiple modernities born of the blending, combining, and juxtaposing of cultural and institutional elements of various civilizations.

3. Many among my interviewees associated specific hair designs with people's ethnic, socioeconomic, and sometimes political conditions. They noted that slaves had specific hair designs, that there were braiding styles worn specially by nobles, warriors, or wealthy people. Unmarried and married women also sported differing styles of coiffures. This information is consistent with earlier observations by European explorers and scholars of Africa. See, for example, Bertho 1950: 71–74, Laugel and Marçais 1954: 113–21, and Sieber and Herreman 2000: 18–23.

4. Some authors tend to assimilate *géer* with agriculturalist or noble. In reality, as argued by A. Bara Diop (1981), the *géer* is negatively defined as those who are not involved in artisan work, in contrast to the *ñeeño*, defined as professional artisans. Besides agriculture, *géer* can work as traders, hunters, or even fishermen. Nor is *géer* a synonym for noble, as affirmed by some authors (Tamari 1997). Caste and nobility relate to different kinds of sociopo-

litical hierarchies: the caste system and the order that relates to the political system.

5. On the effects of the policies of structural adjustment on Senegalese society, see O'Brien, Diop, and Diouf 2002, esp. chaps. 3 and 4; Niang 1997. See also Sassen 2007a (esp. chaps. 4 and 5, 97–163) and 2007b for a broader analysis of the effect of the new global economy on transnational migration. Sassen focuses on "the translocal circuits for the mobility of labor and capital," but her analysis is also relevant for understanding the less conventional trajectory of Senegalese women braiders in the United States.

6. For more on Gey see Babou 2002: 151–70. I also refer to my interview with Gey in Dakar, June 17, 2004.

7. Interviews with Kumba Babou, Mbacké, May 31, 2004, and Fatou Tall, Medina, Dakar, June 28, 2006.

8. The literature on Senegalese international migration is relatively extensive, but it concentrates on the male immigrants and especially on the transnational Murid traders and the immigrants from the Soninke and Fulbe areas of northern Senegal. Women are virtually absent. See Carter 1992; Schmidt di-Friedberg 1993; Ebin and Lake 1992a; Ebin 1992b; Ebin 1993: 101–23; Malcomson 1996: 24–43; Diouf-Camara 1997: 95–115; Riccio 2001: 583–99; and Bava 2003: 69–84.

9. Interviews with the owner of Billy Jean Hair Salon on West 116th Street and Lennox Avenue, Harlem, New York, March 31, 2006. This salon, opened in 1978 by an African American male entrepreneur, is one of the first salons to offer African style braiding in New York City. See also Banks 2000: 144. In informal conversations, African American women refer to African braiders as "the real deal."

10. Interviews with Mbay Caam, New York City, May 17, 1999; Amy Jaxumpa, New York City, March 31, 2006, and Assan Gey, Atlanta, February 26, 2006. All these interviewees are among the first generation of Senegalese men and women to immigrate to the United States. Caam came to the United States in the late 1960s; Jaxumpa and Gey joined their husbands in New York and Atlanta, respectively, in 1988 and 1990.

11. This was the case of Assan Gey and Astu Aac, the two most successful Senegalese female braiders in the United States, who both learned to braid from friends and neighbors.

12. Interview with the owner of Billy Jean in Harlem, March 31, 2006.

13. I thank my colleague Kathy Peiss for calling my attention to the parallel between the impact of French women on white fashion and that of Senegalese on black fashion. Email, January 26, 2007.

14. Interviews with Yaasin Caam, October 15, 2006 Anderson, South Carolina, and Faatu Joob, Philadelphia, October 25, 2006. Both interviewees are salon owners.

15. These numbers are my own estimations but they also reflect the general perception of Senegalese journalists and community leaders I consulted.

16. All the salon owners that I interviewed use this system of payment. Independent braiders also affirm that they are paid based on the number of heads they braid.

17. This is a recurring complaint of the braiders I met during my field research in Atlanta, New York, and Philadelphia. It is also a frequent topic that comes up whenever Senegalese women gather during family and communal celebrations. However, one should not overlook the effect of gender solidarity between African and African American women. It is clear that the hair salon is also a place where clients share with braiders their knowledge about the rights of women in the United States and where to get help in case of espousal abuses. Many Senegalese husbands of braiders accuse African American women of trying to turn their wives into "extreme feminists."

18. The blending of professional and domestic activities seems prevalent among women entrepreneurs in Senegal. I. Guérin observes the same phenomenon among Senegalese Women involved in the micro-finance business. See Guérin 2006: 554. But African American hair salons and barbershops are not different; they also function as places for work, leisure, and socialization. I thank my colleague Nwando Achebe for calling my attention to this. Personal conversation, East Lansing, November 10, 2007.

19. Yaasin Caam mentions that in South Carolina, African women braiders are often referred to by their African American customers as "dumb people." Yaasin, who studied in Canada and is now completing a degree in accounting, takes this as evidence of their ignorance about Africa and Africans as fueled by the popular media. Interview, October 15, 2006.

20. We may be witnessing a process of cultural migration from Senegalese traditional gender roles and toward a more feminist consciousness, which Abuk attributed in the twentieth century to the influence of Western education. See Abuk 2003: 723–40. The new process of cultural migration I am describing in this paper seems to be driven more by money and exposure to American capitalist culture than modern education. In fact, many of the women I write about are illiterate.

21. Interviews in Atlanta with Assan Gey, February 26, 2006, Ndey Njaay, February 27, 2006, and Kine Joob, February 27, 2006.

22. Research made among successful Ghanaian businesswomen has reached a similar conclusion. Personal conversation with Dr. Sandra Barnes, Philadelphia, October 4, 2007.

23. These complaints are recurrent in the many formal and informal discussions that I have had with Senegalese male immigrants throughout the United States over the last ten years.

24. In the case of rural Senegal, it is the pauperization of the head of household, who is no longer able to feed the family because of the drastic neoliberal economic reforms that undermine their masculinity. See Perry 2005.

25. Malick Diagne, like many of the male Senegalese immigrants I have interviewed over the last ten years, reasserted to me how money earned from braiding and other activities have made Senegalese women forget the values they learned in their families back home, and how this is hurting family life in the diaspora. Diagne, like many of his compatriots in the diaspora, however, did not consider how male discomfort with their wives' economic standing may have contributed to the situation. Personal conversation, New York City, November 23, 2006.

26. Donna L. Perry traces this transformation in gender roles in Senegal to the neoliberal reforms of the second half of the 1980s. See Perry 2006: 210. However, although the drastic economic changes ushered in by the structural adjustment programs have had a profound effect on the economic conditions of Senegalese, its full cultural impact, especially as related to the household, seems to have manifested more recently. It seems that the culture of migration that has evolved from the mass migration to Europe and the United States of men and women in the late 1990s and the new household ethics it helped foster played a major role in subverting entrenched gender roles.

27. The Baay Faal, a sub-group within the Muridiyya Muslim order, constitutes an exception. Some disciples of Ibra Faal, the founder of this sub-group, wear dreadlocks. More recently, dreadlocks have become a popular hairstyle among urban followers of Rastafarianism. But these locks are rarely made in hair salons; they are grown naturally or made through the use of chemicals.

28. Interview with Kine Joob, Atlanta, February 27, 2006.

29. Interview with Assan Gey, Atlanta, February 26, 2006; Kine Joob, Atlanta, February 27, 2006.

30. Interview with Kine Joob, Atlanta, February 27, 2006.

31. This section is based on a biographical article on Ndeye Astu Aac ("Success Story" 2003); on an interview with her husband, Mbay Caam, in New York City, May 17, 1999; and on interviews with braiders in Atlanta and New York City in February 2006, and Anderson, South Carolina, in October 2006.

32. Interview with Mbay Caam in Harlem, New York City, May 17, 1999.

REFERENCES

Abuk, C. 2003. "Urbanisation's Long Shadows: Mariama Ba's So Long a Letter." *Journal of Ethnic and Migration Studies* 29(4): 723–40.

Appadurai, Arjun. 1990. "Disjuncture in the Global Cultural Economy." *Public Culture* 2: 1–24.

Babou, Cheikh Anta. 2002. "Brotherhood Solidarity, Education and Migration: The Role of the *Dahiras* among the Murid Muslim community of New York." *African Affairs* 101: 151–70.

Banks, Ingrid. 2000. *Hair Matters: Beauty, Power and Black Women's Consciousness.* New York: New York University Press.

Barnes, Sandra T. 1990. "Women, Property, and Power." In *Beyond the Second Sex: New Directions in the Anthropology of Gender,* ed. Peggy R. Sanday and Ruth G. Goodenough. Philadelphia: University of Pennsylvania Press.

Bava, Sophie. 2003. "De la baraka aux affaires: Ethos économico-religieux et Transnationalité chez les migrants sénégalais mourides." *Revue Européenne de Migrations Internationales* 19: 69–84.

Bertho, Jacques. 1950. "Coiffures-masques à franges de perles chez les rois Yoruba de Nigeria et du Dahomey." *Notes Africaines* 47: 71–74.

Biaya, T. K. 1999. "Hair Statements in Urban Africa: The Beauty, the Mystic and the Mad Man." *Codesria Bulletin* 1/2: 32–38.

Boserup, Esther. 1970. *Women's Role in Economic Development*. New York: St. Martin's Press.

Buggenhagen, Beth A. 2003. "At Home in the Black Atlantic: Circulation, Domesticity and Value in the Senegalese Murid Trade Diaspora." Ph.D. diss., University of Chicago.

Carter, Donald. 1992. "Invisible Cities: From Tuba to Turin: The Senegalese Transnational Migrants in Northern Italy." Ph.D. diss., University of Chicago.

Craig, Maxine Leeds. 2002. *Ain't I a Beauty Queen? Black Women, Beauty and the Politics of Race*. Oxford: Oxford University Press.

Diop, Abdoulaye Bara. 1981. *La société Wolof: Les systèmes d'inégalité et de domination*. Paris: Karthala.

———. 1985. *La famille Wolof: Tradition et changement*. Paris: Karthala.

Diouf-Camara, Sylviane. 1997. "Senegalese in New York: A Model Minority?" Trans. Richard Phicox. *Black Renaissance/Renaissance Noire* 2: 95–115.

Dumont, Louis. 1970. *Homo Hierarchicus: An Essay on the Caste System*. Chicago: University of Chicago Press.

Ebin, V. 1992. "A la recherche de nouveaux 'poissons': Stratégies commerciales mourides par temps de crise." *Politique Africaine* 45.

———. 1993. "Les commerçants mourides à Marseille et à New York." In *Grands commerçants d'Afrique de l'Ouest*, ed. Emmanuel Grégoire and Pascal Labazée. Paris: Karthala.

Ebin, Victoria, and Rose Lake. 1992. "Camelots à New York, les pionniers de l'immigration sénégalaise." *Hommes et Migrations* 1160: 32–37.

Fall, Babacar, ed. 1997. *Ajustement structurel et emploi au Sénégal*. CODESRIA-Karthala.

Guérin, Isabelle. 2006. "Women and Money: Lessons from Senegal." *Development and Change* 37(3): 549–70.

Hubbard, Lee. 1999. "Braiding without a License Still Crime in California." *Final Call* 18: 49.

Irvine, T. L. 1973. "Castes and Communication in a Wolof Village." Ph.D. diss., University of Pennsylvania.

Jackson, Kennell. 2000. "What Is Really Happening Here? Black Hair among African-Americans and in American Culture." In *Hair in African Art*, ed. R. Sieber and F. Herreman. New York: Museum of African Art.

Laugel, A.M.M., and P. H. Marçais. 1954. "Les coiffures à Tindouf." *Université d'Alger travaux de l'Institut de Recherches Sahariennes* 12(2): 113–21.

Lynch, Michael W. 2000. "Hair Trigger: Court Rules against California Regulation of Hair Braiding." Reason, September 15, 2006.

Malcomson, Scott L. 1996. "West of Eden: The Mouride Ethic and the Spirit of Capitalism." *Transition* 71: 24–43.

Mbow, Penda. 2000. "Démocratie et castes." *Journal des Africanistes* 70 (1–2): 71–91.

Muhammad, Charlene. 1999. "Hair Braiders Battle for Right to Work." *Final Call* 19: 2.

Niang, Abdoulaye. 1997. "Le secteur informel en milieu urbain, un recours à la crise de l'emploi." In *Ajustement structurel et emploi au Sénégal*, ed. Babacar Fall, 29–57. CODESRIA-Karthala.

O'Brien, Donal Cruise, Momar C. Diop, and Mamadou Diouf, eds. 2002. *La construction de l'Etat au Senegal*. Paris: Karthala.

Peiss, L. Kathy. 1998. *Hope in a Jar: The Making of America's Beauty Culture*. New York: Metropolitan Books.

Perry, Donna L. 2005. "Wolof Women, Economic Liberalization, and the Crisis of Masculinity in Rural Senegal." *Ethnology* 44: 207–26.

Riccio, Bruno. 2001. "From 'Ethnic Group' to 'Transnational Community'? Senegalese Migrant's Ambivalent Experiences and Multiple Trajectories." *Journal of Ethnic and Migration Studies* 27(4): 583–99.

Sassen, Saskia. 2007a. *A Sociology of Globalization*. New York: Norton.

———. 2007b. "Global Migration and Economic Need." Paper presented at the University of Pennsylvania, October 25.

Schmidt di Friedberg, Ottavia. 1995. "l'Immigration Africaine en Italie: Le Cas Sénégalais." *Etudes Internationales* 24(1): 125–40.

Sieber, Roy, and Frank Herreman, eds. 2000. *Hair in African Art and Culture*. New York: Museum for African Art.

Stoller, Paul. 2002. *Money Has No Smell: The Africanization of New York City*. Chicago: University of Chicago Press.

"Success Story: La saga de Ndeye Astu Athie Thiam." 2003. *Frasques* 581: 4–5.

Tamari, Tal. 1997. *Les castes de l'Afrique Occidentale: Artisans et musiciens endogames*. Paris: Nanterre.

Williams, Monte. 2001. "Bargain Braiders Battle for Heads." *New York Times*, May 18.

13 WHAT THE GENERAL OF AMADOU BAMBA SAW IN NEW YORK CITY

GENDERED DISPLAYS OF DEVOTION AMONG MIGRANTS OF THE SENEGALESE MURID TARIQA

BETH A. BUGGENHAGEN

ELEGANCE

Moments after the shaykh disappeared behind the darkened windows of his SUV and his driver began to pull out of the Marriott Marquis Hotel, a frantic young man in a patchwork cloth ensemble bolted from the crowd. He threw his lanky body across the hood of the car as it pulled into the dense theater-going traffic of Times Square. As he and several others who clung to the doors of the slow-moving vehicle were pulled away and consoled by other adepts, the SUV cut off a group of European tourists on the sidewalk, mostly older women. Near them stood a large group of Senegalese women, resplendent against the bitter, grey November day in layers of iridescent pastel fabrics and gauzy scarves, who had ushered the shaykh and his security entourage out of the hotel. Stunned by the scene they had just witnessed, the European women turned toward the Senegalese and asked, "What play was that?"

The tourists' confusion was confounded by the fact that the Marriot Marquis Hotel was also home to the Broadway Marquis Theater.[1] What they had just witnessed was the last scene in the production honoring Modou Kara Mbacke Noreyni, a renegade leader of the Senegalese Sufi order Tariqa Murid, known popularly as the "le Général de Bamba," referring to the founding figure of the Murid way, Amadou Bamba. What they may not have understood were the performative aspects of the frantic young man's antics and that, although the women appeared to be in theater costume, looking quite conspicuous in midtown Manhattan—where suits of dark, somber colors were the norm—they too were displaying a certain sartorial acumen, a performance central to their devotional practice. These gendered performances of devotion had everything to do with a Muslim soteriology, or doctrine of salvation. As the young man sought to absorb the *baraka* (Arabic, religious grace) of his departing spiritual guide, a quality transmittable through objects, like texts, cloth, prayer beads, or even in this case a car, women sought *tuyaaba* (Wolof, religious merit),[2] through good or wholesome acts such as alms, hospitality, or even their *sanse* (Wolof, sartorial skill). Their objects of adornment were objects of grace, and as such making them visible through bodily display both pointed to and constituted their religious merit. In this performance, women embodied the idea of *jekk* (Wolof, elegance) promulgated in Modou Kara's sermon that day. Being elegant has been associated with conveying the dignity of the lineage (Mustafa 2006: 180), yet in the context in which Kara used it, elegance takes on meanings such as piety, purity, and upright behavior. Elegance had become the slogan of Kara's religious and political movement in and out of Senegal. Here, elegance marked notions of *tahara* (Arabic, purity) central to his claim of moral authority and political leadership in Senegal's political terrain, where political leaders have been increasingly subject to intense moral scrutiny for their corrupt and repressive practices in a sobering economic climate.

In the United States, the mass media image of the Muslim woman in the past few years has focused on various forms of veiling and concealment of the feminine form, portraying Muslim women's dress as lacking in any sartorial skill, imposed mainly by men's anxieties about female virtue and piety. Yet in Senegal, it is *affair-u-jigeen* (French/Wolof, women's business) to *sanse* (Wolof, shine).[3] Women carefully stylize their bodies to convey wealth, status, and piety through consumer choices often driven by fashion trends prompted by Western, West African, and Arab influences, the imported goods provided by translocal traders, and localized notions of beauty. A well-dressed woman might wear copious amounts of fabric, with varying degrees of tailoring and embellishment—reflecting recent trends to draw attention to her neckline, shoulders, and face—over one or more locally woven strip-cloth underskirts that signify a lineage of high status (if she is of a certain age). She is properly accessorized with shoes, a bag, and jewelry, the latter two often chosen to accentuate elegant hands with long fingers, a marker of beauty and thus of grace. She may beautify her face and make it more prominent and luminous with henna or cosmetics, and frame her visage with a headscarf fashioned from a long oblong piece of fabric tied in a large knot at the top of her head. Importantly, she also allows her fragrance of incense or perfume to hang in the air. Dressing well is one of many strategies of display—of beauty, wealth, and individual and collective identities often tied to cloth wealth. Fashionable, thoughtful dress has been vital to Murid women's participation in a number of public gatherings central to their devotional practices, including meetings of religious associations; family ceremonies; pilgrimages to the tombs of Sufi figures; Muslim conferences; and, in cities outside Senegal, the annual visit of religious leaders during the commemoration of Shaykh Amadou Bamba. Dress, I argue, is one of several strategies employed by women to achieve religious merit. Attention to women's sartorial practices and debates surrounding them point simultaneously to the centrality of Islam to women's lives and to the centrality of women in the mission of the Murid way.

Dressing well has been amplified by the increasingly mediated nature of these events, from television to the web to numerous video and digital recordings and photographs that circulate nationally and internationally between those at home and abroad. Devotees avidly watch these recordings to understand and participate in the lives of those at home and/or abroad, to amplify their religious merit, and to absorb the teachings of religious leaders who appear in these visual media. In fact, the savvy use of media has become a central strategy for many aspiring Muslim figures seeking to garner a following and to demand the attention of political and religious leaders in positions of power. While media use (including radio, Internet, cell phones, and visual media) is common in religious circuits across West Africa, especially in light of the liberalization of formerly state run media in many places (Gueye 2003; Schulz 2003; Soares 2005), it has become particularly crucial in Senegal as an increasing number of potential disciples reside abroad.

In this essay I analyze the influence of Murid migration at home by focusing on how the devotional practices of women, how their search for religious merit through their dress and exchange practices in New York City and elsewhere, have impacted the political and religious aspirations of members of the Murid clergy. The increasing number of female disciples making offerings to the Murid order from their earnings abroad has had a substantial impact on the organization of the order itself and the place of women within it. With women's increasing financial potential has come a good deal of debate. Women's sartorial success is linked in part to their exchange of vast amounts of cloth wealth in family ceremonies,[4] and thus have become the focus of much criticism in an era marked by fiscal austerity (Mustafa 1998) as a sign of women's productive and reproductive potential gone awry.[5] At the same time, well-dressed Murid women at home and abroad have caught the eye of the Murid clergy seeking to expand its moral and material might in global Senegal. These debates over Muslim women's dress in and out of Senegal are not unique to the Murid way, but can be found elsewhere in the Muslim postcolony (LeBlanc 2000;

Schulz 2007) and signify important shifts in gender relations, often at the conjuncture of political change, economic liberalization, and calls for moral austerity in tough financial times.

A CIRCULAR MIGRATION? MURID COMMUNITY IN NEW YORK AND THE CENTRALITY OF TUBA

The Murid order is a distinctively Senegalese Sufi way that emerged in Senegal at the turn of the twentieth century, as disciples were attracted to the scholar Amadou Bamba Mbacke. While men and women in the rural Muslim lands of the French colony often sought out the guidance and teachings of Muslim scholars, Bamba promulgated a form of Sufism that enabled mass participation. Young men in particular were attracted to the Murid communes by the promise of land, which the French bequeathed to the Murid clergy in exchange for their cultivation of groundnuts, an important source of oil for French industrialization and in demand for cosmetics and soaps as well. When the price for groundnuts dropped in the world market in the 1970s and the Sahel was faced with drought and declining agricultural production, the clergy exhorted disciples to engage in trade, largely of recycled items. Though the Murid way was initially an agricultural movement, Muslims have long been associated with trade in West Africa (Amselle 1971; Cohen 1971; Curtin 1975; Hopkins 1973; Stoller 2002). For many Muslims, as well as the Muridiyya, trade had a "historical precedent and Prophetic practice; it is inherent in the words of the sacred scripture of Islam, the Qur'an, and thus has, for Muslims, the stamp of divine authority" (Hunwick 1999: 72). What ensued was large-scale rural urban migration out of the Murid peanut-producing regions of Diourbel and Kaolack, toward the town of Thies and the capital Dakar, as many disciples turned dry-season trading into a full-time occupation in the urban areas (Creevey 1985: 715; Cruise O'Brien 1988; Diop 1981; Roberts 1996: 87).

There were external factors at play in shaping Murid transnational migration as well. A labor shortage in postwar France drew many former colonial subjects abroad (Bowen 2004: 44). As former colonies gained independence, a bilateral agreement between France and Senegal allowed Senegalese to move without restriction (Diop and Michalak 1996: 77). While Murid disciples emigrated to France in this period in search of university degrees and wage labor, many more became involved in an international trade in African art (Cruise O'Brien 1988: 139). Yet emigration to France did not mark the first time that the Muridiyya had engaged with the global. Muridyya have always been global, if not through Islam, then by conscription into both world wars, forced participation in *corvée* labor projects, and the cultivation of cash crops for export. Moreover, the

Muridiyya were not the first to engage in long-distance trade in Senegal; Soninke from the Senegal River Valley preceded them (Manchuelle 1997; Adams and So 1996).

By the 1970s the French economy, like the American economy, suffered a recession related to the global oil crisis and immigration to France was suspended in 1974 (Diop and Michalak 1996: 78). Immigrants became seen as competitors for low-skilled, low-paying jobs (Bowen 2004: 44). Many of the itinerant male immigrant workers created permanent immigrant families after immigration was restricted to family members under the 1974 family reunification act. Though the family reunification act did permit many more family members to emigrate to France, in no way did it lessen ties to kin and community at home, especially not religious ties (Kane 2002: 246). French right-wing political parties spoke to insecurity and racism beginning in the 1970s, and by the 1980s conflict grew out of perceived cultural differences between Muslim migrants of the former colonies and French citizens (Bowen 2004: 44). Coupled with fears of violence in the suburbs, where immigrant worker housing had been built, and international terrorism following the hijacking of several international airliners, many Senegalese sought opportunities elsewhere.

Murid migration to the United States was spurred by events in France, in large part but also by structural adjustment and devaluation of the currency in Senegal that began in 1985 (Diouf 2004: 270; Perry 1997: 233). In North American cities many Murid migrants have described their travails as their partaking in the spiritual quest of Amadou Bamba, who was exiled several times by the French, fearing that he would foment an uprising against the colonial power. They described their travel as a form of knowledge based on the example of Amadou Bamba, who used his exile as an opportunity to engage more deeply in his spiritual quest, but also as participating in the *hijra*, the Prophet's migration from Mecca to Medina (Buggenhagen 1997). Though men had started coming to New York City as early as the 1970s (Ebin 1992), the U.S. Amnesty Law passed in 1986 facilitated a greater circular migration of these trade disciples as their status was regularized and the numbers of Murid in the United States grew steadily (Babou 2002: 160). The traders, however, were not all men. As early as the 1980s women traders began to visit festivals in the summer months and by the 1990s, through marriage with international traders, the number of women migrants was growing (Babou 2002: 162; Diouf 2004: 276). More recently, the number of single and divorced women has also increased, perhaps in part due to the steady decline of opportunities for earning a living as well as finding a desirable spouse in Senegal. In New York City, women's financial success can often surpass their male counterparts as professionals, business owners, and hair braiders (see chapter 12 in this volume). As women normally keep their own earnings and then draw on their spouse's earnings to cover household expenses (Babou 2002: 163; Diouf 2004: 276–77), their financial transactions have been the subject of some interest. Women who migrated to the United States and elsewhere invested their earnings in real estate in Dakar (Tall 1994), made offerings to shaykhs in Tuba (Rosander 2004) during the annual pilgrimage known in Wolof as the *Magal,* and were watched keenly by the Murid clergy.

The international migration of Murid disciples, largely as traders but also as university students, wage laborers, and professionals, has in many ways been facilitated by the Senegalese state. The current president, Abdoulaye Wade, a Murid disciple himself, was elected as an opposition candidate after twenty years of rule by the Socialist Party, in part through organizational success of Senegalese, many of whom were Murid disciples living in New York City. Wade pursued the Senegalese business class as well as the many shop owners on 116th Street, speaking to their predicaments in Senegal and in New York City (Salzbrunn 2004: 471). In 2007, despite widespread dissatisfaction with declining economic conditions and political repression of the media in Senegal, Wade was reelected to a second term. In part, his success had much to do with his courting of the Murid way through the granting of diplomatic visas to the clergy, Hajj trips to Mecca, and sorting out the land claims of migrants (Mbow 2008: 162). Wade had noted the importance of migration and remittances to Senegal as the "true motor of Senegal's economy" (Mbow 2008: 161)

The influence of Murid disciples abroad on Senegalese politics and on the central clergy is due in part to their organizational strategies. When Murid disciples first migrated out of the peanut basin to the urban areas of Senegal, they established religious associations known as *da'ira,* the Arabic word for circle (Babou 2002: 154). These associations were gender-based and were fundamental to newcomers offering camaraderie, mutual aid, and spiritual kinship in unfamiliar places. Today the structure of religious associations endures in many global cities where Muridiyya reside. The first *da'ira* was established in New York City in 1986 by Serigne Moustapha Mbacké Gaindé Fatma, a great grandson of Amadou Bamba.[6] Initially the *da'ira* was a means of collectively singing the litanies of the order and collecting offerings to garner an audience with a shaykh in the religious center of Tuba. Today many religious leaders travel internationally in search of new disciples to bolster their claims to spiritual authority and to widen their financial base at home in Tuba. Many *da'ira* seek not only to collect money regularly to support visits by shaykhs but also to contribute to social welfare projects that often bear their name in Tuba (Gueye 2001: 111). There are as many as thirty *da'ira* associations in New York City (Babou 2002: 165), and as *da'ira* usually meet in gender-restricted groups, there are a number of strictly female *da'ira.* One of the most prominent women's *da'ira* in New York City is the Da'ira Maam Jaara Boussou, which has a prominent part in organizing the annual observation of Cheikh Amadou Bamba Day (Babou 2002: 155; Salzbrunn 2004: 484). The *da'ira* not only assists in financing the event, but also plays an important organizational role, providing copious amounts of cooked food; their presence in large numbers in the mediated public gatherings shows the strength of the Murid in New York City to other city dwellers and to their compatriots in Senegal.

Although African Muslims comprise only 7 percent of the six millions Muslims in the United States (Diouf 2004: 268), and the Murid community estimates its numbers at about 1,000 to 2,000 members (Salzbrunn 2004: 479), the Murid community has become quite visible in the Harlem neighborhood of New York City. In addition to the many shops and restaurants on 116th Street, the Muridiyya also utilize space in the Malcolm Shabazz mosque, an important architectural landmark on 116th Street for religious observances. In 2001 they built an Islamic center consisting of a mosque and school at 137th Street and Edgecombe Avenue to receive members of the clergy. The Murid Islamic Center becomes the center of activity annually during the commemoration of their founding figure Shaykh Amadou Bamba in New York City, through a parade and interfaith dialogue at the United Nations (Buggenhagen 2010).

One could characterize Murid migration as a circular migration (Perry 1997; Reynolds 2004: 34; Salzbrunn 2004: 471; Youngstedt 2004: 43) based on the remittances of cash, cloth, and religious paraphernalia to kith and kin in Senegal; the seasonal movement of the disciples themselves as traders (who often return in winter) and as students (who return in the summers); and the annual pilgrimage of the many who travel to Tuba for Magal or for the observance of Ramadan with family. Yet the establishment of Murid community structures such as mosques and Koranic schools for young children—who conventionally are sent back to Senegal for a moral education—and the increasing surveillance of migrants in the United States after the events of 9/11 raise the question of how regularly Murid migrants are able to return to Senegal. Given the current anti-immigrant climate in the United States and the lack of legal avenues for circular migration, many Muridiyya who fall out of status must choose either to remain in the United States indefinitely, risking detention and deportation, or to return to Senegal with a penalty requiring them to wait ten years before reapplying for a U.S. visa.

MERIT AND MOVEMENT

One of the central problems in Max Weber's *Sociology of Religion* is soteriology, or the problem of salvation and how best to achieve it. Scholarship on Islam in West Africa has emphasized the uniqueness of Sufi traditions privileging the authority of religious scholars and leaders in their analysis and of men's attempts to receive *baraka* (Arabic, grace) through initiation and *njebbel* (Wolof, submission)[7] to the guidance of a shaykh. From their male interlocutors, scholars learned that women did not perform this rite of initiation, which, according to Donal Cruise O'Brien, is "the only condition to becoming a member of the brotherhood," and "this makes their position marginal" (Cruise O'Brien 1971: 85–86). While male scholars were correct that religious grace was probably of less concern for women than men, their understanding came in part from their limited access to women's worlds, which they were left to decipher through the discourses of men.[8] As the Senegalese scholar Codou Bop has argued, because women are assumed to lack ritual *tahara* (Arabic, purity) at certain times, such as during menses or after childbirth, they are not permitted at such moments to lead or participate in public prayer, approach the mosque, serve as imams, engage in fasting, or read the Koran (Bop 2005: 1114). As such, it might seem that women are less devout than men, less concerned with their salvation, or that their religiosity is directed or controlled by men.

I focus not on the ways in which men render women marginal to Islam but focus instead on how Islam is central to women's lives, to ask questions about "the ways in which both women and men transform and redefine the spaces available to them in order to gain access to previously excluded options" (Cooper 1997: xiv). Initially, I sought to understand how women were also recipients of *baraka*. Yet when I was engaged in fieldwork in Senegal in the spring of 2000, I was corrected when I asked the *mbotaye* (Wolof, neighborhood ritual association) if their preparation of *ceere bas* (Wolof, millet couscous and beef) to celebrate one's return from the Hajj garnered them religious grace. No, they insisted, offerings of food did not, not for this occasion or on similar occasions such as during Ramadan, life-cycle rituals, Muslim feast days, or *ziyara* (Arabic, pious visits and pilgrimages). Each of the association women took turns trying to explain how these acts were intended to be *baax* (Wolof, good); the acts were *tuyaaba* and as such resulted in religious merit, the accrual of which would secure their place in heaven. I began to suspect that women's mundane search for religious merit, a central Sunni practice not unique to the Sufi tradition in West Africa, has been little noted in the scholarship because there is nothing uniquely Murid or even Sufi about religious merit.

While much scholarship on the Murid way has focused on rites of initiation and the transmission of spiritual grace, here I focus on how women employ the religious idioms of *tuyaaba* and *harakat* (Arabic, movement, act, or deed). *Harakat* is a setting out or movement more commonly used in reference to the Hajj (see, for example, Cooper 1999: 104). As Eva Evers Rosander observes, religious merit may be more available to women than to men, as its acquisition does not depend on the mediation of a shaykh, to whom women may have differential access (2004: 79). Both men and women seek religious merit and the cumulative acts are tallied on the Day of Judgment and will ensure their entry into paradise (Buitelaar 1993: 121; Rosander 2004: 79). Merit can be gained by performing acts that create value, including extending hospitality, giving alms to the poor, providing treats for children, and giving gifts of cloth, and can also be used to describe things that are good and wholesome, such as food, the eating of which is likely to bring merit. The key difference between religious merit and religious grace is that male disciples say that the *baraka* of the shaykh will help them reach paradise; according to O'Brien, "in return for the promise of paradise, the followers regularly made pious offerings . . . to their shaikh on the occasion of pilgrimages . . . to the holy place where he resided" (Cruise O'Brien 1971: 26). *Tuyaaba*, on the other hand, is received directly from God. Through their search for religious merit, women express their concerns for the hereafter, while men's quest for *baraka* is really about the here and now (Buitelaar 1993: 123), largely because of its link to *warsek* (Wolof, luck) and the ways in which male discourse links prosperity with grace. Women, of course, also employ a discourse of *warsek* in relation to business affairs but also in courtship and marriage as well.

As the women at the Kara conference searched for religious merit through sartorial displays and offerings of cash, Kara, like many lesser shaykhs, searched for recognition of his spiritual authority to bolster his position in the Murid hierarchy. Christian Coulon suggests that as the number of clergy members has increased, so too has their need to attract new disciples to build their base.[9] Women have become likely candidates. While they may not have submitted to a shaykh,[10] as Lucy Creevey has recently argued, many have sought out religious figures for advice, offering labor, cash, and attaching themselves to the order (Creevey 1996b: 283). Renowned for their capacity for mobilization and their organizational strategies, which included not only collecting funds but also recruiting crowds and providing an impact for public events by wearing matching cloth, women were often enlisted by religious leaders and political parties. Their numbers and dress would draw pride from an audience interested in both the speech of media savvy religious specialists and the exemplary pious and fashionable dress of the attendees.

In the *da'ira* women gave regular contributions of cash to make offerings to a shaykh, who would be responsive to their needs and raise their status, and to fund their travel to pilgrimages, all-night prayer sessions, and religious visits to tombs of Sufi figures as a group. During these *da'ira* meetings, women not only collected contributions and laid plans; they shared food, admired each other's art of adornment, and promoted their wares; many members were often also engaged in some form of trade.

The organizational structure of the *da'ira* was vital to women's work in promoting local leaders and national political parties, to advancing their interests in areas such as education, health care, and urban development, and to financing their businesses. Women's wealth was evident from the pots of money they stashed in their locked armoires from rotating credit unions, from religious and ritual associations, from the stacks of cloth from family ceremonies, and from the ledgers that recorded these transactions.

In all these exchanges women sought to construct a public persona of movement, mobility, and motion. Such practices were consonant with the idea of *harakat*. They constructed their reputation for mobility through participation in the Hajj and lesser pilgrimages, through the circulation of offerings, and through television, videocassettes, photography, and the Internet from the diaspora to the center, Tuba. Various categories of movement, not just *ziyara* but also migration, one's reputation for generosity, and business acumen, were articulated through these idioms of merit and movement, *tuyaaba* and *harakat*. Women expounded upon the notion of religious merit by arguing that things given to others accumulated *njerin* (Wolof, value) in contrast to things that were *lekk* (Wolof, eaten). This led women to talk about one another's character as *naxari* (Wolof, hard) versus *sawar* (Wolof, active). Persons or actions, they argued, had *njerin* because they set things in motion.

SARTORIAL POLITICS AND SUPPLICATION

The mediated production of Kara's visit to New York City in November 2005 involved not only the conference at the Marriot Marquis Hotel, but also his reception of disciples in his room across the street at the Sheraton. Men and women came from as far away as Michigan to seek guidance in their financial and personal affairs as well as counsel for living an upright life in a non-Muslim land. For many male disciples the visit also presented an opportunity to reestablish one's vow of submission. Commensality is often central to these ritual visits, and food largely prepared by women's *da'ira* associations brought them merit. For shaykhs like Kara the visit offered an opportunity to practice qualities of generosity and munificence that would underpin his claim to an exalted status.

As a ritual practice, then, *ziyara* involves greetings, hospitality, prayers, supplication, and offerings. The ensemble of these was photographed and videotaped, and a segment of his arrival at the airport was even posted on multiple Internet sites.[11] Women played no small part in facilitating the excitement and energy for an event that garnered no more than fifty persons and filled the conference room. Yet these performances and their recording were central to Kara's search for legitimacy. Spiritual authority is conventionally derived from configuring descent from the founding figure of the Murid way, Amadou Bamba (Rosander 1997a: 9), as well as through scholarly learning, performance of miracles known as *karamat* (Arabic, evidence of the divine), and *khalwa* (Arabic, spiritual retreat). Religious specialists were also known to be poor speakers, in part emphasizing their asceticism and otherworldly concerns. Consonant with a Wolof language ideology associating low-ranking persons such as griots with gifted, persuasive, often loud speech, as well as with rapid movement, and high-ranking persons who command others to speak for them with mumbled speech and a sedentary comportment, Murid religious leaders were not adept public speakers (Irvine 1989). While Kara was the grandson of Bamba's youngest brother (Bjarnesen 2007: 7n2), he did not emphasize the chain of spiritual transmission or initiation based on his genealogical ties. Rather, he fashioned his authority from his claim to be the "General of Amadou Bamba," a point driven home by the popular portrait of Kara in military fatigues. His media savvy, his use of visual and aural media such as videos, the Internet, radio, and print media, his persuasive speeches and religious conferences, all were far more evident as a source of his appeal rather than conventional forms of religious authority. Yet this medium was not neutral: his use of media shaped his messages and the audience's reception in large part because he was such an engaging speaker (Schulz 2003: 161). At the New York conference Kara was expressive and warm, speaking for himself audibly, persuasively, and authoritatively at a podium through several microphones (to facilitate the recording of the event), without the mediation of a griot, though he did have the requisite entourage one would expect from most exalted figures. In his speech about elegance, the very quality of his voice embodied the idea of what an elegant speaker should be. In Kara's case, the medium affected the message in that it enabled him to use both the media and his skill at public speaking to attract a largely disaffected sector of Senegalese society—the unemployed youth with massive amounts of time on their hands, those seeking a morally approved interstitial space and far more attracted to the possibilities of new media technologies. His medium also attracted those abroad who sought out the kinds of immediacy that videos and the like provided. What is interesting is that for both of these groups of followers, their adoration for Kara, and their piety in general, is quite publicly displayed in their dress and speech.

Kara also seemed to fashion himself as a public figure through sartorial acumen—portraits of him could be found in various stylized outfits. His varied looks included a pin-striped dark Western suit with a knee-length jacket and a turban, a *jelaba* (the longer austere tunic popular in North Africa), military fatigues, a grand boubou, a bow tie, and even black tie and tails. His outfits were often accented by brimmed woven hats, the knit hats of the modou modou, or embroidered Muslim caps, often combined with scarves, wraps, and capes. His hands, often gesturing elegantly, were often prominently featured in his photographs, which is quite common in West African portraiture. As mentioned, long slender hands have long been associated with high status and beauty, not unlinked here to his platform of elegance in dress, bodily comportment, speech, public personae, and moral virtue. His portraits circulated widely in the news media, on television, and videocassettes and were even for sale in the market, as Murid disciples commonly like to carry a portrait of their shaykh with them (Gueye 2003: 613).

Kara was not only a shaykh on the rise who had engaged in some unusual publicity stunts, such as occupying a downtown Dakar hotel claiming he had been commanded to do so in a vision; he was also a shrewd entrepreneur and aspiring political figure. Kara's disciples established Kara International Exchange to facilitate financial transfers between New York and Dakar in the late 1990s (Gueye 2003: 615; Tall 1996). In 2004, he founded the Parti de la Vérité pour le Développement (PVD) and garnered wide support among young men as well as members of the Baye Fall sect of the Murid tariqa. Kara's claims to political power could be seen as based in part on the position of his wife, Sokhna Dieng Mbacké, a senator appointed by President Abdoulaye Wade (Mbow 2008: 162).

Although Kara was widely known as the "Marabout of the Youth" (Bjarnesen 2007: 7), in his audience in New York there were as many middle-aged men and women as there were young men. It is estimated that there are perhaps as many as two million followers of his movement (Bjarnesen 2007: 7), which challenges both the spiritual hierarchy of the Murid tariqa with the figure of the Khalifa-General at its center as both the political and the spiritual leader, and the secular nature of the state itself with his positioning as a "morally superior political leader" (Bjarnessen 2007: 7).

SARTORIAL PRACTICES

Though Kara made extensive use of the media, he was not alone; Muslim conferences are often broadcast on the national television station in Senegal (RTS 5). One of the key elements that draw women into viewing these productions from within their homes aside from the desire to increase their religious knowledge is to watch television cameras pan the audience of women in attendance. Often there are exclamations of how much the women shined (sanse), which are often followed by a question: did they perhaps shine too much? Was the thin black crocheted netting over one young woman's heavily made-up face a sufficient alternative to the conventional white scarf so many Senegalese women draped over their elegant frames?

At the Kara conference women arrived in large groups, most of them wearing the loosely cut dyed *bazin riche* cloth, a marker of high social distinction (Schulz 2007). They further distinguished themselves with trendy iridescent *mousours* (Wolof, headscarves), trimmed with satin ribbon. They seated themselves on the left side of the aisle with their bags and video cameras in tow, opposite the men, saving chairs for women who arrived late. As they waited some two hours for the shaykh to appear, they busied themselves with discussing each other's sartorial acumen, including feeling the quality of each other's cloth, establishing its provenance, the name of the tailor, and innovations in cosmetics, hairstyles, and their objects of adornment. They took photographs of each other, made videos, and discussed *da'ira* affairs.

These displays of beauty, or *rafet*, were displays of wealth, or *alal*, which alluded to stores of cloth and the desire to bestow these wealth objects on others. These displays were rooted in the notion of a beautiful birth, or *rafet judo*. Such beauty speaks to the cult of elegance that characterized colonial urban Senegal and claims of high rank, or a beautiful birth. For high status women, Irvine (1974) suggests that *alal* is closely tied to Wolof normative ideas about honor, or *kerse*, and birth, as one with high birth would demonstrate the qualities of honor. Because *kersa* involves self-restraint, it is seen as essential to the ability of high-status women to accumulate wealth and to attract dependents (Irvine 1974: 183). Generosity and liberality were essential to attracting dependents and were tied to ideas about the proper comportment of high-ranking women.[12] These qualities are also key to achieving religious merit.

Beautification practices garnered religious merit, but these displays as forms of communication could also be dangerous (Irvine 1989; Calame Griaule 1986). While Deborah Heath (1992) argues that women's more ostentatious displays enabled men to behave with the restraint characteristic of an austere Muslim masculinity, certainly such displays of beauty must be carefully balanced in Muslim Senegal as in Niger, where Cooper argues that "*daraja* [Arabic, respectability] is associated with a certain distancing from vulgar (or rather visible) public display" (Cooper 1999: 95). These displays of beauty are also dangerous because they are expensive. In a time characterized by fiscal austerity ushered in by the neoliberal policies of President Abdoulaye Wade, women have employed inventive means of shining, from borrowing to buying on credit, to create an appearance of affluence (Mustafa 1998). The challenge was how to continue the performance without being charged with *puukare* (Wolof, posing), or extending oneself beyond one's means. Beauty under these conditions would be the inverse of merit.

OFFERINGS TO THE RELIGIOUS HIERARCHY

The Murid women in attendance at the Kara conference hoped to receive *baraka* from Kara himself and *tuyaaba* directly from God (see also Rosander 2004: 79) for their good acts. Once Kara had arrived with his elaborate security and media entourage, the women settled down and carefully followed the series of talks given by several religious scholars. After Kara finally took the podium and delivered a rather short sermon about elegance, women demonstrated their appreciation of him through elaborate performances of rising up and placing money in front of him, they swayed back and forth with their arms waving and snapping their fingers in the air, and they sang his praises. The leader of the women's group encouraged women, as is often common during regular meeting of the religious association, to contribute twice or even three times as the collective energy of the congregation rose. While men in attendance also approached Kara at the podium and gave offerings, there was a comparable lack of organization among them; each appeared to give as an individual and only made a single trip. Their lack of celebratory pleasure seemed to match their drab garb: black leather coats and dark pants stood in stark contrast to the brilliantly colored women's wear. Perhaps the men's fashions were a translation of what would otherwise be austere and rather simple dress, characteristic with religious devotion in sobering financial times.

This ardent performance of generosity by women was captured by videographers who produced cassettes for the faithful in New York and for their leaders in Senegal. These cassettes circulated alongside those produced in Senegal commemorating the annual pilgrimage to Tuba for those in the diaspora unable to journey to the center of globalized networks in which migrants seek their social futures and fortunes. In these cassettes they could view how the proceeds earned from work abroad were invested in the city of Tuba, for mosque construction and embellishment, electrification, clinics, and schools. The visual manifestation of these circuits, my interlocutors would remind me, represented all that Amadou Bamba has provided for them as aspirants to the path to divine union.

For men, offerings brought *baraka*, because they were given to the shaykh in return for the promise of paradise. They were initially made at the time of *njebbel* (Wolof, initiation) and thereafter given on a rather regular and somewhat obligatory basis (Cruise O'Brien 1971: 92). Although Sufism posits that salvation is achieved through asceticism, usually in the form of prayer, Bamba posited a doctrine of salvation, whereby labor in a calling—as a form of ascetic practice equal to prayer—would lead to salvation. Haddiya offerings were introduced by the second Khalifa-General of the order in 1947,[13] intended for the construction of the Great Mosque that was begun in 1927 to fulfill Bamba's vision (Cruise O'Brien 1971: 93). The collection of haddiya in the 1950s also coincided with the movement of Muridiyya away from their agricultural base to the towns and the founding of the early *da'ira* in urban centers. Muridiyya maintain that the practice of haddiya is sanctioned in the Koran, and further commentary on this practice is given in verse 40 of *Masalik-al-jinan,* a well-known *qasa'id* (Arabic, type of religious poem) written by Bamba.

Haddiya can be distinguished from *sarax* (Wolof) or *sadaqa* (Arabic)—alms of sugar, candles, rice, sour milk, and the like—and from *zakat* (Arabic), the practice of setting aside 10 percent of one's income a year for charity as part of one of the five pillars of Islam. Through haddiya offerings, disciples entered into circuits of blessings that were both spiritual and material, for through them disciples gained access not merely to eternal prosperity but also to the this-worldly wealth that made their trade networks viable. Practices of supplication and travel constructed a spatial and temporal domain apart from the mundane.

Haddiya are also collected by local *da'ira* associations offering their disciples assurances of salvation—of ultimately being in God's presence—in an uncertain moral terrain. The *da'ira* links the locality to the Murid hierarchy, and the collected offerings present the possibility of an audience with the shaykh. It is in this context that women are more likely to make offerings. As previously mentioned, women's *da'ira* associations organize collective contributions of cash and cooked food usually for the support of pilgrimages and visits in the diaspora of Muslim shaykhs. The act of offerings, whether of cooked food or cash, brings women religious merit (osander 1998: 152).

Women's and men's *da'ira* associations enabled participation in the broader life of the Sufi way and placed the shaykh at the center of a well-organized network. Offerings indexed a shaykh as a spiritual master of sufficient *baraka,* one who could deliver the benefits of salvation in this world and the next. For younger religious leaders like Kara, the *da'ira* is a crucial means of financial and political mobilization. The number and strength of *da'ira* associations devoted to a particular shaykh underpin one's status in relation to the central hierarchy.

CONCLUSION

Women's sartorial and exchange practices during the Kara visit were central to their search for religious merit in an uncertain land and at a fiscally troublesome time and central to their vision of themselves as being in motion. The devotional practices of women—once considered by scholars to be of secondary interest to the real business of Sufi Islam in West Africa, the transmission of *baraka*—are now taking center stage as lesser religious figures seek to position themselves as leaders in diasporic locations to alter their position in the religious hierarchy. This attempt to raise one's position at home by works abroad is an endeavor in which both men and women, regardless of rank, participate. Indeed, Kara sought to alter the terrain of religious authority at home, through his garnering of a following in New York City. He further sought to challenge the conventional basis of spiritual authority based on genealogical claims and scholarship by employing new media that emphasized his public persona as a persuasive and elegant speaker, promising immediacy to sectors of Senegalese society—youth and migrants—who lack personal access to saintly figures.

NOTES

1. November 20, 2005.

2. I have also written about religious merit in Buggenhagen 2008. Rosander (1998) noted that her female interlocutors emphasized the importance of their quest for "tiyaba," which she defines as a Wolof word. I use "tuyaaba" based on the *Dictionnaire wolof-français et français-wolof* by Jean-Léopold Diouf, which defines the word as "Grâce divine à la suite d'une bonne action." I suspect it may be related to the Arabic *tayyib*, meaning all that is good and wholesome, such as objects, deeds, beliefs, persons, or foods.

3. Mustafa suggests that the Wolof word *sanse* derives from the French *changer*, meaning to transform (2006: 178).

4. I have discussed women's exchange of cloth wealth at length in Buggenhagen 2003.

5. On the subject of control of women's reproductive potential, see also Buggenhagen 2004.

6. www.toubamica.org, Mouride Islamic Community of America, accessed June 16, 2008.

7. Cruise O'Brien translates *njebbel* as "the gift of a person without conditions" (1971: 85n2).

8. See also Rosander 1998: 157.

9. Coulon (1998: 116) further points out that "even if women are excluded from public places of worship, nothing prevents them from having *baraka*, worshipping saints, or becoming agents of a particular marabout." The *baraka* of Amadou Bamba is considered to be transmitted through his daughters as well as his sons, and thus daughters also have the potential to act as *sokhna* (Wolof, spiritual leaders). On this point, Rosander argues that women obtain "less social recognition for the blessing they have inherited from the maraboutic lineage through descent" (Rosander 1998: 151). See also Creevey 1996b: 291.

10. In fact, this statement about the act of *njebbel* is itself in need of quali-
fication, as Cruise O'Brien himself points out that widowed women and
daughters of a shaykh do practice direct allegiance through the act of *njebbel*
(1971:86).

11. Googlevideo.com and myspace.com (accessed June 23, 2008).

12. While it is true that the Murid way drew adepts from slave and warrior castes (Copans 1988: 226; Klein 1998: 198–99) and that some shaykhs
who were relatives of Bamba came from the low-ranking castes, most were
freeborn (Irvine 1974: 450), and many shaykhs began to arrange marriages
with those of royal lineage and thus to identify themselves with the freeborn
(Irvine 1974: 451–52).

13. Initially taking the place of the *sas* (Wolof, duty, offering of labor/cash),
which takes its name from the areas that each person was responsible for
under collective cultivation (Cruise O'Brien 1971: 93).

REFERENCES

Adams, A., and J. So. 1996. *A Claim to Land by the River.* Oxford: Oxford
    University Press.
Amselle, J. L. 1971. "Parenté et commerce chez les Kookoro." In *Develop-
    ment of Indigenous Trade and Markets in West Africa,* ed. Claude Meil-
    lassoux. Oxford: Oxford University Press.
Babou, C. A. 2002. "Brotherhood Solidarity, Education and Migration: The
    Role of the Dahiras among the Murid Muslim Community of New
    York." *African Affairs* 101(403): 151–70.
Bastian, M. 1996. "Female 'Alhajis' and Entrepreneurial Fashions: Flexible
    Identities in Southeastern Nigerian Clothing Practice." In *Clothing and
    Difference: Embodied Identities in Colonial and Post-Colonial Africa,*
    ed. Hildi Hendrickson. Durham, N.C.: Duke University Press.
Bjarnesen, J. 2007. "The Baye Fall of Gueule Tapee. A New Religious Path
    towards Adulthood?" Paper presented at the AEGIS Conference, Leiden,
    Netherlands.
Bop, C. 2005. "Roles and the Position of Women in Sufi Brotherhoods in Sen-
    egal." *Journal of the American Academy of Religion* 73(4): 1099–1119.
Bowen, J. R. 2004. "Does French Islam Have Borders? Dilemmas of Domes-
    tication in a Global Religious Field." *American Anthropologist* 106(1):
    43–55.
Buggenhagen, B. 1997. "Body into Soul, Soul into Spirit: The Commodifica-
    tion of Religious Value in Da'ira Tuba-Chicago." Master's thesis, Univer-
    sity of Chicago.
———. 2003. "At Home in the Black Atlantic: Circulation, Domesticity and
    Value in the Senegalese Murid Trade Diaspora." Ph.D. diss., University
    of Chicago.
———. 2004. "Domestic Object(ion)s: The Senegalese Murid Trade Diaspora
    and the Politics of Marriage Payments, Love, and State Privatization." In
    Producing African Futures: Ritual and Politics in a Neoliberal Age, ed.
    Brad Weiss. Leiden: Brill.

———. 2008. "Beyond Brotherhood: Gender, Religious Authority and the Global Circuits of Senegalese Muridiyya." In *New Perspectives on Islam in Senegal: Conversion, Migration, Wealth, Power and Femininity*, ed. Mamadou Diouf and Mara Leichtman. New York: Palgrave.

———. 2010. "'Killer Bargains': Global Networks of Senegalese Muslims and the Policing of Unofficial Economies in the War on Terror." In *Hard Work, Hard Times: Global Volatilities and African Subjectivities*, ed. Anne Maria Makhulu, Beth Buggenhagen, and Stephen Jackson. Berkeley: University of California Press.

Buitelaar, M. 1993. *Feasting and Fasting in Morocco: Women's Participation in Ramadan*. Oxford: Berg.

Calame-Griaule, G. 1986 [1965]. *Ethnologie et langage: La parole chez le Dogon*. Paris: Editions Gallimard.

Callaway, B., and L. Creevey. 1994. *The Heritage of Islam: Women, Religion, and Politics in West Africa*. Boulder, Colo.: Lynne Rienner.

Carter, D. M. 1997. *States of Grace: Senegalese in Italy and the New European Immigration*. Minneapolis: University of Minnesota Press.

Cohen, A. 1971. "Cultural Strategies in the Organization of Trading Diasporas." In *The Development of Indigenous Trade and Markets in West Africa*, ed. Claude Meillassoux. London: Oxford University Press for the International Africa Institute.

Comaroff, J. L., and J. Comaroff. 1990. "Goodly Beasts and Beastly Goods: Cattle and Commodities in a South African Context." *American Ethnologist* 17(2): 195–216.

Coombe, R., and P. Stoller. 1994. "X Marks the Spot: The Ambiguities of African Trading in the Commerce of the Black Public Sphere." *Public Culture* 7(1): 249–74.

Cooper, B. 1997. *Marriage in Maradi: Gender and Culture in Hausa Society in Niger, 1900–1989*. London: James Currey.

———. 1999. "The Strength in the Song: Muslim Personhood, Audible Capital, and Hausa Women's Performance of the Hajj." *Social Text* 17(3): 87–109.

Copans, J. 1988. *Les marabouts de l'arachide*, 2nd ed. Paris: Harmattan.

Coulon, C. 1988. "Women, Islam and Baraka." In *Charisma and Brotherhood in African Islam*, ed. Christian Coulon and Donal B. Cruise O'Brien. Oxford: Clarendon Press.

Creevey, L. 1985. "Muslim Brotherhoods and Politics in Senegal in 1985." *Journal of Modern African Studies* 23(4): 715–21.

———. 1991. "The Impact of Islam on Women in Senegal." *Journal of Developing Areas* 25(3): 347–68.

———. 1996a. *Changing Women's Lives and Work: An Analysis of the Impacts of Eight Microenterprise Projects*. Rugby: Practical Action Publishing.

———. 1996b. "Islam, Women and the Role of the State in Senegal." *Journal of Religion in Africa* 26(3): 268–307.

———. 2002. "Structural Adjustment and the Empowerment (or Disempowerment) of Women in Niger and Senegal." In *Women in Developing*

Countries: Assessing Strategies for Empowerment, ed. Rekha Datta and Judith F. Kornberg. Boulder, Colo.: Lynne Rienner.

Creevey, L., and B. Callaway. 1989. "Women and the State in Islamic West Africa." In *Women, the State, and Development,* ed. Sue Ellen M. Charlton, Jana Matson Everett, and Kathleen A. Staudt. Albany: State University of New York Press.

Cruise O'Brien, D. B. 1970. "Mouride Studies." *Africa: Journal of the International African Institute* 40(3): 257–60.

Curtin, P. D. 1975. *Economic Change in Pre-Colonial Africa: Senegambia in the Era of the Slave Trade.* Madison: University of Wisconsin Press.

Diop, A. B. 1985. *La famille wolof.* Paris: Karthala.

Diop, M. C. 1981. "Fonctions et activities des dahira Mourides urbains (Senegal)." *Cahiers d'études africaines* 20(1–3): 79–91.

Diop, M., and L. Michalak. 1996. "'Refuge' and 'Prison"—Islam, Ethnicity, and the Adaptation of Space in Workers' Housing in France." In *Making Muslim Space in North America and Europe,* ed. Barbara Daly Metcalf. Berkeley: University of California Press.

Diouf, M. 2000. "The Senegalese Murid Trade Diaspora and the Making of a Vernacular Cosmopolitanism." *Public Culture* 12(3): 679–702.

Diouf, S. 2004. "The West African Paradox." In *Muslims' Place in the American Public Square,* ed. Z. Bukhari et al. Lanham, Md.: AltaMira Press.

Ebin, V. 1990. "Commerçants et missionnaires: Une confrérie sénégalaise à New York. " *Hommes et Migrations* 1132 (May): 25–31.

———. 1992. "A la recherche de nouveaux poissons: Stratégies commerciales mourides en temps de crise." *Politique Africaine* 45: 86–99.

———. 1993. "Les commerçants mourides à Marseille et à New York." In *Grands commerçants d'Afrique de l'Ouest,* ed. Emmanuel Grégoire and Pascal Labazée. Paris: Karthala.

———. 1996. "Making Room versus Creating Space: The Construction of Spatial Categories by Itinerant Mouride Traders." In *Making Muslim Space in North America and Europe,* ed. Barbara Daly Metcalf. Berkeley: University of California Press.

Gueye, C. 2001. "Touba: The New Dairas and the Urban Dream." In *Associational Life in African Cities: Popular Responses to the Urban Crisis,* ed. A. Tostensen, I. Tvedten, and M. Vaa. Stockholm: Nordiska Afrikainstitutet.

———. 2003. "New Information and Communications Technology Use by Muslim Mourides in Senegal." *Review of African Political Economy* 98: 609–25.

Heath, D. 1992. "Fashion, Anti-Fashion and Heteroglossia in Urban Senegal." *American Ethnologist* 19(1): 19–33.

Hopkins, A. G. 1973. *An Economic History of West Africa.* New York: Columbia University Press.

Hunwick, J. O. 1999. "Islamic Financial Institutions: Theoretical Structures and Aspects of Their Application in Sub-Saharan Africa." In *Credit, Currencies and Culture: African Financial Institutions in Historical*

Perspective, ed. Endre Stiansen and Jane I. Guyer. Uppsala: Nordic Africa Institute.

Irvine, J. T. 1974. "Caste and Communication in a Wolof Village." Ph.D. diss., University of Pennsylvania.

———. 1978. "When Is Genealogy History? Wolof Genealogies in Comparative Perspective." *American Ethnologist* 5(4): 651–74.

———. 1989. "When Talk Isn't Cheap: Language and Political Economy." *American Ethnologist* 16(2): 248–67.

Kane, A. 2002. "Senegal's Village Diaspora and the People Left Ahead." In *The Transnational Family: New European Frontiers and Global Networks*, ed. Deborah Bryceson and Ulla Vuorela. London: Berg.

Klein, M. 1998. *Slavery and Colonial Rule in French West Africa*. Cambridge: Cambridge University Press.

LeBlanc, M. N. 2000. "Versioning Womanhood and Muslimhood: 'Fashion' and the Life Course in Contemporary Bouaké, Côte d'Ivoire." *Africa* 70(3): 442–81.

Manchuelle, F. 1997. *Willing Migrants: Soninke Labor Diasporas, 1848–1060*. Athens: Ohio University Press.

Mauss, M. 1990 [1950]. *The Gift*. Trans. W. D. Halls. New York: Norton.

Mbow, P. 2008. "Senegal: The Return of Personalism." *Journal of Democracy* 19(1): 156–69.

Mustafa, H. N. 1998. "Practicing Beauty: Crisis, Value and the Challenge of Self-Mastery in Dakar, 1970–1994." Ph.D. diss., Harvard University.

———. 2006. "La Mode Dakaroise. Elegance, Transnationalism and an African Fashion Capital." In *Fashion's World Cities*, ed. Christopher Breward and David Gilbert. Oxford: Berg.

———. 1971. *The Mourides of Senegal: The Political and Economic Organization of an Islamic Brotherhood*. Oxford: Clarendon Press.

———. 1975. *Saints and Politicians: Essays in the Organization of a Senegalese Peasant Society*. Cambridge: Cambridge University Press.

———. 1988. "Charisma Comes to Town: Mouride Urbanization, 1945–86." In *Charisma and Brotherhood in African Islam*, ed. Christian Coulon and Donal B. Cruise O'Brien. Oxford: Clarendon Press.

———. 1992. "Le contrat social sénégalaise à l'épreuve." *Politique africaine* 45: 9–20.

———. 1996. "A Lost Generation? Youth Identity and State Decay in West Africa." In *Postcolonial Identities in Africa*, ed. Richard Werbner and Terence Ranger. London: Zed Books.

Perry, D. L. 1997. "Rural Ideologies and Urban Imaginings: Wolof Immigrants in New York City." *Africa Today* 44(2): 229–60.

Reynolds, R. 2004. "We Are Not Surviving, We Are Managing: The Constitution of a Nigerian Diaspora along the Contours of the Global Economy." *City and Society* 16(1): 15–37.

Roberts, A. 1996. "The Ironies of System D." In *Recycled, Re-seen: Folk Art from the Global Scrap Heap*, ed. C. Cerny and S. Seriff. New York: Harry Abrams for the Museum of International Folk Art, Santa Fe.

Rosander, E. E. 1997a. *Transforming Female Identities: Women's Organizational Forms in West Africa.* Uppsala: Nordic Africa Institute.

——. 1997b. "Women in Groups in Africa: Female Associational Patterns in Senegal and Morocco." In *Organizing Women: Formal and Informal Women's Groups in the Middle East*, ed. Dawn Chatty and Annika Rabo. Oxford: Berg.

——. 1998. "Women and Muridism in Senegal: The Case of Mam Diarra Bousso Diara in Mbacke." In *Women and Islamization: Contemporary Dimensions of Discourse on Gender Relations*, ed. K. Ask and Marit Tjomsland. Oxford: Berg.

——. 2003. "Mam Diarra Bousso: The Mourid Mother of Prorkhane, Senegal." *Jenda: A Journal of Culture and African Women Studies* 4.

——. 2004. "Going and Not Going to Porokhane: Mourid Women and Pilgrimage in Senegal and Spain." In *Reframing Pilgrimage: Cultures in Motion*, ed. Simon Coleman and John Eade. London: Routledge.

Salzbrunn, M. 2004. "The Occupation of Public Space through Religious and Political Events: How Senegalese Migrants Became a Part of Harlem, New York." *Journal of Religion in Africa* 34(4): 468–92.

Schulz, D. E. 2003. "Political Factions, Ideological Fictions: The Controversy over Family Law Reform in Democratic Mali." *Islamic Law and Society* 10(1): 132–64.

——. 2007. "Competing Sartorial Assertions of Femininity and Muslim Identity in Mali." *Fashion Theory* 11(2/3): 253–80.

Soares, B. F. 2005. "Islam in Mali in the Neoliberal Era." *African Affairs* 105(418): 77–95.

Sow, F. 1985. "Muslim Families in Black Africa." *Current Anthropology* 26(5): 563–70.

——. 2003. "Fundamentalisms, Globalization and Women's Human Rights in Senegal." *Gender and Development* 11(1): 69–75.

Stoller, P. 2002. *Money Has No Smell: The Africanization of New York City.* Chicago: University of Chicago Press.

Tall, S. M. 1994. "Les investissements immobiliers d'émigrants sénégalais à Dakar." *Revue Européen des Migrations Internationales* 10(3): 137–51.

——. 1996. "Kara International Exchange: Un nouvel instrument financier pour les courtiers mourides de l'axe Dakar-New York." Communication au colloque international de l'APAD, June 5–8, Université de Hohenheim (Stuttgart).

Tapper, N. 1990. "Ziyaret: Gender, Movement, and Exchange in a Turkish Community." In *Muslim Travelers: Pilgrimage, Migration and the Religious Imagination*, ed. Dale F. Eickelman and James Piscatori. Berkeley: University of California Press.

Villalón, L. A. 1995. *Islamic Society and State Power in Senegal.* Cambridge: Cambridge University Press.

——. 2004. "Senegal. Islamism in Focus." *African Studies Review* 47(2): 61–71.

Weber, M. 1993 [1963]. *The Sociology of Religion.* Boston: Beacon Press.

Weiner, A. B. 1992. *Inalienable Possessions. The Paradox of Keeping-While-Giving.* Berkeley: University of California Press.

Youngstedt, S. 2004. "The New Nigerien Hausa Diaspora in the US: Surviving and Building Community on the Margins of the Global Economy." *City and Society* 16(1): 15–37.

14

TOWARD UNDERSTANDING A CULTURE OF MIGRATION AMONG "ELITE" AFRICAN YOUTH

EDUCATIONAL CAPITAL AND THE FUTURE OF THE IGBO DIASPORA

RACHEL R. REYNOLDS

Starting in the mid-1990s, I have had several informal conversations with older teens and young adults in the United States whose parents had emigrated from Nigeria. With a few notable exceptions, these youth speak little to no Igbo, despite their parents' own fluency, and despite having been raised in a closely watched and carefully monitored immigrant home. More formally, my recent work has investigated why and how being raised in an immigrant family affects children's choices in education. One particularly surprising finding in studies of language education choice was that all students in an Igbo language course at the college level were children of Igbo people living in the diaspora. That is, they were largely second-generation children of immigrants or members of the "1.5 cohort," those born in Nigeria but who relocated to the United States at a young age.

In a conversation with these five students, I asked why obtaining a bit of fluency in Igbo would be helpful to them. All agreed it would bring them closer to family in Nigeria and abroad; one discussed plans to work in a family import-export business, while another said she wanted to practice medicine in her parents' home area. Soon, however, the students began to talk about what it was like to return to a home that some of them had never or only rarely seen and how their lack of linguistic knowledge in Igbo (and various Nigerian Englishes) was both troubling and inconvenient. Another student responded that lack of cultural knowledge was a problem, telling us how he was "cut" on his wrists as a child by a grandmother, holding his arms up for everyone to see, but that he didn't know what these ritual marks meant. I also asked if these students knew how to conduct kola ceremonies, which are short ceremonies—given often—

which welcome important guests to the home or that celebrate special occasions. The students nodded vigorously for a few seconds, and then one explained that he knew the motions of breaking the kola nut. However, he said that he wanted to know more about the kola ceremony, asking what verbal content might mean in its deeper linguistic and visual symbolism.

This is a brief snapshot of a discussion in which many things were happening, but especially this vignette highlights two important elements: despite the fact that these students carry with them some sense of their families' places of origin—to the extent that some have limited familiarity with relatives, foodways, and the like, and that some even bear physical markings of those places of origin—they have rather limited access to contextually meaningful practices that transmit the experiences of traditional culture known to their parents. These second-generation youth cannot easily gain command of Igbo traditions, traditions that are communal, and collective forms of knowledge, knowledge making, and knowledge transmission. Ironically, it took an institution of American higher education, a course in Igbo language, a classroom of five students, and a visiting American researcher to lay bare an exploratory moment and place where and when a connection to the imaginings of homeland, tradition, and origin could be taken up and examined by Igbo American youth. The second element is that these students were all majoring in international business or pre-medicine and all expressed an intention to work in or for those from Igboland. They all had also strongly expressed an interest in living in Nigeria (or returning to it), and all wanted to establish the kind of international networks of funding, social control, or regional power that would allow them to invest in capital development in their parents' home area.

This essay seeks to open up a range of questions about young immigrants' choices as shaped by access to new forms of global capital, especially in contemporary higher education in the United States. I also seek to join these questions to an analysis of the migratory circumstances of the most recent generation of Igbo "brain drain" immigrants coming to the United States.

INTRODUCTION:
IMMIGRATION AS HUMAN CAPITAL DEVELOPMENT

Scholarship on the post-1965 immigrants in the United States tends to work on an American place-focused and assimilationist point of view, in which the newcomers' integration into circuits of social and cultural capital like schools, neighborhoods, congregations, and workplaces are the central avenue of inquiry (Kasinitz et al. 2008; Foner 2001; Suárez-Orozco and Suárez-Orozco 2002; Portes and Rumbaut 2001). However, new works are beginning to explore the idea that specific groups and populations within sending countries have profound effects on social, political, and especially economic realignments that are occurring between lesser developed areas of the world and the industrial and post-industrial West (Smith and Bakker 2008; Pajo 2008; Foxen 2007; Coe et al. 2011). Of particular interest for this essay are "co-ethnics" whose networks abroad are centered around the pursuit of forms of economic, social, and cultural capital that may be rooted in areas of settlement but are intended in part to be remitted to the homeland. Most obviously, such remittances are economic. Consider Ghana or Mexico, for example, where monies sent home provide both subsistence and rich multiplier effects, including small business capital and tuition for children (UN Habitat 2006; Mazzucato 2008). There is also increasing exchange between receiving and sending areas in the form of human capital, where return immigrants, perhaps westernized or perhaps educated in Western paradigms of economy, culture, and development, convey to their home areas fresh energy and ideas, often with money attached. This field of exchange, or the arenas in which this capital circulates, are places where migrants' vision of their future warrants examination.

Because the practices of international or global communication have shifted radically with new communication technologies, transnational peoples increasingly participate in shared social lives across tremendous distances, sometimes daily, and certainly with greater numbers. Such changes in the social lives of all peoples are articulated, lived, and planned for by individual actors, including youth and their families, on the ground. This planning, in particular, is a central question of this essay: how do transnational communities plan for their futures, when those futures are understood as individual and collective? And how do they plan for futures as particular individuals and as specific families? How might their attitudes toward capital development in their communities—and especially human capital development—be an indicator of and an ideological stance about these actors' imagination of the future in a globalizing world? And most centrally, since Igbo migrations in the United States include large numbers of families with children, how do children experience their sense of self and the practices of growing up that their parents so carefully shape for them?

Since African immigrants in the United States are only now establishing communities with visible economic, geographic, and cultural contours, the second generation is presently entering our classrooms and our workplaces. In this essay, I highlight two things, the first perhaps more completely than the second. The first issue arises out of the historical contexts that tell us how migrations in and out of Africa are by no means new; as many of the essays in this volume explain, there is in the migration literature an overarching need to envision how, with each significant and widescale change in global economy, local economies and the practices of local social life responded. For example, in what ways are African migrations in the late twentieth and early twenty-first centuries responses to state rescaling, the increasing scope and influence of global agribusiness, fluctuations in oil production, or the demand for brain-drain professionals in North America and Europe? Is it fruitful to connect these economic changes to the idea of push-and-pull factors in how migrants make decisions and in how migratory regimes arise? How might one understand the ways that parents migrate at least in part to ensure their children's futures through the education that prepares them for survival in the global future, something they both imagine and they create?

My second pursuit in this chapter involves a few small steps toward an understanding of how a second generation of highly educated African immigrants is experiencing ideological realignments between generations who will be living and reproducing society within the flexible global economy. I seek to lay groundwork for a more detailed and emic approach to how youth in particular negotiate and adapt to the various forces around them (peer pressure, parental pressure, educational and political pressures) to prepare themselves as workers in the near future. I ask about how individuals comprehend and act upon the challenges of survival as global citizens by imagining their future self shaped by new forms of education, the challenges of the transnational or global workplace, as well as religion and biological reproduction. Those challenges are especially pertinent to the grasp of how transnationalism affects the home area, in that the subjects discussed in this chapter are the children of professional immigrants, a group of Nigeria's most educated workers, and people who shaped postwar Nigeria. These children are part of a new generation of global Igbo citizens.

Together the two subjects I mention above—the history of movement both within and in and out of Nigeria in the last century, and the idea of children's future that overtly shapes practices and ideologies in Igbo and other Nigerian communities in diaspora—come together to point toward how the new economies of southern Nigeria and the economies of places such as Chicago or the Washington suburbs of Maryland are not only subtly shaping the migrant experience, but are the social milieu out of which migrants are subtly shaping themselves and their efficacy in the wider world.

DATA AND BACKGROUNDS:
ON IGBO IMMIGRATION TO THE UNITED STATES

In this section, I provide a brief overview of the two data sets out of which my postulations on second-generation children emerge. Then I characterize some of the qualities of Igbo communities (and individuals) living in the United States as they have been formed by the history of migrations within and outside Nigeria.

The most recent data are from a preliminary set of interviews and surveys from college-age Nigerian Americans conducted between 1997 and 2008. Of twenty-two students with whom I have had contact over these years, two had Yoruba immigrant parents; these students' circumstances as immigrant children of "brain-drain professionals" are rather similar to those in the Igbo diaspora. The remainder of the interviews and surveys were conducted with "1.5" and second-generation Nigerian Igbo immigrants who are maturing as educated members of a transnational society. The surveys were part of a project on those immigrants learning heritage languages that are among the less commonly taught languages in the United States (Reynolds et al. 2009). Additionally, field notes from research conducted in Igbo immigrants' hometown associations between 1997 and 2002 constituted a major source of general information on young adult attendance at meetings and on conversations between children and their parents about the "training" of Igbo youth in the United States.

In 1997, I began fieldwork by joining an immigrant hometown association in Chicago. In my publications and presentations, I call this association ONI, or Organization for *Ndi Igbo*/Igbo People, a pseudonym that reflects this very large group's sense of itself as representative of Igbo affairs in the United States and also of the heart of Igboland. This group was in fact more inclusive than other hometown associations one might find in itinerant and multilocal communities in Nigeria that merely draw upon members from a single town or single small region (Trager 2001; Harneit-Sievers 2002). Nonetheless, ONI's formal meeting activities and structure were modeled on these Nigeria-based types of hometown associations. At the time of my research, there were about 140 families in the group. It was indeed the largest home-area group in the region, and families from as far as 200 miles away in the United States came to monthly meetings on Sunday afternoons. Reflecting its members' status as part of the middle or upper middle class in the United States, the organization itself is less about mutual assistance than it is about a social opportunity to come together to share language, gossip, and political talk. Of course, group members do sometimes provide mutual assistance, especially when a family has an emergency such as illness or periods of joblessness. The hometown association is also a venue that ties Igbo activities abroad to title-taking back home. Title-taking is highly variable across African societies, but in this case I refer to voluntary men's and women's associations in which senior members, including those living abroad, can actively position themselves to be elected or approved by group members to receive titles of honor. Generally speaking, good works, community donations, and material and monetary contributions to the association in question can all help the pursuit of a title. The more tangible activities of the group include participation in the Bud Billiken Day Parade (a Pan-African pride parade held each summer on the south side of Chicago), organizing a yearly *Ili-Ji* or New Yam Festival, and providing contact among group members to share wakes, christenings, weddings, housewarmings, and other celebrations. There are at least five such groups in Chicago and many more across the United States and Canada, especially in places like Maryland and Houston. Estimates indicate that in 2007 there were approximately 25,000 Igbo speakers (Nigerian born and raised) in the United States.

A striking contrast between Igbo speakers and other immigrant groups, including immigrant groups in the United States and immigrant groups coming from Africa to other destinations, is their disproportionately high access to capital—both global financial capital and educational capital. Igbo migrants are largely from the upper educational strata in Nigeria who upon entry to the United States attend both less selective and highly selective institutions of higher education. This process involves initially entering the United States on student visas, then continuing through settlement and family reunification. Other older immigrants arrive seeking professional (H1B) visas (see Reynolds 2002 for a detailed description). It should be apparent that this migratory pattern involves a deep involvement in the kinds of educational and social capital that are paramount to professionals. Indeed, Igbo speakers living abroad also indicate that they do so because educational opportunities for their children in the overloaded Nigerian system were unavailable, creating a greater push factor for brain-drain immigrants.

To illustrate, the association of which I was a member was connected to a chain migration anchored at the University of Chicago in the early 1970s. The initial members finished university degrees and then developed technology and venture capital firms. The occupations of group members vary enormously, as do their zip codes across the city and its suburbs. While the group included taxi cab drivers, small store managers, and leaders of small congregations, a majority of its members are in business, medicine, journalism, information technology, corporate management, elementary and secondary education, and social work.

Thus, this Igbo migratory presence that is roughly the same in composition among hometown associations throughout the United States, has arisen from immense educational sophistication. Immigrants from Nigeria and secondary migrants from other locations have knowledge of western education and professional standards of practice that inform them before arrival. Settled migrants have knowledge, skills bases, and professional social networks waiting to help co-ethnics as they arrive. In particular, this helps group members hedge against the kinds of exploitation from which other immigrant groups often suffer, although it should be mentioned that several new arrivals live in marginal neighborhoods and work initially at "monkey jobs" (minimum-wage service jobs) until their professional visa status comes through. Some well-educated people are also underemployed, especially when their degree in Nigeria is not recognized in the United States; such people have a great deal of sophistication and skills that they draw upon to ensure their children's success, even if they may not have a great deal of economic capital. Finally, of course, poorer, less educated, or poorly educated Igbo speakers rely more on the generosity and expertise of their compatriots and sometimes their multi-ethnic congregations to establish a suitable life in the United States or to hedge risk. In sum, Igbo speakers' sophistication in the United States makes living in America easier upon arrival, setting them on a path to future socioeconomic security and achievements, be they monetary, educational, or career-oriented,.

EDUCATION AS SOCIAL CAPITAL AND IDEOLOGY IN IGBO IMMIGRANT COMMUNITIES

One of the most striking phenomena of African migration generally is that Africans living in the United States are variously reported as having the highest levels of education of any migrant group (Swigart 2001). In fact, the reported levels of literacy among Nigerians on the continent of Africa are just a little below those of its near large neighbors Ghana and Cameroon (UNESCO 2002). Also, Igboland and other areas of Nigeria where Igbo speakers have settled have areas of poverty and underdevelopment where education (especially for girls) is sacrificed by families who have to make hard choices, or where peoples' levels of education reflect their work as local farmers and traders (Egbo 2000). And yet, there is a notable migratory order of Igbo speakers with a long history and a great deal of unique characteristics that have laid the groundwork for a culture of migration with a disproportionately high level of engagement with forms of global capital.

This section outlines some of the characteristics that have formed this order, including the history of early diffusion of Western forms of literacy and training; the migratory habitus of the Igbo people coming out of their role in the history of the Nigerian economy and Nigeria's pre- and post-independence relationships with Britain; the effects that the Biafra-Nigeria War had on the current generation of Igbo people now rapidly aging; and a key ideological factor within Igbo culture that naturalizes the movement of Igbo people into the mainstream currents of globalization. These factors are the raw stuff that filters down in bits and pieces to Igbo second-generation youth living in the United States. This second generation, aware of it or not, is a continuation of older traditions of going forth from Igboland to become traders in the north of Nigeria and other regions, or more recently to pursue education and professional work. Thus, what immigrant youth are transforming now into a twenty-first-century tradition of international education soon will be part and parcel of Igbo professional life in diaspora. And yet, these youth are also experiencing fragmentary forms of assimilation into various youth cultures in the metropoles, addressed below.

There is a remarkably long history from the early colonial period onward in British West Africa of Igbo speakers working in—if the anachronism is forgivable—the flexible knowledge-based economy. Because of its location along a portion of the Niger River utilizable for trade and its proximity to the coast, Igboland in southeast Nigeria is an area where colonial missions and government centers were established in relatively large numbers, although most didn't arise until the years 1910–1930 (Afigbo 1974; Crowder and Afigbo 1974). Thus, many Igbo people learned English and received the kinds of training that early on made them in demand as servants, clerks, and even as missionaries in locations sometimes far away from the coast.

As trade throughout Nigeria evolved into exchanges of goods between north and south in the 1920s through the 1960s, very large numbers of Igbo people—including itinerant traders and highly trained teachers, businesspeople, and government officials—began to establish homes in areas outside of Igboland, including the cities of Kano and Kaduna in northern Nigeria. Meanwhile, in the 1950s and early 1960s, some of the best educated native sons of Igboland moved abroad for higher education, generally to British universities, although Nnamdi Azikiwe, president of the First Nigerian Republic, notably went to the United States. Returning home with Anglicized "refinement," they worked as lawyers, politicians, writers, military officers, hospital administrators, and other professionals where bureaucratic, scientific, and international political knowledge served the newly forming nation. They were called "been to"—an emic label still used in Igbo communities. I have heard Igbo speakers living today in North America use the term periodically in public discourse about ideologies of global movement of Igbo and, more generally, Nigerian people.

The "been to" can be glossed as someone who has gone abroad for education and returned to Nigeria, ready to take his or her place in the political, social, and economic elite of the country. However, this is also an opportunity to discuss how most of the people in Igbo immigrant networks in the United States are not from the upper elite of Nigeria. Those elites are either wealthy or politically powerful enough to stay in Nigeria. Rather, members of the ONI group and others are frequently self-selecting educational migrants—children and relatives of paycheck-supported middle-class entrepreneurs and professionals—who have much personal initiative guided and channeled by families that work together to share capital to invest in their children's education. Therefore, the higher status of their families is seen as realized through their children's future. This need to consolidate community and family interests is a central concern for the immigrant association, which is a venue for extended discussions about the human capital needs of Nigeria, the best way to raise Igbo children in the United States, and the political future of Igboland.

The focus on children's future is in many ways key to understanding that the relatively tenuous status of these families undergirds the ideation of how Nigerian young adults living abroad understand their connections to the homeland. The youths I interviewed in Illinois and Pennsylvania are ideologically fused to the "been to" tradition, even though the real "been to" are of elite status that is mostly inaccessible to this professional class. It works like this: these children's grandparents were the same migrants and traders who were the first who were able to afford to educate their parents' generation into the mid-level elite Nigerian class of school teachers, government workers, college professors, medical doctors, bankers, and businesspeople who thrived during the 1970s and early 1980s when the value of Nigerian currency the *naira* was high and the Nigerian economy and infrastructure development was coming along well. This era of prosperity preceded the era of structural adjustment and currency devaluation in the mid-to-late 1980s when there was an acceleration of professional migration abroad due to their inability to practice their professions and afford a suitable lifestyle.

Thus, today's generation of well-educated parents have migrated in order to find some measure of middle-class security, a security they had expected to have and that eluded them in Nigeria in the last decade and a half of the twentieth century (Ogbaa 2003). To this group of parents born from 1950 to 1970, their children's education is expressed as the end-all and be-all for their movement abroad. Thus, students of Igbo descent, unsurprisingly, are pushed and socialized into a sense of being part of the educated elite abroad—"That's what we're here for!" Moreover, these parents work assiduously to connect their children to the Igbo homeland by sending the 1.5 generation home to stay with relatives, or setting the stage for their children to date other Igbo children. Finally, because the parents are for the most part themselves highly educated, they have genuine educational capital to guide school selectivity and enhance their children's experience at exam-taking, admissions, and so forth. These children are therefore socialized into a kind of self-understanding as "educational darlings" whose accomplishments are preparing them to work transnationally and as members of the diaspora.

There are two other elements that are important in grasping how Igbo migrants of the 1970s and 1980s affect their children's sense of future community contributors. One element is that the contemporary generation of adult professionals are survivors of the Biafra-Nigeria war. An in-depth discussion of the ramifications that the war has had on how immigrants see themselves in the diaspora is certainly needed but is beyond the scope of this essay. It can be recorded here from my own fieldwork that the living memory of war among Nigerians abroad most substantially creates strong ethnic ties. Not only does the generation living abroad (born between World War II and the mid-1960s) know intimately what privation means to a community; they also will design to shield their children from that sort of privation by seeking out places of political stability for their children. What further drives this point home is that religious-regional-ethnic riots in Nigeria still periodically occur—a few Igbo people will email far and wide pictures of dead youths with captions that to the elder generation in the diaspora harken directly to the war. Likewise, through their parents' eyes and their parents' reveries about the war, the children see Nigeria as a serious place. Perhaps some see Igboland or Biafra as something like a sacred place, one of deep political consequence in their lives. Interestingly, these children also engage with many of their parents' utopian ideas borne of the Biafran legacy, especially ideas of patriotism and Igboland/Biafra as having the potential to become a model African state. To pick a splashy example, the problem of utopia and the vision of Biafra was potently dealt with by Chimamanda Adichie, herself a member of the 1.5 migrant generation, in her Orange Prize–winning novel *Half a Yellow Sun*.

A final element that is strong enough to push Igbo children living abroad into a specific understanding of their place in the global order involves longstanding, well-studied, and well-developed Igbo political ideologies of diffused power. These ideologies take on new life in the late twentieth and early twenty-first century as tropes of neoliberalism and of Igbo peoples' rightful place in the dominion of global capitalism. Igbo people from various parts (though not all) of Igboland will widely quote the adage "*Igbo enwe eze*" (the Igbo are without kings). The phrase is representative of a trope in Igbo societies centering around the relatively headless political system of Igboland prior to the arrival of the British (Anyanwu and Aguwa 1993). The term is today popularly deployed a number of ways. U.S. Igbo people see the term as referring to a historical system in which autonomous towns were led by a caste of freeborn people who could be elected into leadership roles by other officeholders based on a combination of moral righteousness and success in farming. "*Igbo enwe eze*" is also frequently used today as an ethnic rallying term, contrasting the presumptive democratic impulses of a "people without kings" to other Nigerian ethnic groups with centralized and hierarchical leadership systems who are portrayed as less democratic. In the United States, this trope is attached to the idea that Igbo are especially suited to thrive in the democracy- and freedom-loving culture of the United States, where market forces and individual initiative, rather than an oppressive, corrupt, or exploitative state (or the taking of what is seen as government handouts) characterize their immigrant initiative. Many Igbo American college youth see themselves as part of this tradition. In initial interviews, it appears to be reflected in their choices of major and their feelings about their majors, where studying business is seen as activating an approach to solving problems of the developing world by enhancing free-market practices and politics. These young adults also find much entrée and engagement with their parents' rhetoric of development in the home area.

GLOBAL TO LOCAL PRACTICES OF COMMUNITY IDENTIFICATION: INFLUENCES ON THE SOCIAL LIVES OF IGBO IMMIGRANT YOUTH

The last part of this chapter constitutes a report on the mechanisms of Igbo youth group identification in the United States, although this process is perhaps best put as a kind of socialization into both American and Nigerian networks of actors. This kind of socialization, I propose, involves in part taking the social capital endowments of their Igbo forebears into arenas of American social life, most notably within the environment of elite high schools and college campuses, where such youth constructs a sense of self and, importantly, a sense of future self. There are a mass of complex forces, often simultaneously centripetal and centrifugal to Igbo community, that Nigerian-Igbo second-generation students harness and utilize effectively to be agentive in their world. Also, they are subject to these forces and they struggle to control them. Any kind of organization of this section will give an impression that one factor is more primary or influential than another, and that is not necessarily the case. Thus, in this section I look at the forces of identification and social practice around being an Igbo second-generation and 1.5 generation immigrant teen/young adult, ranging from the most "global" practices and influences to the most "local."

Interestingly, as is the case with other middle-class immigrant youth in the United States, these children are skilled at utilizing various media, a skill that becomes a source of deep connection to their peers within and outside the immigrant culture group (Maira 1999). In the case of young adult Igbo, however, connections through and to the media are characterized by an engagement with pan-African forms of marketing and mass-culture consumption. These students might enjoy web-accessible videos of Nigerian rap artists, but they also have Internet social networking connections to share music across Africa and the diaspora, including, for example, in-depth knowledge of Kenyan Sheng rap artists, South African music videos, and collections of contemporary American rap or R&B. Significantly, these youth are often more nationalistically "Nigerian" (as opposed to Igbo) than their parents in terms of culture consumption. That is, Nigerians produce many and varied popular media products. These products, which are not always interpreted as ethnically marked and instead are merely "Nigerian," or even "African," are heavily consumed and shared by Igbo college students in the United States. Notably, such videos, blogs, podcasts, and CDs are far removed from the classical Igbo education that parents expect their children to have absorbed as a result of merely being "Igbo" children.

As cross-cultural migrants or children of immigrants, the youth have an almost anthropological sense of what it means to be an immigrant. They can gaze at their own otherness and use it as an experimental identity resource. More than monocultural African Americans and European Americans, African second-generation students find themselves conflicted, made more creative, and often comforted by moving between self-representation as African Americans on American college campuses, patriotically American, culturally or ancestrally Igbo, and Nigerians in the wider world. These maneuvers depend deeply on context, of course, and they are built on things like biases that youth are aware of against African Americans within both Igbo communities and white communities. Youth also sometimes find that Americanness is hard to access because of the color line, where unmarked American identity is often acknowledged as belonging to white communities. Other kinds of American identity practices can be difficult to deploy, because unlike many African Americans, they are in general not as deeply socialized into the ability to code-switch across mainstream and markedly African American cultural membership. Likewise, for those Igbo children living abroad who return to Nigeria, they feel that their Africanness can be deeply suspect when back home in Igboland. For example, one young woman told me that family would tease her for her inability to produce Broken English (i.e., Nigerian vernacular English). Family would also ask her embarrassingly forward and sometimes insulting questions about her sexuality, and the student thought that these questions involved expectations about Nigerian stereotypes of American sexuality.

Ultimately, however, between so many identity resources, including linguistic and kinesic and ornamental expressions of group belonging, commodity consumption, and practices of self-expression, students sometimes feel caught up in too many resources and perhaps too many moments where they feel in-between or liminal. A majority of the Igbo

1.5 and second generation solve this problem by joining with other elite students of African and sometimes Afro-Caribbean parents. Indeed, many of the globalized practices in media consumption and identity practice (food, parties, dance, language use, dress) are an earmark of not only the Igbo group of immigrant and recent-arrival children, but their entire generation; they join a large number of their peers in Africa, in London, in Sydney, through various forms of mobility, both virtual and real. These youth are especially joining together in the videosphere, texting friends internationally, collecting compendia of obscure pan-African video products on YouTube, and sharing tales of woe and sometimes superiority as children of demanding traditional parents.

Finally, the fostering of first-generation Igbo youth by adults living in the United States brings together Igbo diasporic youth across the globe and is a developed mechanism for the accrual of educational capital in communities. It is also a means to set the stage to match American Igbo youth with co-ethnic marriage partners. Briefly, older (and idealized) traditions of fostering, in which a mother's brother is expected to help obtain a proper education for nieces and nephews, are extended into the Igbo diaspora in the form of aunts and uncles helping to sponsor relatives in the United States while they attend college or graduate school. Foster children are brought into the homes and lives of 1.5 and second-generation Igbo youth as well, and it is quite common to find newly arrived immigrant youth on campuses well integrated with coteries of second-generation students. The fostering tradition is especially important in knitting together families across large distances and, combined with frequent trips home to stay with relatives, this system of bringing Igbo children together across the diaspora is probably leading to a high rate of marriage between Igbo people in the United States and Igbo people from other parts of the world.

In all, though, there are centripetal forces that remove these children from the homeland and cultural practices that are so idealized by their immigrant parents' generation. Above, I alluded to parents' mentality about the homeland involving one of a classical Igbo education, where by watching and listening children absorb the ability to apply proverbial learning and rituals of ancestral honor to become moral Igbo people. It is sadly ironic that these parents often do not impart to their children the Igbo language upon which so much of Igbo traditional education is based.

There are many reasons why second-generation and even 1.5 generation youth do not always learn Igbo from the previous generation. The first is that Nigeria itself appears to be undergoing a language shift, as evidenced by interviews with some Igbo children raised in Nigeria who come abroad at the age of nineteen or twenty for college and who speak little Igbo (especially so with children raised in cities outside of Igboland). There are many reasons for this kind of shift in immigrant communities, including the primacy of Nigerian English and even Americanized English in many people's homes (this is sometimes driven, ironically, by polyglot parents' idea that using multiple Nigerian languages and multiple dialects of Igbo would confuse children). Also, children sometimes learn varieties of Igbo in early childhood but, like other immigrants, turn away from it in late childhood and early adolescence in an attempt to conform to American monolingual norms. Of course, there is a differential based on whether parents are deeply committed to using the Igbo language and are savvy about the practice of bilingual language transmission (none of my sample had monolingual parents, although I have heard that there are some monolingual Igbo women in the United States rearing families). And some Igbo youth living in the United States may have spent enough time directly in Igboland to arrive in the United States with a solid grounding in the language.

For migratory parents raising families in the United States, there are also multiple challenges to imparting elements of what is regarded as traditional Igbo life, including forms of communicating and performing Igbo group identity through political talk, humorous banter, and exhortations on traditional morality that invoke proverbial wisdom, masquerades, drumming, and dances—all of which occur in ethnic association meetings. Perhaps the biggest challenge is how far-flung Igbo people are geographically. In Chicago or outside Washington, D.C., families live in zip codes that correspond to their work and socioeconomic status, as well their concerns about school systems, crime, and the ethnic makeup of their neighbors. Without ethnic enclaves or tight-knit neighborhoods, Igbo people meet through immigrant associations to assemble and conduct what they see as traditional affairs, especially about the practice of hometown identities and political membership in Igbo communities. Meetings are frequently conducted in multiple languages, including various dialects or features of regional Igbos, and the meetings involve sophisticated political arguments that would be nearly incomprehensible to children. And most important, very few youth are brought by parents to these meetings, or they are brought infrequently. Meanwhile, as indicated, in the home, youth and their parents are very busy; and sometimes childcare is left to older girls, who do not use Igbo with their younger siblings. All these circumstances severely tend to limit the rendering or revealing of collective Igbo traditions to second-generation youth.

CONCLUSION: IGBO YOUNG ADULTS AND THE FUTURE OF A GENERATION OF PROFESSIONALS

Nonetheless, between occasional meeting attendance, family events, daily life practices in the home, and visits to Nigerian relatives, there is a relatively lively field of socialization through which Igbo youth and young adults in the United States become members of the Igbo diaspora. I conclude this essay by fusing issues of human capital development central in Igbo communities worldwide with the idea of how being and acting as an embodiment of the Igbo future affects young people's choices and sense of selves.

One may be particularly taken by students' choices of majors in college, and their positive and premeditative attitudes toward a desire to live and work in Nigeria. Their choices were notable earmarks of an engagement with a disciplined future self, a jet-setting global worker in business, technology, and medicine, and especially as a Nigerian or an Igbo global citizen.

Indeed, a strong indicator of agency and the sense of future self can be seen through children's choice of major and intent to travel to Nigeria. Since 2002, among fifteen Igbo and two Yoruba students, I found that four were majors in engineering, five in pre-med, one in nursing, and five in business. From previous data sets, I found that nursing and engineering were by far the most popular majors for young adults related to Chicago immigrants (oddly, only one was in computer science), and that the two students who majored in English literature were preparing novels and poetry about Nigerian subjects. Talking about their sense of the future, all these approximately twenty-one-year-old youths overtly saw themselves as an upcoming generation of Africans who were jumping into their perceptions of what the "new" economy is: two Nigerian students pointed out they were studying chemical engineering in a program that emphasized either development or sustainability issues.

Importantly, these young adults are choosing to learn what they can at the university level about their parents' home area, squeezing courses like language instruction, history, and anthropology into their crowded pre-professional course schedules. At the last stages of cognitive development, as many students turn to the identity work that typifies the last few years of higher education, the interviewees tell me that they plan to live and work in Nigeria. Others wish to create transnational corporations through which they can live out their sense of a global professional self, not unlike the Chinese "astronauts" of the Pacific Rim (Wong 1998). And yet, ironically, these young adult Igbo children of diaspora must arise to the challenge of operationally obtaining the language varieties of Igbo and Nigerian English, the sense of living Igbo culture in Nigerian contexts, and the maturity to grasp the discrepancies in expectation between political, business, and scientific cultures in Nigeria and the United States. They also must fuse their sense of local and global identities into a self-understanding that fires their aspirations to create a new kind of professional self: from those rooted in the idealized Igbo hamlet or the Biafran utopia, to those of the commoditized pan-African self, to those of the highly educated second-generation American. I strongly suspect that they are fusing flexible knowledge-based economic practices into their identity practices as Africans, and will be seeking to move into the broader world based on this.

REFERENCES

Afigbo, A. E. 1974. "The Establishment of Colonial Rule, 1900–1918." In *History of West Africa, Volume Two,* ed. J. Ajayi and Michael Crowder. New York: Columbia University Press.

Anyanwu, U. D., and J.C.U. Aguwa. 1993. *The Igbo and the Tradition of Politics.* Uturu, Nigeria: Fourth Dimension Publishers.

Coe, C. et al., eds. 2011. *Everyday Ruptures: Children and Migration in Global Perspective.* Nashville: Vanderbilt University Press.

Crowder, M., and A. E. Afigbo. 1974. "West Africa 1919–1939: The Colonial Situation." In *History of West Africa, Volume Two,* ed. J. Ajayi and Michael Crowder. New York: Columbia University Press.

Egbo, Benedicta. 2000. *Gender, Literacy and Life Chances in Sub-Saharan Africa.* Clevedon, UK: Multilingual Matters, Ltd.

Foner, N. 2001. *New Immigrants in New York.* New York: Columbia University Press.

Foxen, P. 2007. *In Search of Providence: Transnational Mayan Identities.* Nashville: Vanderbilt University Press.

Harneit-Sievers, A. 2002. *A Place in the World: New Local Historiographies from Africa and South Asia.* Leiden: Brill.

Kasinitz, P., J. H. Mollenkopf, M. C. Waters, and J. Holdaway. 2008. *Inheriting the City: The Children of Immigrants Come of Age.* Cambridge, Mass.: Harvard University Press.

Kwadwo, K., T. K. Baffour, and J. A. Arthur, eds. 2006. *The New African Diaspora in North America: Trends, Community Building, and Adaptation.* Lanham, Md.: Lexington Books.

Maira, S. 1999. "Identity Dub: The Paradoxes of an Indian-American Youth Subculture (New York Mix)." *Cultural Anthropology* 14(1): 29–60.

Mazzucato, V. 2008. "The Double Engagement: Transnationalism and Integration—Ghanaian Migrants' Lives between Ghana and the Netherlands." *Journal of Ethnic and Migration Studies* 34(2): 199–216.

Ogbaa, K. 2003. *The Nigerian Americans.* Westport, Conn.: Greenwood Publishing.

Pajo, E. 2008. *International Migration, Social Demotion, and Imagined Advancement: An Ethnography of Socioglobal Mobility.* New York: Springer.

Portes, A., and R. Rumbaut. 2001. *Legacies: The Story of the Immigrant Second Generation.* Berkeley: University of California Press.

Portes, A., and M. Zhou. 1993. "The New Second Generation: Segmented Assimilation and Its Variants." *Annals of the American Academy of Political and Social Science* 530 (November).

Reynolds, R. R. 2002. "An African Brain Drain: Nigerian (Igbo) Decisions to Immigrate to the U.S." *Review of African Political Economy* 29(92): 273–84.

Reynolds, R. R., K. Howard, and J. Deák. 2009. "Heritage Language Learners in First-Year Foreign Language Courses: A Report of General Data across Learner Subtypes." *Foreign Language Annals* 42(2): 250–69.

Smith, M. P., and M. Bakker. 2008. *Citizenship across Border: The Political Transnationalism of El Migrante.* Ithaca, N.Y.: Cornell University Press.

Suárez-Orozco, C., and M. Suárez-Orozco. 2002. *Children of Immigration.* Cambridge, Mass.: Harvard University Press.

Swigart, L. 2001. *Extended Lives: the African Immigrant Experience in Philadelphia.* Philadelphia: Historical Society of Pennsylvania.

Trager, L. 2001. *Yoruba Hometowns: Community, Identity and Development in Nigeria.* Boulder, Colo.: Lynne Rienner.

UN Habitat. 2006. "Migration—Remittances: Facts & Figures." www.unhabitat.org/downloads/docs/Media/WHD%20B7%20%20Remittanes%20Facts%20&%20Figures.pdf. Accessed August 7, 2008:

UNESCO. 2002. "Education for All World Monitoring Report." http://portal.unesco.org/education/en/ev.php-URL_ID=13597&URL_DO=DO_TOPIC&URL_SECTION=201.html. Accessed August 13, 2008.

Wong, B. 1998. *Ethnicity and Entrepreneurship: The New Chinese Immigrants in the San Francisco Bay Area.* Boston: Allyn and Bacon.

CONTRIBUTORS

Afe Adogame is Associate Professor in World Christianity/Religious Studies at the University of Edinburgh, where he teaches Indigenous Religions, African Christianity, and Religion in the New African Diaspora. He is General Secretary of the African Association for the Study of Religion.

Cheikh Anta Babou is Associate Professor of History at the University of Pennsylvania. His research focuses on francophone West Africa since the nineteenth century and on contemporary African diasporas in France and the United States.

Beth A. Buggenhagen is Assistant Professor of Anthropology at Indiana University. Her research interests include circulation and value; diaspora and transnationalism; gender and neoliberal global capital; Islam; and visuality.

Donald Carter is Professor of Africana studies and Chief Diversity Officer at Hamilton College. His research interests include cultural theory, racial formation, visual culture, invisibility, and transnational cultural politics.

Hansjörg Dilger is Junior Professor of Social and Cultural Anthropology at Freie Universität Berlin. His research interests include anthropology of religion (especially Pentecostalism and Islam) and medical anthropology (especially HIV/AIDS, anthropology of biomedicine, transnationalization of health, medicine, and healing).

Isaie Dougnon is Assistant Professor in the Department of Social Sciences, University of Bamako. He was a Fulbright Senior Research Scholar at the University of Florida in 2011–12.

Jane Freedman is Marie Curie Chair in the Centre de Recherches Politiques at Université de Paris 1, Sorbonne. Her research has focused on national and European immigration and asylum policies, gender and migration, gender in asylum, and refugee policies.

Cindy Horst is Senior Researcher at the Peace Research Institute, Oslo (PRIO) and leads the Migration Research Group. She is a social anthropologist whose current research interests focus on humanitarian assistance practices; cultures of migration; interactions between forced migrants and the refugee regime; and political transnational practices.

Abdoulaye Kane is Associate Professor of Anthropology and African studies at the University of Florida. His recent research interests cover issues of diasporic identity formation, religious transnational movements, border crossings, and immigration policies.

Loren B. Landau is Director of the Forced Migration Studies Programme at the University of Witwatersrand in Johannesburg, South Africa. A political scientist by training, his research explores migration, belonging, and sovereignty in Africa.

Todd H. Leedy is Associate Director and Senior Lecturer in the Center for African Studies at University of Florida. His current interests include transnational Zimbabweans in southern Africa; urban life, service provision, and city management in Africa; and African modernist architecture.

Rubin Patterson is Professor of Sociology and Anthropology at the University of Toledo. His present and recent research interests include brain circulation, transnational societies, technology and development in southern Africa, and comparative African-Asian development.

Rachel R. Reynolds is Associate Professor in the Department of Culture and Communication at Drexel University. Her work ranges from ethnographic studies of adult (im)migrants to questions of how to research, interpret, and express children's experiences of migration.

Paul Stoller is Professor of Anthropology at West Chester University. In 2002, he won the American Anthropological Association's Robert B. Textor Prize for his book *Money Has No Smell: The Africanization of New York City*.

Bruce Whitehouse is Assistant Professor of Anthropology at Lehigh University. He previously worked for the U.S. Peace Corps in Mali (1997–2000) and the Center for Strategic and International Studies in Washington, D.C. (1993–1996).

Scott M. Youngstedt is Professor of Anthropology at Saginaw Valley State University. His primary work explores the ways by which migrant Hausa create modernities, construct communities in diaspora, and negotiate personal identities in the context of neoliberal globalization.

INDEX

Aac, Ndeye Astu, 234, 239–241, 243n11
Aboubacar, Diakite, 169
academic obligation, 170–171
Achebe, Chinua, 64
Adeboye, Enoch, 187, 188
Adichie, Chimamanda, 279
Adogame, Afe, 10, 13
affair-u-jigeen (women's business), 249
"African Church Plans Christian Disneyland" (Farwell), 173
African Hair Gallery, 240
African National Congress (ANC), 105
African Renaissance, 104
African Union (AU), 83, 86
African-led churches, 178–179, 183, 188, 189
Afro revolution, 233
age of migration, 1
agriculture: rural, 97; sexuality and, 130n7
Ahmadi, V., 226
AIDS. *See* HIV/AIDS
alal (displays of wealth), 260
alienation, 100, 163–167, 169
All African Women's Group, 224
Ambiguous Adventure (Kane), 64
Amisi, B., 106
Amnesty International, 69
Amnesty Law of 1986, 233, 252
ANAPEC. *See* National Agency for Employment Promotion and Skills
ANC. *See* African National Congress
Andersson, Jens, 127
Anduru, Agoro, 116, 124
Anthias, F., 187

anthropological folklore, 124
anthropological studies, 6–7
anti-immigration, 72–73; political ideology, 66; riots, 69
apartheid, 97, 98
artificial hair, 232
Ashimolowo, Matthew, 179, 188
Asia, 80–83, 86, 88
L'Association des Nigeriens de New York, 138
Association of African-Style Hair Salon Owners of Philadelphia, 238
asylum seekers, 66, 68; feminization and, 211–226; gender-related persecution and, 217–224; survival strategies and, 224–225; women as, 212–217
atomization, 103, 106–107
AU. *See* African Union
Augé, M., 177
autochthony, 7

Baay Faal, 245n27
Babou, Cheikh Anta, 12
Baldwin, James, 65
Ballard, R., 106
Bamba, Amadou, 241, 248, 250–252, 254, 258
baraka (religious grace), 249, 255, 256, 261, 263n9
beautification practices, 260
Beck, U., 107
"been to," 277–278
Bellu, Giovanni Maria, 62
belonging, 59, 93–95, 125–127; fragmentation and marginalization and, 99–100; gatekeepers and globalization and, 100–102; new

forms of, 107–109; rural-urban
migration and, 121–123; self-identified host community and, 96–98;
state primacy and, 98–99; tactical
cosmopolitanism and, 102–107
benchmarking, 85–86, 223
Benhabib, Seyla, 71
Berlusconi, Silvio, 72
Biafra-Nigeria War, 276, 279
bias: gender, 218; systemic, 25
bilingual language transmission, 283
Billy Jean (hair salon), 233
black hair fashions, 233–234;
    dreadlocks, 245n27. See also hair
    braiding
Black Seminoles, 55n9
Black Women's Rape Action Project,
    220
blood donors, 129n3
boat journeys, 52
body art, 231
Bop, Codou, 255
Boserup, Esther, 235
Bossi, Umberto, 72
Bossi-Fini, 62
brain circulation, 78–79, 81–82, 84
brain drain, 6, 271; professionals, 274
brain gain, 82
brassage (cultural and ethnic blend-
    ing), 140
Brazzaville, Republic of Congo,
    19–20, 22–24, 25, 31n1
breadwinners, 114
bridewealth, 147
Broadway Marquis Theater, 248
brown areas, 99
Bruni, Frank, 70
Buggenhagen, Beth, 12

Caam, Mbay, 239
Caam, Yaasin, 244n19
care and maintenance, 199–203
care systems, 124–125
Carter, Donald, 5
cash offerings, 256
castes, 231, 238
Castles, Stephen, 1

Catholicism, 67
cell phones, 148–152
Center of Information and Migration
    Management (CIGEM), 51
centers of initial reception, 70
central pillars, of cosmopolitanism,
    102
Centri di Permanenza temporanea e
    Assistenza (CPTAs), 74n8
Centri di Prima Acooglienza (centers
    of initial reception), 70
children, 12, 117; of asylum seek-
    ers, 214; authorization permit for,
    57n27; inheritance and, 119; traf-
    ficking, 53; wealth of, 23. See also
    youths
chira (disease), 122–123
chosen migration, 5–6
Christians, 43, 72, 175
Christian Disneyland, 173, 184, 185
Christian Peoples Alliance (CPA), 182
churches, 10, 67, 105–106; African-
    led, 178–179, 183, 188, 189. See also
    specific churches
Churchill, Winston, 87
Ciampi, Carlo Azeglio, 72
CIGEM. See Center of Information
    and Migration Management
circular migrants, 141, 142–145,
    251–254
citizenship, tactical, 107
civil servants, 28
Claims of Culture, The (Benhabib),
    71
Clifford, James, 54n1, 137, 138
Cliggett, Lisa, 24
Cockburn, C., 226
co-development programs, 36, 50
co-ethnics, 272, 282
Cold War, 80, 225
collective welfare, 23
colonial capital, 2
commensality, 257
Commission on Human Rights, UN,
    223
Committee for Refugees and Immi-
    grants, U.S., 197

communication, *151;* cell phones, 148–152; ICTs, 87–88; strategy, 52; technologies, 9, 272
community identification, 280–283
comprehensive immigration reform, 62
Condition of Post-modernity, The (Harvey), 160
conflict, 19, 215; gender and, 167; religion and, 175; remittances and, 155; sexual violence and, 220; voyage as, 49
contestation, 175
Cooper, Barbara, 260
cosmopolitan consciousness, 102
cosmopolitanism, 100; tactical, 102–107
Coulon, Christian, 256, 263n9
counter-hegemonic strategy, 106
CPA. *See* Christian Peoples Alliance
CPTAs. *See* Centri di Permanenza temporanea e Assistenza
Crawley, H., 218, 219
Creevey, Lucy, 256
Cressy, David, 39
crime, 169. *See also* sexual abuse and violence
cultures, 68; blending, 140; differences of, 167, 221; diversity, 66; dominant, 96–98; geo-cultural spaces, 178; ignorance of, 169; of migration, 4, 21; plurality of, 104; of trade, 165; traveling, 133, 137
cultural anthropologists, 21
cultural anxiety, 59
cultural change, 230–242
cultural competence, 162
cultural erosion, 160
cultural flowering, 136
cumulative effect of migration, 4

da'ira (religious associations), 253–254, 256–257, 262
Da'ira Maam Jaara Boussou, 254
Dallas Morning News, 173
danbe (dignity), 27
danga (curse), 23–24

Dante, Alighieri, 63
data: benchmarking, 86; collection, 85; of Igbo diaspora, 273–276
de Haas, Hein, 54
death, 62–67; inheritance and, 119; of urban breadwinners, 114
definitive migration, 46
democratization, 1
demonstration effect, 21, 25
deportations, 68, 69
desecrated space, 178
desk jobs, 23, 28
destinations, preferred, *144*
Destiny Changing Church, 177
detention camps, 72
detention centers, 69, 70
deviant behavior, 118
devotional displays, gendered, 248–263
Diagne, Malick, 244n25
Diallo, Amadou, 169
diamond traders, 2
diaspora, 54n1, 83, 86–87, 134; core-based, 82; definitions of, 136–137; formations, 139–145; global networks and, 101; identities, 11–14; navigating, 59–73; processes, 136–139; scholars of, 171; typologies of, 137. *See also* Igbo diaspora
Dictionnaire wolof-français et français-wolof (Diouf), 263n2
diffused power, 279
dignity, 26–27
Dilger, Hansjörg, 8, 11
Diop, A. Bara, 242n4
Diouf, Jean-Léopold, 263n2
disease of poverty, 127n2
Disney, Walt, 173
Disneyland, Christian, 173, 184, 185
displacement, 2; dwelling in, 13–14
diversity, 66, 81
Divine Comedy, The (Dante), 63
divorce, 148, 237
documentation, 86
domestic migrants, 97
domestic violence, 219
dominant culture, 96–98

Dominion of the Dead, The (Harrison), 63
Dostoyevsky, Fyodor, 71
Douglas, Mary, 65
Dougnon, Isaie, 4–5
downside of social capital, 22
draconian intervention, 81
dreadlocks, 245n27
dressing well, 249–250
dry-season migration, 137
dual system, 7, 117
Durand, Jorge, 4
Düvell, F., 223
dwelling in displacement, 13–14

Eastern European migrants, 73n3
eco-industrial development, 88
economic activities, 235
economic analysis, neoclassical, 20
economic anticipation, 162
economic dimension, of migration, 3–4
economic domination, 93
economic exclusion, 100
economic globalization, 20
economic polarization, 161
economic restructuring, 125
economistic fallacy, 30–31; overcoming, 19–29
economy, 61; decline of, 147; French, 252; global, 100; human, 30; moral, 127–129
ecumenicalism, 94
education, 21, 114, 115; as social capital, 276–280
educational capital, 270–285; human capital development and, 271–273
Eid al-Adha (feast of sacrifice), 149
elegance, 249
elite youth, 270–285; community identification and, 280–283; human capital development and, 271–273
emergency aid, 199–203
emplacement, 176
endogamy, 231
Enloe, Cynthia, 226n2

entrepreneur's social dilemma, 23–24
erasure, 60, 62
ethnic conflict, 220
ethnopolitical factions, 19
EU. *See* European Union
Europe: Eastern European migrants, 73n3; as fortress, 3, 5–6; immigration crisis and, 59–62, 66; migration to, 2–3. *See also specific countries*
European Union (EU), 50–51, 59, 66, 68, 86; asylum and, 211–212
exclusion, 94–95; economic, 100; fragmentation and marginalization as, 99–100; horizontal, 100; patterns of, 98; process, 65; self-exclusion, 103–104; state primacy and, 98–99
exiles, 106

Faal, Ibra, 245n27
fada groups (formal conversation), 141, 145
families: abroad, *143*; care and maintenance and, 201–202; reunification act, 252, 275; rural, 117–118
Farwell, Scott, 173
Fatma, Serigne Moustapha Mbacké Gaindé, 253
Favell, Adrian, 30
fellowship, 166
female genital mutilation (FGM), 215–216, 218, 222
feminist constructivist analysis, 226
feminization, 11–14, 134, 147; of asylum migration, 211–226; of workforce, 160–161
Ferguson, James, 7
Fesshaye, Semret, 225
FGBFC. *See* Full Gospel Bible Fellowship Church
FGM. *See* female genital mutilation
Fini, Gianfranco, 73
fluid association, 103
forced marriage, 215–216, 218

forced repatriation, 68
foreign policy, 65
fragmentation, 99–100
France, 50–51, 160, 167–168; Muridi-
yya and, 251–252
Francis, Rachel, 118–121, 125
Freedman, Jane, 12
French Institute of South Africa, 95
Friedman, Jonathan, 102
friends, *143*
Full Gospel Bible Fellowship Church
(FGBFC), 126

gatekeepers, 100–102
géer (non-artisans), 231, 238, 242n4
gender, 11–12, 134; asylum seekers
and, 211; bias, 218; expectations
of, 167; hair braiding and, 235–239;
inequality of, 235; persecution and,
217–224; rural-urban migration
and, 121–123; structural inequalities of, 213. *See also* men; women
gender-disaggregated statistics, 212
gendered devotional displays,
248–263; circular migration and,
251–254; merit and movement,
254–257; religious hierarchy and,
261–262; sartorial politics and,
257–259; sartorial practices and,
259–261; supplication and, 257–259
"le Général de Bamba," 248
Geneva Convention, 69, 71, 215,
220–221; Relating to the Status of
Refugees, 197, 217–218
geo-cultural spaces, 178
geographic movement, 93
geographies of place, 178–189
Germany, 220
Geschiere, Peter, 7, 117
Gey, Assan, 234, 243n11
Gey, Sheikh, 232
Gibson, William, 31
gift-giving, 198, 204
Gilbert, Alan, 21
global cities, 9, 21
global economy, 100
global hierarchies, 28–30

global markets, 160
global migration, 80
global networks, 101
global place, 177
global practices, 280–283
global stratifications, of wealth, 31
globalization, 8, 80, 100–102, 127,
276; economic, 20; studies, 134
goals, achieved, *147*
Götz, G., 106
governments, 80–82
grand theory, 85
Great Recession, 161
Greece, 174–175
Gregory, J., 224
grin, 56n20
griots (bards), 231
Guérin, 244n18
Gugler, Josef, 7, 21, 117

haddiya offerings, 261–262
hair braiding, 230–242; Aac and,
239–241; designs, 242n3; social status and, 231–232, 235–239; wealth
and gender and, 235–239
Half a Yellow Sun (Adichie), 279
Hannerz, U., 107
harakat (movement, act, or deed),
255, 257
Harrell-Bond, B., 198
Harrison, Robert Pogue, 62, 63
Hart, Keith, 23
Harvey, David, 160
Has God Forsaken Africa (Kala), 3
Hausa communities, 133–134; cell
phones and, 148–152; demographic
profile, *135*; diasporic formations
and, 139–145; international migration and, 141–142; "left behind"
and, 138; perspectives on migration and home, 138; proverbs of,
137; women, 126, 140, 147–148
health system, 6, 73n7
Heath, Deborah, 260
hereditary status, 231
heritage, 73
heterogeneity, 98

hierarchies: global, 28–30; household, 236; of labor, 28–29; religious, 261–262
high wage countries, 20
hira groups (informal conversation), 145
historical-structuralist approach, 84
HIV/AIDS, 8, 113–114, 118; as disease of poverty, 127n2; economic restructuring and, 125; kinship, belonging, and gender and, 121–123; moral economy and, 127–129; NGOs and, 125–127
Hogon (religious leader), 43
Holy Ghost Congress, 183
home, 159; revaluing, 136–139
Home and Exile (Achebe), 64
homebodies, 8, 138, 146–147
homeland, 137
hometown associations, 274
horizontal exclusion, 100
Horst, Cindy, 10
hospitality, 68
host communities, 96–98
host-country incorporation, 14
houses, 237
households, power structure of, 236–237, 241
human capital development, 271–273, 284
human cargos, 5–6
human economy, 30
human rights, 71, 81, 218, 225
human trafficking, 6, 44, 53–54, 68, 72; of children, 53; of women, 216–217
humanism, 74n9
humanitarian aid practices, 198
Hurston, Zora Neale, 59
hyper-visibility, 65

Ibrahim, Rashid, 199–203
ICTs. *See* information and communications technologies
identity, 104; diasporic, 11–14; religious, 12–13; social, 46–50; spatial, 176–177
Igbo diaspora, 270–285; community

identification and, 280–283; data and backgrounds, 273–276; human capital development and, 271–273; ideology in, 276–280
"Igbo enwe eze" (the Igbo are without kings), 279–280
illegal migrants, 50–52, 53, 66
Immigration and Asylum Act, 224
immigration crisis, 59–62; death and, 62–67; Mediterranean and, 67–73
in-betweenness, 13
inclusion, 108; without membership, 104–106; patterns of, 98; total, 101; urban, 95–96, 98
incorporation, 68
Independence (newspaper), 50
India, 84
industrialized countries, 214
Inferno (Dante), 63
informal sector, 161
informal service providers, 4
information, social networks and, 25–26
information and communications technologies (ICTs), 87–88
integration, 163
intentions, migratory, *144*
international aid, 198–199
International Holy Ghost Festival, 183
international migration, 80, 141–142; historical-structuralist approach to, 84
International Monetary Fund, 232
International Organization of Migration (IOM), 57n25, 78–79, 82, 84–86
international stratification, 29
intolerance, 67
intra-regional migration, 2
invisibility, 65, 72
involuntary homebodies, 138, 147
IOM. *See* International Organization of Migration
Islam. *See* Muslims
Italy, 60–62, 66–67; anti-immigration sentiment and, 72–73; Libya and, 68–69; Mediterranean and, 67–73
Izala reformist movement, 154

Jackson, Michael, 65
jekk (elegance), 249
Jelloun, Tahar Ben, 70
Jenitongo, Adamu, 170, 171
jobo (to flee), 43
Johannesburg, South Africa, 9, 95–96, 97; domestic migrants in, 11; self-exclusion and, 103
Jordan, B., 223

Kabeer, N., 94
Kala, Musa Dieng, 3
Kamara, Ali, 169
Kane, Cheikh Hamidou, 64
Kara International Exchange, 259
karamat (evidence of the divine), 258
Keita, Seydou, 62
Kenya, refugees in, 195–205
khalwa (spiritual retreat), 258
KICC. *See* Kingsway International Christian Center
Kihato, C., 104
kin and kinship: networks, 123, 128; obligation to, 23–24; rural-urban migration and, 121–123; solidarity, 113, 114. *See also* families
Kingsway International Christian Center (KICC), 176, 179–181, 183, 188–189
Kitsantonis, Niki, 174
Krause, K., 177

labor: cheap, 9, 20; global commodification of, 81, 84; hierarchies of, 28–29; market, 55n12; migration, 2, 11, 115; sexual division of, 238; status and, 28
Landau, Loren, 9, 11
language, 163; bilingual transmission, 283; competence, 162; loss, 160; shift, 282; trade, 164–165. *See also* Igbo diaspora
Latin America, 80–83, 86
LDA. *See* London Development Agency
Lee, C. T., 107
"left behind," 134, 138, 146–148
Levi, Primo, 73n6

liberal rights discourse, 218, 221
Libya, 68–69, 70
liminality, 159
linguistic ignorance, 169
liquid cemeteries or tombs, 6, 60
local concepts, of migration, 36–39, 52
local practices, 280–283
localities, 176
London Development Agency (LDA), 180
London Thames Gateway Development Corporation's Planning Committee (LTGDC), 180–182
Lukio, Dishon, 121, 123
Lukio, Francis, 113, 114, 118, 130n11

Macklin, A., 217, 220
Malcolm Shabazz mosque, 254
Malians, 4, 24, 35–40, 45, 47
Mandela, Nelson, 9
Mang'ana, J., 106
marginalization, 95, 99–100
market behaviors, 164
market English, 163
marok'a (praise-singers), 146
marriage, 147–148, 236; forced, 215–216, 218; polygamy, 237, 241; polygyny, 147
Marriott Marquis Hotel, 248
Martelli, 62
Marx, Karl, 100
Masalik-al-jinan (Bamba), 262
masculinity, 237, 260
mass influx, 212
Massey, Doreen, 176, 177, 190n5
Massey, Douglas, 4
Mauss, Marcel, 198, 204
Mayaki, Issifi, 158, 161–162, 163, 165, 167
Mbacké, Sokhna Dieng, 259
Mbeki, Thabo, 9, 104
mbotaye (neighborhood ritual association), 255
media, 9, 36; Muslim women and, 249–250; news media, 8; religious speaking and, 258; youths and, 280–281, 282

Mediterranean, 67–73
Meillassoux, Claude, 56n21
membership, inclusion without, 104–106
men, 11; hair braiding and, 236–238, 241; Hausa, 140; wise men, 47
merit, religious, 254–257
Merrill, Heather, 61
Meyer, Birgit, 126
middle-range theories, 85
migration de prestige, 37
migration for development strategy, 78–79, 81
migration survey, 95–96, 97
migration zero policy, 52
migration-development policy agendas, 83–87
migratory patterns, 2, 3, 139–145
militarization, 66
Miller, Laura, 187
Miller, Mark J., 1
Minima Ethnographica: Intersubjectivity and the Anthropological Project (Jackson), 65
Ministry of Exterior Malians and African Integration, 57n25
minority groupings, 174
Miracle Center, 179
Misago, J. P., 106
misinformation, 25
misunderstanding, 164
mobility, 114–115; moral economy of, 127–129; as phenomenon, 1–3; sexual, 122; socioeconomic, 123; studies on, 117
modernity, 26–27, 31, 242n2
Mollenkopf, John, 161
Molyneux, M., 221
monetization, of African companies, 232
money, 6, 48
Money Has No Smell (Stoller), 164
Moneygram, 150
monkey jobs, 276
moral economy, 127–129
moral integrity, 117
motivations, of migrants, 20–22

Motorola, 151
Mounkaila, Boubé, 164, 165, 166
Mountain of Fire and Miracles Church, 106
Moussa, Kankou, 55n13
movement: geographic, 93; within Niamey, 140–141; religious, 254–257
Movement citizen (NGO), 54n2
"muddling through," 80–81
multidisciplinary approach, to study, 1
murders, 169
Murid Islamic Center, 254
Muridiyya Muslims, 241, 245n27, 248–263; merit and movement, 254–257; religious hierarchy and, 261–262; sartorial politics and supplication and, 257–259; sartorial practices and, 259–261
Murtalla, Sheikh, 241
Muslims, 43, 65, 67, 166, 176; of Athens, 174–175; devotional displays of, 248–263; hair braiding and, 235–236; traders, 13. See also Muridiyya Muslims
Mwinyi, Ali Hassan, 121

National Agency for Employment Promotion and Skills (ANAPEC), 57n26
National Geographic, 49
nativism, 95
naval accident of 1996, 62
Ndour, Yousou, 240
ñeeño (artisans), 231, 232, 242n4
negative impact, 81–82
Nehru, Jawaharlal, 84
neoclassical economic analysis, 20
neoclassical theories, 27
neoconservative ideology, 72
neoliberalism, 133, 161, 279; reform policies, 113, 127, 245n26
neo-Marxism, 37
New Partnership for Africa's Development (NEPAD), 78–79, 83, 86
New Science, The (Vico), 63

New Yam Festival, 275
New York City, 12–13, 158–160;
   devotional displays in, 248–263;
   economic polarization and, 161;
   formal associations in, 138; hair-
   braiding salons of, 233; social life
   in, 167–170
Newell, Sasha, 28
news media, 8
NGOs. *See* nongovernmental organizations
Niamey, Niger, 136; achieved goals
   in, *147*; demographic profile of
   Hausa migrants in, *135*; diasporic
   formations in, 139–145; international migration and, 141–142;
   "left behind" in, 134, 138, 146–148;
   migratory patterns in, 139–145;
   transnational connections and
   adaptations in, 145–154. *See also*
   Hausa communities
Nigeria, 175–176; Igbo diaspora,
   270–285
9/11. *See* September 11, 2001
njebbel (submission, initiation), 255,
   261, 264n10
Nokia, 151
nongovernmental organizations
   (NGOs), 36, 54n2; asylum seekers
   and, 216, 218, 225; HIV/AIDS and,
   125–127; refugees and, 195, 197
non-interventionists, 80–81
non-places, 177
non-*refoulement*, 68
non-state spaces, 99
Noreyni, Modou Kara Mbacke,
   248–249, 256–261
norms of reciprocity, 105
North America, 160–163. *See also*
   United States
Northern League, 72
Notes from Underground (Dostoyevsky), 71

O'Brien, Donal Cruise, 255, 256
ODA. *See* Official Development Aid;
   Olympic Delivery Authority

Odom, Elzie, 187
offerings: cash, 256; haddiya, 261–262
Official Development Aid (ODA), 199
Ofpra, 215
Olivier de Sardan, J., 150
Oluyomi, Dapo, 182
Olympic Delivery Authority (ODA),
   180
Omatseye, Sam, 186
1.5 cohort, 270, 274, 278, 282
ONI. *See* Organization for *Ndi Igbo*/
   Igbo People
oral traditions, 124
Organization for *Ndi Igbo*/Igbo
   People (ONI), 274, 277
original centers, 136, 137
otherness, 9
Ousmane, Mamane, 153
out-migration, 30

pan-Africanism, 103, 104
paradox of migration, 22
Parti de la Vérité pour le Développement (PVD), 259
Parti Democratic Sénégalais, 241
Pasqua law, 51, 57n23
patrilineal kinship networks, 123
patterns: of exclusion and inclusion,
   98; migratory, 2, 3, 139–145; of
   remittances, 10
Patterson, Rubin, 6
peasantry, 100
Pentecostal churches, 10, 105, 126
Perry, Donna L, 245n26
Perry, Rick, 187
persecution, gender-related, 217–224
Piot, Charles, 9
Pisanu, Giuseppe, 72
place: geographies, 178–189; recon-
   ceptualizing, 176–177
place-making, 174, 176
poaching, 6
Polanyi, Karl, 30
polarization, economic, 161
policy-informing research, 83–85
political dimension, of migration,
   3–6

political domination, 93
politics of autochthony, 7
polygamy, 237, 241
polygyny, 147
postcolonial migration, 2, 6
Potash, Betty, 124
poverty, 153
power, diffused, 279
power structure, of households,
    236–237, 241
preferred destinations, *144*
prestige migration, 50
professionalization, of hair braiding,
    232
proof of existence, 72
prostitution, 216
protracted refugee situation, 196–198
proverbs, Hausa, 137
psychological dimension, of migra-
    tion, 3–6
purification, 43
push and pull factors, 4, 37; social
    networks as, 22–25
puukare (posing), 260
PVD. *See* Parti de la Vérité pour le
    Développement

racial classifications, 67
rafet (displays of beauty), 260
Rao, A., 221
rape, 215, 219–220
Rastafarianism, 245n27
rational investments, 154
Razavi, S., 221
RCCG. *See* Redemption Camp of the
    Redeemed Christian Church of
    God
RCCGNA. *See* Redeemed Christian
    Church of God North America
reception centers, 70
Reception Directive, 223
reciprocity, 105, 113
recognition, 71–72
Redeemed Christian Church of
    God North America (RCCGNA),
    184–186
Redemption Camp of the Redeemed

Christian Church of God (RCCG),
    173, 177, 183, 185, 187–189
Redmond, Ron, 69
refugees, 195–205, 217; camps,
    196–197; remittances and, 199–
    203; Somali, 196–198; transna-
    tional assistance practices and,
    198–199
Refugee Council, 225
Refugee Women's Resource Project
    (RWRP), 214
regional intolerance, 67
religion: churches and worship space,
    10; differences of, 166; ethnogra-
    phy, 13, 174; gendered devotional
    displays, 248–263; geographies of
    place, 178–189; hierarchy, 261–262;
    identities, 12–13; intolerance, 67;
    place-making, 173, 176; space and
    place and, 176–177; space contes-
    tations, 175. *See also* Christians;
    churches; Muridiyya Muslims;
    Muslims
remittances, 6, 7, 9, 148–152, *151*;
    assistance practices and, 199–203;
    conflict and, 155; migration and,
    152–154; patterns of, 10
repatriation, 68
returning migrants, 45–50
Reynolds, Rachel, 11, 13
rights, 104–106; human, 71, 81, 218,
    225; liberal discourse, 218, 221
rites of initiation, 255
rites of passage, 5, 39–46, 52
ritual killings, 127
Romero, Simon, 186
Rosander, Eva Evers, 255, 263n2
Rousseau, Jean-Jacques, 71
rural agriculture, 97
rural exodus, 2
rural peasantry, 100
rural-urban migration, 61, 113–118,
    121–123
rural-urban ties and relations,
    117–118
RWRP. *See* Refugee Women's Re-
    source Project

sacrifice, 41, 42
SADC. *See* Southern African Development Community
Sales, R., 224
Samsung, 151
Sanders, Todd, 127
sans papier, 51–52
sanse (sartorial skill, shine), 249, 259
Sarkozy, Nicolas, 5, 6
sartorial politics, 257–259
sartorial practices, 259–261
Sarup, Madan, 65–66
Sassen, Saskia, 161, 236
Schmitz, Jean, 3
Scott, J., 99
seasonal migration, 44, 141, 254
second-generation youth, 271, 273, 276, 280–282
secularization, 183
segmented labor market theory, 20
selecting migrants, 145–146
self-alienation, 100
self-exclusion, 103–104
self-identified host communities, 96–98
self-mobilization, 224–225
Senegalese female hair braiders, 230–242
sensitization campaigns, 36, 51, 53, 57n25
September 11, 2001, 51, 166
Seventh Annual Convention, RC-CGNA, 186
sexual abuse and violence, 213–214, 215, 219–220. *See also* rape
sexual cleansing, 124, 130n10
sexual division, of labor and castes, 238
sexuality, 122; agriculture and, 130n7
shipwrecks, 69–70
Simmel, G., 107
Simone, A., 106
Single Room Occupancy (SRO), 162
slavery, 44
social capital, 22, 24, 98, 235; education as, 276–280

social fragmentation, 98
social identity, 46–50
social life: of Igbo youth, 280–283; in New York City, 167–170
social networks, 8, 97, 127; information and, 25–26; as push factor, 22–25
social relations, 165–166
social status, of hair braiding, 231–232, 235–239
social theory, 134, 136
socialist system, 116
sociocultural dimension, of migration, 3–6
socioeconomic mobility, 123
Sociology of Religion (Weber), 254
socio-religious distinctions, 166–167
sohanci (sorcerer), 170
sokhna (spiritual leaders), 263n9
solidarity, 115–118; kinship, 113, 114
soteriology, 249, 254
Soulay, El Hadj Harouna, 166
South Africa: labor migrants and, 2; post-apartheid, 9; World Cup, 104. *See also* Johannesburg
Southern African Development Community (SADC), 85, 86
South-to-West migrants, 79
space, 175, 176–177
spiritual authority, 256, 258
sponsorship, 145–146, 154
SRO. *See* Single Room Occupancy
state barriers, 50–52
state immigration control, 65
state of emergency, 73
state primacy, 98–99
state weakness, 98
status, 26, 31; labor and, 28; social, 231–232, 235–239
Steans, J., 226
Stoller, Paul, 10, 11, 13, 164
street crime, 169
structural adjustment plans, 7, 121, 232
structural barriers, 87
structural form, of migration, 37
structural-functionalists, 124

subjectivity, 125–127
subsidiary protection, 227n9
Sufism. *See* Muridiyya Muslims
supplication, 257–259
support systems, widowhood and,
    124–125
survey, of migration, 95–96, 97
Survival in Auschwitz (Levi), 73n6
survival migration, 37
survival strategies, 224–226
sustainable development aid,
    199–203
systemic bias, 25

Tabaski (feast of sacrifice), 149
tactical citizenship, 107
tactical cosmopolitanism, 102–107
tahara (purity), 249, 255
talent, migration of, 79
Tanzania, 113–119, 121, 127–129
technology: communication, 9, 272;
    ICTs, 87–88
teenagers, 167–168
terrorism, 50, 51
Tettey, W., 188
Their Eyes Were Watching God (Hurston), 59
title-taking, 274
Todorov, Tzvetan, 71, 74n9
total inclusion, 101
trade and traders, 4, 25, 107; culture
    of, 165; diamond, 2; Igbo speakers
    and, 277; languages, 164–165; Murid, 252, 253; Muslim, 13; unions,
    73n5
trafficking. *See* human trafficking
transient superiority, 103
translocal connections, 6–8
translocational positionality, 187–188
transnational assistance practices,
    195, 198–203
transnational connections, 8–11,
    145–154
transnationalism, 102, 105, 136,
    148–152
traveling culture, 133
Treaty of Schengen, 51

Tufts University, 95
Turco-Napolitano, 62
Turner, Victor, 159
tuyaaba (religious merit), 249, 255,
    256, 257

UDHR. *See* Universal Declaration of
    Human Rights
Ujamaa villages, 116
UNDP. *See* United Nations Development Programme
UNECA. *See* United Nations Economic Commission for Africa
UNHCR. *See* United Nations High
    Commissioner for Refugees
United Nations Commission on Human Rights, 223
United Nations Development Programme (UNDP), 199
United Nations Economic Commission for Africa (UNECA), 86
United Nations High Commissioner
    for Refugees (UNHCR), 69, 195,
    212, 220, 222
United States: Committee for Refugees and Immigrants, 197; hair
    braiders in, 230–242; Igbo and, 280.
    See also New York City
Universal Declaration of Human
    Rights (UDHR), 71
urban anthropological studies, 6–7
urban centers, 99, 116
urban inclusion, 95–96, 98
urbanization, 93–95, 101

value, of migration, 20, 47, 49
vertical villages, 162
Vico, Giambattista, 63
violence, 146; anti-social, 169;
    domestic, 219; by ethnopolitical
    factions, 19; sexual abuse, 213–214,
    215, 219–220. *See also* rape
visa restrictions, 52, 53
voluntary homebodies, 138, 146

Wade, Abdoulaye, 241, 253, 259, 260
wall of shame, 52

war: Biafra-Nigeria War, 276, 279;
  Cold War, 80, 225; against migration, 50–51; World War II, 115
Watson, Stuart, 180
wealth, 5, 23–25, 165; bridewealth,
  147; displays of, 260; distribution
  of, 113; global stratifications of, 31;
  hair braiding and, 235–239; redistribution of, 4
Weber, Max, 254
*Die Welt von Gestern (The World of
  Yesterday)* (Zweig), 56n22
West Africa, 35; alienation and,
  163–167; co-development programs in, 36; New York City and,
  158–160, 167–170; North America
  and, 160–163; traders, 13. *See also*
  Brazzaville; Niamey
Whitehouse, Bruce, 4
"Widow, The" (Anduru), 124
widowhood, 124–125
"Widows in African Societies" (Potash), 124
wise men, 47
witchcraft, 122, 127
Wits University, 95
Wolof society, 231–232, 235–237
women, 11–12; as asylum seekers,

212–217; *da'ira* and, 253–254; dress
  of, 249–250; financial success
  of, 252–253; hair braiding and,
  230–242; Hausa, 126, 140, 147–148;
  Murid, 248–263; patrilineage and,
  123; rights of, 218; rites of initiation and, 255; sexuality and, 122.
  See also feminization
Women Against Rape, 220
World Bank, 24, 84, 150, 232
World Cup, 104
World War II, 115
worship space, 10

xenophobia, 9, 102, 169

Youngstedt, Scott, 8, 11
youths, 1, 36, 44, 45; elite, 270–285;
  Hausa, 137; labor market and,
  55n12; second-generation, 271, 273;
  teenagers, 167–168

Zain, 155n3
ziarra, 13
ziyara (pious visits and pilgrimages),
  255, 257
Zongo, Ousmane, 169
Zweig, Stefan, 56n22